RELIGION AND JEWISH IDENT

IN THE SOVIET UNION, 1941-

For the complete list of books that are available in this series, please see www.upne.com

A Sarnat Library Book *Brandeis University Press* *Waltham, Massachusetts*

Religion and Jewish Identity in the Soviet Union, 1941–1964

MORDECHAI ALTSHULER

Translated by Saadya Sternberg

Brandeis University Press
An imprint of University Press of New
England
www.upne.com
© 2012 Brandeis University
All rights reserved
Manufactured in the United States
of America
Designed by Mindy Basinger Hill
Typeset in 10/14 pt. Calluna

University Press of New England is a member
of the Green Press Initiative. The paper
used in this book meets their minimum
requirement for recycled paper.

Originally published as *Yahadut bamakhbesh
hasovieti: Bein dat lezehut yehudit bivrit-
hamoatzot 1941–1964* by the Zalman Shazar
Center for Jewish History, Jerusalem, 2007.

This publication was made possible with
the cooperation of the Zalman Shazar
Center for Jewish History through the
generous support of the Conference on
Jewish Material Claims Against Germany,
Inc., and Brandeis University's Bernard G.
and Rhoda G. Sarnat Center for the Study of
Anti-Jewishness, which aims to promote
a deeper understanding of anti-Jewish
prejudice, as well as Jewish and non-Jewish
responses to this phenomenon, from both a
historical and contemporary perspective.

Library of Congress Cataloging-in-
Publication Data

Altshuler, Mordechai.
[Yahadut bamakhbesh hasovieti. English]
Religion and Jewish identity in the Soviet
Union, 1941–1964 / Mordechai Altshuler;
translated by Saadya Sternberg.—1st ed.
   p.   cm.—(The Tauber Institute series
for the study of European Jewry)
Includes bibliographical references and index.
ISBN 978-1-61168-271-7 (cloth : alk. paper)—
ISBN 978-1-61168-272-4 (pbk. : alk. paper)—
ISBN 978-1-61168-273-1 (ebook)
1. Jews—Soviet Union—History. 2. Jews—
Soviet Union—Identity. 3. Jews—Government
policy—Soviet Union. 4. Jews—Soviet
Union—Social conditions. 5. Soviet Union—
Ethnic relations. I. Sternberg, Saadya. II. Title.
DS134.85.A4813 2012
305.892'404709045—dc23

5 4 3 2 1

Contents

Preface

This book explores the role of religion in Jewish ethnic identity in the former Soviet Union between the years 1941 and 1964. The study is based on documentary material from USSR archives, which became accessible only after the collapse of the Soviet regime. It examines and analyzes records not only from the central state archives but also from archives in towns on the periphery, which, as we shall see, are crucial, because a large gap existed between the declarations of centralized Soviet policy and the implementation of those laws and policies in far-flung towns and villages. Taken together, these records offer us a new understanding of the place of Jewish religion, among other religions, in the USSR and of the extraordinary range of Jewish religious and ethnic activity, which was heretofore unknown. These findings, moreover, call into question commonly held perceptions in Jewish historiography about Jewish life in the Soviet Union.

The Soviet regime was, from its early foundations, antireligious, and fluctuated between periods of heightened antireligious enforcement and relative leniency. How, then, did the sanctioned religious institutions function within these conditions? What was the influence of religion and its institutions on the wider Jewish public, which was largely not religious and sometimes antireligious? During most of this period, the "congregation" (*obschchina*) and the synagogue constituted the only legal Jewish institution in the state. As the fate of their Jewish brethren in the Holocaust became known, many assimilated Soviet Jews experienced a national awakening. It is then no wonder that masses of religiously nonobservant Jews participated, whether directly or indirectly, in these religious institutions alongside religious Jews, who were in the minority. These religious institutions offered the only context in which Jews could give expression to their ethnic identity. Thus, the purpose of this research is not simply to describe the Soviet bureaucracy's policies against the Jewish religion, as has already been done in Western historiography, but rather to focus on instances of Jewish activity and to explore the contribution of religion to a sense of Jewish nationhood.

The book is divided into two parts. The first is chronological and explores the strategies of the legal, as well as semilegal, congregations to cope with shifts in Soviet policy against religion in general and against the Jewish religion in particular. Against this backdrop, the second part provides a glimpse into the wide-ranging efforts of groups and individuals to maintain and express their Jewish identity. This second part concludes with an examination of the relationship among Soviet Jews, world Jewry, and the state of Israel.

This research was made possible through the extraordinary cooperation of numerous archivists: Dr. S. V. Mironenko, director of the State Archive of the Russian Federation; Dr. O. A. Pirig, director of the Central State Archive of Public Organizations of Ukraine; Ms. Larisa Yakovleva, director of the Central State Archive of the Highest Government Bodies and Directorates of Ukraine; Mr. V. Selimenev, director of the National Archives of the Belarus Republic; and the staff of the district archives of Kiev, Vinnitsa, Zhitomir, Chernovtsy, and Odessa. My deepest thanks are extended to all of them. I also want to thank the following institutions: the Centre for Research and Documentation of East European Jewry, the Hebrew University of Jerusalem, the Central Archives for the History of the Jewish People, the Yad Vashem Archive, and the Central Zionist Archive. I am thankful to Israel Chazani, who edited the Hebrew edition of the book, and to Saadya Sternberg, who translated it into English.

This study was supported by the Israel Science Foundation, the Slavic Research Center, Hokkaido University (Japan), and the Center for the Study of World Religions at Harvard University. Much of this book was written while I was a visiting senior research associate at Brandeis University's Sarnat Center some years ago, and so it is fitting that this book appears as a Sarnat Library Book in the Tauber Institute Series with Brandeis University Press. I enjoyed working on the English-language edition with my former student—and now associate editor of the series—Sylvia Fuks Fried. I am grateful to Golan Moskowitz, who ably edited the bibliography and read proofs, and to the editors and staff at the University Press of New England for their thoughtful attention to every detail.

Jerusalem, December 2011

Introduction

The Soviet Union was the first country in the twentieth century to be committed to an antireligion policy from its very inception. Ideologically and practically, the regime and the Communist Party looked upon religion as a phenomenon whose time had passed and that needed to be combated. To that end, the state set in motion a vast apparatus of education, propaganda, and repression. It likewise considered most religious organizations to be social and political rivals to Communist ideology. Yet paradoxically, the religious institutions were the sole public entities that continued to function and maintain their legal status from before the Revolution and up to the collapse of the Soviet regime. This paradox is especially striking with respect to the Jewish religion, which was allowed to continue to function formally even after all the Soviet Jewish organizations were brutally disbanded in the late 1940s.

Implementation of the fundamental antireligion doctrine was on the whole pragmatic—that is, it took various factors into consideration. To a large extent, the Soviet policy on religion, like its national policy, derived from methods developed to handle domestic problems—political, social, and economic; it was also influenced by foreign policy. It is thus unsurprising that years of fierce combat against religion were interspersed with periods of a certain letup. The scholarship on religious activity in the Soviet Union must therefore deal with the not insubstantial issues of periodization of the more and less stringent times;[1] this said, the boundaries are not always sharp and the changes not manifest equally for the different religions. Yet most scholars note that in the second half of the 1930s a certain relaxation in the public antireligion campaign occurred, following the persecutions of the 1920s and early 1930s of most religious institutions. The vigorous campaigns to shut down houses of prayer in those years, and the sporadic efforts to do so in the periods of relaxation, left their marks. In the mid-1930s, in the entire Soviet Union only slightly more than a quarter (28 percent) of all religions' houses of prayer were still functioning, compared to before the Bolsheviks' seizure of power. Although in the twenties and thirties one does not discern a greater animosity toward the Jewish religion than toward any of the other religions, the data hint that in those areas holding the majority of the Jewish population and containing the vast majority of synagogues, more vigorous efforts were made to shut down houses of prayer than in other areas. Thus, for example, in Ukraine in early April 1936, only 9 percent of all religions' houses of prayer remained open, compared to the pre-Revolution days; in Belorussia the proportion was 11 percent. During the government's 1937–1938 terror campaign, handling of religious affairs was effectively transferred almost exclusively to the security services, whose members needed to fill arrest quotas and find enemies of the state in all places. During this period, church leaders and rabbis[2] were arrested on charges of anti-Soviet activity. Yet all this took place without a vigorous public antireligion propaganda campaign, as such efforts had been significantly scaled back[3] out of consideration for world public opinion. The Soviet Union in those years was engaged in building up an anti-Fascist front in most of the world's countries. This front was meant to hold within it social-democratic parties, liberal intellectuals, as well as figures and entities from religious realms: a public war on religion might have interfered with this aim.

After all the party and national frameworks that dealt with religious affairs had been dismantled, and the subject had been marginalized by the Soviet media, the most vigorous remaining speaker against religion was Emilian Iaroslavskii, head of the "League of the Militant Godless." In an address to the Eighteenth Congress of the Communist Party in March 1939, he called for intensified activity against religion of all kinds;[4] and in a speech to the board of activists of the league in Moscow in April 1939, he stated: "The enemies of Socialism are working via the religious organizations. In those areas . . . where churches, synagogues, and mosques do not exist, often there are 'wandering priests' and similar people of the past."[5]

Defining legal religious organizations as hives of anti-Socialist activity offered sufficient grounds to justify their liquidation by the government and the arrest of their activists. Furthermore, in one of his appearances Iaroslavskii pointed out that in recent years a significant decrease had been seen in applications to the authorities on religious matters, a fact that in his view demonstrated the public's lack of interest in religion. He voiced this opinion at a gathering of workers at antireligion museums in March 1941, where among other things he said: "The number of people making requests or complaints about the closure of houses of prayer is declining daily. In those places where requests of this kind are being made, they are the products of the initiatives of wealthy peasants [*kulaki*], religious service providers, ex–religious activists, and owners of private businesses [*edinolichniki*]."[6] Iaroslavskii thus stressed that religious initiatives were directly tied to anti-Soviet elements and their proponents should be treated like any other enemies of the regime.

In 1939, on the eve of World War II, the Soviet Union, with its 3,028,000 Jews, had a handful of legally operating synagogues remaining, and these had a miniscule number of attendees. Often the number was insufficient for a minyan, since even the elderly who may have aspired to attend services resisted doing so lest their attendance negatively affect their children and other relatives. In the 1937 census (the only one to ask a question about religion), only 281,000 Jews declared themselves as religious (9 percent), and 70 percent of these were older than sixty. One may thus affirm that at this time religion and its institutions had ceased to be a factor in the lives of the Jewish population of the Soviet Union.

Yet between 1939 and 1940, the USSR annexed parts of eastern Poland (western Ukraine and western Belorussia), the Baltic states, Bessarabia, and north Bukovina. All these areas combined housed two million Jews, most of whom were rooted in their religious tradition.

The annexed areas had many churches and synagogues as well as active systems of education and social welfare associated with the religious institutions. Yet for tactical reasons, the Soviet regime did not launch a frontal assault against religion in the annexed areas, just as it refrained from launching a massive collectivization campaign so as not to antagonize the peasantry. It sought rather to weaken the influence of religion mainly through attacks on the religious service providers, who were presented in the media as lackeys of the prior regimes and hostile to the government;[7] the security services had many of them followed and opened files against them for use when needed.[8] The few religious service providers who were actually arrested and exiled in the early years after annexation were mainly people with political involvements (heads of parties, parliamentarians, and so forth). In parallel, the regime sent religious figures from the old territories of the USSR into the annexed areas to "guide" the religious service providers in making their organizations conform to the rules and regulations on religious affairs as practiced in the Soviet Union.

In 1940, accordingly, Shmuel Chubrutskii, the head of the Moscow Choral Synagogue (referred to hereafter as the city's "main synagogue"), was sent to the annexed areas (Soviet citizens were not permitted to travel to the annexed areas without a permit) to offer guidance to the Jewish religious service providers there.[9] Born in Bessarabia, in the town of Benderi, Chubrutskii resided in Moscow from the early thirties on; a tailor by profession, in his youth he had had some religious instruction. A rabbi from the United States who met him in 1940 described him as a "simple enough Jew, who perhaps barely understands a chapter of Mishna, yet a wise Jew of relentless energies and with a natural aspiration to stand at the fore and earn a little respect."[10] When Chubrutskii visited the Turei Zahav (Gold Columns) synagogue in L'vov and saw hundreds of Jews, young and elderly alike, reciting verses of Psalms, he "gazed at this scene with emotion and tears in his eyes." Chubrutskii, who in a roundabout way admitted to the American rabbi that he had ties with the authorities and was supervising matters on their behalf in the synagogue, maintained that these very dynamics allowed the synagogue to stay open and that he himself was thus "carrying out a divinely ordained mission."[11] To the authorities he indeed seemed a singularly apt figure for undertaking the needed mission in the annexed areas. In this capacity he visited several towns of Belorussia and western Ukraine and Lithuania and met with rabbis there. One such encounter, in Baranovichi in July 1940, included at least five rabbis. He also had a certain contact with Lithuanian rabbis[12] so as "to instruct the Jewish religious leaders on how to handle the legal status of the synagogues."

Religious life in these areas, too, was under pressure, not however from the direct action of the authorities against the synagogues but as a result of the formal closure of their associated religious institutions, including the heders, Talmud Torah schools, and yeshivas. Students in these institutions now were obligated to attend Soviet schools, mainly those in which Yiddish was spoken, that had opened in each and every town and hamlet. Yet more than this, the religion was damaged in those areas by the impoverishment of the wealthy Jewish classes whose property had been confiscated and who no longer could support the synagogues and religious institutions that continued to operate openly and with permission. "In most locations [in the areas annexed to the Soviet Union] the synagogues remained standing," notes Dov Levin, a scholar of the period, "and the praying public had to bear the physical costs of their maintenance, which included high taxes."[13] Yet the regime was unable, in so short a time, to uproot the influence of religion in the broad strata of the Jewish public. As one such religious Jew attested: "The condition of Judaism in the areas of the Soviet occupation was not bad. Special persecutions against religious institutions and their trustees did not occur at the time. Przemysl and towns near it had *admors* [Chassidic rabbis] and the Chassidic faithful used to travel to see them as in the past."[14]

The continuing influence of religion on broad sectors of the Jewish public was described in an antireligion Soviet magazine in early 1941 as follows:

In the western areas of Ukraine, great is the authority of the "miracle worker" of Czortków, Rabbi Rokeach, and the Rabbi of Sadogura[,] Fridman[,] as well as the Rabbi of Slobotin. These three Chassidic rabbis have masses of Chassidim flowing to them. The synagogues are full here not only on Shabbat and holidays but also on ordinary days. Even in L'vov [in the Jewish neighborhoods], on Shabbat, the stalls of peddlers, the workshops of the tinsmiths, the shoemakers, the carpenters all are closed. En route to synagogue on the streets strange figures slowly move, with long sidelocks . . . [dressed in] long black clothes and their heads bearing odd-looking hats. In these neighborhoods no one smokes on the Sabbath, or rides the trolley-cars, or lights a fire.[15]

Even if this account contains exaggeration, religion was indeed a significant factor for the Jewish population of the annexed areas, which was not the case in the older parts of the USSR, where there were only tiny groups of religiously observant Jews (Chassidim of Chabad, Bratslav, and others) who kept to themselves and did not have a real impact on the wider Jewish population. That wider Jewish population, more than any other ethnic group, was remote from religion, as is suggested by the 1937 census. The differences were also reflected in the number of synagogues that were officially active in the Soviet Union on the eve of the Nazi invasion of June 22, 1941: 1,050, of which 650 were in western Ukraine and 300 were in western Belorussia. There are reasonable grounds to believe that in Lithuania, Latvia, Estonia, Bessarabia, and north Bukovina, at least fifty additional registered synagogues were still functioning. This is without counting the hundreds of unlisted synagogues that continued to operate in those areas, as contrasted with the pre-1939 territory of the USSR. It is thus reasonable to estimate that in the annexed areas, with their two million Jews, perhaps a thousand registered synagogues were officially functioning, whereas in the prewar USSR boundaries, with its more than three million Jews, at most forty or fifty synagogues were operating with legal sanction.[16] This difference is also striking with respect to the number of rabbis. At a time when the authorities maintained that there were 2,559 rabbis in the Soviet Union, the vast majority were in the annexed areas. In the older areas, very few rabbis operated, most of whom were without appropriate training in religious law.

One may thus affirm that on the eve of the Nazi-German invasion, only a tiny number of the synagogues that had been active before the Bolsheviks' seizure of power remained operating in the pre-1939 boundaries of the Soviet Union, and these were attended by a few elderly Jews; by contrast, in the annexed areas the vast majority of synagogues remained active. In the annexed areas, the regime did not have time to implement its intensive antireligion policy, as it had been doing for more than twenty years in the older parts of the USSR.

On the eve of the Nazi-German invasion, the Soviet authorities thus were employing two entirely different tactics with respect to religion. In the older areas, the continual and consistent practice of eliminating the tiny remnants of religious life continued; this now was done less publicly than before and met with only scant opposition by the population. Judaism was in especially dire straits, as most Jews were urbanites and a large proportion of them, especially the younger and middle-aged, was well integrated into the cultural-scientific, administrative, and technical apparatus of the state. In the annexed areas, by contrast, the regime contented itself with antireligion propaganda, which tended to be ineffective with believers; and the houses of prayer on the whole were allowed to remain open to avoid arousing too great an antagonism from the population. This general policy toward religion was reflected also in the attitude of the authorities toward the Jewish faith.

Part One

FROM RELIGIOUS LENIENCY TO A CAMPAIGN OF OPPRESSION

CHAPTER ONE

Soviet Religious Policy in the Wake of the Nazi Invasion, 1941 – 1948

With the Nazi-German invasion of the Soviet Union on June 22, 1941, the Soviet regime had a new reality to confront in all fields, including that of religion. The regime's policy on, and corresponding attitude toward, religion was shaped primarily by its policy and attitude toward the Russian Orthodox Church. In this new reality, four main factors compelled the authorities to make a practical change (not an ideological one) in its attitude toward religion.

1. Notwithstanding the many years of Soviet repression of religion, the leaders of the Russian Orthodox Church publicly called on their believers to rise in defense of their homeland.[1] They did this neither on the orders of the authorities nor out of fear of persecution; rather, a sense of patriotism overwhelmed their hostility toward the regime, and they called on the faithful in the occupied areas to resist the aggressor.[2] In the churches, prayers were held for the success of the Red Army defending Russia against the foreign invader,[3] and priests called on believers to contribute to the Red Army and to help on the home front. The calls by the Russian Orthodox Church were followed by those of the other religions,[4] first of which was the Jews, whose leaders knew Hitler to be the enemy of the Jewish people. During the war's critical moments in late 1941, prayers were held in Moscow's main synagogue for the victory of the Red Army.[5] In early 1943, the leaders of the Jewish communities of Moscow (Shmuel Chubrutskii) and Kuibishev (Moshe Feigin) telegrammed Stalin to inform him that their communities were raising funds (the former 50,000 rubles, the latter 10,000 rubles) to establish a tank unit and an aircraft unit.[6]

2. The churches, nearly empty before the war, now filled with worshipers. As the situation on the front became increasingly dire and as reports grew on the wounded, dead, and missing, so did the number of those seeking to pray for the recovery of the wounded and for the souls of the fallen.[7] Religion was perceived by broad sectors of the public as the lone shining light in a sea of bereavement, hunger, and misery. A report on the Russian Orthodox

Church notes that during the war, "religious sentiments grew—as confirmed by a significant increase in the number of churchgoers, the number of those conducting religious rites and the number of requests for opening new churches."[8]

In the cities that were absorbing refugees,[9] the existing or newly formed synagogues likewise filled with worshipers.[10] Toward Rosh Hashana of 1941 (September 22–23), as the Wehrmacht drew closer to Moscow, notices were posted at the city's three synagogues and in neighborhoods with large Jewish concentrations listing the hours of prayer and the cantors who would be leading the services. On the High Holidays, the synagogues were full; many of the worshipers now either donned uniforms or were youngsters who may not have known how to pray but who paid close attention to the prayers. Likewise, on Rosh Hashana of 1942 (September 12–13), Moscow's main synagogue was completely packed; about a quarter of the worshipers were in uniform.[11] Here, for example, is how a sixty-five-year-old Jew who had fled the Ukraine and reached the town of Sverdlovsk in the Ural region described the prayers in a letter to his son at the front in 1942: "On the High Holidays the synagogue was not big enough to hold all who came to pray. With a breaking heart and tearful eyes we prayed to the Almighty to bring a swift defeat to the bloody one [Hitler]. . . . We are reciting psalms for the victory of the Red Army and for the survival of our people."[12]

The regime, which sought to draw every shred of support it could find for its war effort, allowed synagogues across the country to open even without official approval. Moreover, the activities of the League of the Militant Godless,[13] until then the symbol of the regime's antireligion policy, were brought to a halt, as was publication of antireligion writings in Russian and other languages.

3. During the war, the Soviet Union was keenly interested in the sympathy of the public in the Allied countries, so its representatives in these countries often emphasized the Soviet authorities' newfound support for a policy of religious freedom. This point was stressed by the Soviet ambassador to Britain, Ivan Maiskii (1884–1975), in his meetings with representatives of Agudat Israel;[14] he even promised to transmit to Moscow the request of the Chief Rabbi of Eretz Israel, Rabbi Yitzhak Halevi Herzog (1888–1959), to free forty rabbis from prison and exile.[15]

4. In contrast with the Soviets, the Nazi-German occupation authorities did not have a coordinated policy on religion in the Soviet occupied territories. Yet for practical or opportunistic reasons, various German authorities encouraged or even initiated the creation of churches. The priests who served in these churches did not hold unitary views: some voluntarily collaborated with the occupier while others aided the partisans. More important, though, was that

the churches filled with worshipers and that baptisms of children and even adults were held.[16] In contrast with the complete restriction of religious studies in the Soviet educational system, the German occupiers permitted or even initiated religious instruction in the Russian primary schools.[17] In areas with large Muslim populations, many mosques were reopened, and large numbers of people took part in religious rites.[18]

It is hard to say to what extent an actual religious revival took place in the Soviet Union and its occupied territories—whether this was a momentary reaction to suffering and distress, or the result of the authorities (both German and Soviet) stirring up the status quo, or an upwelling of suppressed and dormant religious sentiment that now crested and rode the tide of nationalism-patriotism. Regardless of such factors and motivations, the Soviet regime was brought to the realization that religion played a role in public affairs that the leadership could not afford to ignore and on which it had to take a stand.

After the victory in Stalingrad (November 1942–February 1943) and the successful battles of Kursk (July–August 1943), the prospect of a Soviet victory over Nazi Germany felt increasingly inevitable. Correspondingly, Soviet leaders began to consider plans for the shape of the postwar period. Stalin and those around him recognized the immense destruction caused by the war and the need to engage the population in the vast effort to restore the economy. It is in this context, it appears, that the new steps taken by the regime to reorganize religious affairs are to be regarded.

The regime had several options available for dealing with the new situation, in which religion apparently had the power to motivate large masses of people. One option was to return to its harsh suppression of religion; another was to reach a certain understanding with the religious establishment, the Russian Orthodox Church first of all. Thus, certain reprieves could be granted to the church establishment, which in turn would aid, at least indirectly, in the functions of the state and the authorities. Following this latter concept and after suitable preparatory efforts, a brief consultation was held on September 4, 1943, in Stalin's summer home to organize relations between the Russian Orthodox Church and the regime. The meeting's participants included Josef Stalin, Georgii Malenkov, Lavrentii Beriia, and G. Karpov;[19] the attendees resolved to establish a soviet for the affairs of the Russian Orthodox Church, which would exist formally "alongside" the Soviet government (*Sovet po delam Russkoi Pravoslavnoi Tserkvi pri* SNK SSSR). To stress the importance with which the regime regarded the issue, it was decided to invite the leaders of the church to a meeting with Stalin. That meeting included leaders of the Russian Orthodox Church as well as Viachislav Molotov (1890–1986) and Karpov. Stalin launched the discussion by saying that "he himself and the government very much appreciate the work of the Church," and stressed that "the Church can count on the multilateral support of the government in all issues connected with strengthening its organization and development within the Soviet Union."[20] For their part, the church leaders made eight requests: (1) to convene a gathering to elect a patriarch for the Russian Orthodox Church; (2) to establish institutions for training of priests; (3) to publish a church periodical; (4) to build factories for the manufacture of candles (a source of church income); (5) to allow priests to serve as members of the board governing the religious associations; (6) to allow greater freedom in the financial administration of churches, and devote a greater percentage of revenues to the central institutions; (7) to reasonably structure the taxation of providers of ritual services; (8) to find lodgings in Moscow for the offices of the patriarch. Stalin immediately assented to all the requests and even expressed a readiness to consider appeals to release certain clerics from prison and exile. The meeting thus established a kind of "concordat" between the Russian Orthodox Church and the Soviet regime, and on this basis the government, on September 14, 1943, announced the formation of the soviet mentioned before.[21]

The new institution was meant, among other things, to help the church increase its influence throughout the Soviet Union and concurrently to help the Soviet Union increase its influence via the church. Nor did the regime ignore the value of the influence held by the Russian Orthodox Church beyond Soviet borders.[22] Thus, common interests were forged between the Moscow-based church patriarchy and the Soviet imperialist apparatus. The new arrangement was based on two reciprocal principles: leaders of the church, who now had been granted official recognition, agreed to support the regime and let it supervise religious activities through the soviet; for its part, the regime expressed a willingness to address some of the demands of the church and to bolster its central institutions.[23]

On the basis of this new agreement, various amendments were made to the religious affairs legislation of 1929, the most important of which was one that allowed the providers of ritual services to act as members and even heads of the governing boards for the religious associations. An amendment from August 1945 recognizes the religious associations as "legal entities" permitted to lease and acquire properties for religious purposes, to open bank accounts, to hire providers of ritual services, and so forth. In a gesture toward all the religions, the Release Committee Office of the Soviet government decided, on February

26, 1945, that no acting providers of ritual services would be drafted to serve in the regular army or reserves.[24] Accordingly, the rabbis of Chernovtsy sought "the release from the army of all ritual service providers such as rabbis, cantors and beadles of all the synagogues."[25]

The accord reached with the Russian Orthodox Church was made before the agreements with any other religious body. This served to emphasize the church's "eldest brother" (*starshyi brat*) status, as was explained by the chairman of the Soviet for Religious Affairs in a memorandum to the Soviet government in July 1947:

> Almost all the religions that exist in the Soviet Union were born in the West or in the countries of the Middle East, and in relocating to Russian soil [these religions] have historically preserved the foundational dogmas common to them and to the religious associations which are active abroad. This state of affairs objectively creates the possibility of the penetration of influences from the foreign religious associations to their fraternal associations in the Soviet Union. The case is different with the Russian Orthodox Church. It itself transmits . . . a Russian influence abroad by the very maintenance of its Russian uniqueness. The Orthodox Church carries in certain instances a decisive influence and in other cases a weight in the countries of Eastern Europe . . . which no other religion does.[26]

The Russian Orthodox Church was thus the eldest brother among the religions, just as the Russian nation was the eldest brother among the nations of the Soviet Union. Nevertheless, the state could not entirely ignore the "younger brothers," when it came to religion. Accordingly, on May 19, 1944, a "Soviet for Religious Affairs [henceforth SRA] alongside the Government of the Soviet Union [*Sovet po delam religioznykh kultov pri* SNK SSSR]"[27] was established with the aim of bringing order to "the religious awakening caused by the war" and aiding in the Soviet propaganda effort abroad.[28] As part of the latter mission, permission was granted to Muslim groups to fulfill the commandment of the hadj to Mecca.[29] On that basis, in 1947, a group of Jews from four cities in Uzbekistan (Bukhara, Kokand, Samarkand, and Tashkent) sought permission from the SRA to make a pilgrimage to Jerusalem, arguing that this was one of the Jewish religious commandments.[30] The request was denied, but this denial should not immediately be taken as an act of special discrimination against the Jewish religion, since a pilgrimage to the Holy Land does not occupy as central a place in Judaism as the hadj does in Islam.

The person appointed as chairman of the SRA was Y. V. Polianskii, a veteran security services officer. The guidelines he issued, which were approved by the government on May 29, 1945, were modeled on those that applied to the soviet for the Russian Orthodox Church. The SRA and its representatives (*upolno-mochennye*) in the Union Republics and the districts (*oblasti*) were instructed to: (1) meet with representatives of the religious associations and listen to their requests; (2) receive complaints by the religious bodies to the authorities, and discuss them; (3) visit the various settlements to see the activities of the religious organizations and other religious problems (i.e., oversee religious activities); (4) coordinate the efforts of the SRA representative with those of the state and party authorities; and (5) ensure that structures that once were places of worship, yet no longer served this purpose, were transferred legally to other authorities.[31]

The SRA did not have actual executive authority; rather it was meant to serve as the coordinating link between the executive authorities—both central and local—and the religions under its jurisdiction. The SRA preferred open and organized religious activity over a decentralized approach not because of its positive attitude toward religion but because this approach allowed for greater supervision and control. This point was stressed by the SRA chairman in a memorandum of July 1, 1947, to Klement Voroshilov (1881–1969), who from 1946 on handled religious affairs in the Soviet government: "It is preferable to have an open and organized administration of any particular religion, which allows the SRA to have an influence on a movement that is externally amorphous, takes place in secret, and therefore is not subject to control and direction."[32]

During the war, numerous places of worship had opened throughout the Soviet Union; these were augmented by the places of worship in the conquered territories, which continued to function after the entry of the Red Army. Thus, one of the central tasks of the SRA was "to change the nature of religious activity from a stychic . . . to a largely organized phenomenon." The soviet needed to register the religious associations and the structures and property they owned; it also sought to determine "the optimum weight of each religion and correct division of the various associations among the republics."[33] Yet carrying out these tasks was no easy matter.

A relatively small apparatus with various branches was allocated to the SRA, and even the central office in Moscow was not adequately prepared to handle the diverse religions under its control. Functions were delineated only in the late 1940s or early 1950s, when three departments were formed: a department for the Islamic, Jewish, and Buddhist religions, which in the early fifties constituted the largest department; a department for the Armenian-Georgian, Catholic, and Lutheran religions; and a department for the recognized Christian religious sects.[34] Thus this SRA, as opposed to its parallel entity for the Russian Orthodox Church, had to deal with more than a dozen religions and sects, each of which had its own system of beliefs, customs and rites, and traditions. Indeed, a report to the Soviet government by the chairman of the SRA listed, among the special difficulties it faced, the problem of handling "a multiplicity of religions, each of which has distinct dogmas, customs, rites and traditions."[35]

The governments of the Union Republics were in no hurry to appoint representatives of their own to the SRA, and six to nine months passed before the Moscow SRA was able to place its representatives in the republics. Most of those appointed to the post held ties to the security services, although formally they were subordinate both to the soviet in Moscow and to the administrations of each of the Union Republics. The SRA appointee for Ukraine was Piotr Vil'khovy;[36] for Belorussia it was Kondratii Ulasevich. Making such appointments in the districts was no simple affair, as often appointees needed to come from the district bureaucracy and to be paid out of the local budget. Small wonder then that district authorities sought to avoid making these appointments, whom they furthermore regarded as overseers on Moscow's behalf.[37] The reluctance of the district authorities to appoint representatives to the SRA is all the more understandable if one considers that the settlement or township bureaucracy previously had authority over numerous religious issues, and was now being asked to withhold action in these affairs until consulting and seeking approval from the soviet or its representative. Quite a few of the local officials who had previously handled religious affairs either directly or indirectly saw the change as an intrusion in a realm over which they had held exclusive authority. The post of SRA district representative, which often was imposed on the apparatus in the district, was typically staffed by a person who also held another job; he often viewed the role as an added chore and related to it accordingly.[38] Moreover, theirs was a harder job than that of the representative of the soviet of the Russian Orthodox Church: while the latter had to handle a single religious organization, about which he usually also knew a thing or two, the former had to deal with all the district's religions (except the Orthodox Church), including those, such as the Jewish religion, about which he knew almost nothing.

It was natural, then, for the SRA to regard preparing written "instructions" to all its representatives throughout the Soviet Union as one of its duties—instructions that, like all other correspondence on religious matters, were meant to be kept secret from the religiously involved citizenry.[39] Yet even these instructions were insufficient to address the considerable problems faced by the district representative, especially in such areas as Ukraine with its multiplicity of religions and sects. Accordingly, the Ukraine SRA representative summoned the district representatives to a special consultation on September 12–16, 1946, to learn what was being done and to guide the representatives on the different approaches to be taken toward the different religious groups.

For all the difficulties they faced, the SRA officials did not enjoy any prestige from the district bureaucracy. Representatives often complained to their superiors that they were allocated a tiny office, had no secretary, and were not even given office supplies. A few complained that they did not enjoy the same favors as comparable members of the *nomenclatura,* such as superior food coupons, the right to purchase goods in special stores, and so forth. It is unsurprising, then, that the SRA chairman complained to the government of the Soviet Union about the "inadequate estimation of the activity of the soviet by prominent workers of the soviet apparatus at the local level."[40]

On the basis of the experience gained by the SRA during the four years of its existence, and in light of government policy toward religion in this period, the SRA chairman affirmed that:

> Religion in the Soviet Union is lacking in any social roots and has hitherto been preserved among a certain portion of the citizenry of the Soviet Union only as a remnant of capitalism. . . . It is impossible to identify the masses of believers with the ritual service providers which are a closed and isolated group of professional providers of religious services who have special interests.

However, since the majority of the religious people participate in "the building of Communist society," he went on to note, it would be inappropriate to use administrative means in the struggle against religion. In this context he stressed that the different religions should be treated differently, in line with their attitude toward the Soviet regime. The Muslims, the Armenian-Georgians, the Old Believers (*Staroobriadtsy*), and the Lutheran-Reformers were in a process of accommodating themselves to the regime; the Catholics and the Greek-Catholics (Uniates) continue to be opposed to the regime, although "they do so passively." Alongside these religions are "extremist Messianic religious groups which continue to actively oppose the Soviet regime."[41] It may thus be said that even during the short period that has rightly been considered one of regime leniency toward religion (1941–1948), the basic negative approach was unchanged, even as the implementation of this approach varied with respect to the different religions. The question faced by the SRA, thus, concerned the most effective way of gaining control over the religious organizations and of steering them toward the regime's desired path.

Between Decentralization and Centralization

Central bodies of religious institutions lacked a formal position in the Soviet Union. Even the various regulations enacted after the establishment of the SRA did not grant to those bodies a binding status; at most, the regime decided that on certain issues, such as the appointment of providers of ritual services, the authorities would consult with the central bodies. Yet only actual recognition of religious institutions and a certain degree of cooperation with their leaders could demonstrate a significant change in the regime's posture on religion, both to the public in the Soviet Union and to public opinion worldwide. Clearly, then, a granting of recognition and prestige was called for in cases in which central bodies were part of the religion's tradition. The question remained, however, how the regime should act toward religions that historically did not have a central, nationwide body.

One might have thought that the authorities would find it easier to deal with local religious associations, as opposed to a central religious authority for each group. Yet the SRA chairman—Polianskii—who knew well the complaints about the inadequate status and inexperience of his district representatives, preferred central institutions even for those religions that lacked such institutions as part of their tradition. He thus remarked, in a 1947 memorandum to the Soviet government, that for many religions the absence of a center was complicating the soviet's efforts to carry out its duties. In one of his requests for approval of such a center, Polianskii noted that "religious centers almost always have a decisive role in the activity and direction of the religions. Under conditions of good organization of a religious center and in the presence of its considerable authority it is easier to guide the processes which take place within the religious organizations."[42] The chairman of the SRA thus sought to utilize the intrareligious prestige and authority of the centers to organize matters that his representatives and the local authorities could not do on their own. Indeed, in 1945 central religious institutions existed for at least six of the religions supervised by the soviet (two of them in which a hierarchy was traditional, and four in which central institutions contradicted the religion's precepts and history). The existence of these centers let the religious groups enjoy, at least partially, the rights granted to the Russian Orthodox Church, and this sufficed to demonstrate that the Soviet Union was not discriminating among its religions. Accordingly, the chairman of the SRA stressed in his 1947 report to the Soviet government that the existence and bolstering of central institutions for the various religions was an interest of the regime, and that a series of problems had been resolved largely with the help of the appropriate influence of the religious centers and their hierarchies. This state of affairs obligates the strengthening of the religious centers to the extent possible and the raising of their prestige. [This can be done] by granting [those centers] the possibility of publishing religious literature, allowing several institutions of religious education to open, and permitting those centers to maintain international ties.[43]

The writer also stressed that even in the future the intent was "to continue the line of strengthening religious centers and to avoid raising obstacles to the establishment of new ones in necessary cases."[44] Given this policy, it seemed logical to also create a central institution for the Jewish religion, and from 1944 to 1946 the sra indeed worked to ready the ground and to identify the figure who would lead the nationwide institution of the Jewish faith. The authorities believed that this figure should be of high stature in the religious circles of the Soviet Union and also be known outside of it. One early proposal was that the leader should be Rabbi Isaac Levi Schneerson (1878–1944), but he protested that he was too old and infirm. Meanwhile, Rabbi Avraham Yehoshua Heschel Twersky, the Rabbi of Makhnovka, refused to cooperate with the authorities in any shape or form.[45] In light of these refusals, the authorities conferred the role upon Rabbi Shlomo Shlifer.

Rabbi Shlifer was born in 1889 in the Ukrainian town of Smela, half of which (some 7,500 out of 15,000 inhabitants) was Jewish. His father, the town's ritual slaughterer, later served as rabbi of the town of Aleksandriia in the Kherson *guberniia*. Shlomo studied in the heder and continued his studies at the famed Lida yeshiva; in 1913, after receiving rabbinical authorization, he was appointed as rabbi of the town of Voronovo. From there, he went on to serve as rabbi in the town of his youth, Aleksandriia, where he remained until the pogroms of 1919. When the Soviet regime stabilized, he moved to Moscow, where from 1922 to 1929 he served as secretary of the main synagogue. When the antireligion persecutions of the late 1920s intensified, he shifted away from public service and earned his living as an accountant. After the outbreak of the Soviet-German war, Rabbi Shlifer was evacuated with his family to the town of Alpaevsk in the Ural region.

In 1943, the Soviet authorities hoped to influence Jewish public opinion in the Allied countries, and to that end they sent a delegation of the Jewish Anti-Fascist Committee (consisting of Solomon Mikhoels and Itsik Fefer) to countries of the West. From the delegation's reports, the Soviet regime learned of the considerable interest in religious life in the Soviet Union harbored in the United States. In response, the authorities arranged a December 1943 dispatch to the Jewish Telegraphic Agency in New York, signed by thirteen rabbis from the Soviet Union, with an emotional appeal to the Jewish public to aid the Soviet Union in its war against Amalek (Hitler), the destroyer of the Jewish people. This letter does not contain the signature of Rabbi Shlifer.[46] Nevertheless, in early 1944, Rabbi Shlifer was summoned to Moscow and, apparently on orders of the security services, offered the position of rabbi in the capital's main synagogue, a move aimed at showcasing the Soviet Union's treatment of Judaism to the world. The authorities evidently believed that the Jewish Anti-Fascist Committee also needed to be adorned with a rabbinic figure and on April 2, 1944, Rabbi Shlifer first appeared at one of the committee's meetings.

Within a short while Rabbi Shlifer came to be highly regarded by the worshipers in the Moscow synagogue, and communities across the Soviet Union likewise turned to him on religious matters. The SRA staff learned to recognize him as someone "who has a realistic assessment of the situation." It is unsurprising therefore that the authorities viewed Rabbi Shlifer as a suitable candidate to lead a central organization of the Jewish faith in the Soviet Union. However, the rabbi's name was unfamiliar among world Jewry, and the regime sought such recognition. For this reason, the SRA responded favorably to Rabbi Shlifer's request to hold a general fast in memory of the victims of the Holocaust on March 14, 1945—a request rooted in an appeal by the Chief Rabbi of Eretz Israel. That same objective was served by an article of Rabbi Shlifer's published in the newspaper *Hatzofeh* in Eretz Israel on September 17, 1945. Following publication of the article, most of which was devoted to the Holocaust and the duty to fight the remnants of Fascism, Jews worldwide began to recognize Rabbi Shlifer as the religious leader of the Jews of the Soviet Union.[47] The ground was thus set for his appointment as the Soviet Union's chief rabbi.

On the basis of these preparations, the chairman of the SRA reported to the Soviet government on December 1945 that

in the opinion of the soviet now is the time to establish [for the Jewish religion] a Soviet-wide religious center. This center has to be not merely advisory on religious issues (as corresponds to the Jewish tradition of many generations) but primarily an administrative religious center. As it would be headed by recognized Jewish religious figures who carry authority, [people] with a realistic assessment of the situation, the center will need to direct the main part of its activity to keep the religious associations from acquiring a political and nationalist character. To that end, the soviet intends in 1946 to summon to Moscow a conference, which would have the participation of the most authoritative actors in the

Jewish organizations. These will select the Chief Rabbi of the Soviet Union and a Council, and will prepare a uniform statute for the religious communities.[48]

As part of the preparations for this nationwide conference of Jewish religious figures, the authorities encouraged the congregation (*kehilla*) of Moscow's main synagogue to make contact with congregation activists throughout the Soviet Union. To that end, in mid-1945 delegates were sent by the Moscow main synagogue to eighteen cities.[49] So as to complete the preparations for the conference and for the unanimous "election" of Rabbi Shlifer as Chief Rabbi of the Soviet Union, the SRA thought it advisable to fire Congregation Leader Chubrutskii and to appoint Rabbi Shlifer in his stead.

While Shmuel Chubrutskii's proficiency in Torah and halakhah were quite limited, he still often presented himself as a rabbi and he delivered the sermons in the synagogue. Tensions rose between Chubrutskii and Shlifer, with the former pointing out that he was the congregation leader and the latter retorting that he was unsuitable for this task. The synagogue too was divided into two camps. This competition lasted for over a year, without the intervention of the authorities and perhaps even at their instigation. Yet given the regime's plans to have Shlifer serve as the nation's chief rabbi, in 1945, the SRA encouraged Chubrutskii's departure. A special committee was formed to investigate Chubrutskii's activities, and thereafter he was removed from his post. Rabbi Shlifer was then "elected" as congregation leader and rabbi of Moscow's main synagogue.[50]

In the first quarter of 1946, preparations ensued to create a central nationwide administration for the Jewish faith. This sort of centralization ran against Russian Jewish tradition, in which a rabbi's influence was determined primarily by his capacities as a Torah scholar. We may thus suppose that rabbis and other religiously active figures were not excessively enthusiastic about the idea of a central administration, although some indeed did call on the authorities to form a parent organization comparable to those that existed for other religions. In 1946 the leaders of the Uzbek Jewish communities made the case to the authorities that "other religions like the Muslim religion and the Christian-Evangelical-Baptist religion have their own central institution, yet to date [the authorities] haven't arranged any central institution for us and it would not at all be bad if the appropriate steps were taken to arrange a comparable organization for our religion too."[51]

Many of the religiously active figures in the communities were aware of the intent to hold a conference in Moscow, and the rabbi of Kamenets-Podol'skii, Aron Lipin, offered several suggestions for its agenda. These included: "(a) To convene a world conference in the city of Moscow to reexamine [*peresmotr*] the laws of the halakhah; and (b) to decide on the need to teach Jews Hebrew [*drevne-evreiskii*] via language instruction in high school and institutions of higher education."[52] Ideas of this kind also had some support from Yiddish-culture proponents in the Soviet Union, whose interest in religious matters was minimal.[53]

Ultimately, however, it was neither any differences of opinion in the Jewish public about the planned Moscow consultation nor reservations about creating a central religious organization nor qualms about the imposition of a chief rabbi that led to the cancellation of the plan for a central Jewish institution. It appears instead that the regime reassessed the utility it could extract from such an institution versus the complications it could cause, or perhaps the different Soviet agencies held conflicting opinions on the matter. We do not have direct evidence of deliberations in the SRA or other agencies about this situation, but one can reasonably state that the idea of a central organization was discussed seriously and approved in certain ruling circles before it was formally presented to the Soviet government and before practical steps were taken to implement it. We may therefore suppose that between December 1945, when the recommendation was presented, and late 1946, when representatives of the religious communities were to be invited to Moscow for a conference, that Soviet authorities' attitude on whether to build such an institution had endured a shift. In mid-1947, SRA chairman Polianskii wrote that "requests on the issue of forming a center for the Jewish religion are to be rejected due to the lack of political interest in such." He noted further that "the creation of a center for Judaism in Moscow as well as the publication of a prayer book and religious calendar should be regarded as without benefit."[54] The subject was mentioned in a similar context in instructions given to the SRA in 1949, according to which "the formation of a Jewish center in Moscow and the publication of a prayer book and [Hebrew] calendar are to be regarded as misdirected [*netselesoobrazny*]."[55]

Although we lack direct documentation about the change in the regime's position on forming a central Jewish institution, we can speculate on circumstantial factors. In 1946, the SRA was strongly critiqued for its weakness in the fight against nationalist manifestations by religious groups, and those of the Jewish religion in particular.[56] That same year opinions were voiced on the need to disband the Jewish Anti-Fascist Committee, which had served as a sort of public face to the world of Jews of the Soviet Union. Yet eliminating one nationwide, regime-oriented Jewish organization that maintained ties with Jewish institutions abroad seemed illogical, if another, religious one would simply be formed in its place. Presumably these two factors would have been considered—or at least have been part of the climate—in rejecting the plan.

Most scholars of Soviet Jewry describe the failure to establish a central institution for the Jewish faith as a manifestation of a policy of discrimination toward this religion, and argue that this state of affairs had purely negative implications on Jewish communal existence. Yet with the new access to archival materials and the ability to draw a fuller picture of the role of the synagogue in Jewish communal life, this opinion may be called into question. Had a central administrative organization for the Jewish religion been established, the authorities would, presumably, have allowed it to form a rabbinical seminary (indeed, in 1944 the authorities contacted leaders of certain communities on the issue of opening a rabbinical seminary in Moscow).[57] It would also have been allowed to periodically issue religious publications and to represent the propaganda interests of the Soviet Union to Jewish entities abroad. Correspondingly, this sort of administrative-bureaucratic body would have helped the Soviet authorities to impose their will upon the religious communities, and would have reduced or even eliminated local initiatives. Substantial numbers of Jews would have been unable to take advantage of the local conditions and of the oppositions between the center and the different districts to expand the functional realms of their community activity. The nonformation of a central Jewish religious institution may therefore not have been solely detrimental for the communities, at least in the 1940s. Indeed, the absence of a central institution even seems to have contributed to the localities' vigor and allowed for the formation of new synagogues and community organizations.

During the period of the thaw (1954–1958), certain congregation activists advocated revisiting the idea of establishing a central institution for the Jewish faith. During Rabbi Shlifer's August 24, 1956, visit to the SRA, he himself raised the subject, and the SRA representative advised that Shlifer rethink his question.[58] Likewise, Rabbi Leib Levin raised the issue from time to time. At a meeting between Rabbi Avraham Haim Lubanow of Leningrad and the representative of the SRA in Moscow on January 28, 1958, the rabbi said that "it makes sense to organize a center for the Jewish religion in the Soviet Union so as to offer a solution to a series of religious and halakhic questions." To this, the SRA representative immediately offered this diplomatic response: "This is one of those questions that the person making it should think over."[59] In other words, the proposition was rejected right there and then. This was, so far as we know, the last time anyone active in the religious community in the Soviet Union brought up the issue to the authorities; from that time on the issue was raised mainly by Jewish delegations from abroad.

CHAPTER TWO

The Legalization of Congregations and Synagogues

Registration of Congregations: Local Variations

One of the tasks of the SRA was to register and legalize the religious associations that had formed spontaneously across the Soviet Union during the war years. The legalization of these congregations thus became a major focus of Jewish activity in the years 1944–1948.

By a law of April 8, 1929, permission to organize a religious association was granted to citizens ages eighteen and older who lived in a single settlement or multiple proximate settlements "for the sake of the common satisfaction of their religious needs."[1] A prerequisite was that the association have at least twenty persons (*dvadtsatka*), and if one of the twenty members moved to a different settlement or passed away, another person had to register in his place: if the needed twenty individuals could not be mustered, this was legal grounds for the association's dissolution. Each of the twenty members of what was often called the "initiators" or "core" group had to sign the registration request, which included his address, age, and workplace or income source.[2]

From among the "twenty," a governing board of three members would be chosen to serve as the executive body and to represent the religious association externally. The chairman of the board was the association's most influential person and in most congregations he was the *gabbai.* The right to elect people to this board extended to all those who attended services and not just the regular worshipers; this allowed the authorities to influence and manipulate the results (for which reason one should regard the Soviet documentation with caution whenever it speaks of the "election" of a board, chairman, or rabbi). Moreover, any gathering of members of a religious association for aims other than prayer or ritual required special permission from the authorities. The authorities thus retained, even legally, the right to control the religious associations, and officials from the local authorities and "other institutions, whose function [was] to guard the revolutionary order[,]" were authorized to come to any gathering of any religious association.[3] In addition, the local authorities and other institutions had the right to cancel the election of any member of the board, and they tended to avail themselves of this right to ensure a board makeup convenient to their goals.[4] The religious association had the right to act formally only once it was legally registered and approved by the local authorities and, beginning in 1945, also approved by the SRA or its district representative.[5]

The SRA was charged with registering (and approving) the religious associations, including the congregations (*kehillot*). On November 19, 1944, the government of the Soviet Union passed a resolution "pertaining to the opening of houses of worship"—that is, the registration of religious associations[6]—requiring that prayer houses of all religions organize themselves in accordance with the instructions on religious associations. The "initiating group" had to present a series of documents demonstrating as much.[7]

In the early years, two paths existed for such registration—one for existing associations, one for new ones. Existing associations referred to those based in a physical structure and with "religious service providers" prior to the formation of the SRA, and that had been listed by the authorities of the district or republic. Those associations that tended to gather for prayers on a regular basis but may not have used a particular structure were required to register as new ones, with final approval of their status to be decided in Moscow.[8] The request and documentation for registering a new religious association were to be passed to the representative of the SRA in the district and the republic, with the attachment of the opinion of the settlement, district, and republic; all the material, including the opinions, was transferred to the SRA in Moscow.[9] The SRA would carefully analyze the request and pass it on for official authorization to the government of the Soviet Union. In this context, the number of religiously practicing people (*veruiushchie*) in the settlement would be examined, as well as whether "there is an extreme and urgent political necessity" for registering a new religious association.[10] The problem of defining a "religious person" has perplexed quite a few scholars and confounded the SRA representatives themselves, who were obligated to include statistical data in their reports on religious practice in various towns and villages. Hence, most estimates of religious people were based not on verified data but on questionable sources. With regard to the number of "religious Jews," the reference was not to halakhic observance but rather to the keeping of certain traditions defined as religious rites, even when the motivation may have been ethnic identification more than religion. Small wonder, then, that frequent, significant disparities appear in the data from successive periods. The fluidity of these official estimates[11] also allowed the authorities to sometimes declare the presence of an insufficient number of religiously practicing individuals in a given settlement and thereby deny registration of a congregation or call for disbanding one.

Registration of a new congregation involved many stages and unclear standards; this made the chances of obtaining permission very slight. Registration of an existing congregation, on the other hand, was decided at the local level, and for those to whom the survival of the congregation mattered, it was easier to influence the local bureaucracy than the central institutions in Moscow. However, at the time of the founding of the SRA—the official date for counting a congregation as "existing"—many towns had only recently been freed from Nazi occupation and had no congregations and almost no Jews, a condition that contrasted with that of the Christian groups, the activities of which had persisted throughout the occupation.

Furthermore, in 1945 the SRA ruled that houses of prayer, or religious associations, that for whatever reason had stopped functioning for a year would be considered as new ones.[12] This ruling was of special significance to the Jewish religion. While most of the religions, as stated, had kept up activity during the Nazi occupation, even the few Jewish congregations active at the beginning of the Second World War did not function in the occupied areas,[13] meaning that all were required to undergo the complicated process of registration as new congregations. Yet the provincial authorities did not always follow Moscow's instructions. Thus, for instance, the SRA chairman wrote to his representative in Belorussia on August 4, 1947, that he must stop the practice of registering new religious associations as old ones. Such a practice, however, seems to have remained common, so in April 1948 the SRA in Moscow sent a special circular again declaring that "the soviet hereby decisively orders the blocking in the future of any registration of religious associations that had formed before the SRA and which have existed up to the present without its permission."[14] Indeed, as of late that year, almost all permits were granted to congregations solely with the approval of the government of the Soviet Union.

Even earlier, the actions of the authorities in Ukraine and Belorussia indicate variation from central SRA doctrine. In Belorussia, the SRA representative wrote in 1946 that he "is of the opinion that as to the opening of synagogues and registration of Jewish religious congregations, everything must be done through the [Moscow] soviet because such congregations are reorganizing." He then reprimanded his representative in the districts of Poles'e and Gomel', which had registered three congregations on their own initiative.[15] In Ukraine, for its part, the situation was more ambiguous and depended to a great extent on relations between the congregations and the city and district officials. In this republic, quite a few cases were reported of SRA leniency with synagogue registrations.[16]

From 1944 to 1945, in the entire USSR sixty-four congregations won official approval. Another thirty-nine were registered in 1946, followed by sixty-five in 1947. During these years one congregation was dissolved. Out of the 167 congregations registered by early 1948, about 80 percent (136) won recognition as established congregations. From 1948 on, the registration of existing congregations essentially ended; only one congregation was registered in this manner.[17] Of the 161 congregations registered in the USSR by early 1949, fifty-two were in Ukraine (32 percent) and one or two in neighboring Belorussia (about 1 percent). Formal registration of a congregation depended only in part on the zeal with which the local Jews pursued the matter and was determined by the policy of authorities in the republic more than by directives from Moscow. A comparison between Ukraine and Belorussia on this issue highlights these differences.

The two republics were in many respects similar. Like Ukraine, the Belorussian republic contained areas annexed to it during the Second World War. The Jewish population of Ukraine was, by the 1959 census, 5.6 times larger than that of Belorussia. Requests for registration of congregations were made in 124 towns in Ukraine and 23 in Belorussia—so, proportionally, no difference existed between the republics in the number of Jewish attempts to organize congregations. But whereas in Ukraine 42 percent of the requests were answered positively, in Belorussia less than 10 percent were. We can affirm then that Belorussia had a particularly restrictive policy toward such registration, and that this situation stemmed primarily from local policies and not the directives from Moscow. On September 6, 1947, the chairman of the SRA wrote to the Belorussia representative that

> considering that in Belorussia there are only two synagogues [i.e., congregations] and the recent growth in the number of groups of religious Jews holding gatherings in apartments and private houses for prayer . . . the soviet [maintains] that there are grounds for a positive response to a few requests for establishing synagogues [i.e., congregations] in towns where this is desirable practically and politically reasonable . . . with the aim of weakening the influence of reactionary elements on the Jewish population.[18]

The special harshness of the Belorussian authorities toward the Jewish religion as well as the Catholic Church led to the summons to Moscow, in February 1948, of one of the secretaries of the Central Committee of the Communist Party in Belorussia, Nikolai Gusarov, along with Prime Minister

Pantelei Ponomarenko (1902–1984). At their meeting with the SRA chairman, Gusarov asserted that

> the main hostile forces in the Belorussian Soviet Republic are Catholics and Jewish nationalist elements. . . . The Jewish nationalists need synagogues; lacking the ability of engaging in nationalist activity in any other way, they try to turn the synagogue from a house of prayer into a center for advancing nationalist perspectives and sentiments and for propagating them among all Jews. . . . They blame the Russians and Belorussians, [saying] that they could have saved the Jewish people from being destroyed by Hitler. . . . We decided that in Belorussia we would not open a single additional synagogue.[19]

A completely different attitude was shown by the Georgian authorities, who did not regard the petitioners for registration of congregations as "hostile forces." The SRA representative in this republic stated that

> of all the religions [in the republic], the most active is the Jewish religion . . . members of this religion, more than others, show vigorous efforts for increasing the number of synagogues [i.e., congregations] despite the large number already in existence. . . . Georgian Jews are generally fanatic and are prepared to deny themselves many things just so they can have a synagogue. . . . Requests to permit opening new synagogues have not ceased . . . to this day [1952].[20]

It is possible that this state of affairs had some influence on the number of registrations, considering that a circular of the SRA chairman, dated August 31, 1948, required that every report of a request for registration describe "the level of zealousness [of the request] of the religious [people] . . . to open a house of prayer."[21] But ultimately what determined the outcome was the readiness of the authorities to register the congregations, which in Georgia was greater than elsewhere in the USSR. Indeed, this republic, which had 2 or 3 percent of the Jewish population in the USSR, had more than 19 percent (thirty-one) of the total number of registered congregations. We can therefore conclude that the responsiveness of the authorities to requests to legalize congregations was, between 1944 and 1948, to a great extent a function of the attitude of the regime at the level of the republic or even of the district.

Unregistered Congregations

Aside from the registered associations, which were considered the only legal religious bodies, thousands of unregistered religious associations of all faiths functioned in the open.[22] Most of these associations had houses of prayer and were organized broadly along the lines set forth by the regime. The local authorities had ongoing connections with these organizations, even though officially they did not exist. The Vinnitsa district SRA representative complained to the party organization that "the heads of Soviet agencies in these places do not correctly understand the relationship with the religious associations." He went on to note that the head of the unregistered Jewish congregation in Shargorod had been given a permit signed by the subdistrict (*raiow*) head (*raispolkom*) for the expansion of the Jewish cemetery; and a March 1949 letter from the district head (*oblispolkom*) to all subdistrict heads in his district states "that by this action the local authorities have effectively recognized the existence of an unregistered congregation, active since 1945"—when the congregation should always have been regarded as a minyan and treated as such.[23] Indeed, in late 1945 fifteen unregistered Jewish congregations operated in the Vinnitsa district, and in 1947, at least two such congregations did so in the Zaporozh'e district. The Zakarpat'e district, annexed to the USSR after the war, had many unregistered congregations operating until at least early 1949.[24] Even harsh Belorussia, which granted few permits to associations of any religious affiliation, had a few operating in late 1947. For example, the local government in the towns of Borisov and Polotsk maintained contacts with unregistered congregations despite the orders of the SRA chairman "to warn the [district] soviet about the need to strictly fulfill the legal instructions and forbid activities of such congregations if not registered as required."[25]

The existence, at least four or five years after the war's end, of many unregistered congregations was tolerated because in certain towns the local government preferred them over the official ones. The unregistered congregations were completely dependent on the local authorities and this dependence gave the bureaucratic mechanism enormous leverage, sometimes including the ability to extort private favors.[26] The traditional Russian bureaucracy of the tsarist period, so well known to the Jews of that country, had not disappeared even thirty years after the Communist takeover. Now, with the Communists in charge, quite a few local authorities touted their "achievement" in not having their district "tainted" by religious organizations, thus drawing praise from their superiors.[27]

The Jewish public, for reasons of its own, sometimes also preferred an unregistered congregation, which may have had access to a synagogue and in its day-to-day functioning was not actually different from a registered congregation but was not subject to the same supervision. Accordingly, the Vinnitsa district

SRA representative complained in late 1946 that "[certain] congregations are avoiding registration."[28] Registration was a long and complicated process that in many cases ended in rejection. The central SRA in Moscow, which was the final arbiter, turned down many requests for various petty reasons: out of the 171 registration requests coming from all religions considered by the SRA in Moscow, only ten were approved. Many Jews therefore concluded it would be better to "let sleeping dogs lie." The SRA representative for Belorussia wrote in early 1948 that "the religious Jews of Gomel', as no one forbids them from meeting for prayer . . . have stopped their lobbying to open a synagogue and register the congregation."[29]

As noted, a necessary condition for the existence of a congregation (registered or not) was a building in which to conduct the religious rites, and the SRA "instructions" of April 1945 emphasized that "the religious associations . . . which have no house of prayer or whose prayer-house structure fails to meet the building codes—fire prevention and suitable sanitation—may not be registered."[30]

Obtaining a Structure for a Synagogue

Between 1944 and 1948 at least, Jews throughout the USSR worked consistently and continuously to obtain buildings for synagogues. The main way of doing so was to demand the return of former synagogue structures that had been seized in the first decades of Soviet rule.

According to a Soviet government resolution of 1918, the property of religious organizations became state-owned; a 1929 law determined that "in order to satisfy religious needs . . . the religious associations are permitted to obtain a lease for the unpaid use . . . of prayer buildings and special ritual objects, solely for ritual needs." Additionally, "property . . . purchased [by religious associations] or donated for purposes of religious ritual, is considered to be nationalized."[31] On January 28, 1946, the USSR government passed a resolution permitting registered religious associations to build or purchase a building for purposes of prayer along with affirming that "all structures built by religious associations" were owned by the state. Transfer of such a building from its religious use to other uses thus did not require permission from the central USSR agencies: a decision by the local authorities sufficed.[32] Based on this resolution, the Kiev district authorities determined that the district owned the building that the Smela congregation had purchased for 55,000 rubles,[33] and when the Uzhgorod congregation wrote to Moscow that it would not agree to give up its synagogue and find a different building to replace it, the local government was requested to clarify to the writers that "houses of prayer . . . were nationalized, that is to say are state property, which the religious [people] do not own but are only allowed the use of, and hence the transfer of a religious building . . . for public or cultural needs . . . is decidedly legal."[34] The Jews of Pinsk received a similar reply about the confiscation of a structure they had bought with their own funds.[35] Recipients of buildings or other property for religious purposes were required to oversee these structures, to use them only for ritual purposes, to repair them when needed, and to make all requisite payments.[36] Most of the synagogue structures within the USSR's 1939 borders were confiscated between the late 1920s and the outbreak of the Soviet-German war. Some were given to cultural and educational institutions, and some were altered to become residences; quite a few synagogues were converted to workshops and storehouses, while some were torn down when funds for their restoration were lacking.[37] In the battle zones of the Soviet-German war, many buildings were destroyed, some of them former synagogues. In the German-conquered areas, many of the synagogues were converted into residences or demolished so as to wipe out the memory of the Jews.[38]

After the liberation, the condition of the Jewish faith with respect to houses of prayer differed from that of the other religions, particularly Christian groups. SRA data on the Ukrainian Soviet Republic indicates that 4,785 houses of prayer functioned in 1940 (not counting those of the Orthodox Church), the majority in territories annexed to the USSR in World War Two. During the German occupation (1941–1944), this republic had 6,508 functioning houses of prayer, a rise of more than one third (36 percent).[39] In occupied Belorussia, nearly 1,050 Orthodox churches operated, of which 20–25 percent were in structures that had never been churches, and in the occupied areas of Russia there were about 2,150 Russian Orthodox houses of prayer.[40] Most Christian houses of prayer continued to operate for at least a few years after the Red Army's liberation; but all the synagogues in the Nazi-occupied territories were shut down, except a handful that continued to function in Romanian-occupied areas (Transnistriia).[41] The condition of the Jewish faith was thus much worse than the Christian one, a fact that the Jews of Gomel' brought to Stalin's attention in a 1947 letter, in which they wrote, among other things:

> The district authorities have rejected our request to restore to us our synagogue [confiscated in 1930] . . . while at the same time the Slavs got their churches back. . . . We were told that it was the Germans who returned the churches, which makes our request all the more justified.[42]

There were also cases, as in the city of Glukhov, in which the local authorities confiscated synagogues for use as residences by former members of the police during the Nazi occupation, a practice that caused much bitterness among the Jews.[43]

In these circumstances, obtaining a structure for use as a synagogue became a focus of broad Jewish activity in many towns, especially those just liberated from Nazi occupation. In the republic of Ukraine, Jews sought sites for a synagogue in at least 124 towns; in Belorussia in 1944 and 1945, they applied to form synagogues in twenty-three towns. More broadly, from 1944 until 1949, intensive efforts to obtain sites for synagogues were made in at least 147 towns in the two republics, whether in structures that had formerly been synagogues, newly constructed sites, or buildings bought, leased, or rented. The incomplete data available indicates that Jews sought to open synagogues in 289 towns across the USSR.

Quite a few requests to restore synagogues to the Jewish community were rejected by an SRA directive of 1945, which stated that the return of a house of prayer to a religious group may be refused when there is "no possibility of vacating [the structure of] a [former] house of prayer which has been adapted for purposes of culture, security, residence or industry."[44] Nevertheless, the Jewish efforts continued, and a late 1946 report stated that "the activism of the Jewish population [not solely the religious population] has consistently grown."[45]

The refusal to return synagogue structures to the congregation was interpreted by many Jews as discrimination against them, in comparison to treatment of other ethnic and religious groups. The Belorussia SRA representative wrote in his fourth-quarter report for 1947:

During applications [for the return of synagogue buildings] one can hear declarations of this sort: "Why do they allow the religious [people] of other faiths to open houses of prayer and forbid us Jews from praying. Our nation suffered more than all others from the Hitlerite occupiers and we aren't allowed to pray for our victims" . . . thus implying that there is inequality among the nations of the USSR.[46]

This theme recurs in the repeated requests from Odessa on the need to open an additional synagogue in that city, as is clearly reflected in a mid-1945 telegram sent to Stalin by Lieutenant Colonel (*podpolkovnik*) D. S. Frenkel:

I have been a party member since 1918 and am now serving in the ranks of the Red Army. While staying with elderly family members in Odessa, I was greatly upset by their report that churches have been returned to the Russians, and *kostely* [Catholic churches] to the Poles, but synagogues haven't been returned to the Jews despite their requests over nine months.[47]

The feeling of quite a few Jews that the authorities were discriminating against them on this issue, a subject of special sensitivity because of the Holocaust, empowered broader strata of Jews to get involved.

While many towns had more than a single house of prayer for each of the different religions, the authorities refused, at least in Ukraine and Belorussia, to open more than one synagogue even in towns with a large Jewish population and, by official estimates, a large number of religious Jews. In late 1944, hundreds of Jews organized in Odessa seeking to be recognized as a congregation and to be given the former synagogue on Ol'geevskaia Street, which was then occupied partly by a security services archive and partly by a horse stable. Though their application was rejected, the initiators didn't back down and sent letters to Stalin, Georgii Malenkov, and Lazar Kaganovich. The applicants were ready to provide a different building for the use of the archive and, among other things, stressed in their request that thirty Orthodox churches operated in the city versus only a single synagogue, and this did not suffice. But the authorities turned the request down anyway, insisting that the writers had no right to speak on behalf of the city's Jews.[48] For support they cited Rabbi Yosef Diment, who according to the SRA representative's summary had stressed in a discussion with him that "there is no . . . necessity of opening another synagogue in Odessa, as all religious needs are entirely met by the existing synagogue."[49] Neither were the Jews of Vinnitsa content with their single synagogue. Jews of the Sverdlovsk neighborhood testified that they had two to three thousand religious Jews living two or three kilometers from the active synagogue. As a result, they raised funds and purchased a building on Nekrasova Street that functioned regularly and in the open until late 1947. But when the worshipers sought to have the synagogue legally registered, the district SRA representative demanded its closure. The decision was appealed and the appeal denied. Yet the neighborhood's Jews did not accept this verdict and turned directly to Stalin, stating in their letter that "[they] had lost sons, brothers and other relatives on the front in the Great Patriotic War, and find comfort in the prayers for the souls of the fallen."[50] An attempt to open a second synagogue was made in Kiev as well—where most of the Jews lived downtown, while the only functioning official synagogue was in the Podol neighborhood. But the authorities were firmly against this initiative and claimed that one synagogue surely sufficed when only 150–200 worshipers came to prayers each day.[51]

Not just requests for a second synagogue in a city were turned down, so were requests for the first one. Sometimes the rejection was grounded in objective reasons, such as a severe shortage of structures, especially in areas liberated from the occupiers where orders dictated that "priority be given to rehabilitation of industrial structures, buildings for [housing] demobilized soldiers, [housing] for returning evacuated civilians and expansion of orphanages."[52] Transfer of buildings to congregations for a synagogue often involved the eviction of an institution, factory, or inhabitants; this caused difficulties, as the events in the city of Vinnitsa demonstrate. In 1945 the city council decided to allow a synagogue to open in a former synagogue building, in the undestroyed portion of which a single family lived. The congregation agreed to take the building and in 1947 restoration commenced; the congregation signed an agreement with the city council by which the building was transferred to the congregation and regular prayers would be held therein. In light of the many worshipers, the congregation asked the local authorities to see to the eviction of the family. Concurrently, the city council met with opposition from a *trest*—a unit that controlled varying numbers of enterprises—which claimed that it had purchased the building from the local authorities in 1941, paying 35,000 rubles, and therefore opposed evicting the family, whose head seems to have been one of its workers. The municipality and district attorneys sided with the consortium, while the district SRA representative and his superior in Moscow maintained that the city must allocate a residence to the family and hand over the entire building to the congregation.[53]

Given the many difficulties involved in vacating a sound building, the authorities often tried to exploit the funds of the Jewish population for town reconstruction. Unsurprisingly, then, while the authorities refused to hand over a sound building for the purpose of worship, they were willing to consider handing over destroyed buildings so long as the Jews would assume the costs of rebuilding them. This approach was taken in Bobruisk, Mozir, Khar'kov, Kherson, Kamenets-Podol'skii, and other towns.

"In reconstructing a city," wrote the Gomel' district SRA representative, "it is customary to exploit the means and possibilities of public volunteerism. . . . The public interested in the existence of a Jewish congregation can now be used to obtain the means of rehabilitation of structures for synagogues. [For this purpose] one of the destroyed buildings may be allocated."[54] The authorities in Bobruisk gave the Jews a destroyed building to rehabilitate as a synagogue; and indeed, within a short time the congregation collected the necessary funds and many of the town's Jews actively participated in the reconstruction. But when, in 1946, the work was nearly complete, the Jews were offered a different building, also destroyed, to rebuild as a synagogue, with the cost of the repairs coming to some 100,000 rubles. On August 19, 1947, the authorities decided to temporarily close that synagogue, too, and eventually this temporary closure became permanent.[55] The practice of exploiting Jewish financing for reconstruction of ruined towns is also reflected in a case from Mozir. In early 1945, a group of Jews requested the return of one of two synagogue buildings in the town center: one was being used as a residence and the other as a produce storehouse. In July, the SRA representative demanded that the storehouse be vacated and the building transferred to the congregation. In seeming compliance with this demand, the district authorities decided in August 1945 to give the congregation, instead of said building, a "partially destroyed" structure in the Kemirovka suburb, which was about two kilometers from the city center, where most of the Jews lived. The cost of the reconstruction was 30,000–40,000 rubles and the congregation refused to accept the building because of both the distance and the cost. They therefore petitioned the Chairman of the Supreme Soviet expressing a willingness to make do with the second floor of one of the synagogues in the town center. But this request was denied and, instead, the authorities suggested that the congregation build a new structure, at its own cost, on the lot of a synagogue that had been destroyed during the war. The exploitation of religious people's money to restore buildings once used as houses of prayer, contributing thereby to town reconstruction, was not solely a local phenomenon but was in effect authorized by Moscow, which allowed structures to be offered as houses of prayer "if the faithful promise to execute the necessary reconstruction on their own and on their account."[56]

A different means to the same end, which is to say town reconstruction via private financing, involved allocation of vacant plots of land for synagogue construction. This possibility depended essentially on three conditions: (1) a grant of a plot by the government, which owned all the land in the state; (2) a grant of permission by the authorities; (3) the congregation's ability to raise the funds for synagogue construction. Even though grand structures were not contemplated, but rather small, modest ones, the construction of a new building, the ownership of which by law would pass to the state at the local or national level, was an achievement for the local authorities. Thus, for example, in 1945 the city council of Zhlobin allowed a synagogue to be built, and prayers were conducted there on a regular basis; but in January 1947, the Belorussia SRA representative wrote that "only a few days ago it was made known to me that the religious congregation . . . has erected, with permission from the local authorities and without the knowledge or agreement of the [SRA] representative, a building in which rituals are held."[57] In turn, the district authorities refused to authorize the synagogue and it was effectively nationalized.[58] Likewise in the town of Orsha, the local government turned a blind eye to the construction of a building for purposes of prayer but afterward recanted and prohibited its use.[59] In 1946 the local authorities of Mozir suggested the idea of erecting a new structure for a town synagogue. The Mozir congregation agreed to the proposal and even bought building materials, but when the time came for an official decision, the local authorities grew apprehensive about taking this step without Moscow's permission. The answer from Moscow appears to have been negative; in 1947 the local authorities announced the verdict and the investment was lost.[60] In Mogilev, after requests by the Jews to restore one of their synagogue buildings to them were refused, they asked the authorities to allocate a parcel of land for a synagogue, but the request was denied.[61]

Officially, only a registered congregation could seek a permit to build a house of prayer, but registering a congregation was conditional on already having a house of prayer. This was a trap, and so authorities inclined to go along with the Jewish requests would often ignore certain legal niceties. The town of Roslavl, for example, had an unregistered congregation operating in the open; the site for prayers was random—anywhere the congregants could find. To be registered legally, they needed a building, but being officially a "nonexistent entity" meant the application to build had to be entered in the name of a private individual. The local authorities were aware that a synagogue was being sought, especially as the plot requested had been occupied by a synagogue before the war. Even so, the authorities granted the request, and only determined interference by the SRA representative halted the construction, leaving the congregation without a synagogue.[62]

Given the refusal to allocate land and permits to build synagogues, certain congregations preferred to apply for construction permits as private individuals, with funding for construction coming from the Jewish public. Thus, officially the individual was the owner of the building, and he rented or leased it to the congregation for a symbolic sum. The local governments usually knew about these arrangements but tended to look the other way. The Belorussia SRA supervisor, for example, stated as much after his visit to the Vitebsk district in late 1947, when he discovered that the local Jews had built a synagogue structure in the district capital that was listed as the property of a Jewish woman named Shneiwais. When this arrangement was discovered, the district authorities shut down the building, and to keep the Jews from demanding its return, the government quickly filled it with residents. The building erected at the congregation's expense thus became a residential structure.[63] Likewise, the

Polotsk SRA representative learned belatedly that one of the structures being erected in the city was meant to be a synagogue. He visited the site on March 25, 1947, and "in a chat with the carpenters [working on the site], I was able in part to ascertain that the building was being erected on the congregation's account"; he then demanded an investigation of whatever individual had allocated the plot for a synagogue. Tension arose over the issue between the local authorities and the district SRA representative, but ultimately the building was expropriated by the city and turned into a kindergarten.[64]

Aside from obtaining a building from the local authorities, or erecting one, another avenue existed for acquiring a building for a synagogue: by purchasing an existing structure. Thus, for example, after the authorities in Voroshilovgrad refused to transfer to the Jews one of the few synagogues still standing, the SRA representative advised them to buy a house, and they did so, refurbishing it into a house of prayer. After the reconstruction, the synagogue attendees sought to have their congregation registered legally, but "suddenly" it turned out that the SRA representative had deemed the building unsuitable for a synagogue; and in December 1946 the district authorities prohibited its use for such. As a result, the unregistered congregation owned a building but wasn't allowed to use it. In 1949, despairing of its chances to obtain a legal permit to operate a synagogue, the congregation sold the building.[65] In the town of Nikopol', likewise, the local Jews purchased and modified a building and even began to hold regular prayers in it, but when they sought to register the congregation legally, the district SRA representative replied that the town had too few religious Jews (40–180 men and women) to justify having a synagogue. The representative added that the building wasn't suitable, as its floor wasn't tiled, its ceiling was made of wood, its walls were unplastered and a residence existed in its courtyard, contravening the regulations for operating a house of prayer.[66] In Olevsk, the government refused to permit operation of a synagogue in a building bought by the Jews, owing to its proximity to Soviet institutions. In the Zaporozh'e district, the SRA representative advised the Jews to buy a structure for a synagogue away from the residential areas. In line with this recommendation, a building was purchased in 1947 on Artema Street and was reconstructed per the government regulations; the congregation was given a temporary registration permit. Regular prayers were held in this synagogue even after the temporary permit expired; only in 1949 was it shut down.[67] In Tomashpol' in 1945, the town's Jews purchased half a house, with the sellers continuing to live in the other half. The congregation invested large sums to adapt the place for use as a synagogue, and regular prayers were held there for about two years. In 1947 the Vinnitsa District Authority refused to allow the synagogue to continue functioning because "it is under the same roof as an apartment," contravening the regulations on houses of prayer. Nevertheless, the synagogue continued to function until 1950.[68]

As mentioned, certain congregations preferred to purchase structures and list the buyer as a private individual; but this move allowed the authorities to claim fraud and hence tag the action as criminal. For example, in late 1949 an SRA representative learned that the small Jewish community of Prokof'evsk in Western Siberia had collected 16,000 rubles and purchased a villa (*osobniak*) for use as a synagogue under the name of Lifshits. Once the local authorities "discovered" this fact, they confiscated the building and converted it into a teachers' residence, even threatening Lifshits with criminal prosecution.[69] So as to prevent—as much as possible—the nationalization of buildings they had purchased, certain congregations preferred to keep the properties they bought officially listed as belonging to the seller, as an SRA representative reported in 1946:

> The religious Jewish congregation of the town of Borisov has applied to open a synagogue in a building seemingly given [to] them for this use by a private individual. Actually they bought the building, but they're worried that the structure might be nationalized and hence don't want to admit to it publicly.[70]

Highly limited possibilities existed for buying a structure for a synagogue partly because of the very low supply of buildings and partly because of the high costs. Most of the buildings purchased by Jews functioned as synagogues only for a few years and then were closed down by the government for one reason or another.

Yet another way to open a synagogue was to lease or rent a building or part of one from private owners. Leases ran for at least five years while rentals were for shorter periods. But this was not an easy option for two main reasons: (1) There was a serious building shortage in the USSR in general, and it was even more severe in areas near the front of the war with Germany. (2) The authorities had strict requirements as to location and technical specifications, and few structures met their standards. Jews thus tried renting or leasing only once they had given up on recovering a former synagogue building or once the local authorities, seeking to free themselves of pressure from the Jewish community, directly or indirectly recommended such a course. Against this background, we can understand the attitude of the Ukraine SRA representative, who agreed with the local authorities not to give the Jews of Tul'chin one of the former synagogue buildings, writing that "the Jewish congregation of Tul'chin may be registered . . . in a leased private house." But when in 1947 the Jews leased the first floor of such a house, the authorities refused to authorize it as a synagogue, since the owner continued to reside on the second floor.[71] In the towns of Mogilev-Podol'skii, Konotop, Ovruch, and Novograd-Volynskii, the authorities also preferred that synagogue space be leased over the option of allocating the congregation a former synagogue building.

All government-imposed limitations on synagogue structures also applied to buildings leased or rented. Thus, sizable operating expenses were involved, which only some congregations could sustain; usually such synagogue structures were much smaller than the ones used previously. On the issue of returning a former synagogue versus leasing a new space, the local authorities usually opposed the stance of the SRA in Moscow or in the republic's capital. The former were in daily contact with the Jewish population, which sought the recovery of synagogue buildings, even as the granting of such requests was complicated by the overall building shortage or the need to evict residents or institutions. Lease or rental of a built space was therefore a convenient solution for quite a few authorities. Thus, for example, the local authorities of Orsha accepted the lease of a building for a synagogue, after having confiscated a building that the Jews had built and paid for. But intervention by local and central authorities prohibited its use as a synagogue, and in early 1948, the building stood empty, the key in the hand of the congregation's leader.[72]

The SRA in Moscow and its representatives in the republic capitals, on the other hand, saw the lease or rental of buildings for synagogues as an undesirable phenomenon. They worried about the "damaging influence" of a synagogue on the surrounding population. Thus on September 6, 1947, the SRA chairman wrote:

> The opening of synagogues in private buildings via leases is to be allowed only in extraordinary cases. [This is to occur only] on condition that the leased building is empty of all residents, both inside the structure and nearby it (i.e., in the courtyard it shares), and that there be no schools, clubs or other educational institutions in its vicinity.[73]

These requirements were often used as the reason for rejecting congregation applications. Thus, for example, the authorities refused to permit the opening of a synagogue in the town of Dzhurin, because there was a kolkhoz club nearby, and in Ovruch, because of the nearness of the subdistrict Soviet school.[74] The authorities in Enakievo, Konstantinovka, and Kazatin also forbade the opening of synagogues in residential buildings.[75] In Shpola, on the other hand, the town authorities ignored the synagogue, which existed in a residential building, until the Kiev district SRA representative expressed his vigorous opposition to it.[76] Many of the leased and rented synagogues also did not meet the authorities' technical standards, but even in the few instances they did, the authorities did not always allow them to be run as synagogues. In Polotsk for example, the Jews leased a building from R. Y. Ostreich, "located outside the city, with no public or cultural institutions nearby, and suitable from the technical point of view[,]" for a synagogue, but the authorities did not allow it to operate, ostensibly because of its small size.[77] More generally with the leased or rented synagogues for which operation was refused, it is difficult to determine for certain whether technical specifications were actually unmet or whether authorities simply wanted an excuse to justify refusal.

Behind every registration of a congregation and every procurement of a structure for a synagogue is a serpentine tale of decisions, sometimes opposing ones, by different authorities (city halls; district authorities and district head [oblispolkom], the SRA representative, and others), that the Jews had to navigate while exploiting the various possibilities that presented themselves and enlisting the most possible resources to assist them. The few examples cited here hint at the obstacle course and the vast efforts Jewish congregations made to obtain legal authorization and procure a synagogue structure in hundreds of USSR towns. The applicants and petitioners for synagogues and registration of congregations were usually simple people: artisans, service workers, and low-ranking Soviet clerks; most were pensioners and some were living with their adult children. An examination of 238 signatories (among them 40 women) to applications for the return of synagogues in seven cities in 1945–1948 shows that only 10 percent were younger than forty-five, 19 percent were forty-five to fifty-four, more than a third (34 percent) were fifty-five to sixty-four, and more than a third (37 percent) were sixty-five and older. However, these people were only the external face presented by the community; in practice wide ranges of Jews were involved, a state of affairs that did not pass unnoticed by the authorities, as the following description from Odessa in 1948 shows:

> The congregation has people who do much more for it than those officially designated as its activists. It was enough that the congregation decided to paint the walls of the synagogue with oil paint . . . that inside a week it was painted beautifully. It was enough that the congregation decided to install electricity in the synagogue, and within two or three days it was better lit than any Soviet institution in Odessa. . . . Within two weeks the synagogue was furnished with

furniture which any Soviet state institution . . . would envy. All this was done by people . . . who can be called a secret band of activists.[78]

This "secret band of activists," a not insignificant part of the Jewish public, was usually the central element in persistent efforts to register a congregation and obtain a structure for its synagogue. This activity required the intensive use of legal procedures—applications and complaints to the authorities; exploitation of internal contradictions in the Soviet apparatus; and often circuitous means such as personal connections (called *blat*) and even the direct bribery that was common enough[79] even if only faint traces of it appear in the archival documentation.

In the procurement of synagogue buildings, as in the registration of congregations, large portions of the Jewish public were involved who had no personal need for a synagogue as a place of religious ritual. Such activity thus became an important element in the formation of a sort of clandestine infrastructure in Jewish public life.

CHAPTER THREE

The Formation of Prayer Groups (Minyanim)

Unlike the unregistered congregations that functioned in the open, usually in a structure meant for prayer and with the partial recognition of the authorities, minyans were gatherings for prayer held in private apartments. Any gatherings in private homes for the purposes of religious ritual, except those at the home of the dying or deceased, were deemed illegal if the participants lacked an explicit permit from authorities, including the locales and the dates of the gatherings.

Confusion has surrounded the legality of such gatherings. In the 1929 legislation on religion in the USSR, two terms for religious organization appear: "association" and—for settlements with fewer than twenty religious people (the minimum needed for an association)—"group" (gruppa). The latter term is extremely vague and, in the copious documentation available to us, is almost never mentioned in reference to the Jewish faith. Yet this term has misled certain Western scholars into concluding that both authorized and unauthorized minyans operated.[1] On very rare occasions, the documentation refers to "minyans under surveillance" (miniany na uchete),[2] meaning not that these operated legally but rather that the authorities knew of their existence and had them under observation. For the most part, the authorities used the Hebrew term (miniany) for the minyans, sometimes also using the phrase "illegal synagogue,"[3] "underground synagogue," or "illegal congregation." Gathering to pray on a regular basis generally required the existence of a registered house of prayer, but in special cases and only with the permission of the local authorities small groups of acquaintances were allowed to gather to pray regardless.[4] All minyans, accordingly, were unauthorized gatherings for the purpose of religious observance and, as such, illegal. That said, as Soviet publications from the "Perestroika" period reveal, gatherings by Muslims and Buddhists did take place in private homes and "for decades . . . the local Soviet authorities assented to it silently because they didn't want a confrontation with the religious [groups]."[5] Likewise, regular minyans operated throughout the Soviet Union that the authorities knew about but did not break up, at least until the late 1940s.

A potential division of minyans into types, therefore, would distinguish not between legal and illegal but between *regular* and *holiday* minyans. Minyans of the first type met for prayer every day, several times a week or on Shabbat: in other words they constituted a sort of synagogue, as defined by the 1948 report on Jewish religious activity: "They are essentially synagogues, the only difference being that they meet in private houses and operate illegally."[6] For prayer in such a minyan it sufficed to have a Torah scroll, and any participant could lead the prayers. It seems that most such minyans did have Torah scrolls, probably privately owned or purchased by the minyan regulars; almost certainly some scrolls were given to these minyans by synagogues.[7]

Participants in long-running minyans grew to know each other, formed social ties, exchanged opinions, and the like. The regular minyan was therefore a social unit, in which prayer was only a part of a broader framework of social bonds. In keeping with Jewish practice in various countries of Eastern Europe, where synagogues were organized on the basis of the members' professions, in the Soviet Union, too, certain minyans formed along professional-occupational lines. Two such minyans were described in late 1945:

> In the city of Bershad'. . . we discovered two religious groups which de facto had become special trade unions [*tsekhy*] of shoemakers and tailors . . . the people in those groups [i.e., the minyans] are workers in Cooperatives [*artel*].[8]

We can assume that these two minyans, which built professional-economic as well as social ties, were not the only such instances in the USSR. All the same, minyans based on a symbiosis of religious ritual and professional-economic interests do not seem to have been very common. Still, those who came to the regular minyans participated in a gathering that was formally regarded as illegal, and they consequently developed relations of mutual trust and understanding. The owners of the apartments where such prayers took place received a certain fee, paid by all the members; by this means a mutual assistance infrastructure took shape. A minyan was thus not only a place to pray but also a social unit, differing, in this respect, from the minyans that met only for the holidays.

During the High Holidays, the need to pray was great—especially in the Yizkor service (for remembrance of the dead) and especially after the Holocaust. The representative of the SRA in Belorussia stressed that many Jews "said that they need to organize minyans to pray for their relatives who were murdered in the time of the Great Patriotic War." At a meeting between an SRA supervisor and a minyan organizer in Gomel', the latter affirmed that "[i]n the days of the Great Patriotic War he lost a son and a daughter on the front and that he was conducting a 'memorial service' for them."[9] Although participation in holiday minyans also called for a certain degree of trust, gatherings that met a few times a year, usually by a changing group, inherently did not produce the intimacy that characterized the regular minyans.

Regular minyans could be found not only in cities without a congregation (registered or unregistered); towns with authorized synagogues had them too.[10] This was most likely due to three main reasons: (1) the large distance between residences and the synagogue and the difficulty of getting to it on Shabbat and holidays; (2) differences of opinion and mutual suspicions between minyan organizers and congregation heads; (3) the personal preference of some people to pray in relative privacy rather than in public in the synagogues.

Relations between the registered congregations and the regular minyans were complicated and differed from town to town. Mostly these relations did not turn on the varieties in prayer service or religious approach (Chassidim and their opponents—the Mitnagdim—and the like), but rather had to do with the personalities of the minyan organizers and congregation heads. In Minsk in 1948, for example, the registered congregation had "representatives" in each of the seven regular minyans; in Novograd-Volynskii the registered congregation helped organize the minyans;[11] and in Kiev a minyan for the High Holidays was formed by those who opposed the synagogue's use of a loudspeaker.[12] At times the congregations played a role, either directly or indirectly, in breaking up those minyans that they viewed as competition. Thus, for example, the SRA representative reported to the Bershad' subdistrict authorities in 1945 that, according to information given him, apparently by congregation members, a minyan was held in an apartment fifty meters from the synagogue, whose members were former collaborators with the Nazi regime in the ghetto through work in the Judenrat and police.[13] This information forced the authorities to act immediately, given their suspicions of any Jew from a Nazi-occupied area who had survived.[14] Not surprisingly, the minyan in question was disbanded and the "ritual equipment," probably Torah scrolls, was transferred to the official synagogue.[15] As noted, however, closure of minyans by bureaucratic means did not become widespread until the late 1940s.

In certain localities, relations between the minyan members and the synagogue administrators turned prickly precisely at the beginning of Khrushchev's thaw. The rabbi of the Minsk synagogue complained in 1954 that "the minyans are asserting themselves" and that many worshipers have left the synagogue, formed minyans of their own, and are now thumbing their noses at the synagogue administration. Yet the authorities did not hasten to take concrete action against the minyans.[16]

Since assembling in a minyan was illegal, the police could be summoned to shut it down and bring the organizers to trial. Yet doing so was not easy. As the Ukraine SRA representative admitted: "[T]he battle against the minyans is difficult, almost impossible. . . . Finding out who the organizers are and putting them on trial is difficult because such groups are internally cohesive, and putting all the prayer participants on trial wouldn't be right."[17] Clearly the authorities did not hasten to use the police to disperse minyans.

Religious groups that performed their rites regularly in private homes, of which the minyans were only the Jewish form, were so widespread that in June 1947 the SRA in Moscow saw fit to issue a secret directive for their immediate dispersion.[18] This order was aimed not just at Jews but at all the religious groups. An investigation in Belorussia revealed that "in almost all the towns where Jews reside there are religious groups and assemblages who gather illegally for prayers in private homes." The SRA representative in this republic thus directed all his subordinates to ensure that organizers and homeowners "who allow prayer gatherings in their homes be brought to trial."[19] Yet it was not only Belorussia, which had almost no registered congregations, that was rife with minyans; so was Ukraine. The SRA representative in the latter republic even supposed that "there is a subversive central leadership . . . organizing the minyans. The careful thought and the legal care used in the selection of the organizers . . . indicate that the organizations are not spontaneous but [planned]."[20] This Soviet bureaucrat, trained to act on directives, did not comprehend the social and psychological motives that drove so many Jews to join minyans, and assumed that some kind of central management must be guiding them.

The SRA, through its representatives in the republics and districts, was the main government body to fight the minyans. Enforcement could be done in two principal ways: summoning the police to prevent or disperse minyans, and punishment of minyan organizers and apartment owners. In certain communities the SRA certainly tried to get the security services—Ministry for Internal Affairs (MVD) and Ministry for State Security (MGB)—and the police involved. Yet the security services, at least until the early 1950s, did not attach much political significance to the minyans and so refrained from vigorous involvement, at times remaining content just to issue warnings; nor did the police embrace the task with enthusiasm. Thus, the SRA representative in the Polotsk district complained that despite the district authorities' instructions to the "city's police commander . . . to forbid gatherings of religious Jews in private apartments and to charge violators . . . violations of the District Committee decision continue."[21]

It may be assumed that the minyans became a source of private favors for quite a few bureaucrats in many localities, possibly explaining why many such bureaucrats did not hasten to use all means at their disposal to disperse the minyans. Perhaps taking strong measures against all or most minyan attendees would have aroused overly strong resentments among the Jewish population and accusations of antisemitism, which may also help explain why SRA representatives preferred to limit their efforts to the organizers and apartment owners. From a legal standpoint, someone who held a minyan in his home or organized one could be fined or sentenced to up to thirty days of forced labor. The fine, per the criminal law in Ukraine in mid-1947, was one hundred rubles—by no means a difficult sum for minyan participants to cover. Nor was the other punishment—forced labor—publicly comfortable to enforce, as most of the organizers and apartment holders were elderly and unemployed. For example, of Kiev's roughly seven regular minyans in 1947, the heads of five were over seventy, one was sixty, and one was fifty-nine.[22] The authorities thus preferred[23] to fight the minyans not by fines but through the tax system and the municipal residential rights laws.

Each inhabitant of a particular town had to be listed as its resident. The right of residence in large cities or towns with a military industry was restricted, and unlisted inhabitants could be deported. Moreover, during the war and the years that followed, many people settled in cities and for one reason or another did not get listed as residents. At any rate, as noted, in 1947 the Ukrainian authorities attempted to fight the minyans through the residential rights laws. The police were instructed to check whether organizers of minyans had the right of residence in their towns. While it isn't clear to what extent this check was actually carried out, one report stated "that the investigation [of minyan organizers] as to compliance with passport regulations [right of residence] showed that all were legally entitled to residence. Hence it is impossible to take steps against them using the residence laws."[24]

Another seemingly promising method of restricting minyan activity involved taxation of income, real or fictitious. On May 7, 1947, Kiev SRA representative I. M. Zaretskii (apparently a Jew) approached a municipal treasury official claiming that he had figures showing that the two minyans he had investigated comprised sixty members, each of whom paid fifty rubles per prayer meeting; as there are forty-nine prayer days per year . . . the minyan organizers must have been taking in 137,000 rubles a year. The Belorussia SRA representatives made similar reports to treasury officials relating to the 1947 holiday minyans in the provinces of Minsk, Vitebsk, and Gomel'.[25] However, action on these suggestions or demands made mainly by SRA representatives required the cooperation of treasury officials, and many of them were reluctant to offer it. Thus, for instance, the treasury officials in Dnepropetrovsk stated in 1948 that "you don't make millions running a minyan" and refused to tax the apartment-owners. A similar statement was made by a treasury official in Odessa that year when refusing to tax an apartment owner.[26] In Dnepropetrovsk, the vigorous intercession of the town's Communist Party committee was needed to force payment of nine thousand rubles by two minyans. In Leningrad, treasury officials were compelled to put apartment-renters for minyans on trial for tax offenses, but after lengthy legal deliberations the defendants were acquitted, as the treasury had not properly supported the case.[27] In Gomel', conversely, the authorities didn't need the courts, deciding on January 31, 1949, to tax the apartment owners. But as an additional ruling from four months later (May 9)[28] shows, the ruling was not enforced, nor probably was a subsequent ruling. It thus seems that the "tax grinder" was not a simple or especially efficient means of dispersing the minyans either. A statement made in 1948 by the Belorussia SRA supervisor confirms that

> the existence of so many illegal religious associations [minyans] stems from the fact that the local authorities do not take sufficient steps to forbid their activity and the treasury agencies fail completely to tax the organizers and landlords who offer up their houses [for this activity].[29]

Given the involvement of assorted Soviet agencies in the fight against the minyans and certain oppositions among them, bribery was one means of ensuring the minyans' survival. The Ukraine SRA representative reported that one of the minyan organizers in Kiev was paying the neighborhood policeman three hundred rubles a week, and the manager of the building (*upravdo-mom*) where the minyan met was getting two hundred rubles a week in "hush money."[30] Of course for most cases of bribery no traces appear in the archival documentation, and we learn of it only when things went wrong. One such case involved Zaretskii (the Kiev district SRA representative until 1949), who permitted Davidov—a Jew over seventy years old—to hold a minyan in his home until April 1946, after which Zaretskii demanded that it be dispersed. Accordingly, in 1947 fifty Jews (in their sixties and seventies) sent a petition to Ukraine Communist Party secretary Lazar Kaganovich, stating that the great distance from their homes to the synagogue and the associated transportation difficulties compelled them to seek permission to maintain the minyan. The request was passed back to Zaretskii, who summoned Davidov and forbade him from holding the minyan in his home. Davidov then attempted the "tried and true" means of "softening" Zaretskii. On July 20, 1947, one of Zaretskii's old friends came to his house and asked to speak with him about the Davidov minyan. According to Zaretskii, he advised his guest "not to lobby for Davidov," and if the latter wished to discuss the subject he should come to his office. Davidov indeed came to Zaretskii's office two days later. The events that ensued were described by Zaretskii in a letter to the Ukraine SRA representative:

> I made it clear to him [Davidov] that on the issue [of keeping the minyan] the conversation was over. I got up and went to the cabinet to put back the file. When I turned around, I saw that Davidov had put a packet of cash under the inkwell on my desk. When I saw this I asked him to wait a moment and went to the door to summon someone who could serve as a witness to Davidov's attempt to bribe me. But Davidov grabbed at my feet from behind and while on his knees, begged me not to prosecute him and promised he would not give more money and wouldn't tell anyone. . . . [A]t that moment Sazonov, who had heard the noise, came into the room. When Davidov saw Sazonov he got up quickly, ran to the desk, grabbed the money and fled the room . . . so quickly that we weren't able to catch him. . . . In view of the attempt to bribe me with money . . . it would be fitting if the appropriate institutions would take the appropriate steps . . . against this vile, criminal man.

This tragicomic episode need not be taken at face value; it is quite possible that this Sazonov had interrupted Zaretskii's receipt of the bribe and made it necessary for the latter to devise this story. Nor is the elder man's swift flight credible. Yet whatever the accuracy or inaccuracy of the story, it tells something about the role of bribes in the survival of minyans.[31] Once Zaretskii came under suspicion of corruption, he tried to demonstrate his righteousness: on October 5, 1948, he turned to Ukraine's minister for internal affairs demanding that the police take appropriate action to disperse the minyans that were about to assemble for the High Holidays. Yet the minister contented himself with a casual response in a letter dated November 2 (after the holidays) that the appropriate measures had been taken, even though no measures at all had been taken. Zaretskii also demanded of the Kiev police that it act as follows against minyan organizers (minianshchiki): (a) impose heavy taxes on minyan organizers and those renting apartments to that end; (b) banish from town those who continue to organize minyans after being warned about the practice; (c) indict those who take bribes from minyan organizers—which is why the organizers operate with impunity.[32] Yet Zaretskii's demands were not only ignored, they even gained him enemies in the local bureaucracy.[33]

In Minsk, seven regular minyans that "in practice had become synagogues" were functioning in 1948, and regular minyans operated in the cities of Lepel',

Vitebsk, Slutsk, Brest-Litovsk, and Mogilev. Gomel' had seven regular minyans in January 1949. There were four minyans in Bobruisk in which a total of nearly three hundred people prayed every Shabbat; the local authorities did not act "to close down the illegal synagogues [i.e., minyans]." Regular minyans were to be found not only in towns with relatively sizable Jewish populations but also in those with very small ones. Thus, for instance, the towns of Mikashev-ichi and Bragin had regular minyans, and Rechitsa had two, even though two years earlier the Belorussia SRA representative had written to the authorities demanding that minyan organizers and apartment owners be heavily taxed.[34] Even the small Jewish community in the town of Melitopol' in the district of Zaporozh'e had a regular minyan running since the end of the war. The authorities dispersed it in 1948, and the local Jews petitioned the Chairman of the Supreme Soviet of Ukraine, writing that "we Jews will be forced to hold our national prayers under the open sky in the Jewish cemetery, where our Jews are resting who were killed by the Fascist murderers." The response to this letter was that "holding prayers outside of a structure designated for such is absolutely forbidden."[35] Nevertheless, prayers continued to be held in the more-or-less regular minyans in many towns of the Soviet Union.

Partial figures indicate that in Belorussia alone, some thirty regular min-yans operated in thirteen cities and towns between 1944 and 1948, with each municipality having between thirty and seventy people gathering for prayer on Shabbat. It would not be excessive to estimate the number of Shabbat minyan-goers in Belorussia at 1,500–2,000, exceeding the number who prayed at the republic's two official synagogues. The number of regular minyans was large not only in Belorussia, but also in Ukraine, which during 1944–1948 had some seventy registered and unregistered congregations. Very partial data suggest the presence of at least seventy or eighty regular minyans, spread across twenty-three settlements, which the authorities knew about and are mentioned in the documentation.[36] According to our partial figures, these Shabbat minyans had not just the requisite ten men but an average of seventy men and women. In Ukraine, therefore, some 5,000–6,000 worshipers at-tended Shabbat minyans, counting both men and women. Across the entire Soviet Union, hundreds of minyans may well have operated. Almost certainly, the minyan activity did not involve only those who came to pray but also their sons and daughters, quite a few of whom would have had positions of status in Soviet society.

On holidays, the regular minyans did not have enough room to hold all those who wished to take part. The numbers of Jews who wanted to participate had grown considerably due to the Holocaust, since many sought to commemorate their family members who had perished in such cruel circumstances. Unlike the regular minyans, holiday minyans in a private home were, in theory, permitted by the SRA regulations, and a group of people had the right to apply to the local authorities or the SRA representative to perform a religious rite, in this case prayer, in a private house on a specific date or dates. The response of the authorities to applications of this sort depended on how intense the antireligion policy was in the Soviet Union at that moment, as well as on local conditions. Thus, to thwart calls of this kind in advance of the High Holidays of 1947, on September 3, the Belorussia SRA representative sent a circular to all the district authorities stating that many Jews would be seeking permits for minyans and that these were not to be granted by any means; that where minyans are nevertheless held they are to be fined and taxed heavily; and that "the district authorities and the police are to prohibit all unregistered religious congregations from holding any assemblies whatsoever." Yet most local authorities seem to have ignored this circular, and a few contented themselves with issuing a circular of a similar kind accompanied by no particular action.[37] All this correspondence was kept secret, however, so it is unsurprising that the next year Jews in certain towns applied to the authorities for permits to hold minyans for the holidays. A Jew from Baranovichi, for example, sought permission to hold a minyan. When asked whether he himself was a religious person, he replied "religious/nonreligious."[38] In Grodno in September 1948, twenty-one Jews applied for permission to gather for prayers on the High Holidays. Similar applications were made in Kazatin, Kamenets-Podol'skii, and Mikashevichi.[39] Yet most of these applications were denied. Jews interested in prayer in public accordingly preferred not to make formal applications but to follow the hints of the local authorities. Indeed, despite the September 3 circular of the SRA representative for Belorussia, during the Sukkot holiday of 1947, six minyans operated in Minsk alone—in addition to the seven regular minyans—and prayers in holiday minyans were held in at least seven other cities in Belorussia.[40] In 1947, holiday minyans were held in Ovruch; for the High Holidays of 1948, minyans in addition to those held regularly were organized in Moscow, Leningrad, Tashkent, Gorkii, and Kiev.[41]

As the holidays approached, the minyan organizers would typically rent a room or an apartment from a private individual, and would bring to it a Torah scroll and the needed furniture. But in other cases, apparently quite a few, an agreement of a different sort was reached with Soviet agencies. One such case is the agreement made by one of the minyan organizers in the town of Dnepropetrovsk before the High Holidays and Sukkot of 1948. The chairman of the town's workers union offered the Jewish worshipers the use of the town culture hall in exchange for their willingness to repair, at their expense, the oven and the floor of the clubroom.[42] Thus, the minyan's worshipers prayed in a spacious hall, which quite likely had pictures of Lenin and Stalin adorning it and walls covered with Soviet and perhaps antireligion slogans. This setting can serve as a graphic illustration of some of the contradictions of religious practice in the Soviet Union.

The regular minyans owed their existence to the will of the thousands of Jews who preferred, for whatever reason, to pray there rather than in synagogues (where synagogues existed). These people were willing to reach into their own pockets to cover the expenses of keeping the minyans, a share of the fines and taxes imposed on the organizers and apartment owners, and part of the bribes, too, when necessary. The survival of the minyans depended also on the hundreds of organizers who acted mainly out of ethnic-religious motives, although the apartment owners no doubt derived income from their role. The broad activity of the regular minyans as well as the holiday minyans was possible in these years mainly because the center was unable to impose its will on the district establishments, and many Soviet agencies were unwilling to act firmly and vigorously to shut down the minyans. For several years, Jewish social groups were thus enabled to exist under the surface. The large number of minyans organized for the holidays, as well as the growth in the size and number of the regular minyans, arose out of the deep spiritual need of many Jews to commemorate family members who had been murdered by the Nazis.

CHAPTER FOUR
Jewish Spiritual Needs in the Aftermath of the Holocaust

Between 1944 and 1948, broad sectors of the Jewish public participated directly or indirectly in the formation of congregations and the opening of synagogues. This prompts an obvious question: are we to regard this phenomenon as a case of a true religious revival among the Jews of the USSR, or should it be explained in terms of the special conditions of the time and new roles taken on by the religious congregations?

During the Soviet-German war and the few years afterward (1942–1948), Jews were represented to the authorities and to world Jewry by the Jewish Anti-Fascist Committee, a Moscow-based organization of relatively few members drawn from the Jewish cultural elite, most of them active in Yiddish language circles. The committee did not have branches in the provinces and had scant room for the initiatives or active involvement of Jews from more peripheral areas and towns. Jews from those areas could, at most, approach the committee with suggestions or complaints, which, following Jewish intercessionist tradition, would be forwarded to the local or district authorities, without the committee taking an official role in responding to them. Some correspondents of the committee's newspaper (*Eynikayt*), who to an extent represented the committee, tried to report on Jewish life in the periphery, but the articles, which were subjected to a double censorship—self-imposed by the author for self-protective reasons, and again by the editorial board—rarely gave voice to the urgent needs of many Jews, such as for immediate material assistance, the desire to memorialize Holocaust victims, and the like.[1] The second legitimate Jewish institution existing in the Soviet Union in those years was the Yiddish writers' sections of the Writers' Union of the USSR. Many of the writers were indeed somewhat aware of the needs of the Jewish population, and because of the Holocaust a few felt increasing anguish at any further Jew lost to assimilation; yet a majority kept their feelings to themselves or at most expressed them among a limited circle of friends.[2] The open activity of the writers thus was limited to occasional public invitations for discussions on literary topics, and naturally this interested only a small audience. Events of this kind took place mainly in Birobidzan, Moscow, Minsk, and Kiev, and infrequently in other towns. But they could not fulfill the spiritual need of many Jews for a vibrant, relevant encounter.

The three Yiddish magazines published in those years[3] might conceivably have supplied the Yiddish reader with a source of ethnic identification, but they could not sate the spiritual need for "togetherness" that grew especially strong after the Holocaust, and of course they did not reach the large segment of the Jewish population who didn't know Yiddish.

The third legitimate Jewish institution in the USSR of those years was the theater. There were four such professional theaters—the Jewish state theater (GOSET) in Moscow; the Jewish state theater in Minsk, Belorussia; the Jewish state theater in Chernovtsy, Ukraine; and the Jewish theater in Birobidzan. Actually the theaters were the only places where large numbers of Jews could meet each other. Unsurprisingly, then, the theaters were packed at each performance, and the atmosphere was as follows, in the words of the assistant to the director of Ukraine's Jewish theater on a 1945 visit to Kiev:

> The theater, stalls and gallery, full to overflowing . . . the audience: writers and poets . . . doctors and painters, workers and artists, people of many professions . . . the space was hushed . . . a black curtain was raised and in glowing white letters were the words in Hebrew: "The People of Israel—live." Suddenly the audience rose as one to its feet . . . the thunder of applause shook the theater building . . . with the applause rising like an electric current passing through the audience came the cry: The People of Israel—live . . . The People of Israel—live . . . the applause is unceasing . . . choked back sobs are heard . . . women weep . . . men's eyes well up with tears.[4]

Yet this sort of experience was limited primarily to Jews who lived in the three cities with theaters; and increasingly the requests by theater companies to tour as many cities as possible were met with objections from the authorities.[5] For Jews in the outlying towns, the congregation and synagogue were the only places left to act and meet in a Jewish context. This was particularly noticeable in the areas recently liberated from the Nazi occupation.

With the liberation of each city and town, the Jews who had been hiding among the non-Jewish population emerged into view. From these individuals, the Jewish officers and soldiers learned of the fate of the Jewish population—in most cases, this fate was brutal annihilation in antitank ditches, mines, and pits dug near the municipalities especially for mass burial. One by one, often within weeks of the liberation, the Jews reassembled—those from villages where they had found a shelter during the occupation, those few who had survived the Nazi concentration camps, and those who emerged from the forests where they had fought alongside the partisans. In time they were joined by Jewish officers and soldiers of the Red Army who had been discharged due to wounds or other factors and been sent to their own homes or those of their relatives. What they all shared was a loneliness and sense of orphanhood—each and every one had lost family in the Holocaust and had known the hostility of the surrounding population. These people, singly or as parts of families, searched for others who had gone through similar experiences and felt similar feelings—that is, Jews like themselves. This need was recognized even by Nikita Khrushchev—who served as first secretary of the Communist Party of Ukraine beginning in 1938 and as Ukraine's prime minister beginning in 1944—who visited one of the cities immediately after the liberation. He noted in a letter to Stalin that Jews "who meet each other in the street kiss one another with tears of joy in their eyes."[6]

The government in the liberated areas worked to quickly restore economic and administrative activity, and even though the authorities, especially in Ukraine, discriminated against Jews in the granting of permits to return to the liberated areas, growing numbers of Jews returned anyway. Like their forerunners, those Jews confronted the results of the Holocaust, and feelings of "togetherness" characterized many of them as well. Jews who only four or five years earlier had viewed themselves as integral to surrounding Soviet society now felt alienated from it. The Jewish-Russian writer Gregory Svirsky (b. 1921) touched on this alienation in his novel *Zalozhniki,* which is subtitled *The Personal Testimony of a Soviet Jew.* As the war ends, the novel's heroine (b. 1924) visits her hometown (Shirokoe, near Krivoi-Rog in Ukraine), which she had left for Moscow on the eve of the war. There she meets friends who witnessed the murder of her mother, father, and brother, and finds that several of the neighbors are using possessions from her family's home. The young woman keeps quiet, but feels deep within her the unraveling of the ties that had bound her to this society;[7] her alienation grows under the influence of the antisemitism common among certain strata of the non-Jewish population.[8] Many Jews felt rage toward the surrounding population for either calmly looking on as their relatives were sent to their death or, in some cases, taking an active role in their murder. This situation created a social and psychological atmosphere conducive to public Jewish activism not only by a few writers, journalists, and members of the elite, but also by numerous Jews from the peripheral regions.

The only local, legal framework for such public activity was the congregation, and the physical entity symbolizing its existence was the synagogue. The congregation and the synagogue thus became a wide locus of activity for the expression of ethnic Jewish sentiments that may not have been decidedly religious in nature. This ethnic aspect of Jewish organizational activity was pointed out by the SRA chairman in one of his first reports to Soviet prime minister Molotov (December 1945), in which he wrote:

> What uniquely typifies the Jewish religious congregations is their obvious aspiration to grant their organization more of a social-political meaning than a religious one; [an organization] that expresses and bears the [ethnic-] national interests of the Jewish people as a whole. Incidents have been reported in which applicants and lobbyists for opening a synagogue explicitly say that they themselves, and those they represent, are remote from religion and that they are active in the congregation only because [they view] the organization as the sole form for [achieving] national unity.[9]

This perspective on synagogues was further made clear by the SRA chairman at a meeting of his representatives at RSFSR:

> Based on the special historical conditions of the development of the Jewish people, religious Jews, in contrast to those of other religions, see the synagogue not as a house of prayer, meant only for the public performance of religious rites, but also as a religious-political, religious-social organization—or more exactly a political-religious, socioreligious and sometimes purely sociopolitical [organization].[10]

The speaker thus stressed that the social or public aspect, and not the ritual-religious one, was the primary impetus for Jewish activism toward forming synagogues. In his summary of the SRA's work for 1946, he also mentions the growth of ethnic identification on the part of the Jewish population following the Holocaust:

> The tragic victimization of the Jewish people during the war has caused a significant increase in national sentiments. A special "Soviet" Zionism has emerged, the representatives of which do not see the ways and means of the problem which for some time has been solved in the USSR, viz., the Jewish problem, and declare that "the synagogue is the only place for national [ethnic] assembly and the only focus of the ethnic culture." This is the basis on which a gathering around the synagogues is taking place not only among religious Jews but also in many cases among people who have nothing to do with religion, even Communists.[11]

Another summary stressed that Jews were engaged in especially widespread activity for the opening of synagogues with the intent of turning them into "centers of Jewish public life."[12] Here it is worth noting that from the early 1930s on, the authorities did not acknowledge even the concept of Jewish public life, even as Jews were recognized as one of the peoples of the USSR. The phrase "Jewish public life" itself was considered an ethnic-chauvinist expression, not to mention any pretension by Jews themselves to speak out for their community interests. This helps explain why the Jewish Anti-Fascist Committee did not use this phrase: at most it spoke of Jews or the Jewish population.

The unique ethnic-national character of Jewish religious activity was also pointed out by the Ukraine SRA representative in his mid-1947 report:

> Daily observation and study of the internal processes of the religious congregations decisively confirms the uniqueness of this religion, which explicitly strives to give [the religious congregations] a meaning and form not so much of religious associations but of sociopolitical organizations, which bear and express the interests of the Jewish people. There were cases in which the opening of synagogues was handled by people quite remote from religion; their interest was that they viewed the religious congregations as the only form of [ethnic-] national union.[13]

Likewise, the Moldavia SRA representative stated in January 1948 that

> the activity of the Jewish religious congregations is blatantly permeated by national aspirations. This is clearly manifested in the appearance of the congregations as representatives not only of religious people but in the name of all the Jewish population in the congregation's area. . . . The leaders of the Jewish religious congregations seek to turn the prayer house [synagogue] not only into a place where the devout can satisfy their ritual needs but their cultural needs [as well]. The rabbi of the Kishinev congregation—Rabbi [Yosef] Epel'boim—frequently raised the question of holding in the synagogue . . . concerts in Yiddish [evreiskii iazyk], on the grounds that Kishinev has no Jewish theater. . . . A long line of rabbis have demanded that a school for Jewish children be arranged in the synagogue, on the argument that as the Jews are assimilating and forgetting their mother tongue and customs the synagogue must attend to this."[14]

In L'vov, for example, the nonreligious activists who were closely involved in synagogue life, led by Lev Serebriany the *gabbai*, insisted that the congregation take upon itself the job of broadening Yiddish cultural activities. The congregation should arrange lectures in Yiddish, found a library, and even see to the formation of a Jewish theater in the city.[15] In Leningrad, too, the congregation wished to found a library, and when its members were asked whether the library's books would be religious texts, they answered that they wanted journals and literature in general.[16] Based on this information, the SRA chairman, in a summary delivered to the USSR government in June 1948, noted:

> The clerical-nationalist elements . . . use the particularity of the Jewish faith, in which religious rites frequently mesh with national aspects; [they] strive to turn the synagogue into a social-ethnic organization. The representatives of these congregations usually appear speaking in the name of the Jewish people and seek to develop broad charitable activities at the scale of the whole Jewish community; they run fundraising campaigns among the entire Jewish population for the upkeep of cemeteries; sponsor the erection of monuments to Jewish heroes and victims of the Great Patriotic War; form ties with other congregations in the USSR and abroad; and seek to bring as many Jews as possible under the sway of the congregation, regardless of their religious views.[17]

Though we ought not accept the SRA chairman's simplistic explanation that broad Jewish involvement in congregational life resulted mainly from the efforts of "clerical-nationalist elements," his account does correctly suggest the mingling of ethnic and religious motivations. It thus seems that the SRA chairman had a deeper understanding of the broad Jewish congregational activism than his representative in Belorussia, who on November 25, 1947, wrote to his superior in Moscow that "after the war religious fanaticism increased among the Jewish population . . . and people . . . who before the war behaved as complete atheists had now become strictly observant Jews."[18] The SRA chairman replied as follows:

> [T]he activity [of the Jewish congregations] is manifested mostly not on the part of the religious masses . . . [and so] it is doubtful that we can conclude that religious fanaticism has grown among the Jewish population. . . . It is more correct to assume that the synagogue is concentrating the Jews around it, not because they are starting to have a greater need for religious rites but because the synagogue has begun to take upon itself more of the roles of a sort of center of Jewish public life.[19]

This analysis is supported by reports of concrete cases. Thus, for example, in late 1947 the Belorussia SRA representative reported that after permission had been denied to operate the Orsha synagogue, "several employees from Soviet institutions came to me and asked, 'why is it so hard for you to register the congregation?! Let our old folks pray.' They often add the justification that 'we are the people that has suffered the most and we wish to pray.'"[20] The SRA representative who visited Mogilev in March 1948 likewise stated that

> lately, we can see a significant increase in town in the initiators of Jewish religious activity, who seek to grant the congregation . . . a character not so much religious as ethnic. Convincing evidence to this effect is the list of names submitted to me by the congregation. . . . [I]t includes many young citizens and clerks who are not religious and who were included in the list . . . to expand . . . the numbers of the latter.[21]

Of the Khar'kov congregation, the Ukraine SRA representative reported that "the local intelligentsia, which is not part of the religious public, takes an active part in synagogue life and tries with all its might and means to influence the synagogue in a narrow [ethnic-] national direction";[22] an activist from that congregation, Rivlin, told the SRA representative that "the town's intelligentsia is joining us, most of it nonreligious people . . . who love their nation." The congregation wanted to arrange a general meeting of the town's Jews in the synagogue to raise funds for a Jewish old age home and for the needy, but the authorities forbade it.[23] Indeed, the Ukraine SRA representative stated in his 1947 report that "there were cases of applications to open synagogues by persons far removed from religion, who were interested in this only because they view the religious congregations as the only form of national unification."[24]

Thus, characterizing the synagogue activity in the USSR after the Second World War as a religious awakening seems hasty; rather the activity should be regarded primarily as an ethnic-national awakening consequent to the Holocaust. The congregation and synagogue were the only legal, local venues in which nonreligious as well as religious Jews could give expression to their sense of belonging as Jews.

The considerable diversity of activists for social and cultural causes in the framework of the congregation—which embraced the religious and nonreligious, the intelligentsia and the common folk—was a potential source of tension. And the border was at times blurred between a desire for status and influence and the wish for emphasis on a particular realm of activity. While the intelligentsia (mostly nonreligious) and the religious agreed in full in quite a few realms—most notably the desire to memorialize the victims of the Holocaust—points of friction were not in short supply. Some of a congregation's activists wanted to give priority to the religious-ritualistic aspects, while others saw the congregation mainly as a framework for activities unrelated to the narrow religious field. Each side sought the encouragement and support of the authorities, chiefly the representatives of the SRA, who usually supported the groups that focused their interest on the religious-ritualistic aspects. Indeed, the SRA representative wrote to the USSR prime minister that

> attempts by the heads of certain religious Jewish congregations to grant the synagogue a strictly religious nature are meeting the fierce opposition of the elements with nationalistic tendencies, who accuse [the former] of a policy of "assimilation" and indeed of the destruction of Judaism as a people.[25]

These tensions, well known in various countries, were not evaded by the Jews of the USSR in the period in question, and they indicate the significance of the congregation not only to the religiously observant groups, who were extremely small in number, but to wide swaths of the Jewish public. Yet ultimately it was neither differences of opinion, nor of principle, nor any personal conflicts, that constituted the chief cause of the breakup of the congregations, closure of synagogues, and dispersion of minyans. The cause, rather, was the shift in Soviet policy, which became apparent in the late 1940s.

CHAPTER FIVE

Stalin's Final Years, 1949 – 1953
PERSECUTION AND THE THREAT OF LIQUIDATION

Shifts in the Policy toward Religion

In late 1948, signs pointed to a change away from the government's stance of relative tolerance toward religion,[1] stemming almost certainly from a combination of domestic and foreign policy shifts in the USSR. In the late 1940s, the battle against "nationalistic aberrations" had intensified and the security services gained in power. The number of prisoners in the Corrective Labor Camps (*Ispravitel'no trudovye lageria*) almost doubled (from 786,441 in 1947 to 1,533,767 in 1951) and likewise the number of Jewish internees grew by almost 50 percent (9,530 to 14,374).[2] The government had increasingly less need for the services of the Russian Orthodox Church, a change in relations that was echoed in interactions with other religions as well. In the authorities' view, the Orthodox Church had ended its assigned functions: to bring the Orthodox churches in areas annexed by the USSR in World War Two under the control of the Muscovite Patriarchate and to dismantle the Greek-Catholic Church in Ukraine, a focus of Ukrainian nationalism.[3] In this context, voices of intolerance toward religion within the Soviet establishment grew louder. These groups, mainly activists of the Komsomol (Communist Youth movement), struggled to reconcile the contradictions between the Communist Party platform and the situation on the ground. The party platform asserted the aspiration "to liberate the laboring masses from religious prejudices . . . and is organizing antireligion propaganda . . . of the broadest kind." On the ground, however, widespread religious activity was taking place, which had the increasing participation of the youth.[4] This situation produced confusion, as the secretary of the Communist Party for propaganda in the Stavropol' area (*krai*) reported: "Certain Communists are confused about the attitude of our Party toward religion and even are expressing their opinion that the Party platform ought to be changed." Grassroots activists, encouraged by central figures in the Soviet leadership, sought a decision to launch an antireligion campaign, but Stalin wasn't interested in such an intensive public campaign, including one against the Jewish religion.[5] Still, the intent to restrict religious influence was expressed in a decision critical of the Soviet for Russian Orthodox Church Affairs; and the Ukraine SRA representative likewise "admitted" in 1949 that his institution had made mistakes in the past, and that henceforth vigorous measures would be taken against those who violate Soviet laws and regulations on religion "so as to shrink the number of religious organizations."[6] Meanwhile, the religious associations themselves, chiefly the Russian Orthodox Church, had lost their value as tools of propaganda and foreign policy relations owing to the Cold War and Soviet disinterest in world public opinion. Exceptions to this rule did exist, however, as when the government held the Congress of Religious Representatives for Peace in Zagorsk in May 1952, with participants including the rabbi of Moscow's main synagogue, Shlomo Shlifer (who also served as a panelist),[7] and Rabbi Yitchak ben Hersch Shekhtman of Kiev, who spoke at the concluding ceremony. In his address, Shekhtman stressed the words of the prophets on peace and the daily *amida* prayers, which end with a blessing of peace; he also spoke of the murders at Babi Yar, Maidanek, and Treblinka, though without mentioning that most of the victims were Jewish.[8]

The government thus enacted a policy of minimizing the influence of religion, but without involving the public—that is to say, not through a broad propaganda campaign but rather through quiet repression. This was Stalin's preferred method in other realms as well.

The general policy of reducing the number of prayer houses had special repercussions for the Jews, because the Jewish religion is also an ethnicity and any damage to it had extra impact. This was especially true given that other forms of community existence had been stripped from the Jews with the dismantling of the Jewish Anti-Fascist Committee and Yiddish Writers' sections of the Writers' Union of the USSR in late 1948, leaving the theaters as the last vestiges of Soviet Jewish culture in 1949. Meanwhile, an "atomization" policy toward the Jewish population was implemented, making the congregation the sole authorized remnant of Jewish public life. The authorities followed an increasingly stringent policy meant to reduce the number of congregations (synagogues) across the country on the one hand and, on the other, to confine Jewish religious activity to sacramental observances. This approach was reflected in the instructions of the Ukraine SRA representative in advance of the 1949 autumn Jewish holidays (High Holidays and Sukkot) to heighten the supervision of synagogues, as the Jews were likely to break the law in their prayer houses; the SRA representative also demanded that these instructions be transmitted to the local authorities so that they would take corresponding measures.[9] The trend was likewise quite clear in the circular sent out by the SRA chairman before Passover 1950. He instructed his representatives in the republics and districts to pay attention to "nationalist propaganda" and to the "nature of the sermons" and required these representatives to "warn the congregation heads that sermons must have exclusively religious content."[10] In turn, the rabbis were careful to ensure that their sermons contained nothing that could be interpreted as having hidden "nationalistic" significance. Increasingly, the authorities applied pressure to "purify" the Jewish religion of its historical and ethnic references. Now the enemy was Zionism, displayed as one of the most dangerous arms of imperialism and as an enemy of the USSR; any expression of ethnic-national sentiments rooted in the past or present was seen as an expression of Zionism. The Ukraine SRA representative thus affirmed in April 1949 that "internal study of the Jewish religious congregations shows that many congregations are exploited by certain elements of religious types [tserkovinki] that have infiltrated the congregation leadership and turned it . . . into hotbeds of nationalist expression." As an example of such activity, the writer cited efforts to commemorate the Holocaust.[11]

The words in the previous passage were carefully formulated by someone who knew Soviet policy well. If the writer had unambiguously stated that congregations were "hotbeds of Jewish nationalism," the natural conclusion would be that they must be shut down, as had been done to the Soviet Jewish institutions; the writer thus preferred to state more ambiguously that "certain elements" had infiltrated the congregations and were exploiting them for nationalistic purposes, while the congregation itself was not specially nationalist and remained within the bounds designated by the government. In the same spirit, the Zhitomir district SRA representative wrote in 1949 that "nationalistic elements" had taken over the Berdichev congregation and that "it . . . has gone beyond the religious domain and seeks to play a role of a Jewish-nationalist entity."[12] To prevent such a drift, the authorities in various cities decided that the doors to the synagogues must remain locked except during times of prayer and that sleeping therein was forbidden.

The synagogue buildings in Eastern Europe were not only places of worship but also of study, gathering, and even lodgment for guests, attributes the authorities now sought to restrict or prevent. After the Holocaust, many Jews wandered from town to town, some of them alone, in search of relatives and the possibility of making do in a different city; accordingly, these people sought to connect with local Jews who might help them. The synagogue was often the only place for such meetings, and some of the itinerants, lacking other possibilities, would be given a place to sleep in the synagogue. By the late 1940s the numbers of such wanderers had declined, but others such as ritual circumcisers from other towns, fundraisers, and plain beggars still found shelter in the synagogues. These people, who drifted from congregation to congregation, were a source of information about happenings in other places—a fact not pleasing to the authorities, who thus sought to restrict the practice.[13]

Synagogue leaders tried to prevent conversation during prayer partly because it was a distraction and partly out of fear of the evil eye, but during the "third feast" on Shabbat, when a glass of wine or vodka was usually sipped, tongues loosened and the few congregants exchanged opinions—a practice frowned upon by the authorities. Perhaps unsurprisingly, in 1951, the Ukraine SRA representative approached his superiors in Moscow and suggested prohibiting the third feast in all the synagogues. The SRA chairman, who must have consulted his experts on Jewish religion to ascertain that the third feast is a religious commandment, replied that the feasts could not be prohibited outright "but if the third feast will be used for purposes unconnected to religious ritual, then the guilty [parties] . . . must accept the consequences."[14] Notwithstanding this ambivalent ruling, the authorities in certain cities forbade the feast, and when the American rabbi Isaac Ozband[15] was asked if the feast should be celebrated anyway, he answered that "this is not a decree aimed to force Jews to violate their religion. . . . [The authorities] are forbidding all assemblies and their main intent is [to stop] the assembly and not the upholding of the commandment. . . . [Accordingly] there is not an obligation here [to sacrifice practice for its sake]."[16] Somewhat ironically, the SRA representative stressed the religious character of the feast while the rabbi, fearing the fate of those who might resist this edict and incur the repercussions on religious life, stressed its social aspects.

The authorities were thus conscious that synagogues were playing more than simply a ritual-religious role. Along these lines, the deputy chairman of the Ukraine SRA directed all his subordinates that "in cases where the SRA representative receives information of nationalist-Zionist tendencies on the part of the activist members of the synagogues, all material must be passed immediately to the institutions of the Ministry of State Security (NKGB)."[17] There were indeed cases in which persons inside or outside the congregation supplied information of this kind to the authorities. For example, the Vinnitsa district SRA representative received an anonymous letter stating that "in 1945 students distributed leaflets in the Zhmerinka [synagogue] about Israel, and [the *gabbai*] failed to report this while downplaying the incident." (Many years later, the distributors of the leaflets attested that "the synagogue's *gabbai* immediately gathered the leaflets and passed them to the authorized bodies.")

The informer's letter also noted that the head of the congregation invited a cantor with a choir of four singers from Vinnitsa for the High Holidays; that such words as "Jerusalem" and the "Land of Israel" were heard during prayers; and that the cantor "sung some of the prayers to the tune of the Israeli national anthem."[18] In the case of Jerusalem and the Land of Israel, the terms were interpreted by the authorities as Zionist propaganda.

In this period, therefore, Soviet policy with respect to the Jewish religion seems to have tended toward separating out elements of society who had less interest in Judaism's ritual-religious aspects and viewing the congregation as primarily a context for ethnic-nationalist activities. This tendency is apparent in a 1950 report by the Ukraine SRA representative stating that his agency was tasked, among other things, with stopping "the activity of the organizers and activist cadres of the minyans, and [collecting] information about synagogues which maintain ties with Zionist groups and other nationalist circles."[19] This stand was reiterated more explicitly by the Ukraine SRA representative in his report on religious activity for the final quarter of 1952.[20] In that year, the Poltava district SRA representative observed that "a characteristic phenomenon among many of the religious is to protect the synagogue at any cost, and to broaden it to the extent possible because the synagogue *is a certain type of Jewish organization,* despite it being religious [emphasis in original]."[21] Indeed many synagogue activists, especially those who helped out behind the scenes, supported the synagogue not solely because it was a religious institution.

The authorities' approach was somewhat conflicted: on the one hand, they regarded the congregations as Jewish organizations with a nationalist-Zionist complexion while on the other they were reluctant to go so far as to disperse all the congregations and shut down all the synagogues. Consequently, the government agencies made efforts to reduce the numbers of synagogues and in some cases move them away from the cities so that they would not serve as a focal point for gatherings of Jews.

Given the increasingly heavy hand leveled against religion in general and the Jewish religion in particular, the authorities, and especially the SRA, instituted a combined action between 1949 and 1952 that had three aims: (1) to remove the ethnic and historical aspects from Jewish ritual activity as much as possible; and to distance Jews with positions in the local Soviet bureaucracy—starting with Communist Party members—from the synagogues; (2) to increase persecution of the minyans and the people associated with them; and (3) to reduce the number of legally registered congregations and shut down the unregistered synagogues.

TAMPING DOWN NATIONALISM:
DISTANCING THE NONRELIGIOUS FROM CONGREGATIONS

The Jewish religion contains quite a few ethnic-nationalist aspects, the most obvious of which is the expectation of "deliverance," as symbolized in part by a return to the ancestral land. Many prayers and texts refer to the Holy Land; these were perceived by Soviet interpretation as "Zionist" in character. In his report on the Jewish "autumn holidays" of 1951, the Ukraine SRA representative wrote, among other things:

> In the past three years we have discovered that on Passover and Yom Kippur . . .
> the prayer that ends with the words "next year in Jerusalem" [transliterated in
> Cyrillic from the Hebrew and translated to Russian] is specially emphasized.
> Until the foundation of the bourgeois-nationalist state of Israel, this prayer
> was treated truly as a prayer, but now it is exploited by the nationalist-Zionist
> elements for their ends.[22]

This statement reiterates a formulation from a 1950 report stating that in the Kiev synagogue the cantor had stopped reading this phrase (per the instructions of Rabbi Shekhtman) but that in other cities it continued to be read. The phrase, according to the statement, ought to be forbidden, and prayer books containing it should be removed from the synagogues.[23] There are grounds for supposing that in many synagogues the concluding Yom Kippur service ended without the traditional call by the cantor, "Next year in Jerusalem." Still, certain worshipers may well have continued to call out these words in full voice, as their fathers' fathers had done.

Nor is it a coincidence that the SRA representatives paid special attention to the Jewish festivals tied to the history of the Jewish people in the Land of Israel—which they called "half holidays"—primarily Tisha be Av (Ninth of Av) and Hanukkah (Feast of Lights). In mid-1951, the Ukraine SRA representative wrote:

> Until the state of Israel was founded, the [days of Hanukkah] were almost
> indistinguishable from weekdays. But now they are celebrated as "a very
> important" holiday. . . . Until the state of Israel was founded, [Tisha be Av] was
> observed only as a fast. But now it has become a day of mourning, as if "to
> commemorate all the tortures and sufferings of the Jews [throughout the ages]."
> It is therefore no coincidence that this day closes with the slogan "Next year in
> Jerusalem."[24]

It follows that the authorities were expected to relate very strictly to the "Zionist significance" of these holidays, and SRA representatives now tried to demonstrate to their superiors their vigor in the struggle to counteract such "significance." The representatives thus suggested increasing restrictions: the Ukraine SRA representative, for instance, suggested removing the Star of David from cemetery headstones and forbidding stonemasons from carving the symbol henceforth. The authorities tried to dissociate Jewish religious practice not only from meanings that might be connected with the state of Israel but also from the congregations' own histories.

In the seventeenth century, the Council of Four Lands, a Jewish self-governing body, had identified the Twentieth of Sivan as the day for commemorating the events of 1648 and 1649—when Bogdan Chmielnicki's brigades had massacred the Jews of Nemirov—as well as the Crusader-era pogroms. Quite a few congregations in Polish and Russian areas, and in Ukraine especially, observed a fast and recited prayers in memory of those events. But over the generations, the custom had fallen somewhat into disuse only to be revived in certain Ukrainian congregations following the Holocaust, perhaps in response to the Ukrainian assistance to the Germans in their slaughter of the Jews. Yet the Twentieth of Sivan now was seen by the authorities as an expression of Jewish nationalism and an offense against unity among the ethnic groups, especially given that Chmielnicki was regarded as a national hero for Ukrainians. In this context, the congregations of L'vov and Kiev were forbidden from holding a commemorative fast on the Twentieth of Sivan; the Ukraine SRA representative even asked Moscow if such observance shouldn't be prohibited for all the congregations of the USSR. Moscow responded that while "the holiday ought not to be prohibited," steps should be taken to ensure that the prayers contain no expressions of nationalism.[25] These few examples suffice to demonstrate the government's inclination to dissociate Jewish religious practice from its historical bonds and ties to the Land of Israel—a nearly impossible feat. Accordingly, a state of affairs was created in which every religious practice could be viewed as having hidden Zionist significance. And in certain cities—Moscow, Leningrad, Odessa, Rostov-on-Don, Vinnitsa, Simferopol', Kiev, Chernovtsy, and Riga—the congregation heads and activists were arrested. In other towns, too, synagogue service providers were arrested on various charges. Thus, for example, an activist from the Uzhgorod congregation was arrested because during a 1948 trip to Moscow to handle the affairs of a closed congregation, "he contacted a spy ring of a bourgeois state and acted to the detriment of the USSR." Subsequently another congregation activist, Landau, was arrested on similar accusations. In August 1951 the Minister for State Security (MGB) sought permission from Communist Party secretary Georgii Malenkov to arrest Rabbi Shlifer on charges that he had formed ties with the Jewish Anti-Fascist Committee and the Israeli embassy; this permission was denied.[26]

Congregation and synagogue life, as noted, had the considerable involvement of Jews who held positions in the local Soviet apparatus, including members of the Communist Party. So as to limit the influence of this uniquely Jewish entity (the congregation) as much as possible, the authorities tried to keep such people away from the synagogue. The Belorussian Communist Party secretary, V. A. Tomashkevich, ordered the republic's SRA representative to examine the lists of people who had ever applied to the authorities on any matter connected with congregational activity in Minsk. The names of 422 men and women were found, among them three Communist Party members then living in the city. The three were summoned to a party hearing, at which they claimed that their names had been entered in the lists without their knowledge. The rabbi of Minsk, Yaakov Yosef Berger, was then required to hand over the names of the people who had dared to include Communists in the lists of synagogue activists. Yet the rabbi—who in many cases had complied with official requests—this time refused to do so, as lives were at stake. The investigation and demand made of Rabbi Berger raised fears among some of the congregation activists and those connected with it, and consequently nineteen people, most of them relatively young, asked that their names be removed from the lists.[27] Likewise, in the city of Ludza (Latvia) the lists of congregation activists were examined and found to contain "many names of party members, Komsomol members and senior workers."[28] Actually these persecutions did not lead to the breakup of most congregations, although they did cause some of their activists to withdraw from involvement.

MINYANS

The closure of the permanent minyans and suppression of holiday minyans became a focus of SRA activity during the late 1940s and early 1950s.[29] On February 22, 1949, the SRA sent all its representatives a special bulletin calling on them to act vigorously to stop minyan activity. In line with this bulletin, the Belorussia SRA chief wrote to his representatives in June 1949 that minyan members "hold ties with the USA and with the State of Israel and write letters requesting help and deprecate conditions in the USSR. They receive from abroad magazines and publications with nationalist-religious content."[30] These harsh accusations sufficed to cause the minyan organizers to be regarded as political enemies who had to be combated. Accordingly, the Vinnitsa district SRA representative appealed to the district authorities demanding that they immediately close the minyan that had been operating in Nemirov for several years. He also demanded that strong measures be taken, in keeping with the February 22 bulletin, against the minyan's rabbi and the apartment owner leasing it.[31] The Belorussia SRA representative, on September 5, 1950, ordered that special efforts be made to locate the minyans and immediate steps taken to shut them down. Thus, when word spread of minyans in Minsk for the High Holidays of 1949, apartments owners renting out their units were summoned to the police, and minyan organizers were warned that serious consequences would result from holding the minyan. Nevertheless, before Passover 1950, minyans were again organized in Minsk. The authorities were now more alert than in previous years to any plans to organize minyans, and when they learned that minyans were being arranged for Passover 1952 in Odessa, Pervomaisk, Savran, Kodyma, and other towns, the organizers' and owners' homes were visited by treasury officials with police escorts and the former were taxed heavily in advance.[32] The battle against the minyans became especially harsh because the authorities viewed them, even more than the registered synagogues, as hotbeds of "nationalism and Zionism." In early April 1953, the Vinnitsa district SRA representative wrote that "the minyans are underground synagogues with rabbis, cantors and preachers. . . . With the Jews the prayer gatherings are exploited by Zionists and other anti-revolutionary groups for nationalist propaganda." As the persecution of the minyans intensified, the SRA representatives insisted that the police take the lead in dealing with the issue. Yet in October 1949, the Vinnitsa SRA representative complained to the district party secretary that the police were doing absolutely nothing about the matter, even though he had supplied them with addresses of the minyans diligently collected by the security services. Accordingly, on March 15, 1953, sixteen Jews who belonged to a minyan were arrested in Vinnitsa and accused of "membership in an anti-Soviet, nationalist Zionist organization."[33]

In the tense climate thus created, fewer and fewer Jews were willing to risk organizing minyans for the holidays without explicit permission, and the number of applications to gather for prayers grew.[34] Yet almost all the applications were denied, usually with the additional warning "that if [the requestors] gathered [for prayer] illegally, landlords allowing the gatherings . . . will be held responsible for breaking the Soviet law on religion." Thus, for example, when the Jews of Sokiriany approached city hall and asked for permission to hold prayers for the "autumn holidays" in a private home, the district SRA representative replied that "this is absolutely forbidden by law because [such a gathering] is an illegal-underground synagogue and the guilty parties will stand trial and be punished to the full severity of the law and face expulsion from their town." The same individual responded similarly to applications by the Jews of Chernovtsy, Khotin, and Sadgora, and he even contacted the police in those towns to demand that they take strong measures against such gatherings. In Pinsk, the authorities decided to prevent gatherings of minyans for the High Holidays of 1950, assigning the task to the security services.[35]

The SRA representatives who had long led the charge against the minyans now usually had the cooperation of the local authorities, including the police and security services, on the grounds that all gatherings of Jews had a political significance. The police and security services, among other activities, now tracked the movements of minyan organizers to scare them and also to learn where they were likely to meet. In this new state of affairs, the minyans took on an underground aspect,[36] as contrasted with their almost open existence until the late 1940s, and the authorities, especially the SRA, expended much energy on locating their meeting places. Thus, for example, in the town of Baranovichi, an underground minyan formed, which for some days was not discovered by the Soviet representative; only on the last day of Sukkot–Simchat Torah (1950) did this official discover its location. He described his actions and the response of the worshipers as follows:

> I summoned a policeman and pointed out the apartment [where the minyan was held] to him so he could purportedly check identity cards and residence permits of the residents [*pasportnyi rezhim*]. . . . While he was checking the papers, two Jews left the apartment and five minutes later I saw how people who had been participating in the prayers started to jump out the window and run away. Eight people jumped out the window. . . . I hurried to enter the apartment . . . when I asked the owner, Turetskaia, "What is going on here? Why are people jumping out your windows and running away?" another two young women came in and together with Turetskaia, started shouting and argued that I had no authority whatsoever to speak in that manner. . . . [I entered] . . . the room where the prayers had been held earlier. Five old people were sitting there, there was a Torah scroll on the table, and prayer shawls were scattered about . . . and on the table candles were burning. In answer to my question "What is going on here and why did you come here?" the old people answered that they came to pray to God . . . to the question "Who led the prayers?" they answered that no one did, that each prayed alone. . . . I ordered them to gather the things into the cabinet [where] they were usually kept and in that cabinet discovered a shofar . . . afterwards we left the house and documented [the event] as required, [and the records] were passed to the proper institutions [meaning the security services] for processing.[37]

Despite this outcome, the diligent SRA representative did not rest content, adding to his report that his observation post was the residence of a policemen and party member who told him that such gatherings occurred in that apartment every now and then. The SRA representative accordingly complained that the policeman hadn't reported this to anyone; he also mentioned that "the party member treated all the goings-on casually, as if [they were] of no consequence and didn't concern him." The writer of the report furthermore complained that one of the Treasury Department employees—Mendel'—had said taxing the minyan organizers was nonsense; the SRA representative accordingly submitted a complaint to the party institutions against Mendel', and evidence suggests the man was punished in some manner.[38] This account offers a sufficiently vivid illustration of the battle waged by the authorities against the minyans, a battle in which each party member was required to pass information and quite a few did.

Yet even in the newly menacing atmosphere, and as hinted in the previous account, worshipers at times reacted with rage when interrupted in prayer. Thus, for example, the Bobruisk SRA representative showed up at one of the minyans organized for Passover 1950 and "three men approached him . . . and began to shout: 'Get out of here, you are bothering our prayers, we don't recognize your authority, you shut down our synagogue, we'll turn to Stalin.'"[39]

Despite the vigorous campaign against the minyans, the authorities were unable to stamp them out and ultimately learned about only a small number of them. On the exact magnitude of the phenomenon, the documentation offers conflicting evidence. Some SRA representatives believed that the number of holiday minyans had diminished compared to previous years, while others said the number (and that of their participants) had actually increased. But while the data is very incomplete, it does show that the holiday minyan gatherings were widespread even during the last years of Stalin's government. In 1949, in Kiev alone, fifty minyans met over the Passover holiday, and nearly seventy did so in the Kiev district. During Passover of 1950, at least twenty-eight minyans held prayers in this district and the following year the authorities knew of twenty-five minyans.[40] One of the minyans for the High Holidays of 1951, held in a house near the "old Jewish market" in the city center (probably the "Besarabka" market), was described thus: inside the house the men prayed "while the women sat in the yard, dressed in their finest, chatting amongst themselves. . . . [T]he worshipers included members of the intelligentsia who feared going to the synagogue where they might be seen and who felt more comfortable at the minyan."[41] The women, it seems, were also there to warn about unwanted "guests." For Passover of 1952, prayers were held in at least fifty-two minyans in thirteen towns of the Vinnitsa district, in seven towns of the Zakarpat'e district, and in three towns of the Kirovograd district; and such numbers reflect only partial data. In early 1953, the Belorussia SRA representative estimated that thirty-five minyans were operating in that republic.[42] Hence, the government's broad crusade to stamp out the minyans had not succeeded.

Relations between activists of the registered synagogues and the minyans were complex. For example, authorities in Mukachevo justified the closure of the synagogue and breakup of the congregation in 1952 on the grounds that "during the Jewish religious holidays . . . [the congregation] wasn't satisfied with gathering in the synagogue but held group assemblies in various parts of town with ten to fifteen people per minyan.[43] The implication was that the congregation was responsible for the minyans, although it is quite uncertain that any connection existed between the members of the congregation and the minyan organizers. With accusations growing that members of the registered congregations were assisting the minyans, some congregation heads, seeking to protect their congregations, became indirect partners in the minyans' suppression. Thus, in 1950 the rabbi of the Minsk congregation complained to the authorities "that all his lobbying and warnings against holding minyans—for organizers would be charged with having illegal gatherings—[were to no avail, as the minyan organizers] would reply: 'we prefer that the registered congregation be dissolved, as it interferes with our gatherings.'"[44] Hinting clearly that the minyans were endangering the very existence of the registered congregations, the authorities sought to turn the congregation heads into active participants in the dismantling of the minyans, which now went underground. In a successful manifestation of such a tactic, Kiev's Rabbi Shekhtman helped move Torah scrolls from the minyans into the recognized synagogue.[45] It isn't hard to imagine the hostility this action must have generated among minyan participants, who now viewed the congregation heads as the government's direct collaborators, not to mention as antagonistic to Judaism and religion. For their part, the congregation leaders thought it was better that the Torah scrolls be housed in the synagogue than hidden in some shed, and believed they were thus saving the congregation and synagogue—the last legal Jewish institution in the Soviet Union.

CONTRACTION IN NUMBERS OF REGISTERED CONGREGATIONS AND CLOSURE OF UNREGISTERED SYNAGOGUES

In many cases, registered congregations were dissolved and synagogues closed without any real reasons being given—the SRA representatives contented themselves with such standard formulas as "inadequate compliance with laws on religious affairs," "failure to comply with regulations on use of a synagogue structure," and the like. In cases where factual records exist of the "sins," these usually involved events that in the past had been tolerated and about which the authorities had only issued cautions, whereas now the practices were cited as cause for the closure of a synagogue or the breakup of a congregation. Thus, for example, in the town of Smela a synagogue had operated unobjectionably since 1946 in a building purchased by the congregation. But in 1949 the charge was made that "the congregation . . . had purchased the house through indirect and illegal methods" and that contributions had been solicited from former town residents now living in Moscow—an action prohibited by Soviet law. The congregation was also charged with having "received various gifts from America . . . which they distributed not only to religious Jews but to the entire Jewish population."[46] Though these "sins" dated to 1945–46, they served as a pretext for breaking up the congregation only in the late 1940s. Likewise, the registered congregation of Vinnitsa was accused of having organized

> an illegal committee called Bikur Holim to help poor Jews. . . . [T]he chairman of the administration—Haim [Ben Leib] Shoifet—organized a group of thirty men to study Talmud; adjacent to the congregation there was an illegal burial society. The congregation also invited a cantor named Belov from Moscow, who exploited the synagogue for nationalist goals. . . . [I]t organized a network of "collectors" to raise funds for the synagogue in private apartments, sold seats in the synagogue during the Holidays and drew payment for Torah readings, called "aliya."[47]

Similar charges were brought against the Berdichev congregation, along with the additional "sins" of founding a temporary cooperative for baking matzah in the synagogue and holding a cantorial concert that included "the Jewish nationalist song "Ikh vil ahaym" (I want to go home), viewed by the authorities as containing veiled Zionist hints.[48] Accusations of express or implied Zionist activity thus served to justify the dispersal of congregations and closure of synagogues. For example, the Odessa district SRA representative argued in 1951 that the synagogue in the town of Belgorod-Dnestrovskii should be shut down because the members of its administration "were in the past [before the Revolution] agents of large merchants, have ties with Zionist organizations, have maintained ties with America and some of them continue with these even now."[49] Yet often the reference was not to a particular synagogue administration, but rather to the synagogue itself as a Jewish institution.

In quite a few cases, the authorities justified the dispersal of a congregation and closure of a synagogue by pointing to the failing administrative structure and decreasing number of worshipers. Due to the various pressures, sometimes fewer than the required minimum of twenty signatories to keep a building in use as a synagogue were on hand. Thus, for example, in the town of Novoselitsa the authorities charged that the signatories had been asked a misleading question, that most of them didn't intend to be synagogue activists, and that thirteen of them had notified the authorities of these irregularities in writing. This combined charge sufficed for the dispersal of the congregation.[50] An especially cynical use of this accusation was the episode leading to the dispersal of the Khar'kov congregation and closure of its synagogue. The congregation had invested a great deal of funds to rebuild a ruined house for use as a synagogue since 1947, but on February 19, 1949, the Ukraine SRA representative wrote that "according to information in our hands the Jewish congregation is systematically violating the laws on religious affairs, consequently we find it necessary and proper to temporarily close the synagogue." The authorities promised that the congregational activities [the synagogue] would be renewed after the election of a new administration, one not responsible for breaking "Soviet laws on religious affairs." Twenty individuals, then, who had not been in the previous administration subsequently submitted an application to take over the synagogue. But instead of receiving a positive reply, the city responded with its plans to give the building to the Shevchenko theater. These maneuvers elicited great bitterness from some of the congregation's members, which they displayed in a manner not common in the USSR. The members in question responded by holding prayers in the street and on the porch facing the street. The impression on passersby left by a minyan of elders wrapped in prayer shawls, standing and praying, is not difficult to imagine. The worshipers were admittedly very elderly, but the initiators associated with the congregation were among the intelligentsia. The yard of the locked synagogue thus became a sort of demonstration area, where people gathered almost every day. Despite this, the SRA in Moscow authorized the closure of the synagogue in February 1950 on the grounds that the congregation had "basically fallen apart."[51]

In certain cities where for local reasons or fear of an especially sharp reaction by the Jewish public the authorities did not close the synagogue, they tried at least to have it moved to the outskirts of town. Quite a few towns had the synagogue located centrally, a reality that obviously contradicted contemporary Soviet policy, which dictated that if synagogues (like other Jewish entities) were not shut down, then at least their profile would be lowered and their influence minimized. In other towns, structures serving the congregation were confiscated and different plots were given to them in exchange—mostly small and peripherally located—such as in Chernovtsy in the Vinnitsa district and Balta in the Odessa district. The explanations proffered for closing these synagogues centered on their illegality and the local officials' lack of authority in transferring the building to the congregation's use—for example, owing to lack of plots in the city and so forth. In some towns, like Mukachevo, the steps taken by the authorities were meant to serve multiple ends simultaneously. There the authorities decided to combine the registered congregation with an unregistered synagogue on the outskirts of town and thus remove the registered synagogue from the city center.[52]

Contrast between the Center and the Periphery

Usually the authorities in Moscow and the republics would grant almost automatic approval to decisions made by the local authorities with respect to synagogue closures, but in isolated instances, central agencies intervened to dampen the overzealous moves of the local authorities. This happened in Nikolaev and Kherson.

The synagogue in Nikolaev operated from 1946 in the same courtyard as a factory-training school (FZO) without any friction between the institutions. But as the trend to isolate the synagogues intensified, the congregation was obligated to build a wall between the synagogue and the school. The school demanded that it get the lion's share of the yard, despite resistance from the congregation. Instead of dealing with the complexities of the situation, the district SRA representative "recollected" that "the religious congregation . . . had frequently and crudely broken the laws on religious affairs." He subsequently announced that as of August 1, 1949, "I am removing Rabbi Fuks and the congregation's administrative body from their posts, canceling the [congregation's] registration and declaring its dispersal. . . ."[53] The charges leveled by the district SRA representative were so patently false that his superior in Kiev commented as follows:

> Before this, you didn't notify us that the congregation's administration [was] systematically and crudely breaking the laws, which creates the impression that you are suddenly taking a harsh step. . . . [Y]ou must take into account that a harsh step of this sort . . . *may only be taken with the permission of the* SRA *which is alongside the government of the* USSR [emphasis in original].

The Ukraine SRA representative agreed with his subordinate that "there was room to remove any clerics in the group with nationalist leanings who had taken over the synagogue administration," but removing the rabbi and electing a new administration would have sufficed in achieving this end, and there was no need to forbid the activity of the congregation. He therefore instructed "that the synagogue be opened immediately and the congregation recognized as active, and henceforth not to permit temporary closures of the house of prayer *without the knowledge and permission of the* SRA" [emphasis in original].[54] The Ukraine SRA representative took this unusual step chiefly because he saw the actions of the district representative as surpassing the bounds of his authority. The Nikolaev congregation subsequently returned to activity and the synagogue was not shut down until the early 1960s.

In Kherson, a synagogue had been operating from early 1946 whose members hoped to install their rabbi in the adjacent guardhouse (*storozhka*). But the resident there didn't want to move out and was systematically nasty to the worshipers. According to one source, "[The tenant] set up a pigsty in the synagogue yard and would slaughter and smoke pork near the synagogue windows, and when the rabbi told him that his actions desecrate and mock a holy place, [the tenant] answered rudely: 'your place is the cemetery.'" Small wonder, then, that the congregation demanded the guardhouse be transferred to its possession, as stipulated in the agreement designating the structure as a synagogue. But instead of responding favorably to this request, the city decided to cancel the agreement, claiming that it was illegal because the clerk who had signed it lacked sufficient authority. The issue was passed to the SRA in Moscow for final determination and to the surprise of the city and other institutions in Ukraine—which approved its moves—Moscow ruled that the city's action was illegal, on the grounds that outbuildings are to accompany a main structure that has been designated a house of prayer. The SRA subsequently supported the congregation's claims and enabled the operation of the synagogue until the early 1960s.[55]

As these cases attest, conflicts persisted between the government's different arms in the late 1940s and early 1950s. Yet the general trend emphasized shutting down synagogues that operated in the open and reducing the number of registered congregations.

Given the increasing pressure on the unregistered synagogues to register and the absolute refusal of the local authorities to register such congregations without approval from Moscow, such requests to the SRA bureau grew. In 1948, seventy-five requests were made to register a congregation, most of which were denied; the number dropped to thirty-seven in 1949 and to only ten in 1950.[56] Many SRA representatives thought that in light of the policy toward religion, bothering the Moscow authorities with such requests was pointless; the Ukraine SRA representative, too, reacted this way in response to the application of the Jews of Zhdanovo.[57]

The campaign to break up the registered congregations and to close synagogues, begun in 1949, was in the first year implemented harshly in Ukraine mainly for two reasons: first, because this republic contained about a third of all registered congregations, and second, because Ukraine had the largest number of unregistered congregations. Indeed, that year twice as many registered congregations were dissolved in Ukraine as in the USSR as a whole (14 percent versus 6 percent). The authorities focused especially on the Zakarpat'e and Chernovtsy districts, which had many synagogues. In 1949, twenty-two synagogues operated openly in the Zakarpat'e district, only two of which were registered. The Ukraine SRA representative wrote that "we have reached the conclusion that we must disperse the unregistered congregations [synagogues] gradually and leave only four registered congregations." Indeed, seven unregistered synagogues/congregations were shut down in the Zakarpat'e district over three years.[58] In the Chernovtsy district, four registered congregations were broken up between 1949 and 1953, and even in the district of Kiev, which had only five registered congregations, two were broken up in the same years, one of them in Uman', a site of pilgrimage for the Bratslav Chassidim from all over the USSR.

The authorities now wanted to show off their achievements in shutting down synagogues, so the Vinnitsa SRA representative announced in 1950 that his diligence was to be credited for the closure of thirteen synagogues, to which about 5,500 worshipers came, and that the remaining four synagogues had a membership of merely 1,500–2,500.[59]

The general policy of reducing, if not stamping out, the number of congregations resulted—between January 1949 and January 1951—in the dissolving of nineteen registered congregations, or 12 percent of the total. Between early 1949 and January 1, 1953, twenty-five registered synagogues (congregations) were closed, or 15.5 percent of the total. And Jews were hit much harder by the campaign of closing prayer houses than were other religions: for comparison, of the openly operating synagogues (both registered and unregistered), 20.9 percent were closed in 1949, versus only 5.7 percent of the Russian Orthodox churches.[60]

While the overall policy was to reduce the number of registered congregations and shut down the unregistered synagogues, certain local variations existed in how this policy was implemented. Latvia, which had an especially active Jewish population and a local bureaucracy not keen to strictly follow orders from Moscow, had two congregations registered during this period that had previously functioned without registration. In the Slavic republics (Ukraine, Belorussia, and the Russian Federal Republic—though not including the autonomous republics therein), where the anti-Jewish crusade was especially harsh and the local bureaucracy was not entirely free of antisemitic sentiment, eighteen out of eighty-six registered congregations (21 percent) were dissolved during this period (1949–1952); the Republic of Moldavia, which actually was formed only after the war, had two out of thirteen dissolved (15 percent); the republics of Central Asia and the Caucasus, to which should be added the autonomous republics of RSFSR (Dagestan, Tataristan, and Kabardino-Balkaria), which in many respects were like those of Central Asia, had seven out of forty-nine (14 percent) registered congregations dispersed. Most of the dispersed congregations constituted the only one in town (except in Moscow and Chernovtsy), but all the same the Georgia SRA representative set the goal in 1952 of having "in every town no more than one synagogue."[61]

Notwithstanding the persecutions against the Jewish religion, then, the authorities, until early 1953, allowed 136 registered congregations and (at least) 144 synagogues to continue to operate. These congregations represented the only expression of Jewish public life in the Soviet Union, with every other form having been eliminated.

This state of affairs calls for an explanation. Why, after all, were the congregations and synagogues allowed to exist? To the best of our knowledge, no discussion of this subject occurred within the highest ranks of the regime; in any case, no documentation appears to exist of such discussions, even in the many memoirs published over the last decade. Any treatment of this issue is thus necessarily hypothetical, but that does not free us from the need to raise the question.

Presumably, the synagogues were allowed to exist because closing them would have produced a widespread, negative response in the free world. Yet it appears that world public opinion may *not* have been regarded as a decisive factor, for two main reasons: (1) This period (1949–1952) represented the height of the Cold War, and the USSR barely considered world public opinion and even that of Communist parties abroad. (2) The free world's media, both general and Jewish, showed little interest in the Jews of the USSR; if any mention was made of the topic, it appeared in only a few Yiddish newspapers, mostly in connection with the disappearance of Yiddish-language writers. The general media, to the slight extent it did deal with the issue, discussed the official Soviet policy of struggle against "cosmopolitanism." Needless to say, the political institutions of the Western states made no mention at all of the Jews of the USSR.

Until the Soviet archives were opened, it was still possible to argue that synagogue attendees consisted just of a minyan or two of very old Jews, pensioners from the lowest parts of society who busied themselves with prayer—in other words, that the synagogue had no public influence and therefore the Soviet authorities felt no reason for concern. But, as previous chapters have shown and as will be discussed further, the synagogue's activities were not limited to prayer: the synagogue filled an essential role for the Jewish public, and broad classes of Jews in the USSR participated in their activities. This state of affairs did not pass unnoticed by the authorities, as the wide documentation attests.

Other currents within the Soviet Union help illuminate the fate of the synagogues. In the years being considered (1949–1952), a broad campaign in the country was under way to remove Jews from positions of power in various fields. This was known as "the struggle against cosmopolitanism," and for this campaign a partnership of sorts formed between the government and certain groups in the population. After the war, nationalism and antisemitism grew in the USSR, spreading widely in the management class and even among the professional and scientific elite. Due to the relatively high numbers of Jews in administrative positions and in scientific and cultural roles, dozens or hundreds of letters were received by various government agencies, with the writers maintaining that the USSR's "main" ethnicities were being pushed out in favor of the Jews. These communications reflected not only anti-Jewish sentiments but also envy and a desire to take over the positions held by the Jews. Antisemitic attitudes were also common at high levels of government, and the Jews there were perceived as a foreign element with Western leanings. As the Cold War worsened and in response to certain sentiments of the populace, the authorities launched a campaign to reduce the role of Jews in various fields, and thus to win public support.

This did not directly affect congregations and synagogues. To the best of our knowledge, the non-Jewish public showed no interest in Jewish religious life. at least until early 1953; and the overall government policy toward religion was to minimize its influence but not to remove all its institutions. The government thus preferred to permit the existence of open religious bodies, which could be supervised more fully than if they were clandestine. Relations with the Catholic Church offer an excellent illustration of this approach: the Pope and the Catholic Church were characterized as the USSR's sworn enemies, and even so Catholic churches in the USSR were not closed. The synagogues also benefited, for a while, from this overall strategy.

The elimination of institutions operating legally in the USSR usually had the involvement of the security services, and their "findings" would usually be brought to the decision makers, led by Stalin, for authorization. In this period, there was competition between the Ministry for Internal Affairs (MVD) and the Ministry for State Security (MGB) in the hunt for spies and apparent terrorist operatives working for foreign countries, so synagogues were not prioritized for investigation. Still, the synagogue administrations were strongly cautioned to avoid any sort of foreign contact, and even the few official requests received from abroad—mostly by the synagogue in Moscow—were immediately passed to the authorities, who would offer a verbatim response. The synagogue administrations had quite a few people who reported regularly on their doings, and ironically it was these people, who were naturally disliked by their fellow congregants, who contributed, consciously or not, to the indirect persistence of the only legal Jewish institution in the USSR that served as a focus for ethnic identity. Yet in early 1953 this situation began to change.

Eve of the Liquidation

On January 13, 1953, the Soviet media reported the arrest of a group of prominent doctors, mostly Jews, accused of working for the security services of the United States and with the American Jewish Joint Distribution Committee (the Joint) to assassinate the political and military leadership of the USSR. The propaganda campaign launched following this announcement was meant to prepare public opinion for a show trial of the sort familiar from the 1930s. Rumors were also spread that the trial would result in the exile of most Jews of the USSR. The tens of thousands of meetings held on the subject across the country included large numbers of people from all walks of life, from the intelligentsia down to the plain factory workers and farmers. In some of the meetings, organized to condemn the "murderers in white coats," the speakers also demanded that pressure be increased on the synagogues, which were supposed focal points of anti-USSR plots and activities. At a January 1953 meeting of workers in a secret machinery factory in Dnepropetrovsk, for example, it was resolved among other things that "all the synagogues should be specially supervised." The Communist Party secretary of the city of Dneproderzhinsk noted in his January 20, 1953, report that "a special investigation must be made of the Jewish congregation in town as it is suspected of taking orders from the Joint." Subsequently, the security services launched an "investigation of the activities of the congregation . . . which is suspected of being one of the organizations of the Joint." A welder in one of the tractor and agriculture machine stations told an informant from the Kiev Communist Party that "the Soviet government services must increase supervision over Jewish prayer houses, where there are many mysterious goings-on."[62]

The depiction of the synagogue as a locus of subversive activity was, it seems, readily embraced by the broad public because such a characterization largely matched historical stereotypes about the Jews. Broad classes of the public in Leningrad, correspondingly, believed rumors that the city's Jewish cemetery, maintained by the congregation, had buried in it a large cache of weapons, photographic equipment, and radio transmitters. The rumormongers also knew to tell that a tunnel had been dug from the cemetery to the "Bolshevik" factory, one of the large military facilities, with the subversives aiming to blow it up.[63] The synagogue was thus portrayed as a center for spying and sabotage. This was the context for the closing of eight synagogues for three months (January–March), among them that of the town of Poltava, in which the Jewish population numbered about ten thousand souls. The congregation's members were accused of working for private favors and of being swindlers (*deltsy*) and petty crooks (*zhuliki*).[64] Nor did Georgia, where the Jewish religion was treated with special consideration by the authorities, evade the closure of synagogues during those months. On February 12, 1953, the Moscow SRA affirmed the Georgian government's decision to close two synagogues in the republic's capital, charging that foreign currency was found in them and that there were "violations of regulations on structure usage."[65]

The linkage of a synagogue to the Joint, depicted as an American organization for spying and subversion, significantly increased its chances of closure; the Kiev district SRA representative hinted as much when he wrote that

> behind . . . the registered Jewish congregations and their synagogues hide certain dark powers and it is possible that nationalist elements are exploiting the Jewish religious movement as a camouflage for their various goals, to which I assume our special institutions [i.e., the security services] will pay attention.[66]

Indeed, in those months the security services widened their arrests of congregation activists. In this context, K. D. Davidashvili, the forty-five-year-old *hakham* (rabbi) of the Tbilisi synagogue, was arrested on charges that during 1945–1946 he used the synagogue to promote immigration to Israel and organized religious studies for Jewish children. In Ordzhonikidze, one of the congregation heads, D. L. Denenberg, was arrested on charges of Zionism and racism because in prayer he said, "You chose us from among all the nations," and in Passover prayers in previous years he had said, "Gather our exiles from among the peoples and our dispersed from the edges of the earth." A. M. Stankevitch, born in 1875, was arrested in that town on similar charges: as *chazan* in 1947, he had also uttered those prayers.[67] Since these and similar verses are to be found in many prayers, any rabbi or *chazan* reading them in public could be found guilty of racism and Zionism—serious political crimes. The leaders of the registered congregations of Odessa (Rabbi Yosef Diment) and Simferopol' (Rabbi David Berkovitch) were arrested in those months, as was the *chazan* of the synagogue in Rostov-on-Don.[68] The various authorities thus readied the ground for eliminating the congregation—the sole remaining legal Jewish institution in the USSR. Most Jews of the USSR, as a result, lived in daily anxiety and fear of mass exile—whether or not there existed a practical plan to this effect—and the numbers of synagogue attendees dropped.

On March 6, 1953, the Soviet media reported the death of Stalin, and many Jews, like the majority of USSR citizens, received this news with mixed emotions. They sensed that a change was imminent, but couldn't predict its nature. The expectation was not at all upbeat: "after his [Stalin's] death, a dark fear gripped our brethren, children of Israel, for what was to come."[69] This situation cast its pall over preparations for the impending Passover holiday. In contrast with previous years, most synagogues were not repainted or repaired, "matzah was baked only in homes, except in Moscow and Minsk. Nor were *chazanim* invited to most of the synagogues, as was customary every year." Threat of exile, the sword of Damocles that hung over Jewish heads, was manifest in the low numbers of worshipers in the synagogues on the first day of Passover (March 31), well down from the previous year. The falloff in attendees in Astrakhan's synagogue on the first day of Passover was explained by its rabbi: "Religious Jews are afraid to go to the synagogue because of the situation in the country connected to the medical workers' affair. Many religious Jews prefer to pray at home." Of course he wasn't speaking only of religious Jews, but preferred this formulation in his presentation to the authorities. During evening prayers on the first day of Passover, stones were thrown at the windows of synagogues in Leningrad and Kuibishev,[70] making the overall atmosphere oppressive—more like Tisha be Av than Passover. However, with the April 4 announcement of the release of the doctors, the synagogues returned to their former status as a venue of mass gatherings.

In the late 1940s and early 1950s, the authorities pursued a policy of reducing the number of congregations and synagogues and pushing the latter to the fringes of towns. In some places the synagogues were shut down first and only afterward were the congregations dissolved; in some places the reverse happened. At the same time, the authorities made efforts to completely halt the activity of the unregistered synagogues. In 1953 the MVD and the Ministry of Justice in Belorussia, and almost certainly in other republics as well, prepared secret instructions noting that members of unregistered religious organizations could expect a sentence of five years' imprisonment or exile, and confiscation of their property.[71] One may accordingly say that during the days of the Doctors' Plot, synagogues were on the brink of closure across the USSR.

CHAPTER SIX

Public Displays of Jewish Identity
DEMONSTRATIONS IN THE SYNAGOGUE SQUARE

During the "black years" of 1949–1953 the synagogue served as an important center for the public display of Jewish identity. On the Jewish New Year and especially on Yom Kippur, genuine demonstrations were held around many synagogues, a practice virtually unheard of previously in the USSR. One of the government's goals was to "atomize" the Jewish public—that is, to isolate its component members—and yet in those dark days thousands and sometimes tens of thousands of Jews would assemble in mass demonstrations in front of the synagogues. The authorities seem to have been aware of this role of the synagogue, as may be hinted by the secret memorandum "On the Autumn Festivals of the Jews in 1949" sent to Klement Voroshilov (who headed the USSR's SRA file, covering religious Jewish affairs) and to Mikhail Suslov (a Communist Party Central Committee secretary and editor of the *Pravda* newspaper—one of the decisive figures on the "ideological front"). This memorandum stated, among other things:

> This year a special awakening is noticeable in the activities of the Jewish religious congregations with respect to preparation and organization for the holidays. The activities took place and were supported not so much out of religious motives as from the desire of the nationalist-minded clerics and other persons who play upon the nationalist sentiments of the Jewish population, who were interested in drawing as many Jews as possible to the synagogue irrespective of their religious views. . . . Thus, for example, in the town of Nikolaev, Rabbi Fuks, eighty years old, paid daily visits to the houses of religious and nonreligious Jews to remind them of the approaching holidays and ask them to attend the synagogue to memorialize their relatives who died or were killed [in the days of the Holocaust].[1]

Indeed, the SRA chairman had to admit:

> The number . . . of attendees this year [1949] in the synagogues during those days [the New Year and Day of Atonement] was larger than last year. At the memorial

for the dead on October 3 at the main synagogue in Moscow, no fewer than 10,000 people came. The synagogue was packed full and in addition, religious people crowded into part of the Spasko-Galishchenskii Lane next to the synagogue, and as a result interfered with pedestrian and bus traffic.... [I]n Kiev ... on Yom Kippur, not only was the synagogue full of religious Jews, but also the yard and part of the adjacent street.... [T]he number present at the synagogue that day is estimated at 8,000–10,000, two or two and a half times more than in the previous year. There was also a similar significant increase in the number of worshipers in those days in the synagogues of Leningrad, Odessa, Kishinev, Riga and Tbilisi.[2] The increase in attendance at the synagogues of religious Jews this year was seen not only at the synagogues mentioned above ... but also in the much smaller synagogues such as those of Tashkent, Prunze, L'vov, Chernovtsy, Zhitomir, Berdichev and other cities.... [In Irkutsk] more than a thousand people attended at the time of prayer.... [A]t the back of the synagogue one could see people whom you meet during work hours in Soviet offices: in the courts, in the prosecutors' offices, in shops, offices and the like.... [M]ost of the attendees of the synagogues were elderly and middle aged, but young people also attended, and in certain synagogues the number of young people grew significantly from last year. This phenomenon is particularly noticeable in the synagogues of Moscow and Leningrad.... [I]n certain synagogues, especially in that of Leningrad, the presence of Navy persons was felt ... and MVD [security services] personnel. In certain synagogues, members of the Communist Party and the Komsomol attended.[3]

Describing the atmosphere of the Odessa synagogue during the High Holidays of 1949, the Ukraine SRA representative noted that those assembled held lively discussions about the necessity of unity with the state of Israel, with one attendee openly declaring: "I am not religious but I am a Jew and I cannot fail to appear [at the synagogue for] the Jewish holidays."[4] The SRA representative of the Poltava district therefore pointed out:

> [The] Jewish congregation [of the city] numbers sixty individuals, mostly pensioners and very elderly people. How therefore to explain ... the number of visitors in the synagogue ... in the days of the great holidays (New Year, Passover, Yom Kippur and others)? This fact cannot be explained by any special religiosity of the Jewish population nor by [an] increase in its religious fervor.... On the religious holidays not only the religious elders, but many others not among the congregation, attend the synagogue. [On ordinary days, at most ten or fifteen persons come to the synagogue], but on holidays, *masses* [emphasis in original] of the Jewish population ... may be seen there ... workers in Soviet institutions and organizations and also the intelligentsia.[5]

The Belorussia SRA representative also mentioned that during the High Holidays of 1949, "The more religious—old men and women—were in the synagogue [of Minsk], and in the yard were the middle-aged and young." The atmosphere in the yard of the Minsk synagogue on Yom Kippur of 1952, which was packed with about 350 people, as compared to 150 inside the building, he described thus:

> The crowd paid no attention to what was going on in the synagogue, except a
> few who tried actively to get close to the windows . . . in order to listen to the
> prayers . . . most of the people here were of middle age. They stood in groups and
> discussed various subjects. Many of them spoke Russian. . . . [I]t was therefore
> possible to deduce that more than half of them came to the synagogue not out
> of religious conviction, but from a feeling of [ethnic-] national solidarity and the
> traditional customs of the Jewish public which drew them to the synagogue.[6]

Although quite a few SRA representatives understood at least a part of the motives attracting so many Jews to gather in the synagogue and its vicinity, it was convenient for them to explain the happenings as resulting mostly from the deliberate exertions of the religious service providers, as was noted in the report on the High Holidays of 1950:

> The religious service providers and the religious people [*religiozniki*] put out wide
> propaganda on the obligation of Jews to visit the synagogue no matter what their
> religiosity . . . because the synagogue is the only place Jews can join together and
> maintain contact with each other. To that end the religious service providers and
> religious people visited [Jewish] homes in certain towns to remind them of the
> coming holiday and to invite [the public] to come to synagogue.[7]

In 1950 those assembling in and especially near the synagogue included "people of all strata of the population . . . in certain cases uniformed soldiers and officers took part in the prayers."[8] In addition, one saw dockworkers from the river ports in Riga, "railroad men and the like [in Kherson]; and in the synagogue of Birobidzan, prayer book in hand, prayed a policeman in uniform."[9]

The district SRA representative wrote that "in the town of Kherson *the number of visitors to the synagogue in the Jewish holidays of 1951 grew significantly by comparison to 1949 and 1950* [emphasis in original]." Even in cities where the SRA representatives had cause to rejoice because synagogue attendance for the High Holidays in 1951 had decreased compared to previous years, thousands of

Jews gathered around the synagogues. Thus, for example, about four thousand persons gathered around the synagogue in Odessa in 1951 as opposed to five to six thousand in 1950 and nine to ten thousand in 1949. News of the gathering at the Kiev synagogue spread, as was described by the SRA representative:

If on Yom Kippur of 1949 only about 6,500 persons came to the synagogue and in 1950 about 7,000—this year [1951] 20,000 people assembled at the synagogue. I personally was witness to the following facts: starting at the Palace of Culture [*Dvorets kul'tury*], located four blocks from Shchekovitskaia Street where the synagogue is, [Jews were walking]. Mezhigorskaia Street had a *continuous stream* of Jews marching toward the synagogue [emphasis in original]. Many cars were parked in Shchekovitskaia Street and the adjacent streets, which took their owners to and from the synagogue. In my three years on the job I've never seen a concentration of people like this. There were people here of every age.[10]

This lively account of the goings-on in town on Yom Kippur seems to be a faithful depiction, although estimates of the size of the crowds may contain inaccuracies. The rabbi of the Kiev congregation answered the question "Were the masses of people surrounding the synagogue all religious?" with the response: "No. They're not all religious, but come to the synagogue because it is their national custom [*iz za svoikh natsonal'nykh obychaev*]."[11] While the license plate numbers of vehicles driven by Jews attending Yom Kippur services were recorded, and it may be assumed that many suffered for their "sin,"[12] in the late 1940s and early 1950s, it must be noted, very few USSR residents drove vehicles for private or official purposes, and only those of the highest class used them. Thus, Jews from the elite of Soviet society were coming to the synagogue. Further evidence of the mass gathering of Jews in Kiev on Yom Kippur of 1951 comes from a statement by an elderly Jew, Lipnitskii, who said that he had

never seen so large a number of Jews in and near the synagogue as this year. . . . [It] isn't necessary to come to the synagogue but it's enough to stand for an hour or two near it or near a minyan during the holiday *and you feel you are a Jew* [emphasis in original] . . . these aren't religious Jews but they come to the synagogue out of their ethnic feeling.[13]

This immense gathering around the Kiev synagogue in 1951 specifically was no coincidence. That day marked the ten-year anniversary of the largest mass-murder of Jews by the Nazis in the USSR. In Babi Yar, on the outskirts of town, more than 30,000 Jews were murdered around Yom Kippur 1941 (September

29–30), and ten years later almost every Jewish family remaining had lost a close relative whom they wished to commemorate on that day. The day of the Babi Yar slaughter became a sort of "Holocaust Day" in many towns of the USSR, on which Jews who otherwise never set foot in a synagogue attended one or at least gathered around it. Unsurprisingly, then, the Dneptopetrovsk SRA representative reported that on Yom Kippur of 1951 he "saw the Communist Leizerman—deputy manager of the district commercial department—getting out of his car [near the synagogue] with a group of Jews, while from another car emerged the Communist Katerbarskii."[14]

The Belorussia SRA representative was also compelled to admit that the gatherings at and mainly around the synagogue were growing in size over the years, but preferred to blame this phenomenon on the activists of the religious groups and purported Zionist activities, and wrote thus in this report of the second half of 1952:

> The activities of the religious groups not only have not ceased, but in certain places have taken a more vigorous form than in the past few years. It cannot be ruled out that under cover of religion these groups are being exploited by Zionists for anti-Soviet activities.[15]

Given the large assemblies outside the synagogue, the synagogue leadership needed to find ways to ensure that at least some of the prayers would be heard outside. Thus, the Soviet representative complained that the head of the Chernigov congregation chose

> to hold the prayers [for the High Holidays of 1951] with a large gesture: the head of the congregation himself would lead the prayers in the synagogue, and from the porch facing the main street, a cantor would pray, whose voice was as that of a nightingale. All this so that the entire crowd would hear the prayer . . . "Our Lord, hasten our return to Zion, to Jerusalem."[16]

Other congregations wanted to broadcast the prayers via loudspeaker, although religious law forbade it. But the authorities prohibited this on the grounds that religious ceremonies must be held only in the structures designated for such.[17]

The majority of the reports, even if they contain certain exaggerations, attest that from 1949 to 1952 the number of attendees in (and mostly around) the synagogues grew. These growing assemblies do not indicate, in our opinion, that religiosity was on the rise among the Jews. As the chairman of the control board of the Cherkizovo congregation in Moscow put it: "They say about us [Jews] that many of us are religious; yet what unifies us is not just religious views *but also national sentiments* [emphasis in original]."[18] Indeed, many who gathered about the synagogue came out of "national sentiments": blending the memory of the Holocaust, in which many of them had lost family, with their protest against antisemitism.[19]

Confronted with the mass demonstrations of Jews in various cities, the authorities put in place a special system of pressures to prevent these demonstrations from occurring. Special memoranda were sent to the local authorities with precise dates of the Jewish holidays, and workplaces were told that under no circumstances should they grant leave on those days. A well-oiled machinery of pressures and threats was activated, primarily against Communist Party members and persons filling important jobs. Thus, for example, the SRA representative made sure to announce in advance to the Communist Party committees about party members likely to participate in synagogue gatherings during the High Holidays, and the committees, naturally, took steps to prevent such participation from occurring. Nevertheless, there was no appreciable reduction in the size of the demonstrations around the synagogues in 1952 (except in Kiev), and their makeup did not change significantly either:

> There were many people from the commercial realm here, doctors (among others, I personally saw my senior doctor, a Jew, dermatologist, who works in the MGB clinic of Ukraine), people of various cooperatives, communications workers, people of the administration of the Dnepr River fleet, et cetera. There were several people in military uniform, among them one in the uniform of the fleet with the rank of major who had with him a child of four or five . . . two to three hundred people came with children under school age. As in previous years, people filling important and responsible jobs in our society [attended the synagogue], among them scientific workers, doctors, professors and the like. Therefore we can judge by outward appearance and by their manner of arrival [to the synagogue], [some came in] official cars, private vehicles, taxis. The number of "responsible" and "scientific" professionals of this type was a bit smaller this year than in previous years . . . they also distributed charity to beggars generously.[20]

The mass gatherings around the synagogues during the High Holidays did not go without insults from passersby, though very little documentation attests to such insults. In one extant example, on Yom Kippur of 1952 a passerby near the synagogue in Kiev shouted loudly:

Behold gathered here the idlers and extortionists . . . you can plow the soil with them [*na nikh mozhno zemliu kopat*] but they'll idle away, and beggars . . . here, they give alms proudly. Do you think that those giving away money generously earned this money by their labor!? . . . [L]ook, see: here goes a sharp-looking bloke, well dressed. He gives each at least a ruble [or even two] or three, not missing a single beggar. Is he really scattering his own money? Not in the least!! That's our cash, [the cash] which we earned with our labor.[21]

We can assume that such statements drew a response from the crowd congregated around the synagogue, but as noted, only in extreme cases were these incidents recorded in the Soviet documentation. One recorded case happened in L'vov. On Yom Kippur of 1949 (October 3), 1,500 people gathered in and around the city's synagogue. The adjacent street was packed when a peasant on a cart appeared. The crowd demanded that the peasant turn around, but the latter insisted on his right to pass with his cart. A hot argument broke out between the crowd and the carter, both sides using insulting language and curses, and a woman spit in the carter's face. The incident might have passed without notice if the district SRA representative hadn't been in the synagogue at that time. As he came out of the synagogue he saw, as he reported, the crowd blocking the path of the cart. All this happened at about two in the afternoon, during the Yizkor prayer, for which many had come to the synagogue specifically to recall their relatives murdered in the Holocaust, some with the help of Ukrainian collaborators. Unsurprisingly, the atmosphere was highly charged.

The SRA representative supported the carter, which only made things worse. Presently a man from the crowd approached the SRA representative demanding that he leave the place; when the latter identified himself as the SRA representative, the former answered "with contempt" that he himself worked for the Ministry of the Interior (MVD), shouting in the heat of the moment that he would kill him and even grabbing him by his coattails. The SRA representative left the scene and immediately reported the events to the security services, as did the head of the congregation, Makhonetskii, in a letter in which he stated "this was done by a group of irresponsible people, Jewish hooligans of a nationalist orientation, who come to the synagogue once or twice a year."[22]

The brief investigation conducted by the security services revealed that the man involved in the incident was (Lieutenant) Baruch ben Khaim Shlepak, born 1912, who appears to have fought either in the Red Army or the partisan movement. Shlepak had been employed by both the police, which fell within the MVD, and the Ministry of State Security (MGB) since 1946. For his offense, he stood disciplinary trial and was sentenced to ten days' arrest and banishment from the police.[23] Shlepak's reaction was uncommon but also indicates the pain and anger that unified many of those assembled around the synagogue during the High Holidays. Most women and men in the crowds around the synagogues were good citizens of the USSR who saw it as their homeland; they were not heroes and they were not written about in the newspapers. Yet at least once a year they wished to give expression to the offense against their basic human pride caused by the Soviet government's ignoring of the murders of their families during the Holocaust, as well as to protest the policy of discrimination.

The Soviet authorities linked the huge rise in synagogue attendance during the High Holidays to the vigorous activity of "religious activists," but this simplistic explanation does not stand scrutiny. Attempts at encouraging Jews to come to synagogue had occurred in past years, but with little success; anyway the presence of nonreligious Jews in the house of prayer could be seen as tainting the truly pious adherents. Further, it might be argued that in those years the Jewish population underwent a significant religious awakening; but the accounts of the synagogue attendees and their behavior do not bear this out. It is more reasonable to seek the reason for the increase in synagogue attendance in the desire to remember the Holocaust, on one hand, and the political and social condition of most of the Jewish population, on the other. Experiences associated with the Holocaust were part of the personal and familial experiences of many Jews, and the antisemitic attitude of the surrounding society and the authorities was in absolute contrast to the expectations of the Jews after the war. The gatherings in and around the synagogues were therefore mass demonstrations against antisemitic policy, demonstrations unparalleled in the USSR. Given such demonstrations, even if held only one day a year, the Jews of the USSR do not deserve the designation "the Jews of silence" even during the "black years."

A certain change in this state of affairs occurred after the Doctors' Plot amid the climate of pending mass expulsion of the Soviet Union's Jews. However, after the doctors were released, synagogue attendance rose again.[24] The sudden shift of most of the Jewish population from fear and depression to hope and high spirits was noticeable also in synagogue attendance during the seven days of Passover. In Moscow, Leningrad, Kishinev, and other cities, the synagogues could not hold all the arrivals, many of whom spilled into the street; many such attendees were Jews who normally would not go to synagogue on Passover. Quite a few held the newspaper of April 4 and read aloud the announcement of the doctors' release. In many towns, the number of minyans and their visitors grew. The head of the Kursk congregation declared that the

Jews of his town "can breathe more easily now," while at the Minsk synagogue a Jewish woman shouted with joy, "We are all saved!" Between 1,500 and 1,800 people came to the synagogue that day, according to the estimate of the SRA representative, and on May 4 he wrote:

> When I asked the head of the Jewish congregation, la. S. Makhnovetskii, to explain the large participation this year in contrast to the previous year, he replied to me that "many nonreligious Jews came to the synagogue out of curiosity and mainly because in those days the people were in a good mood owing to the government's announcement. . . . This announcement rescued us from the depression we were in. You cannot imagine the emotional experience we underwent. . . . Now our people feel secure, vigorous and happy and that is why so many came to the synagogue.[25]

CHAPTER SEVEN

Khrushchev's "Thaw," 1954 – 1959

The announcement of the release of the doctors on April 4, 1953, restored some courage to many Jews, who now dared to demand that synagogues be opened.[1] But in the regime's attitude toward religion in general, and the Jewish religion in particular, there was little immediate change.

In the Kremlin, a fight began over the spoils of the dictator, a fight that spread to the lower echelons of power and led to the replacement of many district SRA representatives. As part of this struggle, on July 7, 1954, the Central Committee of the Communist Party passed a resolution addressing "serious deficiencies in the atheist-scientific propaganda, and the means to improve it." This resolution harshly criticized the administrative branches, as well as the media and propaganda apparatus, for assuming that religious influences would disappear by themselves and hence not paying proper attention to them. The various government organs were charged with waging an antireligion propaganda campaign "most methodically and vigorously, via methods of persuasion, explanation, and an individual approach toward religious people."[2] This language may seem to contain a hint of moderation, but any such moderation was swallowed up in the details of the antireligion propaganda requirements imposed on all the governmental agencies.

The resolution, reminiscent in wording and tone of similar resolutions from the early 1930s, was drafted by figures within the Soviet apparatus who had sought to intensify antireligion activity dating to the 1940s: Mikhail Suslov, Dimitri Shepilov, and Aleksandr Shelepin.[3] Conceivably, too, the resolution was meant as a response to reports from around the country that young people whose "God" (Stalin) had died were now searching for different "Gods" among various religious groups and outside the framework of the established church, rumors that struck some in the leadership as dangerous. The resolution may also have been aimed at enlisting fresh support for the regime, whose old slogans elicited dimming enthusiasm from the Soviet people. Whatever the reasons behind it, this resolution filtered down through the different Soviet agencies and was regarded as an instruction, or at least as permission, to intensify the attacks against religion. In this context, special seminars were held for antireligion propagandists, and for five or six months the apparatchiks increased their pressure against religious activity. The Belorussia SRA representative instructed his men throughout the republic to visit various towns during the "autumn Jewish holidays," which ran from September 28 to October 20, 1954, so as to uncover "groups operating illegally among the Jewish population [minyans]."[4] Yet the period of heightened antireligion propaganda was short-lived, and its influence in the field was limited.

On November 10, 1954, the Central Committee of the Communist Party published another resolution on "Mistakes in Implementation of the Atheist-Scientific Propaganda among the Population,"[5] which may be seen to mark the beginning of a "thaw" with respect to religion. This resolution was different in spirit from that of July 7 and it began with the declaration that the Church, that is to say religion in general, was loyal to the state, unlike the situation that had obtained during the country's civil war. The resolution went on to address the ideological contradiction between religious and the scientific worldviews, while stressing, on five occasions, that harm must not be done to "the sensibilities of the religious." This statement implied that no heavy hand was to be taken against religious organizations, as vigorous oppression of a religion would inherently involve harming "the sensibilities of the religious." The resolution also noted that most religious people contribute to the state and that it was entirely wrong to cast aspersions on them or even on the religious service providers. Moreover, the resolution criticized the regime's agencies for "administrative interference in religious activity." The tone of the resolution thus indicated that the antireligion campaign, launched only a few months earlier, was now about to end, and many of the clergy viewed it as such.

Following the November resolution, the number of antireligion lectures and publications declined sharply and a certain shift was noticeable in the government's attitude toward religion. The emphasis in the Central Committee's resolution on noninterference in the internal affairs of religious organizations, as well as a Soviet government directive of February 17, 1955, dictating that the ultimate authority in decisions to open or close a house of prayer rested no longer with the USSR but with the governments of the Union Republics, was meant to stress that a change was under way in the regime's views on religion. But this was mainly a change of climate and not a fundamental change, since all the rules and regulations in this field remained in force.

The heads of the Moscow congregation tried to exploit the relative leniency toward religion to arrange a convention of rabbis and congregational leaders in the context of a celebration of Rabbi Shlifer's sixty-fifth birthday. Rabbi Shlifer's secretary, S. V. Artski, applied to the SRA in this connection on January 28, 1955, requesting permission to invite some twenty people from outside the city as well as members of the Israeli embassy. The SRA replied that while indeed they would not interfere in the congregation's internal affairs, the event would best be celebrated more quietly, as "it isn't the anniversary of a person who is conducting broad public activity beyond the borders of Moscow."[6] This response sufficed in persuading the sponsors to cancel plans for the convention. Among the internees released from Soviet internment camps in these years were religious activists, including Jews arrested in Stalin's final years. These for the most part had not served in the registered religious organizations, but some had been key figures in the unofficial religious activity.[7] Indeed, SRA representatives in a consultation in Ukraine on November 13, 1957, noted that people were now expressing their religious sentiments more openly.

Given the partial changes in the atmosphere of the Eastern bloc nations, Western interest increased in religious life in the USSR, and the Soviet authorities took this factor into account, allowing some visits by religious delegations.[8] During those years the number of tourists visiting the USSR also grew, as did the number of Western publications on religious subjects written in the various languages of the Soviet Union and sent by post or brought in by tourists. Quite a few tourists met with religious functionaries in both the official and unofficial religious organizations, and through various methods they brought money to help fund religious activities.[9]

In this overall atmosphere of increased freedom, many congregations made special arrangements for the High Holidays of 1954. The SRA representative described the preparations of the Bershad' congregation as follows:

> The preparations for the autumn holidays of the Jews began in the month of August. [The congregation] thoroughly repaired the synagogue building inside and out. . . . The activists reminded the worshipers during prayers that the autumn Jewish holidays were approaching and showed them a handwritten Jewish calendar. . . . As cantor [for the holidays] Zusia Shoier was invited, a Bershad' native now residing in Khar'kov.[10]

The number of worshipers in the synagogues grew, as was clearly noted by the Belorussia SRA representative in his report from late 1954.[11] This trend continued and expanded after the Twentieth Communist Party Congress in 1956. Given the intense disappointment on the part of the intelligentsia with Communist ideology and the manner of its implementation, members of certain intellectual circles pursued religious-oriented worldviews beyond the confines imposed by state-regulated Church institutions. This offered the general context for the visit to the USSR by a group of rabbis from the United States. The visit signaled to many Jews a significant change in the government's approach to religion, though the Ukraine sra representative characterized the visit as fueling "provocative rumors":

> After the visit by the rabbis from the usa, provocative rumors were spread by religious Jews in some Ukrainian towns . . . that the government had ordered the return to the religious Jews of all their former synagogues and [that] in Kiev the building of the main synagogue now lodging the puppet theater had already been returned.[12]

The widening of Jewish religious activity and the voicing of unacceptable opinions bothered sra officials. The Ukraine representative wrote as follows in his report of 1957:

> The activists [of the Jewish religion] . . . are seeking to turn the synagogues into a center for gatherings where, in addition to religious affairs, it will be possible to conduct nationalist activity. A few clerics and certain groups of Chassidim wish to turn the synagogue into a supposed "House of Peace," and have set themselves the goal of granting religious services not only to the religious but to the entire Jewish population, through provision of kosher meat and matzah and also reinstating "burial societies" alongside the synagogues . . . and establishing groups for the study . . . of Mishna and Gemara. It is no accident that certain "activists" from the religious associations are expressing their wish to turn the synagogue into not only a place of prayer but also into a place where Jews can gather, where they can debate public affairs.[13]

Affected by the prevailing climate in the Jewish community after the doctors' release, the Odessa congregation demanded its synagogue building be replaced and in Kiev congregants raised anew their demand to open a second synagogue.

In Odessa the congregation argued that the former synagogue building in Babelia Street should be restored to it in place of the assigned building on the city's outskirts, which required a three- or four-hour walk for Jews who abstained from vehicular travel on Sabbath. This synagogue was also adjacent to a factory that spewed toxic gas and was not large enough to hold all those who came on holidays. Furthermore, the synagogue had to endure attacks by hooligans: congregation members wrote in 1956 that "there were often attacks by hooligans residing in the quarter . . . insults to the religious, stones thrown at windows during prayers and the like."[14]

The renewed application to open a second synagogue in the central part of Kiev gave rise to a fierce dispute within the congregation. The faction demanding that a downtown synagogue be opened was led by Joseph Bernshtein,[15] who had strained relations with the official head of the congregation, S. I.

Bardakh. Some of the activists left the synagogue on account of this acrimony, an occurrence that naturally didn't contribute to the cause of opening another synagogue downtown.[16] Yet the split didn't adversely affect the number of Jews gathering around the synagogue during the High Holidays, as most such attendees were not involved in the day-to-day affairs of the congregation and had nothing to do with the dispute.

The authorities do not appear to have been behind the dispute in the Kiev congregation, but they did benefit from it, as it freed them from having to seriously address the request for another synagogue in the city center. As to the dispute itself, the SRA stressed that this was an internal issue of the congregation and that it would not interfere.[17] Yet such a response does not mean that the SRA or other authorities indeed never interfered in decisions regarding congregations' leadership, even if they now did so in a less direct way than before. Thus, for example, two members of the board (Kharam and Gutkin) offered to resign their posts in the Kherson congregation so as to "end the discontent and disputes among the religious," yet the district SRA representative opposed their resignation because

> the present leadership of the congregation . . . agreed at my recommendation not
> to invite cantors from other districts and suchlike, while the opposition plans
> to elect undesirable people to the new composition of the executive committee
> [board] . . . activists of a more determined nature [*nastaivaiushchie*].[18]

The continued involvement of the authorities in the selection of congregation leaders is also shown in the events in Vinnitsa in 1958. In May of that year, congregation head Shteinvas took a health-related trip and temporarily transferred his authority to another board member, Tabatchnik. On his return to Vinnitsa, the substitute did not agree to relinquish the position, arguing that he had the support of most of the congregation. Yet the district SRA representative opposed this "election" of Tabatchnik, explaining that the "'neighbors' [*sosedi*, a nickname used for the security services] and ourselves find it convenient that Tabatchnik be removed from the leadership of the congregation."[19]

In line with the slogan of a return to "socialist lawfulness," the authorities now were required to explain their responses to applications by religious associations and not to limit themselves to general formulas. Indeed, certain congregations seeking restoration of synagogues pursued the tactic of stressing the legal aspects; this was done by the congregations of Mukachevo, Cherkassy, and others, as well as by thirty-eight Jews from Khar'kov.[20] When the authorities wanted to officially confiscate the building of the Mozir synagogue building, owned (as was also the case in Korosten') by a private individual, the authorities now had to hold trials. As these deliberations were public, the issue of confiscation of synagogues, especially in smaller towns, became a common topic of conversation and drew many Jews, directly or indirectly, into the efforts to recover them.

During this period, the regime showed more openness to the world and greater consideration of Western public opinion, which was why Rabbi Shlifer was sent to France for the ceremony marking the unveiling of the Monument to the Unknown Jew.[21] USSR authorities, perhaps unsurprisingly, also began taking Western public opinion into account on the subject of the synagogues in the large cities, which were visited by tourists and members of the diplomatic corps. Jews who were aware of this reality mentioned it at times in their requests to the authorities. Thus, for example, the group of Jews who wished to open a second synagogue in Kiev wrote that many visitors from abroad were asking why there was no synagogue in the city center, when so many more Jews lived there than in the Podol area, where the synagogue was sited.[22] The response of world public opinion to the absence of a synagogue in a major city with a large Jewish population was mentioned also in the correspondence with the authorities over the reopening of the synagogue in Khar'kov.

In July 1954, a group of Jews in Khar'kov formally requested the restoration to them of one of the six buildings that had once been synagogues. Their request was turned down by the municipality. The members of the congregation persisted and wrote to the central institutions in Ukraine and Moscow. The final decision went to the government of Ukraine, which received the request on April 25, 1956.[23] The republic's SRA representative, who better grasped the broader implications of a lack of a synagogue in Khar'kov than did the municipal authorities, wrote on May 14, 1956, to the deputy prime minister of Ukraine:

[I]nformation available to us suggests that the ambassador of Israel has connections with the religious activists, who no doubt keep him advised as to the situation of the synagogue in the city of Khar'kov [which was closed at the time]. Taking the large number of religious Jews in Khar'kov into account, and also the fact that many groups of tourists from abroad visit this city, we believe that it would be helpful to register the Jewish congregation in this city and to require the district authorities to allocate one of the buildings which once served as a house of prayer to be a synagogue.[24]

But the Ukrainian government, especially the district authorities, did not hasten to respond to the recommendations of the SRA representative, and Moscow's intercession was needed. In August 1957 the SRA chairman wrote to the district:

In light of the presence in the city of Khar'kov of a Jewish population numbering a hundred thousand persons, thousands of whom are religious, and also taking into account the fact that many tourists, diplomats and political and public figures from abroad take an interest in this city . . . all these factors together make it necessary to reconsider the subject of opening a synagogue in Khar'kov.[25]

Despite the recommendations of the Ukraine SRA representative and the clear position of the Moscow chairman, the district authorities refused to allocate a structure for a synagogue or to register the congregation legally.

The possible reaction of world public opinion to the lack of synagogues, especially in the large cities, which were mostly open to tourists, was indeed taken into account by the Soviet authorities. On the other hand, the transfer of money in various ways from abroad to certain synagogues or to some of their leaders appears to have exacerbated old and new controversies in certain congregations. Such dynamics almost certainly factored in to the dispute that broke out in the Leningrad congregation in the mid-1950s.

The rabbi of the Leningrad congregation at the time was Rabbi Meizeson; he had strained relations with congregation head Gedalia Pecherski (b. 1901 and serving as head since 1954). Unlike the rabbi, who apparently wished to keep the synagogue restricted to ritual observance, Pecherski wanted to have Yiddish, Hebrew, and Jewish history courses taught alongside the prayer regimen. Pecherski, who in his youth had been active in Zionist movements, contacted the Israeli embassy in Moscow, and was given funds as well as materials about Israel. When Pecherski and the rabbi of Dnepropetrovsk (probably Rabbi Shpern) were on holiday at a hotel in Kislovotsk, they plotted the removal of Rabbi Meizeson and his replacement by the Dnepropetrovsk rabbi. But effecting such an outcome would require the permission of the district SRA representative, who was not on good terms with the congregation head. The SRA representative backed those who opposed Pecherski, mainly due to the latter's acceptance of funds from abroad and distribution of them to his supporters. Pecherski's opponents complained about him to the SRA in Moscow; he in turn would discuss them in the presence of foreigners as agents of the security services, informers, and the like, although no real evidence to this effect has been found to date. Because of the complaints, Pecherski was summoned to the SRA in Moscow and told that while the soviet does not interfere with internal congregational matters, nevertheless, the recommendation was that Avraham Haim Lubanov be appointed ("elected") rabbi and congregation head to improve the atmosphere. Pecherski agreed to this and was appointed deputy head. But the factionalism in the Leningrad congregation continued during the following years.[26]

Money matters were also the basis of dissension in the Moscow congregation known as Marina Roshcha. Meir Glik, seventy-six years old and a member of the congregation's board, went to the Moscow district SRA representative on February 9, 1955, charging that deputy congregation head A. G. Esterman was taking for himself funds tourists had donated to the synagogue, and that since Rabbi Natan Olevskii was aged and infirm, the deputy head was in effective control of the congregation's finances and was distributing funds as he pleased. Esterman had once been a Chabad *mashpia* (emissary to yeshivot), and it appears that monies from this movement's branches abroad were sent through him. Yet some individuals in the congregation rebuffed Glik's complaints and expressed full confidence in the deputy head; they insisted that his actions should not be interfered with. "If Esterman is taking money, he must know whom to give it to," was the reasoning. Because of his actions, Glik was boycotted by worshipers in the synagogue.[27]

Quarrels and disputes within congregations are not unknown elsewhere in the world and are hardly specific to the USSR; what was different there was that each side in a dispute would try to draw in the government agencies on which the entire existence of the congregation often depended. Moreover, each party would often accuse the other of being an "informer" and "traitor," language that would raise the pressures in the congregation, sometimes aiding the authorities directly or indirectly.

Ostensibly to correct the ills done during Stalin's last years, in 1954–1955 Jews in at least twenty-two towns sought registration for their congregations and the return to them or the opening of synagogues. Only two of these applications were granted.

At the time, Vinnitsa had a population of some 20,000 Jews, quite a few of whom evidently were interested in having an official synagogue in their city. After repeated applications, the Moscow SRA decided in November 1956 "to allow the representative of the soviet in the Vinnitsa district to [legally] register the Jewish religious association [i.e., congregation] as having a house of prayer in Nekrasova Street."[28] A similar response was given to the request from one of the cities in Uzbekistan. In contrast with these positive responses during the 1955–1958 period, two synagogues were closed in RSFSR and one in Latvia. In Ukraine as well, a congregation was dissolved and the synagogue in the town of Il'nitsa (Irshava area in the Zakarpat'e district) was appropriated.[29]

Whenever the question concerned reopening synagogues that had been closed in the late 1940s and early 1950s, and all the more so opening synagogues in towns that previously didn't have them at all, the authorities' position reflected little change even during the days of the thaw. In early 1954, there were 135 registered congregations in the entire USSR; in January 1959, the figure was 133. The main change on the part of the authorities had to do with the manner of response to the various applications and the new requirement to supply grounds for rejections. A corresponding significant change involved the attitude of many Jews and the broadening range of individuals who demanded that synagogues be opened. A certain change also occurred in the tone of the applications: some of them noted the contributions of Jews to the USSR while others hinted at the antisemitic aspect of the attitude of the authorities. Thus, for example, in the city of Khmel'nitskii, about a thousand Jews had no option but to pray in private homes illegally, even though

> everyone knows that the Jewish religion and the religious Jews have done much
> to raise funds in the war days . . . in order to defeat the Fascist invaders. The
> religious Jews have raised their voices against any form of aggression [a reference
> to the Sinai campaign] and against atomic weapons, and have been advocates of
> peace in the whole world.[30]

A more strident tone in the request to open a synagogue is noticeable, for example, in the August 1956 letter sent by the Jews of Mukachevo to the Ukraine SRA representative, in which they complained about the refusal of the local authorities to relinquish a particular building for use as a synagogue:

> All the structures that were formerly synagogues, more than thirty . . . have been
> given to the municipality. But when it comes to allocating one structure as a
> house of prayer, it turns out that the city is not sufficiently empowered to transfer
> a single shed to a different place. . . . It is absolutely clear to us that with reference
> to satisfying the needs of the Jewish religious community . . . incomprehensible
> foot-dragging and a hidden lack of will to respond to our needs continue. . . . The
> autumn Jewish holidays approach . . . and we are again forced . . . to gather in
> minyans and to pray in private homes as rejected citizens, deprived of the right
> of public prayer. . . . In the last three years our government decisively spoke on
> the issue of resolving outstanding issues concerning religion. . . . If it is forbidden
> for Jews to pray in an organized fashion, this should be said explicitly and not
> manifested by delays; if the Jews are not included in the citizens who have the
> right to organize in groups of "twenty" [to operate their own house of prayer] as
> per the constitution, then this must be announced openly.[31]

One Vinnitsa congregation activist, Idl Tokar, declared to the SRA representative that "closure of the synagogue in the chief town of the district was done only because we are Jews. . . . This is just like the Beilis trial."[32] The reference was to the 1911 blood libel charge against Menachem Beilis, who was accused of killing a young Christian in Kiev and using his blood for matzah. Beilis was acquitted in 1913.

In those same years, Jews continued to gather around the synagogues on the High Holidays; in nearly all towns that had a synagogue, massive assemblies were held. One of these gatherings, on Yom Kippur of 1956 in Dnepropetrovsk, was described by the SRA representative as follows:

> On Yom Kippur—in the second half of the day—it was hard to tell which age was more prevalent: elderly or middle-aged; women or men. . . . One could clearly see that near the synagogue there were many youths, mostly girls. . . . By 2 p.m., the synagogue hall, with its 750 or so seats, was full; there were four hundred persons in the sukkah in the yard, and in the yard itself no fewer than three hundred more. In the street, near the synagogue, there were over five hundred people standing. From 3 p.m. on, there was an incessant stream of further groups of religious people. Individuals and families walked—old and young. There were also quite a few children of kindergarten and school age who came along with their parents. Everyone was dressed festively. At 5 or 6 p.m., the entire street was . . . packed with a mass of people, at least 2,500. At both ends of the street no fewer than thirty buses stood, awaiting passengers. All of them dispersed at 7 p.m.[33]

According to a report by the Jewish Telegraphic Agency, that New Year about 2,500 people gathered at the main Moscow synagogue, even though the Jewish population of that city was three times that of Dnepropetrovsk. Those assembled near the synagogue included soldiers as well as other young men and women, many of whom bore the Komsomol insignia on their shoulders. Likewise in Vilnius, the Lithuania SRA representative noted that during the High Holidays of 1957, the assembly around the synagogue included Jews who worked in the town trading system (*Gortorg*), Jews employed in the film studio and publishing house (*Politizdat*)—who were in large measure in charge of ideological indoctrination—and even one man who was formerly on the government staff. Describing the types of people who gathered around the synagogues during the High Holidays, the Moscow SRA representative wrote that "there are many who don't come at all to the synagogue during the year, and even some who call themselves atheists."[34] The Western print media and Soviet summaries noted that the gatherings around synagogues in Moscow, Riga, and in Belorussia drew also youths and children in school uniform. By the authorities' estimates, about 80 percent of the Jews near synagogues on Yom Kippur usually never attended synagogue.[35] In certain towns, the number of synagogue-goers increased greatly due to the relaxation of the antireligion campaign and the overall climate of thaw. Some congregations went so far as to put loudspeakers in the synagogues to broadcast the prayers to the crowd in the street, although in most cases the authorities removed such equipment on various procedural grounds.[36]

In this general climate, the permanent minyans resumed operation almost in the open. The Belorussia SRA representative wrote in this connection in 1954: "Although minyans exist anywhere there are forty or fifty Jewish families, due to the Communist Party Central Committee's decision of November 10, 1954, I don't view these groups as breaking the laws of religious affairs, because most of them had several times requested legal status and were denied."[37]

Holiday minyans were held in almost every city and town that had Jews,[38] even in those where registered synagogues existed. In Korosten' at least five permanent minyans resumed operation; by the estimates of the authorities, about a third of all the town's religious Jews (about 270 men) prayed in them. Likewise in Kiev many minyans were restarted; one of the accusations against the congregation's rabbi, Avraham Panich, a charge that led to his dismissal, was that he had ties to the minyans.[39]

Tensions at that time increased between the congregation heads and the organizers of the permanent minyans. Almost certainly this owed to two factors. Some of the minyan activists, among them people recently freed from Soviet detention camps, viewed the congregation heads as collaborators with the regime, and resented them as such. For their part, the congregation leaders viewed the minyans as competitors that eroded synagogue attendance as well as synagogue income: quite a few tourists visited the minyans and donated to them funds that would otherwise have gone to the registered congregations. This context explains perhaps why the rabbi of the Minsk congregation "reported to us about the minyans in town," as the SRA representative wrote in early 1956. The head of the Kiev congregation likewise gave the SRA representative the names and addresses of organizers of one of the city's largest minyans, where, as he put it, "office and factory workers [pray] who want to hide their religiosity from their colleagues and so don't go to the synagogue but instead to a minyan"; he even went on to say that contributions were solicited in that minyan to assist the former Zionist Shchukin. The head of the Korosten' congregation, Moshe Ushman, regularly informed the municipality about the existence of minyans operating from monetary motives.[40] Despite these reports and their like, the minyan organizers were not arrested, and the authorities preferred to fight them mainly by financial means.

As noted, the partial expansion of religious activity in the period in question does not indicate a fundamental shift in the regime's attitude toward religion; rather it reflects a thaw that affected many realms. A much more significant change took place within the Jewish public, which now dared to assert its rights under Soviet law. A certain openness on the part of the Soviet regime toward the West also encouraged quite a few Jews to express their religiosity and permitted some aid from abroad to reach and support religious activity. However, the relaxation of the antireligious stance was relatively short-lived, and already by the late 1950s a new propaganda campaign against religion had been launched.

CHAPTER 8
The Public Campaign against Religion

In January 1959, the Twenty-first Congress of the Communist Party of the USSR convened, and First Secretary Nikita Khrushchev announced that the country was entering a new stage in its passage from Socialism to Communism, and to that end must intensify the battle against "manifestations of bourgeois values and ethics." Resolutions passed at the congress stressed the need to increase the atheist-scientific and antireligion propaganda aimed at the public. In keeping with these resolutions, on February 5, 1959, the SRA sent a circular detailing "the main tasks and the work-plan for 1959 for the SRA and its representatives in the republics, regions [krai], and districts."[1] Among other tasks, the work-plan included the complete elimination of unregistered religious groups—in our case, the minyans; cessation of the activities of preachers; and current reports to be submitted to Communist Party institutions on actions being taken in the area of religion.[2] In line with the renewed campaign against religion a series of resolutions were passed between 1959 and 1964.[3] On March 16, 1961, the USSR government passed a resolution "to increase oversight of the implementation of religious affairs laws" and criticized local institutions for having weakened the antireligion propaganda efforts.[4]

The campaign against religion that began in the late 1950s differed from the suppression of religion as practiced during Stalin's final years. In Stalin's time the antireligious activity was primarily administrative and was not accompanied by a broad propaganda effort; and the government was not interested in the public's involvement. In the final years of the Khrushchev government, conversely, the campaign's purpose was not solely to root out religious ideology but also to "develop a scientific worldview and Communist ethics, which are impossible without combating religious ideology."[5] That meant challenging the traditions and modes of behavior of millions of people—something that was to meet with considerable resistance.[6]

To implement this plan, an increase in antireligious articles appeared in the Soviet newspapers, scholars from the humanities and social sciences were recruited,[7] courses on "scientific atheism" were introduced into the higher education curriculum, and the Society for the Spread of Political and Scientific Knowledge (Znanie) was assigned the task of managing the antireligion propaganda. In many towns, "atheist houses" were established along with "atheist soviets," societies, and support groups (*gruppy sodeistviia*).[8] These groups were required to report every violation of USSR law on religious affairs including those concerning the minyans; additionally, an army of propagandists and lecturers on atheism was set to work. In this context, the Soviet authorities bragged that thanks to their activities the conduct of religious rituals had dropped significantly.[9] Yet this may not have been so—in reality, rituals practiced openly in previous years were now being held in secret.

Seminars were organized for the army of propagandists, in many of which lectures against Judaism were held; yet occasionally complaints appeared in the newspapers that this effort was insufficient and that more Jews ought to be recruited for the propaganda campaign.[10] Thus, for example, one journalist wrote:

> The Kuibishev branch of Znanie, in the eight months of this year [1961], held ten thousand lectures . . . but in the thirteen years of this society's existence there was not a single lecture about the reactionary significance of Judaism. Kuibishev has Jewish science workers, teachers of social subjects, some of whom are experts on scientific atheism. Who if not them, who know the tradition, the psychology and the special characteristics of their tribe . . . ought to be helping their brothers and sisters liberate themselves from the shackles of the past? But to our regret they show no initiative in this direction.[11]

Indeed, it wasn't always easy to draw Communist Jews into this sort of activity, as the authorities would sometimes admit in closed sessions. In a consultation with the directors of party propaganda departments, the head of the Mogilev-Podol'skii department was asked why no propaganda efforts against the Jewish religion were being made in his city, when three permanent minyans were operating there to draw upon. His reply was that "none of the Jews wants to give such lectures . . . and it is the same in other districts as well."[12] While it seems exaggerated to say there was such a blanket refusal, some Jewish Communists appear to have felt discomfort at uttering crude statements against Judaism that sometimes bordered on the antisemitic.

So as to promote the anti-Jewish lectures, the Communist Party Committee of the Zhitomir district organized a local seminar in 1960 and held a nationwide seminar in Odessa in late 1963 devoted to the "Critique of Contemporary Judaism."[13]

More broadly, the propaganda campaign against the Jewish faith had religious and national-ethnic themes—defined as Zionism—interwoven into it, so that the campaign came to contain elements of anti-Zionism, despite the latter's being a national-political movement rather than a religious one: ideologically, Zionism had since Lenin's days been regarded as a reactionary movement linked to imperialism. In addition, the propagandists had no trouble linking the Jewish religion to Zionism because the Zionist movement and the state of Israel had embraced quite a few ideas and symbols from religious sources, although in many cases these were infused with new content. The Jewish religious bodies in the world were thus represented as "linked to Zionism, which is the agent of American imperialism in the Middle East."[14] The Jewish religion was represented as racist and the rabbis, together with the Zionists, were accused of collaboration with the Nazis.[15]

In the West, special attention was paid to a book by Trofim Kichko titled *Judaism without Embellishment.* The publisher—the Academy of Science in Ukraine—described this book as an account "of the essence of the Jewish religion, one of the oldest religions in the world, which has absorbed and concentrated all that is reactionary and antihuman in the writings of all the religions of our time."[16] Given the negative reaction to this book in the West, some criticism of it was also made in the USSR. Yet some members of the Soviet propaganda apparatus now felt that in the context of the campaign against religion and its political-Zionist dimensions, the most extreme opinions could be expressed against the Jews and Judaism. The propaganda war against the Jewish religion was therefore fiercer and more toxic than that against any other legitimate religion, and more extensive in terms of the number of publications.

An examination of the lists of books and pamphlets defined as "antireligious literature" published in the USSR between 1959 and 1964 reveals 1,847 publications meeting this description. Of these, 1,176 were directed at religion in general, most of them also containing criticism of Judaism; and of the 671 directed against a particular religion (as attested by their titles), the breakdown was: 43.8 percent against the Christian religions, 21.8 percent against Islam, 26.4 percent against religious sects, and 8.0 percent against the Jewish religion. The proportion of anti-Judaism titles was thus seven times larger than the proportion of Jews in the population (1.1 percent by the 1959 census). The special intensity of the anti-Judaism efforts is seen even more clearly in the print runs. The average number of copies of books and pamphlets of this type directed against the Christian religions was about 27,000; against religious sects, 18,000; against Islam, 6,000; and against Judaism, a remarkable 46,000. Thus in the years 1959–1964, about two and a half million copies of books and pamphlets were published in the USSR to combat Judaism,[17] not counting the anti-Zionist and anti-Israel publications that usually also included content about religion. The intensity of the propaganda campaign against Judaism didn't stem from Jews' closer practice of the faith than others', but instead owed to the ideological and political precepts that the Soviets associated with this religion.[18]

In the Western countries, the propaganda struggle in those years for the rights of Soviet Jews, which had made significant strides among world public opinion and political leaders, focused on religious persecution. This situation was not a comfortable one for the USSR, which to a greater extent, unlike in the last years of the Stalinist period, now took world public opinion into account. It is unsurprising therefore that Soviet representatives sometimes assumed a defensive posture. On the first of July 1959, the SRA chairman issued a memorandum to all his subordinates requiring that they honor Soviet laws and regulations when approaching religious issues so as "not to let bourgeois propaganda exploit this for attacks on the USSR."[19] In this respect, world public opinion provided a shield of sorts against closure of synagogues in the major cities, where tourists and members of the foreign embassies visited. But the special interest that world public opinion took in the plight of Soviet Jews also raised the ire of the Soviet bureaucracy, which regarded this as a sort of demonstration that the religious institutions were focal points for politically significant Jewish activity. Correspondingly, one official defined Judaism as a "troublesome religion [*bespokoinyi kul't*]"[20] and the Ukraine SRA representative wrote as follows to the vice president of the republic in 1962:

[T]he Jewish religion, like the Catholic religion, attracts special attention from "tourists" of various types and official figures from many embassies in the USSR, especially the embassy of the state of Israel. The ambassador of Israel and his colleagues have invested, and continue to invest, great efforts so as to turn the synagogue in Ukraine (and it seems other Soviet republics too) into a center for political espionage and a source of information for anti-Soviet propaganda. Accordingly there is special importance for us to supervise the activities of the Jewish religious congregations (as well as the Catholic ones). . . . There is an obligation for daily and unrelenting supervision over the inner life of the houses of prayer—the synagogues and *kostely* [Catholic churches]. . . . With the closure of the L'vov synagogue [in 1962], Israeli political espionage lost one of its prime sources of information . . . [a tough blow] to the security services of Israel.[21]

Synagogues thus appear to have been perceived as important foci of political espionage, as purportedly demonstrated by the Pecherski affair in Leningrad, which drew a lot of attention from the Western press. Pecherski's house was searched in Passover 1959 and some of his notes on the condition of Soviet Jewry were found, notes he had been passing to the Israeli embassy; despite his advanced age, he was arrested and sentenced to many years of prison.[22] This backdrop helps frame the instructions (*instruktsii*) given by the Ukraine SRA representative in consultation with the SRA representatives of six Ukrainian districts in November 1960, which noted that "oversight of the congregations must not be relaxed, and always one must remember the increased interest given those congregations by the Israeli embassy and various tourists from abroad."[23] One justification for dismantling congregations and closing synagogues was thereby that "nationalist elements are concentrated [in them]" and many tourists and Israeli embassy personnel come there "who incite nationalist feelings and emigration tendencies."[24] Here an opposition of sorts formed between the apparatchiks who ran the antireligion campaign and those involved in Soviet public relations abroad. Whereas the latter were committed to international agreements and were compelled to allow a certain mobility to embassy personnel, foreign journalists, and tourists, the former strove to limit such activity as much as possible. Thus, the Ukraine SRA representative applied to the republic's government "seeking to lobby in the appropriate pipelines to keep the ambassador of Israel, his attachés, secretaries, and counselors from visiting Ukrainian synagogues during the holidays when the masses attend."[25] Though requests of this sort were usually not granted, the field activists nevertheless worked energetically to close synagogues, especially in towns less open to foreign visitors.

In this incarnation, the campaign against the Jewish religion was waged in ways that considerably resembled antireligious efforts of the 1920s. As in the twenties, the authorities ensured that newspapers and magazines published articles against Judaism written by Jews. An examination of 191 signed headlines and articles that appeared between 1960 and 1964 on Judaism in the broad sense of the word (including the Bible) reveals that 65 percent (123) were signed by authors with Jewish names.[26] The Soviet authorities gave special prominence to notices from Jews, some of them congregational activists, about the abandonment of their religion. Most of these declarations contained similar wording and almost surely were dictated by the authorities.[27] As in the 1920s, the authorities in certain cities organized public trials and antireligious meetings, and instigated the writing of letters to newspapers demanding synagogue closures.[28] However, unlike in the 1920s, when the bulk of the antireligion campaign was in Yiddish, now it was conducted in the local languages, increasing the manifestations of antisemitism that culminated in blood libels[29] as well as acts of violence.[30]

The campaign against the Jewish religion was also affected by the battle against "black marketeering and parasitism" that began in 1961. Ostensibly there was no connection between the two. But many actions of the Jewish congregations or persons connected to synagogues, aimed at satisfying religious needs, could be regarded as infractions of economic laws. In the propaganda against the Jewish religion, the monetary issue took on an ever larger role, and a number of synagogues, for example those of Riga, Samarkand, L'vov, and other cities, were defined as centers of illegal commerce. Congregation activists were described as persons for whom the chief aim was not promotion of religion but personal gain.[31] The synagogue in L'vov became, so the authorities maintained, "a sanctuary for crooks, who commit crimes under cover of religion." The closure of this synagogue in late 1962 was thus connected with the arrest of several activists, who were condemned to long prison terms for trading in foreign currencies.[32] Without going into whether those indicted indeed traded in foreign currencies, the mere presentation of the synagogue as a nest of illegal commerce carried a whiff of antisemitism. In this context, we can understand the statement to foreign journalists by Rabbi Leib Levin and the head of Moscow's main synagogue, Nahum Feler, that commerce in the ritual objects left in the synagogue by tourists could bring about its closure.[33]

In order to reduce the number of synagogues and congregations as much as possible, the authorities used a technique that combined encouraging dispute and dissent among the worshipers, on the one hand, and, on the other, "convincing" those responsible for supporting the synagogue to announce their resignation. As part of the anti-Judaism campaign, a group of propagandists held a lecture series in the Jewish neighborhoods of Kremenchug, in the context of which private discussions were also held with congregation activists, and their relatives living in other cities were brought in to persuade the activists to cease their Judaism-related efforts. Special pressures were applied to sons and daughters of congregation activists to influence their parents to end their involvement in synagogue life.[34] The angst is not difficult to describe in the discussion between an elderly father and his son, when the father's resignation from the "twenty" could cause the closure of the town's sole synagogue, and yet the son tells his father that the father's continued activity in the congregation might be preventing the son's career advancement, resulting in critiques targeting him from his Communist Party cell and the like. Unsurprisingly, in quite a few cases members of the "twenty" did indeed resign without anyone being found who was willing to replace them.[35] A lack of a twenty-person quorum, which was responsible for the upkeep of the synagogue and the congregation's existence, or alternatively the small number of worshipers, was often used as the justification for dismantling a congregation and closing the synagogue. Under various pretexts, fifty-eight synagogues were closed in

1959.[36] Official data indicate that ten synagogues were closed in Ukraine in 1960.[37] The campaign continued in 1961 with the shuttering of synagogues in Khotin, Kherson, Romny, and Malin.[38] Insufficient worshipers were cited for the closure of the Balta synagogue.[39]

The paucity of worshipers and the building shortage in Belaia Tserkov' were mentioned as the main reasons for closing the synagogue there, although on Yom Kippur of 1960 more than a thousand men and women were reported to have gathered in or near the synagogue. For those wishing to pray, the authorities suggested a trip to Kiev, with public transportation traveling there every quarter hour. Such ridiculous suggestions were meant to demonstrate that the authorities were not preventing Jews who wished to pray from doing so.[40] Where the claim of too few worshipers was hard to make, as in the city of Zhmerinka, the authorities used a different tactic. They sent a committee to inspect the physical state of the building, which determined that a major rehabilitation must be carried out. Thereafter, the authorities demanded that the congregation's management do this work as a precondition for using the synagogue. The remodeling costs were too great for the small congregation to raise. Some members of the management were thus forced to resign, declaring formally that they had no way to rehabilitate the structure; this was then used as a legal basis for closing the synagogue.[41] The synagogues of Iampol' and Nikolaev were closed on similar grounds.[42]

Sometimes the authorities used "old sins" as the pretext for closing synagogues and dismantling congregations. Thus, for example, the Zhitomir district SRA representative maintained in the early 1960s

> that in March 1949 the religious congregation [of Berdichev] applied to the district authorities seeking permission to bake matzah in the synagogue. . . . [The district authority refused], yet nevertheless the congregation's management took . . . the path of fraud, and via Jews who worked in Soviet institutions . . . founded a "cooperative" [Artel'] of seventeen individuals to bake matzah in the synagogue, registering the cooperative in the town's treasury department.[43]

The writer then went on to point out that the congregation's administration took fat wages for itself, charging seven and a half rubles for baking a kilogram of matzah, and that the overall income from matzah-baking in 1949 came to 21,000 rubles.[44] "Sins" of this type, committed more than a decade previously, thus warranted the congregation's closure.

Some synagogues were also casualties of the extensive building projects in certain towns of the USSR. The area of the Minsk synagogue was included in an urban renewal program, and in February 1962 congregation head Gorelik was summoned and notified by the local authorities that the synagogue was slated for destruction and that a multistory building would be erected on its site. The congregation was instructed to collect the ritual objects and store them in a basement. The congregation's request that one of the town's previous synagogue structures be restored to them was immediately rejected, and the authorities suggested instead that they lease a private home for use as a synagogue. The congregation resisted this suggestion and applied to the republic's authorities, saying:

> Since many tourists from abroad and journalists from the US print media visit Minsk and some of them visit the synagogue . . . the complete eradication of the Minsk synagogue . . . will be exploited by the American journalists for anti-Soviet propaganda.[45]

After this appeal was rejected, the congregation approached Khrushchev and here, too, emphasized the damage that the USSR would incur by closing the synagogue.[46] International repercussions indeed were probably the primary factor preventing closure of the Minsk synagogue. Yet this did not apply in towns that did not draw the interest of world public opinion, such as Beregovo, Zhitomir, and Cherkassy.

As part of the renewal of Beregovo the authorities erected a large statue of Lenin on Ivan Franko Street near the synagogue. The Zakarpat'e district SRA representative had claimed that "when important events need to be noted the place should have a festive look" and hence proximity to a synagogue was undesirable; he suggested that the congregation move its site to a side street and make use of a structure that was once a Jewish house of prayer. This suggestion was made during the thaw, but now the authorities decided to close the synagogue and hand the structure over to be used by the district archive.[47] In Zhitomir the wooden synagogue was located in an area slated for apartment blocks; the city decided to destroy it. Cherkassy, which in 1954 was upgraded from a subdistrict town to a district city, carried out a widespread urban building project that resulted in the destruction of the synagogue building in 1959.[48]

As mentioned earlier, a different tactic meant to spur closure of synagogues and keep the public away from them was the fostering of quarrels and dissent within the congregations. In May 1961, twenty Kiev residents were elected to be responsible for the city's synagogue; they included members of the intelligentsia, who wished to be counted among the twenty. The election was conducted in large measure under the influence of M. L. Iurovitskii, who mostly put his own associates on the ballot. The twenty chose a congregation board from among themselves, including their congregation head, Gendel'man, who was to replace his longtime predecessor, S. I. Bardakh. A dispute ensued between the supporters of the new and the old congregation heads, and six of one group wrote a sharp complaint about the congregation's management to the Ukraine SRA representative, demanding the establishment of a committee to investigate the "management activities and finances from 1960 until late 1963."[49] It is of course impossible to know to what extent these events were coordinated by the authorities, but the government very likely made use of them in their battle against the synagogues, as it did of the quarrel that erupted in the Moscow congregation, described next.

In October 1958, a group of worshipers from Moscow's main synagogue, among them members of the "twenty," complained about Rabbi Levin's disrespectful attitude toward the synagogue activists and also about financial irregularities. In response, the rabbi removed several individuals from the oversight committee who sought to also gain supervision of the Moscow yeshiva's budget. In support of his ruling, the rabbi maintained that the congregation had no standing in the affairs of the yeshiva, which was an independent institution, not part of the congregation. When the dispute escalated, Rabbi Levin resigned as head of the congregation and Feler was elected (appointed) in his place. The latter was summoned by the authorities and told that commerce in ritual objects was taking place around the synagogue and that such petty trade could bring about its closure. Subsequently, on one Shabbat the congregation head made a speech in the synagogue condemning commerce in ritual objects.[50]

The deep divisions in the Kiev and Moscow congregations did not lead to closure of the synagogues in those cities, mostly because of the impression this would have made on world public opinion. Yet in smaller towns that were less accessible to foreign visitors, the disputes often served as a pretext for implementing closures, as in Priluki[51] and elsewhere. Around this time, sharp quarrels erupted in the associations of various religions, and some have argued that the authorities placed professional informers into the congregations to erode them from within. Still, decisive evidence of such practices is absent, so it seems wise to refrain from related accusations, especially given that particular individuals are named. What we can say is that the internal struggles in quite a few congregations eased the path for authorities who sought to reduce the number of synagogues.

There were also cases, albeit not many, in which the authorities did not close a synagogue but sought to have its physical space reduced. In Odessa, for example, the authorities decided not to dismantle the congregation, perhaps sensing the repercussions from world public opinion to closure of the only synagogue in a city with 120,000 Jewish residents. The SRA representative therefore suggested that the Jews take turns with Baptists in holding prayer services in a building that had formerly served as a synagogue. This peculiar suggestion was rejected by both parties, and the synagogue remained open in its former location. Similarly, the congregation of Khust, in December 1961, objected to exchanging its synagogue in the city center for a building one tenth the size on the outskirts of town. The Jews sent requests and complaints to the state leaders, in one of them writing as follows:

In the Great Patriotic War many nations suffered . . . but no nation or religion suffered as did we—the Jews. It can be said that what our nation went through . . . is a suffering unparalleled in history. The suffering of our people showed the whole world the barbaric face of Hitlerism. . . . [W]e, in making the horrible sacrifice of the loss of so many souls, contributed to the enlistment of humanity against Fascism and to the victory over it. Every one of us has family relatives, women and children, whom we weep over to this day and, in accordance with our religious traditions, hold a special religious ceremony for them on Remembrance Day.

Such passages suggest that the Holocaust served as the primary justification of the need for synagogues in the 1960s as well, at least within certain congregations. However, it was not this justification that led the authorities to decide not to move the synagogue from its current location, but rather the difficulties connected with evicting the tenants from the building to which it was meant to move.[52]

The methods used in the campaign against the Jewish religion in the late 1950s and early 1960s differed from those used during Stalin's last years. As part of the trend toward protecting "socialist legalism," the closure of synagogues and dismantling of congregations was justified by a series of legal arguments, quite a few of which combined various stratagems with one end in mind: to reduce the number of synagogues and congregations. But the results of this campaign were more extensive than those of the period of repression against the Jewish religion during Stalin's final years—something USSR representatives tried to hide through disinformation and delivery of conflicting data.[53] Whereas in the late 1940s and early 1950s, 19 percent of synagogues were closed—on

January 1, 1948, the USSR had 168 registered congregations/synagogues and on January 1, 1953, it had only 136—from January 1959 to January 1964, 32.3 percent were closed—on January 1, 1959, the USSR had 133 registered congregations/synagogues and on January 1, 1964, it had only 90. Local factors were notable within this overall trend. Synagogue closures were greatest in Moldavia (from eleven to two, or (81.8 percent) and in Ukraine (from forty-one to thirteen, or 68.3 percent). By early 1965, fourteen of Ukraine's twenty-five districts, where some 264,000 Jews resided according to the 1959 census, were without a synagogue. In RSFSR, 11.1 percent of synagogues were closed from 1959 to 1964 (from twenty-seven to twenty-four), and in Latvia, one was closed. In the remaining Soviet republics, except Kazakhstan, the number of functioning synagogues had not changed until this antireligion crusade. In the wake of the campaign, 29 percent of all remaining synagogues in the USSR were in Georgia (twenty-six out of ninety), although according to the 1959 census, Georgia was home to only 2.3 percent of the USSR's Jews. RSFSR, where about 39 percent of Soviet Jews lived, had fewer synagogues than Georgia.

In contrast to Stalin's last years, when only a few Russian Orthodox churches were closed, during this antireligion crusade, the Orthodox Church, too, suffered blows. Still, among all religions, Judaism was hit hardest, and even the vigorous efforts by Western Jews to stop the synagogue closures had only limited success—particularly in cities open to tourists and journalists from abroad.

With the closure of the synagogues in those years, the persecution of the minyans also intensified. In Kiev, police invaded an "illegal gathering of persons of the Jewish nationality [i.e., a minyan] . . ." and confiscated twenty-two books "in an unintelligible language"—prayer books. Another permanent minyan in the city was forcibly dispersed by the police.[54] In response, most minyans went underground and periodically switched their place of gathering. To try to discover these minyans, atheist "support groups" were enlisted. The authorities held limited knowledge about meetings of the permanent minyans, and even less knowledge about holiday minyans, yet they estimated that in early 1965 in Ukraine alone, sixty-six permanent minyans were operating, with the participation of some 25,000 individuals.[55] By the authorities' estimates, then, each minyan held an average of 350 to 400 persons, so we must assume that these data are exaggerated.

With the increasing persecution of the minyans, Jews occasionally attempted to register as a congregation, though the chances for success were slim. Thus, for example, the Jews in the towns of Narovlia, Novo-Belitsa, and Vitebsk[56] all made such an application; in one, the applicants pointed to the discrimination against the Jewish religion as contrasted with other religions:

The Russian and Baptist churches function freely in the city . . . but the Jewish population has currently no [house of prayer]. In our Soviet state there is no quarrel between nationalities or any discrimination among races. The national minorities are entitled to equal rights here. It would therefore seem that the Jewish national minority in the town of Vitebsk has also the right to a house of prayer.[57]

The Jews of Vitebsk even expressed their willingness to build a synagogue at their own expense. This was the answer:

The *oblispolkom* [district authority] cannot allocate construction materials for the erection of a synagogue because of the lack of construction materials for building residences. Likewise the *oblispolkom* cannot allow building from materials procured in an illegal manner by private persons because this matter is related to the theft of public and state property.[58]

The struggle against the black market was therefore used indirectly as a sort of justification for rejecting the request.

The closing of synagogues and dispersal of minyans was accompanied by the widespread confiscation of Torah scrolls, prayer books, and ritual objects. All the closed synagogues and dispersed minyans contained Torah scrolls, prayer books, shofars, and the like—and all these were considered, per Soviet nomenclature, "equipment for religious rites" that by law was state-owned. All such items were taken from the closed synagogues and some were given to museums or archives where they were preserved in part; most, however, were stored in rooms and cellars without care or oversight, so that the sacred objects gradually disintegrated. With the 1962 closure of the L'vov synagogue, which held antique holy objects, the authorities took care that private individuals would not acquire these objects and transferred them all to the Museum of Religion and Atheism. In Chernovtsy the local Jews succeeded in moving the Torah scrolls from a minyan to a synagogue; when the synagogue, too, was closed, the scrolls went to the district museum.[59] Quite a few books were simply destroyed, as in Beregovo, where the holy books were loaded onto a truck and sent to paper factories.[60] While dispersing one of the minyans that had gathered in Khar'kov for the New Year of 1959, the authorities confiscated the Torah scroll. Because the confiscation took place in a private house, the Jews claimed the scroll was private property and demanded its return; the authorities responded that it was "equipment for religious rites" and thus, by the law of 1918, state property.[61] The authorities' suspicions of Jewish books were so great as to sometimes border on the absurd. Thus, for instance, after the closure of the synagogue in the city of Stalino, an edition of the *Siddur Hashalom* prayer book, printed in Moscow in 1956, was found. Suspecting that the book might contain "unacceptable contents," the authorities handed it over to experts for special examination.[62]

Synagogues as Meeting Centers

Even during the years of the vigorous antireligion campaign, with its overtones of antisemitism and anti-Zionism, the synagogues served as meeting places for Jews. The gathering of thousands of Jews around the synagogues for Rosh Hashana and Yom Kippur, and partly also for Passover,[63] continued, in a way, a tradition that had formed over a decade in many USSR cities. This time, in contrast with the 1950s, gatherings in the synagogues and their environs were given some coverage in the Western media, but the West's focus on the main synagogue of Moscow did not reflect events across the country.

> The situation changes markedly [during] the holidays [reported the SRA representative in 1964] . . . on Rosh Hashana and particularly on Yom Kippur. . . . [T]he synagogue buildings fill from wall to wall and cannot hold all who wish to take part in the prayers. . . . Some hundreds and even thousands of the religious gather near the buildings of the synagogues and in this way they fulfill their religious needs.

On Yom Kippur of 1964, between 25,000 and 30,000 people gathered around the synagogue in Kiev, as did large numbers in Odessa, Dnepropetrovsk, Simferopol', Zhitomir, and other towns. Those who assembled there were

> Jews of various ages, wishing in some way to mark the holiday, at least by their presence near the synagogue. If, on a regular Sabbath, only the elderly are in the synagogue, on the High Holidays the majority are of early and middle age, employees in jobs that contribute to society. Present are laborers and white collar workers, people of various trades and professions. Young people and schoolchildren do not come to synagogue and are not present at the prayer gatherings.[64]

The large number of Jews present thus sought to express their ethnic identity and to symbolically remember their relatives murdered in the Holocaust. Arieh (Liova) Eliav, the first secretary of the Israeli embassy in Moscow, described the atmosphere of the Kiev synagogue on Yom Kippur of 1959 as follows:

With great difficulty I made my path into the house. . . . [T]housands of people, 10,000 or perhaps even more packed together in unbelievably. . . . I saw how they came there separately, one by one or in couples. . . . The people in the street . . . don't often speak with one another. . . . There are a lot of middle-aged people and also youths . . . the Jews standing outside and in the street weren't praying . . . Somehow the sound "*Izkor!*" [Remember!] passes through—the thousands inside [the synagogue], around it and along the street fall silent . . . you see how each one is mentally joining . . . with their dear ones who are no longer alive.[65]

Concurrent with these gatherings, in the late 1950s a new tradition began in certain cities of gathering around the synagogues on Simchat Torah. This gathering was different in composition and form from the gatherings of Yom Kippur, as reflected in the nature of the respective holidays. During the *hakafot* (rejoicing with the Torah scrolls) on the eve of Simchat Torah, an atmosphere of levity inspired youths to gather at the synagogue, and especially in the nearby streets. These young people's character had been molded during the post-Stalin thaw, and they gave expression to their Judaism in ways resembling those of their non-Jewish peers. Like the "flower children" in the West, the youths gathered in the plazas of Moscow and Leningrad, listened to songs that contained antiestablishment, antiregime nuance, danced, and sang to the strumming of guitars. Such an expression matched the youthful spirit. The Simchat Torah holiday struck the young people as most appropriate for a sort of Jewish "happening," and the best place for such an event was the synagogue. Tourists who visited the USSR in 1959 thus related how on Simchat Torah eve, the young people gathered around Moscow's main synagogue, dancing and singing Jewish and Israeli songs until the small hours of the night. The authorities were compelled to block off a few streets to allow for the revelry. The number of youths who gathered around the synagogues in those cities grew from year to year. In 1960 the foreign media estimated that more young people had gathered around Moscow's main synagogue than in the previous year; in 1962 that number was estimated at six thousand;[66] and at Leningrad's synagogue, about ten thousand gathered, twenty-five of whom were arrested briefly for obstructing traffic.[67] The gatherings around the synagogues on Simchat Torah reverberated in the Western media[68] perhaps because they expressed, more than those of the High Holidays, a new form of Soviet Jewish identity, one far more liberated than that of their repressed parents.

Though part of a broader antireligion effort, the campaign against Judaism was harsher most probably for the following reasons: (a) The Jewish religion and the synagogue were seen as focal points for Jewish nationalism, Zionism being among its most prominent expressions. (b) Within the Soviet establishment, even at the highest level, there were persons hateful toward Jews. (c) As the USSR opened itself to tourism, Jewish tourists came, some of whom were specially sent by Israeli and international bodies working on behalf of the Jews of the USSR. These tourists visited synagogues, as these were the main places where one could meet Jews, and such encounters were looked upon with hostility by the authorities. (d) Israeli embassy personnel in Moscow, especially members of Nativ (Israel-based group, discussed later) who now had greater freedom of movement, made efforts to visit the synagogues and distribute both religious and secular literature. (e) The persecution of the Jewish religion in the USSR attracted much attention in the Western media, and non-Jewish journalists, too, considered a visit to a synagogue to be a "good story"; now the embassies of various countries saw fit to report to their governments about this subject. As the Western interest in Jewish religious life in the USSR increased, so did the suspicions of the Soviet security services and the efforts to reduce as much as possible the number of synagogues defined by the Soviets as focal points of "political espionage."

The ouster of Nikita Khrushchev in 1964 as prime minister and first secretary of the Communist Party brought with it a certain relaxation in the intense campaign against religion in general and against the Jewish religion in particular.

Part Two

BETWEEN THE PRIVATE AND THE PUBLIC SPHERES

CHAPTER NINE

Rabbis and the Congregational Establishment

Soviet regulations on religious service providers (*sluzhiteli kul'ta*) were geared mainly toward the traditions of the Russian Orthodox Church, in which a priest was appointed by the senior religious authority and as such had considerable influence in the Church. In 1929 when the regime sought to restrict the role of religion in the state, it passed laws saying that religious service providers could not be appointed to boards of religious associations. When the regime wished to ease its strictures, one of the arrangements it made with the Orthodox Church was to permit priests to join these boards, in actuality to lead them. The status of the rabbi in a Jewish congregation was different: he was not appointed by any sort of religious authority but rather was hired by the heads of the congregation. He was thus dependent on the active figures in the congregation, and usually did not get involved in day-to-day synagogue operations but instead focused on issues of Jewish law. When Soviet policy toward religion became more lenient, rabbis too were allowed to be part of the congregation's management, and that, too, allowed rabbis to serve as heads of the board. There was no uniform policy on this matter: in some cases the authorities preferred that the rabbi serve also as congregation head, or *gabbai*, while in others they preferred that two leaders serve, a *gabbai* and a rabbi. Each arrangement had its advantages and disadvantages. A rabbi who filled both roles obviously had greater responsibilities in the congregation, but his involvement in administrative and financial affairs would occasionally spark resentments and accusations of impropriety from the congregation. Moreover, salaries of official rabbis were paid from the congregations' budget, so a rabbi who served also as congregation head largely determined his own salary. This ability almost certainly would have damaged the rabbi's spiritual standing. Yet even when the rabbi didn't serve as congregation head, he nevertheless was reserved a prominent place in it.

For the vast majority of rabbis who served in the hundreds of congregations in the Soviet Union in the first decades after WWII, almost no biographical information was available until the Soviet archives were opened, even though these rabbis played a substantial role in the lives of the Jewish population.[1]

As hinted in part one of this text, a great many rabbis in the Soviet Union never received *smicha* (rabbinic ordination) and many had never studied in a yeshiva; they simply had a certain familiarity with the religious laws and customs, knew the prayers, and sometimes also had experience in kosher slaughter and circumcision. Nevertheless, they filled a very important role in congregational life and we shall consider them as rabbis, even if in other circumstances their claim to the title would have been dubious. Up until the Revolution, two sorts of rabbis operated in the Russian Empire: official rabbis (*kazennyi ravin*)[2] and "spiritual rabbis" (*dukhovnyi ravin*). The former depended on approval by the authorities, while the latter gained their status solely through the Jewish public. On the surface, this situation appears to have continued during the Soviet period. Yet while the tsarist regime was not antireligion and did not persecute religious groups as such, the Soviet regime considered any activity of rabbis not approved by them to be illegal. Moreover, the rabbis authorized by the Soviet regime were subject to immeasurably greater oversight and control than anything the "official rabbis" had been subject to prior to the Revolution. Thus, as early as October 1945, the chairman of the SRA wrote to all his subordinates as follows:

> Candidates for the position of religious service provider who are dangerous elements or have questionable politics are to be rejected immediately and the communities advised not to even suggest them.[3]

Likewise, after being appointed the rabbis depended on the authorities if they wanted to continue serving the public. Consequently, in many respects rabbis in the Soviet Union may be divided into two categories: "official rabbis"—that is, those who served in this status in their congregations—and "unofficial rabbis," spiritual guides who were perceived by their religious communities as authority figures even if they had no formal status whatsoever.

By Soviet rules and regulations, registration of a religious association (a congregation) was conditioned on the presence of a religious service provider recognized by the regime; indeed some SRA officials threatened to dissolve congregations that lacked such a figure. Thus, for example, the district SRA representative overseeing the congregation of Rostov-on-Don informed members that if they did not present the needed documentation for registration of a rabbi, the congregation would be disbanded.[4] Yet public prayers—"sacramental rites," in Soviet terminology—could not be conducted without an officiating figure. So the SRA representatives of various locales turned to Moscow for guidance on how to handle religious associations lacking religious service providers, and whose "sacramental rites" were led in turns by individuals from the religious association. The SRA chairman, in February 1945, responded that such an association should not be registered until it had a religious figurehead approved by the authorities. Such authorization could typically be given by the SRA after consultations with the security services and the amassing of considerable information on the candidate's past and character. The fact that the congregational rabbi was in effect an appointee of the authorities, even if formally he was "elected," caused consternation among quite a few congregations seeking legal recognition. For applications of this type, the SRA chairman, in October 1945, wrote:

> [People from congregations] vigorously present the stance that there is no obligation that each congregation have a registered rabbi. [They claim] that this demand [for a rabbi in each congregation] derives from the SRA being unfamiliar with the Jewish religion. Yet a closer examination of these claims always reveals that the true reason is the desire to grant the congregation a special national-social aspect and not so much a religious one. Against trends of this kind, which are all too common, a struggle must be waged and the decisive demand made that in each congregation there be a rabbi.[5]

The SRA chairman also noted in his letter that congregations are to be notified that they must deliver the names and personal details of the people serving as religious service providers within three months; failure to do so would cause the religious association to be dissolved.

As has been implied, tensions often arose between the rabbi, whose appointment involved the authorities, and the congregation activists. While the former wanted, or was compelled, to restrict the functioning of the congregation to the realm of ritual alone, as defined by the Soviet authorities, many congregation activists especially in the first years after the war sought to cast the congregation as the local center of Jewish life and not solely as the site of religious ritual.

By the Soviet regulations on religious affairs laid down after the war, any appointment of a religious service provider had to be done through consultations with the central religious body in the USSR of the appropriate religion to establish the candidate's suitability on religious grounds. Likewise, for rabbinical appointments the SRA chairman instructed that one must "demand . . .

that the rabbi be in possession of the traditionally acceptable certifications to officiate."[6] Such a statement raises the question of who is authorized to certify the religious suitability of a rabbinical candidate: at times the authorities were content to allow a rabbi from a different congregation to approve the figure. Yet since religious suitability did not especially interest the authorities, they also approved for the rabbinate persons who had no religious educational certification whatsoever. A representative of the SRA thus wrote to a subordinate in Nikolaev that a "rabbi is elected by the assembly of the religious congregation and the protocol of the assembly of the congregation is a sufficient certificate for the registration of a rabbi and there is no need for additional documentation."[7] Yet even with this method of certifying rabbis, too few people were found who were both acceptable to the authorities and embraced by the congregation. Consequently, the SRA representative in Ukraine was compelled, in January 1946, to announce to his subordinates in the republic that "a congregation can select a rabbi from among its people . . . and the absence of a rabbi cannot serve as a reason for denying the registration of a congregation."[8] The conflicting instructions on this issue permitted the local authorities to sometimes ignore the absence of an official rabbi as the pretext for disallowing registration of a congregation and to allow a congregation to be registered anyway, or to permit listing the cantor to fill the role as the obligatory "religious service provider."

Before the Revolution, every synagogue tended to have a rabbi of its own, yet in parallel each *town* had its own rabbi, called the *av beis din* ("head of the court"), whose legal verdicts may not have been binding on all the rabbis in that town, but who was perceived by broad circles of area Jews as carrying authoritative weight. In the Soviet period, conversely, each congregation (synagogue) was considered to be a separate religious association, and the status of the rabbi of each was equal to that of every other rabbi in town: the authorities vigorously opposed granting any sort of preferential status to a single rabbi over others in the same settlement or forming an association of rabbis across multiple synagogues. Small wonder, then, that the application of congregation heads in Uzbekistan to permit the appointment of a rabbinical head in a certain town was rejected. (In 1946 the heads of several congregations in Uzbekistan requested that every town with multiple synagogues have a single appointed "town rabbi" so that "synagogues of the different congregations would, on religious matters, behave in accordance with the instructions of the [town's] chief rabbi.")[9] The elimination of the rabbinate in the Chernovtsy district may be viewed in the same context.

Around the time of the liberation of Chernovtsy from German occupation

(February–March 1944), a town and district rabbinate was formed, consisting of eleven members. For more than a year, this rabbinate represented the synagogues in the district and applied to the authorities on issues of congregational registrations. This rabbinate, however, was weakened considerably when some of its members moved to Romania in mid-1945, and it was formally disbanded in autumn 1945, yet even then the links between the district's synagogues and its rabbis did not break. In place of the rabbinate, Rabbi Mordechai Shiber was elected as trustee of the district's synagogues, and almost certainly maintained close contact with most of its rabbis. But his office was shut down in early 1946.[10]

Any formal association of rabbis from different congregations in the same town, not to mention an association that linked multiple communities, was prohibited by the Soviet regulations on religious affairs: the authority of each rabbi was to be limited to the synagogue in which he served.

Over the course of twenty years (1944–1964), at least 137 rabbis officiated throughout the republic of Ukraine. Some served for relatively long periods while others were removed from their posts after a short while. The majority served in small-town synagogues, and information on their experience is scant. We will thus have to content ourselves with a few facts about rabbis who served in the central cities. One such figure who officiated in Kiev for about a decade (1945–1954) was Rabbi Yitzchak Shekhtman (b. 1877). He had both *smicha* and a high school education. The authorities described him as a man "who belongs to groups of religious activists, who understand the necessities of life and the need to introduce this or that reform in Jewish ritual. Shekhtman's progressive views permit making use of him to carry out certain reforms in the ritual."[11] Shekhtman's approach was, not surprisingly, less popular with many synagogue attendees, who complained to the authorities "that the chairman of the congregation . . . and the rabbi . . . have forgotten the needs of the Jewish population. They do not extend material aid to the needy and have forgotten the wounded Jewish veterans . . . they limit the activity of the synagogue to the conduct of rites and prayers."[12] Shekhtman's behavior may have pleased the authorities, but opposition to his leadership grew at the start of the thaw and eventually led to his dismissal. Substantial turnover then marked the tenures of the rabbis who followed him in Kiev.[13]

Rabbi Yosef Diment (b. 1874) officiated in Odessa, having received his *smicha* in one of the yeshivas of Vilna, and between 1896 and 1931 served as a rabbi in the towns of Ukraine. In 1931 he moved to Odessa, where he earned his living as an accountant and where he was rabbi of the city's congregation on the eve of the Nazi occupation, at which point he fled to the interior. He returned to Odessa following the liberation and again was appointed as rabbi of the synagogue. Rabbi Diment also served as the synagogue's *gabbai,* a fact that earned him the resentment of quite a few worshipers. In 1949 the authorities accused him of sending fundraisers to Jewish homes to solicit donations for the synagogue, as well as of inaccurately reporting his income. Arrest followed for the rabbi in early 1953, on the charge that between 1948 and 1952 he had recited "Next year in Jerusalem" in the synagogue, a slogan considered to be Zionist. The indictment stated, among other things, that the rabbi "is systematically involved in the dissemination of anti-Soviet ideas of the Jewish national bourgeoisie"; in May 1953 Diment was sentenced to ten years in prison. An appeal reduced his sentence to two years and later the term was shortened further; by July 1953 he had returned to serve as the rabbi and head of the Odessa congregation. Yet the authorities remained displeased with the rabbi's behavior, and the district SRA representative suggested that he resign from the post of congregation head and serve only as rabbi. In September 1958 Rabbi Diment was dismissed as the head of the congregation in Odessa; he passed away four years later and the congregation was left without a rabbi.[14]

In the city of L'vov in the first postliberation years, turnover among rabbis was high, as many of them were immigrating to Poland. Immigration also occurred from within the USSR to this city; thus Iankel Gurari (b. 1892) arrived at L'vov and was appointed rabbi of its synagogue. Gurari had received *smicha* in 1925 in the illegal yeshiva of the Habad movement in Kremenchug. From 1925 to 1928, he ran the yeshiva in Romny, for which he was sentenced to a five-year prison term. Presumably as a consequence of his imprisonment, Gurari kept away from public activity and returned to it only following WWII. When the head of the L'vov congregation was arrested in 1947, Gurari moved to Romny, where he also served as the rabbi; he returned to L'vov in the late 1940s and for several years again was the rabbi there.[15]

During the period with which the present study deals, at least twenty-five registered rabbis officiated in Russia (RSFSR). A few were well known and had a certain influence beyond their communities, such as the rabbis of Moscow's main synagogue: Rabbi Shlifer and his successor, Rabbi Leib Levin. Rabbi Shlifer (b. 1889) served in this capacity from 1944 until his death in January 1957. For Rabbi Levin's (1894–1971) part, he was trained at the Knesset Bet Yehuda yeshiva in Kovno, where he received his *smicha.* From 1923 to 1944, he was active in religious activity in Georgia and Uzbekistan, and from 1945 to 1953 he served as rabbi of the synagogue in Dnepropetrovsk. He came to Moscow at the invitation of Rabbi Shlifer.[16]

The second synagogue in the capital of the Soviet Union was located in

Marina Roshcha, at which Rabbi Natan Olevskii officiated. Born in the Volynia *guberniia* in 1871, he was trained in the yeshivas of Vilna and from 1906 on served as a rabbi in various towns in Siberia and Central Asia. He was the rabbi of Marina Roshcha from 1945 until his death in 1967.[17]

A famed prodigy in Torah and master of Jewish law, the rabbi of the synagogue in Malakhovka (Moscow district), Rabbi Isaac Krasil'shchikov (1888–1965), received his *smicha* at the famous Mir yeshiva. Until 1917, he served as a rabbi in various towns of Ukraine and in the late 1920s moved to Moscow, where he earned a living as an accountant. During the war he resided in the town of Krasnoiarsk and with the war's end he returned to Moscow. After leaving rabbinical service (evidently in 1948), he devoted his energies to a large work, a commentary on the Jerusalem Talmud, which he completed just before his death. At that time he wrote to one of his friends that "I have decided to submit for publication [my composition] both here in our state and in another country, with the approval of the government." Needless to say, the work was not published in the Soviet Union. Only in 1980 was it published in Israel.[18]

Between 1945 and 1954, the synagogue in Leningrad, the city with the second-largest Jewish population in Russia, was served by rabbis Mordechai Belous (b. 1877?) and Meizeson. Severe rifts in the congregation in 1954 led to the appointment as rabbi and congregation head of Rabbi Haim Lubanov (1888–1973), a recent internment camp inmate who was born in Belorussia and after the First World War served as rabbi of the town of Lepel'. In the 1930s he moved to Leningrad, where he worked as a guard in the synagogue. During the war he managed to flee the besieged city with his family, arriving at a *kolkhoz* (collective farm) in the country's interior. So as to keep Shabbat, Lubanov worked as a night guard at a granary. But when a fire broke out at the granary, the rabbi was accused of being responsible and sentenced to two years in prison. After the liberation he returned to Leningrad, only to learn that his only son had died defending the city. In 1951 Rabbi Lubanov was imprisoned once again; he was released after Stalin's death and returned to serve as rabbi of the Leningrad community. He was described as a person "who does not like wealth, deals with the needs of the public and loves human beings." Rabbi Lubanov was a rabbinical scholar with full mastery of the halakhic sources, as became apparent in his sermons on the two days of Rosh Hashana of 1958, which he devoted to discussing the significance of blowing the shofar and to the synagogue's role as the primary mainstay of the survival of the Jewish people.[19]

The congregations of the mountain Jews of the north Caucasus usually were served by rabbis from the local community. The synagogue at Buinaksk was led by the *hacham* (authoritative rabbi, in Sephardi communities) Rabbi

Moisei Agarunov (b. 1890). Rabbi Agarunov was fluent in Hebrew and fully conversant in Russian; he addressed his congregation in the Judeo-Tat language. The rabbi of the town of Nal'chik was the *hacham* Shamuil Amirov (b. 1880). In 1919 Rabbi Amirov organized a group of Zionists from his community who tried unsuccessfully to immigrate to the Land of Israel. Owing to his close familiarity with the religious customs of his community, he was chosen to be rabbi of the synagogue after the war.[20]

From 1941 to 1964, Belorussia had at least four official rabbis. The rabbi of the Minsk congregation, from its formation after the war until 1956, was Yaakov Berger (1892–1959). Born in Minsk, Rabbi Berger received *smicha* in 1914 from a yeshiva in Kovno. He was the rabbi of a synagogue in Minsk from 1915 to 1918, and from 1918 to 1925 he served in Kiev. From 1925 to 1927, in the same city, he worked as a laborer in a chemical plant and from 1928 to 1941 as a slaughterer of fowl. He fled when the Germans invaded and reached the town of Kurgan-Tiube in Central Asia; toward the end of the war he returned to Minsk, where he served as rabbi and congregation head. In the early 1950s, Rabbi Berger became involved in frictions with the organizers of area minyans. The conflict widened to encompass the revenues from kosher slaughter, with the daughter of one slaughterer describing Rabbi Berger as "an informer and favorite of the Gorsovet [municipality]." The dispute in the congregation eventually did lead to Rabbi Berger's dismissal in 1956.[21] For at least the three years after the rabbi's dismissal, the congregation persisted without a registered rabbi. In 1958 the head of the congregation sought approval from the authorities to hire Aizik Perzin, who previously had served in the rabbinate in Penza and had moved to Minsk with the intent of being appointed rabbi there. Before making the appointment, the SRA officials in Belorussia sought information on Perzin from their colleagues in Penza, advising that the security services also be consulted. The verdict from Penza was that no evidence posed an obstacle to his appointment and that the main reason for his relocation to Minsk had been to earn a higher salary.[22] This narrative clearly demonstrates that no authorization of a rabbi took place without the agreement of the security services.

In the early fifties, more than half (52 percent) of those registered rabbis in the three Slavic republics (Ukraine, Russia, Belorussia) whose birthdays were available were over seventy years old, and 17 percent were over eighty.

The age range of the rabbis in the Central Asian republics and the Trans-Caucasus was slightly more favorable, because the fierce battle against religion had begun there later, and Jewish religious instruction of some sort was still taking place as late as the 1930s. In the early 1950s, the republics of Uzbekistan,

Kazakhstan, and Tajikistan were served mainly by rabbis (*hachamim*) from the Bukharan community; in the two republics of the Trans-Caucuses (Azerbaizhan and Georgia), the rabbis were mainly Jews from Georgia and among the mountain Jews. At the time, at least twenty-three rabbis were registered in Georgia and these had a great influence on the entire Jewish population.[23] The town of Kutaisi was considered an important religious center in Georgia thanks to the Davarashvili brothers, who served as official rabbis. Moshe Davarashvili (b. 1898), known as "little Moshe," studied in the yeshivas of Jerusalem and around 1917 returned to Russia; he served as a rabbi between the wars and continued in this task after the Second World War. He immigrated to Israel in the early 1970s and passed away in 1980. His brother Yaakov, called "*hacham Yaakov*," was born in 1902 and after WWI appears to have studied for a time at the Chabad yeshiva in Rostov-on-Don. In the early 1970s, he too immigrated to Israel, where he passed away in 1985.[24] The republic's capital, Tbilisi, had two synagogues, one for the Ashkenazi Jews and one for the Georgian Jews. The rabbi in the former synagogue was Chaim Kupchan (b. 1879), who was accepted also by the Georgian Jews. He was arrested in the early 1950s and passed away in 1963. The Georgian Jews' congregation had as its rabbi the *hacham* Emmanuel Davidashvili. He was arrested during Stalin's last years, but resumed his post after his release.[25]

Of the thirty-five official rabbis of Central Asia and the Trans-Caucuses on whom ages are available, 40 percent appear to have been over seventy (including a few about eighty); yet other rabbis were in their forties and fifties.

The three Baltic republics and Moldavia, which were annexed to the Soviet Union during WWII, had at least twenty-two rabbis officiating during the period in question. One of the well-known rabbis was Mordechai Varkulis (or Varkul) of Kovno, who studied at the Slobodka yeshiva, where he received his *smicha*. With the outbreak of war he fled to the interior of the USSR, was drafted into the Red Army, and served in the Lithuanian division, winning several medals. The rabbi's military service alongside members of the regime aided him later in arranging various matters on behalf of the congregation. Rabbi Varkulis filled his post until immigrating to Israel in the early 1960s.[26]

In the Moldavian republic, formerly part of Romania, several rabbis had held public positions as clerics before the war. The most prominent of these was Rabbi Yosef Epel'boim (1893–1962). In the mid-1940s, Rabbi Epel'boim officiated as rabbi of one of the synagogues in Kishinev. In the 1920s he had been active in the Agudat Israel Party and did much to strengthen the "youths of Agudat Israel" movement. He is considered one of the founders of the Beis Yaakov school for orthodox girls and in 1938 published his book *Pninei Dat*

(Gems of Religion), a sort of abbreviated, systematized *Shulkhan Aruch* for students. Rabbi Epel'boim was also the editor of the Haredi Yiddish monthly *Der shtub-zhurnal*. The Soviet authorities, however, did not think fondly of the highly active Epel'boim, and opined that "he considers himself one of the representatives of the Jewish people, who feels the pains of the nation." These allegations sufficed to have Epel'boim booted from the rabbinate in 1949; the authorities used a letter against him sent to the SRA in Moscow by several worshipers at the synagogue. After his dismissal he did not abandon his religious activities and continued to conduct weddings, oversee divorces, and the like.[27]

Rabbis were considered to be independent business people (*edinolichniki*), and they had to pay income tax both from their salaries and from any revenue from other services performed such as marriages, funeral services, memorials, and so forth. According to a regulation of the Supreme Soviet of the USSR of April 30, 1943, regarding "income tax from the population," rabbis had to pay taxes under Section 19 or, at a lower rate, under Section 5. In quite a few cases the finance officials in various towns used Section 5 while the SRA tried to convince them that Section 19 should apply to the rabbis; when the SRA succeeded in this endeavor, the rabbis would be charged retroactively for the unpaid taxes. Thus, in 1948 Rabbi Berger of Minsk had to pay more than ten thousand rubles to make up for the supposedly mistaken tax collections from previous years.[28] Taxes therefore represented a tool with which the authorities could apply pressure against the rabbis, although this tool was not the most important available.

The official rabbis were charged with ensuring that the synagogue was used for ritual observance only, as defined by the Soviet authorities. This role often caused tensions between the rabbis and some worshipers. To preserve the legal existence of the congregations, the rabbis had to remain in constant contact with the regime's authorities and report to them on the goings-on in the synagogue; to certain circles of Jews in the USSR, this demand made the rabbis suspect. Sometimes rabbis took steps that seem perplexing in retrospect, but we must understand them in their context and climate. A case in point is the behavior of Rabbi Shlifer at the time of the Doctors' Plot.

Rabbi Shlifer apparently knew that he was being observed by the security services, so he sought to preserve himself and the continued existence of the Moscow synagogue. It is in this context that we should view his meeting with the chairman of the SRA on February 20, 1953. The protocol of that meeting, as preserved in the archives, describes the rabbi as having taken the initiative on his own to discuss the supply of matzah for Passover, during which he showed Polianskii [chairman of the SRA] an anonymous letter stating that after the discovery of the hive of terrorists and spies [the "murderous doctors"], it would be desirable that he, Shlifer, would organize a gathering to protest these vile deeds. He asked comrade Polianskii if he should do this. Shlifer in addition asked if he should not in his sermon denounce the awful explosion in the Soviet embassy in Israel and condemn that vile act. Comrade Polianskii responded to Shlifer that his suggestions were good and wise and should be thought about.... We will discuss this [he said] and consult and perhaps will invite you in the very near future for a practical examination.[29]

The next day Rabbi Shlifer was invited to return and at this meeting related that several persons from his congregation had proposed that the members of the Israeli embassy leaving Moscow, following the severing of diplomatic ties, should be stoned with rotten eggs. This suggestion did not elicit a response from the SRA chairman, most likely due to the Soviet disinclination to encourage mass gatherings of Jews. As to the sermon, the host requested that the rabbi clarify the manner and form in which he planned to denounce the doctors. The rabbi promised to prepare the sermon in writing and to present it within a few days. On February 25, Rabbi Shlifer presented the draft of the proposed sermon, with which his host was not satisfied; the rabbi was asked to bring an amended draft, which he indeed presented on February 26. This seems to have been the draft that was read on the synagogue podium. Then when Stalin died, and the sword of exile and synagogue closure hung over the heads of all Jews, Rabbi Shlifer appeared in the offices of the SRA expressing his grief and sorrow over Stalin's death. He said that psalms would be recited for a full week at Moscow's main synagogue to honor the soul of the "Genius of Humanity," and even sought permission to lay a wreath at the funeral in the name of Moscow's Jewish community.[30]

We shall never know the thoughts, let alone feelings, of the 223 official rabbis who served during the period from 1941 to 1946.[31] The most we can do is characterize the conditions under which they worked. These people lived and functioned under the terrible vise of Soviet religious persecution. The authorities went so far as to try, at various periods, to use sons and daughters to influence their parents to desist from rabbinical work; they also made use of the tax grinder to induce economic harm.

The situation of the official rabbis was extremely complex and at times too difficult to endure. In order to keep alive any permitted religious activity, they had to please the authorities and to meet the regime's demands with respect to restriction on religious activity. During the thaw period, the rabbis also had to mediate between the conflicting aims of the tourists and visitors from abroad, who sought to meet Soviet Jews directly, and the unequivocal demand of the authorities to prevent such contact. The Israeli representatives likewise had reservations about the majority of these official rabbis, mainly on account of the latter's publications supporting Soviet foreign policy and condemning Israel.[32] This picture helps show why so few of the official rabbis, in contrast with the first activists of the Jewish national movement in the Soviet Union (the neo-Zionists), active in the late 1960s and early 1970s, earned the support and enthusiasm of world public opinion. For what is was worth, a handful of these leaders' names appeared in the media outside the USSR only in the context of the antireligion campaign of the late 1950s and early 1960s. Yet these rabbis, each in his way, were doing the best they knew how—they believed that theirs was the only way to sustain the sole Jewish institution allowed to function legitimately in the Soviet Union. Their every interest was to protect the institution of the synagogue. We may thus view these rabbis as tragic figures who contributed in a substantial way by aiding the survival of the last legal remnant of public Jewish life in the USSR. The time has come for a renewed estimation of their efforts, untainted by either false idealization or undue disparagement.

The Unofficial Rabbis

Given the complex and difficult situation, one should not be surprised that so few religious figures were willing or able to fill the role of the official rabbi. Less dependent on the regime were the unofficial rabbis, although the authorities, on the whole, knew many details about them and treated them as the heads of their communities. Some of the unofficial rabbis had broad knowledge of the Jewish tradition and at certain intervals served also as official rabbis, while others were simple folk who knew a little about the customs or just enough to lead prayers.

Among the unofficial rabbis of the more experienced sort was Leizer Fridland of Bobruisk. Born in 1896, he studied at the town's heder and later at its yeshiva, where he received his *smicha* in 1912. During WWI and subsequent years, he officiated in one of the Bobruisk synagogues, and with the renewal of religious life after WWII served as rabbi of Bobruisk's unregistered congregation. After that congregation was disbanded, he continued to be thought of as a spiritual authority both by the religious community and by the authorities, who considered him the leader of many minyans.[33] A comparable spiritual leader of minyans in the town of Gomel' was Shmuel-Gershon Sorkin. Born in

1898 in the town of Novo-Belista, he received his religious education in heder and apparently studied for a while in a yeshiva. With the intensification of the antireligion persecutions of the 1930s, he worked in a slaughterhouse, where he performed kosher slaughter. After wwii he returned to his native town, but in the absence of Jewish life there moved to Gomel', where he was accepted as a figure of religious standing. The authorities considered him the moving force behind the minyans, and in mid-1955 Sorkin was summoned to report on the minyans being held in town and their organizers. Despite the risks to his own well-being, he refused to give any information. Unsurprisingly, Sorkin later became a target for attack by the Soviet media during the intensification of antireligion policy in the late 1950s. Articles appeared in the local newspapers accusing him of engaging in kosher slaughter for pecuniary gain and even of forcing parents to circumcise their children.[34]

The city of Chernovtsy had Hersh Spivak as the rabbi of its registered congregation, but the city's spiritual authority until his immigration to Israel in 1970 was Rabbi Pinhas Litvak, who earned his living as a bookbinder. A similar status was held in Kutaisi by Rabbi Khaim Eliashvili, a native of Jerusalem (b. 1888), where he studied in several yeshivas before coming to Georgia in 1909. Up until 1921, he worked in religious instruction in various towns of Georgia; he was arrested in 1933 while trying to escape from the USSR and a few years later was arrested again, to be released only in 1944. Up until Eliashvili's death in 1965, many of Kutaisi's Jews considered him the town's "chief rabbi" even though he filled no official role.[35]

The unofficial rabbis had no income from their rabbinical work except from whatever their followers gave them; their efforts on behalf of the public were driven by a profound sense of religious obligation and a fierce desire to aid the Jewish community wherever its members lived. These individuals were also, on the whole, the first to feel directly any changes in Soviet policy toward the Jewish religion. In 1947, for example, when the Soviet authorities sought to curtail the direct ties between Jews in the USSR and Jews in the United States, the authorities summoned Iuda Agranov, then an unofficial rabbi in the town of Zhlobin (Gomel' district), and told him that not only was he an illegal rabbi but that he was also corresponding with Jews in the United States and that he had even received a Jewish calendar in the mail. Following this warning, the rabbi promised to stop his public activity and even offered to hand in the calendar to the authorities, after he had copied its contents. While the available documentation does not tell what later became of this man, it is fair to assume that his influence on the town's Jews persisted in subsequent years.[36]

Among the unofficial rabbis, Rabbi Mordechai Fridman (b. 1882) may also be counted. He studied at the Lubavitch yeshiva and with it relocated during WWI to Rostov-on-Don, where in 1935 he was arrested for religious activity. After the war he settled in Pinsk, where in 1950–1951 he was the rabbi of a permanent minyan and also worked as a kosher slaughterer. He was ordered to cease his rabbinic activity and to this responded proudly, "I shall not abandon my guard post." In December 1955, after the thaw, Rabbi Fridman approached the SRA representative in the district demanding that the congregation be registered formally, since it had effectively been operating on a regular basis since 1945.[37]

The unregistered rabbis were the first figures against whom the authorities took repressive measures each time the battle on religion intensified. Many were summoned and warned that continuation of their activity would result in severe punishments. Some SRA representatives demanded that officials not settle for warnings but take concrete measures. For instance, in March 1959 the SRA official in the Minsk district wrote:

> [I]t is desirable that the workers of the prosecution and other agencies of the regime . . . decisively call to order the unregistered religious service providers and the itinerant preachers, who openly violate Soviet law. . . . If two or three of them were punished with a year of remedial labor as per criminal law, that would be more effective [than the assorted warnings].[38]

The information on the unofficial rabbis is even more scant than on the official ones, and the distinction between an unofficial rabbi and an observant Jew who was not considered a leader by the public is not entirely clear. More clear is that tension existed between the official and unofficial rabbis, at times reaching outright hostility—even though both types of rabbis were struggling to keep alive the embers of Judaism that happened to give warmth, directly or indirectly, to quite a few nonreligious Jews.

CHAPTER TEN

Cantors for Hire

In most synagogues, an individual from the congregation or the rabbi led prayer services on weekdays and Sabbaths; only a few of the large congregations employed a cantor year-round. Certain synagogues had choirs, which usually performed only on holidays. Thus, for example, the authorities learned in 1958 that the choir members of the Kiev synagogue were receiving a monthly wage of 250 rubles, sparking worry as to whether these were employees of the congregation or ordinary worshipers. Permanent cantors who drew a wage were considered "ritual service providers" and were required to be registered, as were the rabbis.[1] Cantors brought in only for the holidays, and who made a living most of the year by other means, were not.

Leib Spector worked as a permanent cantor in the Vinnitsa synagogue until the congregation's dispersal in 1949. The closure of the synagogue forced Spector to leave town for Simferopol', where he worked as a cantor and *shochet* (ritual slaughterer). During the thaw he returned to the Vinnitsa district, settling in the town of Gaisin, where he served as a cantor in one of the minyans and also continued to work as a *shochet*. Given his commitments, we can understand his rejection of the offer to lead High Holiday services in 1958 as a cantor for the Bershad' synagogue.[2]

An especially popular cantor was Paltiel Grinberg (b. 1918), who had worked as a musician in Chernovtsy's doctors' club and until mid-1948 was also a regular cantor in the city's synagogue on Barbius Street. In 1948 he left that synagogue and became the cantor of the Wilson Street synagogue: a short while later, however, the administration replaced Grinberg with Mendel Malkin as cantor, sparking a dispute within the congregation. In response, Grinberg's supporters threatened—according to complainants' testimony—to use physical force against the congregation's administration. The SRA representative supported the hire of Malkin and stated that "[Malkin] is registered . . . and he has permission to conduct religious services . . . while Grinberg isn't registered and is nothing but a fraud." Despite not being registered, Grinberg continued to work as a cantor and occasionally filled this function at the Odessa synagogue, too, as well as later in Zhitomir, where he was the synagogue's cantor from 1954 to 1957. In the late 1950s, Grinberg again found himself at the center of a dispute in which one faction, led by Rabbi Yosef Diment, wanted to continue employing Grinberg while another, led by congregation head S. P. Orach, sought to have him replaced by C. Y. Kleiner, then the permanent cantor of the Kiev synagogue. Rumors of Kleiner's pending departure from Kiev's synagogue seem to have inspired opposition there, and information was passed to the district SRA representative stating that Kleiner was set to receive large sums of money in Odessa as well as revealing that he plied his services in minyans. Using this information, the Kiev district SRA representative turned to his Odessa counterpart and sought to block Kleiner's employment application there. However, the security services in Odessa had an interest in advancing Orach, so they made sure Kleiner was given a residency permit (*propiska*) in Odessa and signed to a year's contract at 20,000 rubles. The tension between the two congregations, Kiev and Odessa, played into the authorities' desires to reduce religious activity as much as possible and to select people in the congregations who could be easily manipulated. Once Kleiner left Kiev, the congregation considered hiring Grinberg as its permanent cantor, and he was invited to lead the services for Passover 1959. But the cantor and the Kiev congregation didn't reach an agreement, and Grinberg ended up signing on with the Leningrad congregation for an annual sum of 65,000 rubles as well as 25,000 rubles for travel expenses.[3] In 1957, Yaakov Yankelevich (b. 1894) moved to Tashkent to serve as the synagogue's cantor for an annual salary of 18,000 rubles.[4]

Because permanent cantors were considered ritual service providers, as the antireligion struggle intensified the authorities tried to pressure them to abandon their occupation. One approach used by the regime, similar to that used against the rabbis, was the tax grinder. Thus, for example, finance officials in Kiev filed suit against the city synagogue's cantors, S. S. Glazman and C. Y. Kleiner, charging that in 1960–1962 they had supplemented their congregational salary with earnings from minyans, which were considered illegal gatherings. The SRA representative notified the cantors that these transgressions meant they would be fired from their congregation and would be required to pay a sum of 37,000 rubles on their earnings. Likewise, in Dnepropetrovsk in 1962, a Section 19 tax was levied against the cantor and the ritual service providers—not only for their income from congregational work but also retroactively for their income from other sources.[5] As these additional income sources were not clear, the authorities determined the back-tax amounts arbitrarily, as an overall means of discouraging the employment of cantors.

The selection of cantors has caused intrigue in congregations worldwide, with disputes tending to be resolved within the congregation. In the USSR, by contrast, the authorities played a major role in cantorial appointments—that is, in those few congregations that could afford to employ permanent cantors. The situation was otherwise with the holiday cantors.

It was common practice in Eastern Europe for congregations to enlist a cantor for the High Holidays, and sometimes also for Sukkot and Passover; this practice continued during the Soviet period. As described elsewhere in this text, many Jews gathered in and around the synagogues on holidays, and since the cantors were seen to attract crowds, the authorities tried to create obstacles to their participation, particularly when the antireligion campaign expanded. For many attendees' part, a certain nostalgia for the shtetl, awakened by the Holocaust, may have brought them to the synagogues on holidays to hear the melodies that represented to them their fathers' and grandfathers' past homes and way of life.

Even in the USSR, the usual practice for the holidays was to invite a cantor from a different town, and this sort of invitation required the consent of the SRA representative, who almost certainly would consult the security services on the subject.[6] It follows that the invitation of a cantor depended considerably on relations between the congregation and the local authorities as well as on the general attitude of the regime toward religion at the time. It is unsurprising, therefore, that when the struggle against religion eased to some extent between 1955 and 1958, the head of the SRA wrote that "there is no basis to prohibit the invitation of cantors from other towns for prayers on the special [Jewish] holidays (Passover and autumn holidays)." But the authorities also stressed that cantors must not deviate from the standard prayer service and that the appearance must not turn into a cantorial concert. Rabbi Shlomo Shlifer elicited such a response from the deputy SRA head when requesting permission for the singer Mikhail Alexandrovich to be invited to lead services in the main synagogue of Moscow on Hanukkah 1946. This opinion was seconded definitively by the Ukraine SRA representative, who wrote that "the practice of the synagogues to hold religious concerts (with or without payment), as a way of collecting the means to maintain the synagogue, charity and such things must be absolutely stopped." Yet the practice did not disappear at least until the late 1940s. Thus, for example, in May 1947 a cantorial concert was held in the Zhitomir synagogue, "which included songs dedicated to the memory of the victims of Fascism[,]" and the cantor, Mechenovich, who performed in early June, brought "many to the brink of hysteria."[7]

As the antireligion policies grew harsher, the authorities tried, not always with full success, to block the invitation of cantors from other towns. In 1949, not only was the congregation of Kherson forbidden to bring in a cantor for the High Holidays, but the SRA representative warned the congregation against even raising the subject. In spite of the admonition, in 1950 the congregation brought in a cantor from Irkutsk without permission from the authorities. The applications of six other congregations (Odessa, Novosibirsk, Kishinev, Bel'tsy, Tiraspol', and Bendery) to allow the cantors from other towns to be brought in for the High Holidays of 1950 were rejected out of hand on the grounds that the invitees had no association with the requesting congregations. Similar requests for invitations to cantors for the Passover holiday of 1952 were also rejected. The Odessa congregation nevertheless applied for authorization to invite cantor Yaakov Yankelevich from Tashkent to lead the High Holiday services and, when this request was denied, applied to invite Yaakov Munis of Leningrad. (Munis, born 1889, was a member of a shoemakers' cooperative.) This request too was rejected on the absurd grounds that Munis was not a resident of Odessa.[8]

During the thaw as well, quite a few SRA representatives continued to frown on invitations to outside cantors for the holidays, despite instructions from the SRA chairman not to forbid the practice. But in contrast to the previous period, such requests received more affirmative responses. Also of significance, congregations now often dared to bring in cantors without explicit permission. Thus, for example, the L'vov congregation hired the cantor Baruch Leib Shulman for the High Holidays of 1958 and paid him 6,000 rubles. Also, singers from the secular world began to serve as holiday cantors, although the official response to this phenomenon was sufficiently negative. Thus, for example, the Dnepropetrovsk congregation invited an opera singer from Khar'kov, Shmuel Budilov, for the High Holidays of 1956. After the holidays, congregation head Rozin was summoned to the office of the SRA representative and told that if such an occurrence happened again, Rozin would be forced to resign. The Zhitomir district SRA representative also reacted harshly to the invitation of a cantor for the High Holidays of 1958 without his permission, even though he had approved the same invitation the year before. For the High Holidays, the Zhitomir congregation wanted to employ a cantor from Chernovtsy (Kuperman) who was also an opera singer and in previous years had gained high popularity when leading services in the Berdichev synagogue. As was customary in Jewish communities, the cantor was invited to Zhitomir to perform in the synagogue so that the congregation could assess his performance, following which they signed him to a contract. But when these activities became known to the SRA representative, he immediately notified the police in the cantor's town of residence that the cantor was residing in Zhitomir without a residency permit (*propiska*) and demanded that he be fined for this infraction. The cantor, as a result, had no choice but to break his contract. Yet the congregation didn't give up on finding a cantor for the High Holidays and now sought permission from the SRA representative to bring in another cantor from Chernovtsy, Goldman (b. 1901), a request that was categorically denied. While the SRA representative was out of town, the congregation applied to the Kiev branch of the SRA and did not meet with any explicit opposition. On that basis, a cantor was brought in from Berdichev (Frenkel', b. 1905); he led the High Holiday services and was paid 2,500 rubles for his efforts.[9]

Notwithstanding these negative responses from SRA representatives, they and the local authorities elected on quite a few occasions to ignore the importation of holiday cantors. Thus, for example, the congregation of Zhmerinka invited Asher Lerner from Vinnitsa to its synagogue for Passover, and for the High Holidays of 1957 invited A. S. Lenkovskii, a member from the Chernovtsy tailors' cooperative. In Chernovtsy's Barbius Street synagogue, an opera singer from the capital of Moldavia (M. A. Kogan) led services publicly on the High Holidays of 1955 without having been granted explicit permission. That same year in Berdichev, services were led by M. L. Gutrats (b. 1908), a worker in a Chernovtsy craft cooperative, and in Zhitomir by Aharon Blot of Chernovtsy (b. 1920). In 1956, High Holiday services in the Chernigov synagogue were led by Yaakov Chervatskii, an accountant in a Chernobyl factory. The opera singer M. A. Kogan appears again, this time in Nikolaev, performing services along with the artist Moshniager of Kishninev. Though the authorities knew about all these activities, they looked the other way because of the new climate.[10]

The subsequent shift in religious policy in the late 1950s and early 1960s resulted in the hardening of attitudes toward inviting cantors. Just prior to the High Holidays of 1960, the leaders of the Vinnitsa congregation were summoned (as were, it seems, heads of other congregations) and given harsh orders not to bring in cantors from out of town. The SRA representatives of various districts took pride in reporting that their vigorous activities had led to reduced cantor visits and, in turn, diminished synagogue attendance.[11] Besides pressing the congregations not to invite cantors for the holidays, the authorities made efforts to discourage others as well from leading the services.

Most of the cantors who performed in the synagogues did so not out of pure religious motives but rather for the extra income. The SRA representatives, accordingly, made sure to report this employment situation to financial officials in the cantors' place of residence so that stiff taxes could be imposed on them there, thus reducing the number of people willing to lead services. Thus, for example, the Chernovtsy district SRA representative wrote to his colleague in Vinnitsa:

I request via the finance officials that a nonlabor income tax be levied from Yaakov Makval, born 1906 and residing in the town of Mogilev-Podol'skii [Vinnitsa district] . . . who in the holidays of the New Year and Yom Kippur led services in the synagogue on 53 Russkaia Street in the city of Chernovtsy and was paid 10,000 rubles.

Indeed, the Vinnitsa district SRA representative applied to have the cantor legally taxed, but the tax authorities had no desire to take part in such trifles and imposed a diminished fine only after pressure was exerted by the local authorities. SRA personnel thus became the primary informers to tax officials about cantors' incomes. And so, on March 25, 1949, the Vinnitsa district SRA representative sent the following letter to his colleague in the Zhitomir district:

> I hereby request through the finance institutions that a nonlabor income tax
> be levied on the cantor M. V. Levitas, resident of Ovruch, Zhitomir district. The
> aforesaid Levitas was a cantor in the synagogue . . . in the city of Vinnitsa and
> received a sum of 6,000 rubles, and in Mogilev-Podol'skii in an unregistered
> synagogue . . . received 4,000 rubles.[12]

Indeed, following the imposition of an exceptionally high tax on one of the popular cantors of the late 1940s, Kamentskii—and, it seems, also a threat that he would be dismissed from his regular job as a singer with the Kiev philharmonic orchestra—the singer wrote an extensive letter of disclosure about various congregations, in which he asked "that his declaration be believed that he would no longer allow himself to serve as a cantor for any sum in the world." Thus, with the application of various pressures, the number of cantors willing to work in the synagogues on holidays decreased.[13]

Bringing in a prayer leader from out of town, we can therefore deduce, required the official permission of the district SRA representative. To gain this permission, the congregation had to use various inducements (gifts, personal connections, and the like) and, even then, the results were not always favorable.

As mentioned earlier, cantors led services not only in synagogues with congregations but also in minyans, and the authorities knew of the wages they received there as well. It is therefore no wonder that with the intensified struggle against religion generally and against the Jewish religion in particular, taxes were increasingly used (along with other mechanisms) to prevent people from serving as cantors during the holidays. The authorities did not limit themselves to prohibiting the invitation of out-of-town cantors but also made efforts to sharply condemn treasury officials who for their own reasons failed to tax cantorial earnings. Thus, for example, in January 1959 a rather harsh letter was written to the Treasury Department in Chernovtsy about its failure to tax those holding prayers in Jewish cemeteries, performing religious weddings, and receiving "large sums" for doing so.[14]

It seems, accordingly, that congregations in the USSR required the consent of the authorities if they were to hire a permanent cantor or bring one in for the holidays from out of town—even when they had the means to pay for such.

CHAPTER ELEVEN
Financing Religious Activities

The broad literature published in the West on religion in the USSR, and even publications on the subject in the former USSR, scarcely addresses the sources of funding for religious activities. This seems to be due to the paucity of direct documentation on the subject: even the SRA representatives had little trust in the records of income and expenditure that, by the 1929 regulations on religious affairs, all religious associations were required to maintain, including congregations.[1] Yet on the assumption that donations to a congregation (synagogue) also represent some sort of expression of identity, this chapter is aimed at investigating the subject to the extent possible.

Revenue Sources

In discussing revenue sources for congregations, we must divide the years under discussion into two periods: 1945–1954 and 1955–1964. During the first period the congregations did not, to the best of our knowledge, receive material support from abroad, except for isolated congregations that had packages sent to them; this is the period to which most of this discussion will be devoted. By contrast, during the second period many tourists came to the USSR and the Jews who did so regularly visited synagogues and donated their own money or funds transmitted by others. These donations for the most part benefited congregations in the large cities that were open to foreign tourism, while the burden of supporting congregations in small and midsize towns fell entirely upon the local Jews. When the campaign against religion expanded in the late 1950s, the authorities sought to reduce these sources of income as much as possible. One effort involved tourists' cash donations in foreign currency. In such cases, for instance, the Ukraine SRA representative directed all the congregations in the republic to transfer such cash to the Soviet representative who would deposit it in the bank in a state account.[2]

The 1918 law of separation of church and state dictated that all religious activity had to be funded through private donations and not by public or government bodies or property incomes. This restriction was very significant for the churches but marginal for Jewish religious activity, which even before the

Revolution had been based largely on donations. Such donations came first of all from the wealthy, who bore most of the financial burden of the congregation. Yet this class was destroyed in the Revolution, and even the small shop owners who in the 1920s could afford to donate significant sums disappeared in the 1930s when private commerce was eliminated. We thus cannot speak of a Jewish middle class in the post–World War Two USSR that was capable of covering the main expenses of the congregations; financing came mostly from the small contributions of many Jews.

Fundraising in the period under discussion was done in seven primary ways, the first of which was collections from synagogue attendees. A law of April 1929, valid also in subsequent years, stated:

> Members of religious associations are allowed to raise funds among themselves [*proizvodit' skladchiny*] and to collect voluntary donations in the prayer house and outside it only from members of the religious association and only for the purpose of maintaining the house of prayer, maintaining the ritual property and paying the salary of the religious service providers and the executive board [of the religious association].

It thus follows that funds could be raised outside the prayer house walls only from members of the religious association, which is to say, from the "twenty" who signed the agreement to maintain the prayer house or those who signed the request to register the congregation or open a synagogue. These people were usually elderly—pensioners with very small incomes—many of whom needed material assistance themselves, and whose ability to financially support the activities of the congregation was quite limited. It was permissible to collect donations for the congregation from those attending the synagogue on a daily basis, and perhaps those who attended only on the Sabbath also contributed. But weekday attendees numbered a few dozen at most, and their ability to contribute to the congregation was limited. In this respect they were not substantially different from the synagogue activists. Fundraising outside the prayer house from those not considered "members of a religious association" *was allowed* under certain conditions, as specified in the October 1, 1929, directives of the People's Commissariat for Internal Affairs (NKVD) of RSFSR (which applied in effect to the entire USSR):

> Collection of voluntary contributions from nonmembers of the religious associations may be done by that association only after obtaining a special permit, granted on the basis of a decision by the Central Executive Committee and the People's Commissariat of the USSR.[3]

In line with these regulations, in 1948 the congregations of Zhitomir and Novograd-Volynskii applied for a onetime permit to solicit donations toward refurbishment of the synagogue buildings. The district SRA representative was inclined to support the application and wrote to his superior in Kiev as follows:

I believe that it is possible to allow a onetime collection [of donations] on the basis of receipts given by the congregation. This will grant legal status to the illegal collection now enjoyed by shady characters [*temnye lichnosti*], who in addition are engaged in nationalist, anti-Soviet activity. Placing fundraising under our indirect supervision will force the congregations to give an official accounting of the contributions. I believe that granting legal status to clandestine forms of activities of the Jewish congregation will provide us in the future with information which will make it possible to uproot it.

The Ukraine SRA representative wrote throughout his response that "contributions [will be] within the walls of the synagogue,"[4] thus effectively voicing his objection to the district SRA representative's proposal. Correspondingly, the congregation's application for a wider fundraising drive never made it to the central institutions of the USSR. Given the faint chance of being granted permission to conduct fundraising for any purpose connected to religious institutions, congregations in general did not apply again to the government on this matter.

As noted, aside from onetime contribution drives, the religious association, in our case the congregation, was permitted to receive internal contributions from all attendees, including nonmembers. Indeed, every synagogue had collection boxes into which any visitor could slip contributions as he wished. The SRA representative described the boxes at the Kalinkovichi synagogue as follows: "The congregation has a special metal box for collecting money, which during prayers is hung on the wall of the synagogue and into which the Jews insert their contributions. . . . [T]he monies, as per documentation, go toward heating and synagogue maintenance, municipal taxes, et cetera."[5]

Regulations held that the donor himself, and not an intermediary, should make the donation. The Odessa district SRA representative reported in 1958 on the unacceptable method one synagogue used to transfer donations made for *aliya* to the Torah into its cash box: "In a discussion with the chairman of the executive committee [of the congregation] . . . he told me . . . that during the reading of the Torah . . . they put the money on the table, one of the members of the administration pockets it . . . and only afterward transfers it to the synagogue."[6]

The sums collected in the boxes on ordinary weekdays and Sabbath were, it seems, very small. In 1955 the rabbi of the Uzhgorod congregation complained that the three to four hundred rubles collected each month weren't enough even to cover regular expenses, let alone special ones.[7]

The situation was different during the holidays, when many Jews would gather in and especially around the synagogues. The gatherings included quite a few people from the upper stratum of the Soviet middle class, whose ability to contribute was much greater than that of most of the congregation; the system of anonymous contribution, which didn't break Soviet law, suited them well. On those days, people with collection cans would walk about the area surrounding the synagogue, and quite a few Jews, some of whom never entered the synagogue building, would contribute.

Because the sums collected on such occasions were often considerable, many congregations had to report them to the SRA representative. While we may assume that the amounts reported were smaller than what was actually collected, the available data does indicate general trends. Records from five congregations in Ukraine during the High Holidays show that, rather than declining during the difficult years of 1951–1953, donations actually rose by 19 percent.[8] This increase can be viewed as an expression of Jewish identity on one hand and as a protest against anti-Jewish policy on the other.

With the thaw, and especially the hopeful climate that followed the Twentieth Congress of the Communist Party, donations to the synagogues during the High Holidays increased yet again. In 1957 they rose in eleven synagogues by a combined 27 percent over the previous year—from 308,000 to 390,900 rubles. Possibly some of this increase can be attributed to donations by tourists. In breaking down the numbers, we find that revenues during the High Holidays of 1957 in the two Moscow synagogues grew by 26 percent (180,000 rubles from 143,000 rubles in 1956), and in Kiev by 102 percent in 1958 compared to 1956 (90,000 rubles from 44,5000 rubles). Revenues also grew in the smaller communities not reached by tourists. In six towns (Irkutsk, Zhmerinka, Evpatoriia, Nikolaev, Chernovtsy, Rostov), contributions during the High Holidays grew by 33 percent (118,000 rubles from 88,500 rubles).

Once the vigorous antireligion campaign of the late 1950s began, however, revenue from visitors to the synagogues during the holidays decreased, at least as reflected in the official documentation. Thus, for example, holiday donations in L'vov dropped by 10 percent in 1960 compared to the previous year. Kiev too experienced a decline: 90,000 rubles were collected in 1958 against only 7,900 rubles in 1962.

The second source of revenue was "selling aliyot" to the Torah—with the aliyot being auctioned off to the highest bidder. This method was considered to violate the Soviet regulations on religion, and consequently the SRA announced, on April 22, 1947, a total ban on selling aliyot. Following this ban, the auctioning of aliyot indeed seems to have been discontinued in most synagogues; and whoever made an _aliya_ to the Torah would discreetly give a donation to the synagogue.

The third way of gathering funds for the synagogue was selling seats. In advance of the holidays, especially the High Holidays, when the synagogues were full, indoor seats were offered for sale. Larger donors would receive a better place on the "Eastern" wall, but smaller donors and nondonors still had the right to enter the synagogue and pray as they wished. This custom lasted, in many congregations, through the war years and afterward, and in many synagogues, reserved seats were marked with the names of the donors. However, the practice was perceived as contradicting the Soviet rules and regulations on religion, according to which it was forbidden to demand any payment for participation in a religious ritual. So the SRA directed, on April 22, 1947, "that it is forbidden to permit the selling of seats in a synagogue."[9] The authorities ignored the prohibition—which was based on a special directive of the Commissary of Internal Affairs in 1929—until the late 1940s, but even after they began enforcing it in the years of heightened antireligion policy, congregations continued to sell seats, while using various tactics to disguise the practice. Thus, for example, the Odessa congregation sold seats indirectly. After a certain person donated or promised to donate to the congregation, the donor would declare that a seat should be reserved for him in the synagogue on holidays and that he be given an entrance ticket. This method limited entrance to the synagogue to donors only, which caused quite a few complaints.[10] Most congregations avoided this extreme approach, even as they too continued to sell seats in the synagogue secretly. The practice often drew legal action from the authorities and was even used, at times, as a pretext for breaking up the congregation and closing the synagogue.

A fourth source of income was the recitation of the kaddish. Because many Soviet Jews did not want to appear in the synagogues or did not know the prayer, quite a few contributed to the synagogue so that worshipers would say kaddish on behalf of their relatives who had passed away. The _yohrzeit_ custom was well rooted in the tradition of Eastern European Jews, so even Jews for whom this was the only expression of their Jewish identity tried to maintain it; certain congregations would take the trouble of reminding them of the anniversaries of their relatives' deaths. The authorities knew of this practice, which seems to have been widespread, but until the late 1940s preferred to ignore it. Only during the time of the Doctors' Plot did the SRA representative raise the subject in a memorandum to the Central Committee of the Communist Party, writing that "One of the synagogue workers [in Kiev] maintained in his house a file on Jews who died, and sent postcards to relatives inviting them to the synagogue or the cemetery so as to perform the religious ritual for the dead who had been buried in a civil ceremony."[11]

The fifth source of revenue was the donations collected either in Jewish cemeteries or in the Jewish areas of general cemeteries. It was customary in cemeteries and purification houses to place a collection box with the words "charity saves from death"; the funds collected in this manner would pay for synagogue maintenance, plots for the indigent, and the wages of burial service workers. Through such boxes, even people who never set foot in a synagogue could contribute money, including members of the Soviet regime and the intelligentsia who came to visit their parents' graves. People connected to the congregation would also collect contributions for prayers to be made at specific times at the graves of their loved ones—this on top of the fees for holding religious rituals at cemeteries. Not inconsiderable sums, therefore, accumulated in collection cash boxes of this type, and even though such contributions went astray of official Soviet regulations, the authorities ignored them until the late 1940s. That said, authorities began to notice large sums gathering in the collection boxes—such as an average of 15,000–20,000 rubles a month in Moscow's cemeteries, 3,000–5,000 a month in the Odessa cemetery, and 1,000–2,000 a month in the town cemetery of Korosten'. These sums alarmed the authorities, some of whom took measures to forbid the placing of charity boxes in the cemeteries. Thus, the Ukraine SRA representative argued to his superiors in 1950 that charity boxes should be forbidden; however, this practice seems to have continued in subsequent years.[12]

The sixth source of income was visits to Jewish homes. Fundraisers would go around to homes, as volunteers or for a fee, and convince people to donate to the synagogue. In 1947 the Belorussia SRA representative wrote:

> Now the religious Jews have the custom of collecting revenues through home visits [_obkhod kvartir_]—which draws some involvement in the congregation also on the part of nonreligious Jews. I am of the opinion that this practice of collecting funds for the congregation's needs should be stopped, to thus forestall the possibility of increasing the activity of the religious Jews who won't be able to build a synagogue.

The practice seems to have been sufficiently widespread without drawing much attention from the local authorities, but in the late 1940s efforts increased to end it. In late 1948, the Belorussia SRA representative reported, "I warned the chairman of the congregation (who is also the rabbi) [in Minsk] that solicitation of contributions by home visits must be stopped." But congregation activists nevertheless continued to visit Jewish homes while avoiding homes in which Communists lived.[13] Along with the intensified campaign against the Jewish religion came harsher demands to cease home contributions, and on January 15, 1949, the Ukraine SRA representative sent all his district subordinates a special letter, stating:

> It has become clear to us that the Soviet representative in the Odessa district . . . has failed, to this day, to prohibit the synagogue management from collecting funds for the synagogue outside the synagogue walls. . . . We made it clear more than once . . . that it must be categorically demanded from the synagogue boards that there will be no "collectors" [*inkassatorov*], which is to say persons . . . who occasionally tour the apartments where Jewish families live to collect money for the synagogue[,] even from people who never visit the synagogue (professors, doctors and the like). . . . All this indicates that certain SRA representatives have nicely filed away [*akkuratno podshili k delu*] the SRA directives [from Moscow] and forgot about them. I hereby warn that if this sort of thing continues in the current year we shall raise the question of punishment and prosecution and party responsibility for negligence of state interests.[14]

A directive like this indicates the increased pressure, from 1949 to 1953, on congregations as well as Communists and other persons of status in Soviet society to cease contributing to the synagogues and to turn down the requests of the fundraisers who visit their homes. After the directive was issued, several Jewish Communists in Minsk whose names were entered on the lists of contributors without their knowledge wrote to the authorities and demanded that the congregation activists, headed by Rabbi Yaakov Yosef Berger, be tried for using their names illegally. So as to defend himself against these severe accusations, the rabbi let the congregation's accounting books be reviewed by the SRA representative. This investigation, which lasted three days (August 31 to September 2, 1949), revealed an interesting picture of contributions to the synagogue, a picture that almost certainly applied in many congregations. The books listed the names of the donors, the fundraiser, date of payment, and donation amount, which in the official listing is listed as *vocher*.[15] These were, then, weekly and—even more typically—monthly donations to which the donor committed, with his or her name and address appearing in the account books. According to this list, a Mrs. Kaminsky, Communist Party member, donated twenty rubles in 1947 and six rubles in 1948; her husband, not a party member, donated twenty rubles in 1948. Mrs. Sotzkover committed to donating twenty rubles to the synagogue in 1947 but in fact donated only fourteen rubles over several payments. In September 1948 Mrs. Sotzkover paid a different fundraiser fifteen rubles, because she had relocated to another residence. The donation was listed under her name since she wasn't a party member; her husband, Nissim Rojinski, *was* a party member and held a high position in the town's financial administration. The government report stated that "Rojinski, as a Communist, is responsible for the poor reeducation of his wife[,]" a failure for which he was reprimanded. Likewise, Mrs. Zelkinson, who worked as a technician in the Belorussian government garage, paid *vocher* in the sum of twenty rubles in 1948, though the sum was listed as coming from her mother, a pensioner. In September 1947, Josef Kazinetz committed to giving the synagogue a monthly *vocher* of twenty rubles, but in the course of about a half year he could only muster a total of fifty-five rubles.[16] An examination of the account book of the Minsk congregation leads to at least five conclusions: (1) congregation activity was supported in part by Communist Party members, who were declared atheists; (2) certain Jews promised to make a weekly or monthly contribution to the synagogue; (3) the congregation fundraisers didn't visit Jewish homes only on the eves of holidays, but did so more frequently to collect promised sums; (4) the city was divided into fundraising sectors, and when a person moved to a different house, he also moved to a different fundraiser; (5) the donations were very small and, given the large expenses of the congregation, we can conclude that support for its continued existence was expressed by many Jews in this way.

As pressure grew from the authorities to stop synagogue fundraising through home visits, the practice seems to have diminished. When fundraising did occur, pretexts were given more often, such as that of selling Hanukkah candles. But certain congregations, such as the one in Poltava, saw home donations as essential to their survival, and hence continued using this method at least until 1952, despite the associated dangers.[17]

With the thaw, the practice of collecting funds for the congregation through visits to Jewish homes was revived, and fundraisers now dared to visit public places as well. Thus the SRA representative of the Kiev district complained in late 1957 that individuals from the congregation had solicited donations for the synagogue from the city's hairdressing salons, and that almost all the workers had contributed and were given receipts for their donations. But with the antireligion campaign of the late 1950s, accusations again focused on the illegality of collecting money in homes and workplaces.[18]

The seventh source of income for the congregations was indirect. While the first six sources were direct, revenues were also derived from the baking and selling of matzah, whether in the synagogue or in cooperative associations, as well as from kosher slaughtering.[19]

As noted earlier, the only legal mode of fundraising entailed collections from the worshipers inside and surrounding the synagogue, as well as donations from visitors. All other kinds of revenue were either explicitly outlawed or existed in a gray zone of permissibility and prohibition based on Soviet regulations on religious activity. Accordingly, during the relaxation of the antireligion campaign, the authorities regarded this type of activity as tolerable, but during periods of crackdown they invoked various clauses to repress congregations, as well as to sometimes dismantle them and close them down.

Expenses

The expenses of the congregations may be divided into three main areas: (1) investment in infrastructure; (2) periodic expenses; and (3) regular expenses.

1. Most of the synagogues operating in the USSR were opened between 1944 and 1948. The structures handed over by the authorities for this purpose were often only skeletons of buildings, and even supposedly sound structures needed large investments in order to fit them for prayer. Official data on expenses for rehabilitation or purchase of nineteen synagogue buildings indicates that almost a million rubles were spent to this end, but we may assume that actual expenses were much greater than those listed in the Soviet documentation, since some of the building materials were bought on the open market, where the prices were much higher than those on the official list. Furthermore, congregation heads were likely careful not to state the exact sum of the outlays so as to avoid raising the authorities' suspicions about the funding sources. Even those sums relayed to the authorities often elicited astonishment from the SRA staff, one of whom, for example, wrote:

> If we take into account the number of religious people in the synagogue [in Belaia Tser'kov] it is approximately three hundred people and the sum raised for the rebuilding [of the synagogue] is 30,000 rubles, the conclusion is that there was much activity on the part of the religious and that not only the religious, but nonreligious Jews are contributing to the rehabilitation of the synagogue.[20]

The amount spent on synagogue rehabilitation indeed seems high if we take into account that the monthly salary of a lecturer in a teachers' college, with an advanced degree and at least five years' seniority, was 650 rubles, and the salary of the dean of an institution of this type, where at least 180 students studied, was 1,000 rubles.

Infrastructure costs for synagogue buildings came mainly during 1944–1948. In those years many congregations, especially in the areas liberated from the Nazi occupation, would fence and rehabilitate cemeteries and also sometimes build body-purification sheds. Significant expenditures were involved—five congregations (Chernigov, Zhitomir, Kiev, Odessa, and Voroshilovgrad), for example, spent more than a quarter of a million rubles combined for this purpose. Because the congregations weren't legally required to engage in such work, we may assume that the actual expenses far exceeded what is reflected in the partial data in the Soviet documentation. Likewise, quite a few congregations in the areas liberated from the Nazis memorialized the victims of the Holocaust, both directly and indirectly, through landscaping gestures on sites where murders occurred and construction of monuments, most of which indeed did not survive. Such memorials cost a lot of money. Scarce help from foreign sources in those years meant the construction and upkeep of synagogues and cemeteries fell to Soviet Jews who both practiced their religion and hardly did at all.

2. Periodic expenses may be defined as special expenses for the "autumn holidays." Many congregations would repair their synagogue before the holidays. They would paint, fill cracks in the walls, fix floors and furnaces, and restore lighting systems. These expenses added up to tens of thousands of rubles, and sometimes a hundred thousand rubles or more. Most of the congregations would also invite a cantor for the holidays, paying fees of between three and ten thousand rubles depending on the cantor's fame; for some cantors the fees were much higher.[21] Based on very partial data from seven synagogues, we can deduce that cantors earned about 9,000 rubles to sing during the High Holidays.

3. More regular, to some extent, were the operating expenses for the congregation and synagogue. Every congregation needed a "religious service provider" (rabbi), whose salary was paid from its funds. The salaries of rabbis varied according to the size and ability of the congregation, but, on average, they earned between 24,000 and 60,000 rubles a year.[22] The congregation heads (*gabbais*) were not paid salaries, to the best of our knowledge, but they were often reimbursed for expenses associated with the congregation. Several congregations had permanent cantors, who in the 1950s earned roughly between 20,000 (Odessa, Nikolaev) and 90,000 rubles (Leningrad) a year; other synagogues had paid "Torah readers" in addition. Each synagogue also had a

shamash (beadle) whose yearly salary was between 5,000 and 52,000 rubles. In addition, most congregations had a paid administrative staff, the costs of which varied according to each congregation's size and ability. Thus, for example, administrative expenses in the Odessa congregation in 1960 came to 26,500 rubles.[23] Municipal taxes and insurance for the synagogue buildings, which were owned by the state or city, also fell on the congregation; utilities, such as lighting and heating, cost money as well. The expenses described until now all accorded with Soviet regulations applicable to religious associations. However, the congregations also had regular expenses which did not accord with the regulations, even if the authorities knew of and ignored them. One such expense was related to burials and maintenance of Jewish cemeteries or Jewish plots within the general cemeteries.

Some congregations, mainly the larger ones such as those in Moscow and Odessa, employed several people with monthly salaries for burials. Thus, for example, in 1960 the Odessa congregation employed seven gravediggers, whose annual salaries amounted to 26,500–30,000 rubles apiece.[24] Salaried cemetery guards were employed by most congregations, as robbery and vandalization continued even after the war.

Charity and support for the needy, distributed by many congregations, also counted as expenses. In the postwar years, when the antireligion campaign eased, such activity didn't get much attention in the Soviet documentation, but once the campaign reintensified, the Ukraine SRA representative wrote in February 1953 to the republic's Central Committee of the Party:

> Through exploitation of various methods and means, in order to draw the Jewish public to the synagogue, some of the heads [of the Kiev synagogue] are taking illegal steps to collect monies from believers and have created an unlisted fund for giving help to certain persons of Jewish nationality.[25]

Given the severe restrictions on the congregations regarding collection of money and the unceasing pressure applied to people, especially members of the Communist Party and persons with status who wanted to contribute, one cannot speak of transparency in the financial records of the congregations. The very partial data available suggests that the various expenses incurred by the congregations were much higher than reported, directly or indirectly, to the authorities. Most donations, it would appear, came in small sums, meaning that very many Jews participated in some way to support the continued existence of a synagogue. And, as noted, the donors included quite a few who in no way may have been defined as religious or even traditional. What caused these people to contribute, we may only guess. But we may assume that some sought in this way to express their support for the only recognized Jewish institution in the USSR, and that various fundraisers may have evoked for them a parent or grandparent who was murdered in the Holocaust. A mixture of feelings and memories, and perhaps an inclination to protest against the USSR antireligion policy, may have driven these many nonreligious Jews to contribute, in assorted ways, to the synagogue's well-being. The existence of a small group of people who were tirelessly dedicated to the continued existence of the congregation, on one hand, and of masses of Jews willing to support their various activities, on the other, allowed hundreds of congregations to persist and function financially.

CHAPTER 12
Religious Studies and the Moscow Yeshiva, 1957

Torah study is considered one of the most important values of Judaism. From a very young age, Jewish boys across Eastern Europe were sent to what the Ashkenazim call a *heder*, a private institution of sorts where the boys received their initial education in basic religious obligations, prayer, and reading. Since not all parents could afford to send their sons to private heders, over the years Talmud Torahs (traditional schools) were established primarily to serve the children of the poor; these were maintained by funds from the Jewish public.

By the late nineteenth and early twentieth centuries, the heders and Talmud Torahs were not the sole educational settings in the tsarist empire, with many Jewish children studying in non-Jewish schools and other less traditional frameworks (the Russian-Jewish school, the reformed heder [*heder metukan*], and also the nascent Yiddish school system). Nonetheless, until the Bolsheviks took over, most Jewish boys still studied in the traditional setting.

From the outset, the Soviet regime prohibited giving religious instruction to minors. In the first years, it forbade this practice in schools and afterward in other frameworks as well. The laws and regulations ultimately dictated that only the father or grandfather could give religious instruction to his minor progeny, and all group study was forbidden. But this concept was not embraced equally in all the Soviet republics nor were the laws enforced with equal determination. Correspondingly, between the World Wars, a semiunderground religious instruction system developed in some Central Asian republics and in Georgia. The Jews, too, benefited from this situation, and in those republics certain Jewish children, though only a marginal proportion, were given religious instruction in small groups.[1] In the areas annexed to the USSR in WWII, heders continued to operate almost openly, serving the many Jewish children who didn't go to the new Soviet schools or who studied religious subjects in addition to those they were taught in the public schools.

With the change in Soviet policy toward religion following the German invasion of the USSR, the heder or quasi-yeshiva phenomenon increased in areas of Jewish concentration in Central Asia (especially in the cities of Samarkand and Tashkent). Many refugees had reached this region, including quite a few Jews from both the original areas of the USSR and those annexed during the war.

The latter included Jews from Poland, who fled there after Germany's invasion of the USSR or who were freed from exile as a result of the agreements between the Polish government-in-exile and the USSR (July 30, 1941). Many sought to provide their children with a Jewish education. One of the Polish Jews who arrived in Bukhara was the Gaon of Tshabin (Rabbi Dov Berisch Weidenfeld); he opened a sort of yeshiva in which youngsters could study Talmud and Poskim (Jewish legal arbiters). After the government prohibited the Gaon's institution, the work was carried on by his son-in-law, Rabbi Baruch Shimon Schneerson.[2] Given the demand for this sort of education, on the one hand, and the shifts in Soviet policy on religion, on the other, quite a few groups for religious study seem to have operated more or less regularly in Central Asia. Thus in early 1945 the head of the Moscow congregation announced to the Western media that there were several yeshivas in Central Asia headed by former students from the great Lithuanian yeshivas (Mir, Slobodka, and others).[3]

The refugees or evacuees to Uzbekistan included quite a few Chabad Chassidim—the most organized Jewish religious group in the USSR. Following the severe famine of winter 1941–1942, some of them, led by Rabbi Menachem Mendel Puterfas, resumed work as tradesmen, while donating a portion of their profits to financing yeshiva activities. Thus in 1943 a yeshiva opened in Samarkand, with some 190 boys and young men studying under Rabbi Puterfas. In Tashkent a similar institution was founded with some sixty youngsters learning Gemara and Tosefot (Talmudic commentaries).[4] Such an institution was against the law of course, but given the disorder in the area and the relatively liberal policy toward religion, the authorities didn't pay close attention to the yeshiva and it operated almost openly. With the establishment of the SRA in 1944, however, the SRA did begin to track the yeshivas in Uzbekistan.

Yet I would argue that the primary and exclusive cause of the yeshivas' closure was not the authorities but rather the diminishing numbers of Jews interested in their continuation. In 1946 a great number of Jews returned to Poland, and most of the Chabad Chassidim living in the Uzbek towns made their way to L'vov en route to Poland. The few remaining yeshiva boys in those towns were transferred to a small similar institution that operated for a time in the town of Kutaisi in Georgia, where Chabad had been active since early in the century.[5]

Toward the end of the war, some in the Soviet establishment appear to have contemplated the need to establish a yeshiva in Moscow to prepare rabbis for the registered congregations, and in the city of Chernovtsy a yeshiva indeed operated. In September of 1945 that city's rabbis delivered to the authorities a list of fourteen yeshiva students, over half of whom were fourteen to sixteen years old and over a third age seventeen to nineteen: only one was thirty. However, this yeshiva either was shut down or fell apart when many of the city's Jews migrated to Romania, and from then on no yeshivas operated in the European parts of the USSR. In Asia, conversely, in quite a few cities (Bukhara, Samarkand, and others), religious instruction in small groups continued within private houses, which may be viewed as existing at the border of a heder and a yeshiva.[6]

In many cities of Georgia, the "holy tongue" (Hebrew) and religion were taught almost openly in nearly every synagogue, at least until the early 1950s; the republic's authorities took no steps against this phenomenon. The Georgia SRA representative, who viewed himself as a sort of supervisor of religious activity, thus had to apply to his superiors in Moscow to seek their intervention to end this practice.[7]

In certain towns, following the liberation from Nazi occupation in 1944, the religious education of minors resumed. This phenomenon was especially common in areas annexed by the USSR during WWII, mostly in the Chassidic areas of Bukovina, Karpatorus', and Bessarabia. In these areas, under Romanian or Hungarian governance during the war, comparatively more Jews had survived the Holocaust than in the Baltic lands and in the areas annexed by the USSR from Poland (western Ukraine and western Belorussia). Some of these Jews sought to give their children a Jewish education. And certain heads of congregations and rabbis in these areas were unaware of the Soviet laws and regulations on religion, and considered it completely natural for the congregation and its associates to occupy themselves with the religious instruction of the young generation. Thus, for example, the rabbis of Kishinev, Bel'tsy, and Orgeev more than once raised the idea with the Moldavia SRA representative of establishing a school next to the synagogue.[8] It goes without saying that these proposals were rejected by the authorities. Yet the phenomenon didn't disappear, and when the Zakarpat'e SRA representative visited the city of Beregovo in early 1959 he was surprised to find that almost all the Jewish children knew how to read Hebrew (_drevne evereiskii_). Whether or not this statement exaggerated the reality, we do know of two groups of youths in the city, each of which numbered between twenty-five and thirty students, whose parents were paying tuition (to instructors named Zakerman and Lieberman) in the amount of fifty rubles per student per month. The authorities threatened to convict the teachers: by the criminal code of RSFSR and its counterparts in the other republics, the teachers could expect a year of forced labor. Yet the religious instruction of minors wasn't confined only to the annexed areas; apparently it took place also in certain cities of the "old" USSR. Thus, for example, a Talmud

Torah operated in the city of Zhitomir until early 1947, organized by Sh. A. Pesel'zon; it was broken up only as a result of the vigorous intervention by the SRA representative. The authorities came to know that a heder was operating in the city of Novograd-Volynskii, and an SRA official of the Zhitomir district was sent to look into the matter. This heder, according to the teacher, gave instruction mostly to orphans whose parents had perished in the Holocaust. The classes took place in the house of Nachum Keller, age eighty-three, who had been a Hebrew teacher before the war. When Keller was summoned by the authorities, he maintained that he chiefly taught the children how to recite kaddish for their parents and that he took payment for this in money or in foodstuffs. After warnings and pressures, Keller and congregation head Shmuel-Ber Bronshtein signed a commitment to cease running the heder. The SRA representative nevertheless passed the report on to the public prosecutor.[9]

In the first years of the thaw, certain congregations sought a permit, and therefore legal permission, for some of the religious studies activities that had been taking place underground. Thus, in 1956 the Chernovtsy congregation applied officially to the authorities seeking permission to open a heder. Needless to say the authorities rejected the application out of hand.[10]

Nonetheless, religious instruction in small groups seems to have taken place in quite a few towns of the USSR. The authorities' internal correspondence, for its part, makes only tangential mention of the religious instruction of children, either for lack of information or a preference not to deal with the subject. Yet this religious instruction, even if it didn't disappear completely, was an extremely marginal phenomenon that lacked any significance for most Jewish children.

While teaching religion to minors was illegal in the USSR, voluntary group study by adults supposedly did not conflict with the laws and regulations. And as study was considered by Jews to be a positive value and a commandment, in many congregations a custom took root in which synagogue attendees would study Mishna between afternoon and evening prayers. The study group made sure that at least a quorum was present so that they could recite kaddish following their studies. This practice of study followed by recitation of kaddish was taken up by many families during the customary seven days of mourning after a loved one's death. This created some consternation among the Soviet institutions that dealt with religion: according to the 1929 laws on religion and subsequent amendments, burial prayers were allowed to be conducted in the home of the deceased, and the question therefore was to what extent Mishna study could count as burial prayer, and whether it could be conducted in the synagogue and whether the practice constituted a religious study circle.

Group Mishna study was conducted in the synagogues of Odessa, Khar'kov, Kiev, Kherson, and perhaps elsewhere as well. Because these and similar groups met on a regular basis, they formed in effect a "Mishna society" (*khevrat mishnayot*); and since the group leader had to spend time and effort preparing for each meeting, each student was required to pay a sum of twenty to twenty-five rubles to take part. In the Odessa synagogue, there was even a designated person who, according to an official report, was paid a monthly wage of five hundred rubles to conduct Mishna study with a group or groups arranged in the synagogue.[11] The Soviet authorities often ignored this phenomenon, which seems to have been widespread, so long as there was some laxity in the present antireligion policy. But with the intensification of the antireligion campaign, the Ukraine SRA representative sent out special memoranda on this subject, on the thirteenth and fifteenth of January 1949, requesting reports about Mishna study in the synagogues and stating:

> Given that *mishnayot* is not included in the ritual of the synagogue and that activists arrange [such study] for profit, thereby contravening the Soviet legislation on religious affairs, I suggest breaking up these groups [that meet] in the synagogues, and warning the synagogue administration that noncompliance with this order could lead to breakup [of the congregations] and in extreme instances to the closure of the synagogue. If the leaders of the study groups persist, tax them."[12]

Such advisories prompted the authorities to become more stringent on this issue, but Mishna study didn't completely cease even in the more difficult years—though it seems to have taken on a different aspect. For example, the Odessa district SRA representative reported that the city's synagogue had no Mishna study group, yet "during the break between Mincha and Maariv prayers the rabbi reads prayers and also Mishna and Talmud."[13] Thus when the pressures against religion were especially severe, the authorities tried to prevent synagogue attendees from engaging in any form of study, whereas in times of relaxation they tended to ignore such attempts. However, such study was not likely to cultivate individuals with sufficient learning to take over the basic tasks of running the synagogues.

The Moscow Yeshiva

As Jewish learning fell to almost nonexistence in the Soviet Union, the number of religious service providers able to fill the basic roles in the congregation dropped correspondingly. Traditionally, men had trained for such roles in yeshivas, and the few yeshivas still operating half-legally in the USSR of the 1920s ceased existing in the 1930s. The need to prepare religious service providers grew ever more urgent; even the Soviet authorities handling religious affairs recognized this need. Correspondingly, after Stalin's death and during the general climate of thaw, the authorities tended to be more attentive to the requests of rabbis, first and foremost the rabbi of Moscow's main synagogue, to open a yeshiva. Jewish organizations from outside the USSR also occasionally passed requests to the heads of the Soviet government to allow a certain number of men to travel abroad for training. The foundation of a yeshiva in Moscow could improve the USSR's image in the West, something the USSR cared about at that time. The ultimate decision to establish a yeshiva in Moscow came in 1955.[14]

The decision to open a yeshiva in Moscow was followed by rumors across the USSR, and quite a few Jewish residents were interested in the possibility of studying there. Yet the local SRA representatives knew nothing about the yeshiva's inception. Moreover, the prospective students who answered the call rather disappointed Rabbi Shlifer; it seems the Jewish youths with spiritual leanings to religion (then a common phenomenon among the intelligentsia) didn't wish to be associated with a religious institution run under the oversight of the authorities. The rabbi also doubted the religious faith of the candidates and their readiness to devote themselves to religious activity in the congregations.[15] Furthermore, Rabbi Shlifer, who knew how things worked in the Soviet Union, understood that among those seeking to sign up for the yeshiva would be a number of potential informants. The rabbi thus had quite a few quandaries in deciding among prospective candidates.

After a thorough but uneasy sifting, Rabbi Shlifer selected ten or twelve students to study at the yeshiva, and despite the small number, a festive inauguration of Yeshivat Kol Yaakov was held on January 6, 1957.[16] Rabbi Shlifer viewed the opening as the jewel in the crown of his public activity, but within three months this founder and guiding spirit of the yeshiva died suddenly, on March 31, 1957.

His colleagues and the authorities were interested in the continued existence of the yeshiva for opposing reasons: while the former saw it as the only forum for preparing religious leaders for the Jews of the USSR, the latter viewed it mainly as a valuable propaganda tool.[17] Rabbi Yehuda Leib Levin, who viewed himself as heir to Shlifer's role, was installed as yeshiva head during what turned out to be a period of much harsher enforcement against religious activity. In line with the new policy, the authorities sought to cut the number of students in the yeshiva as well as the number of administrators, although they didn't officially close the institution, fearing the response from the West. However, from its inception, the yeshiva was challenged by difficulties involving education, location, financing, and the students themselves.

All teachers and employees at the yeshiva were subjected to a close background check by the authorities prior to their appointment, a check most of the teachers were almost surely aware of and that forced them to behave with great circumspection. Study periods, which took place between ten in the morning and two in the afternoon and resumed from three to seven p.m., were conducted in three languages: Russian; Hebrew in two dialects—Ashkenazi and Sephardi—and Yiddish. The yeshiva students themselves held widely varying levels of knowledge: while some were just learning the Hebrew alphabet, others delved into complicated Talmudic issues. Due to these differences in ability as well as language difficulties, studies were conducted in small groups of three to five students. Much time was devoted to study of the laws of ritual slaughter and circumcision and to obtaining practical experience in these areas.

The yeshiva officially opened before it had a suitable space for regular teaching or living quarters for the students from outside the city. Initially students lived in private houses in different parts of the city, and after a while a place was arranged for them in one of the dark rooms next to the synagogue. Classes were held in a shed connected to the synagogue, an arrangement uncomfortable for both the synagogue attendees and the yeshiva students. There was discussion of building a special structure for the yeshiva where studies would take place and where the students would live. Although at first the authorities didn't reject this idea altogether, the increasing harshness of the antireligion policies led to its abandonment. In the mid-1950s, a kosher restaurant was officially opened in Moscow where tourists from abroad could meet with the synagogue attendees and the yeshiva students.[18]

From the start, the yeshiva faced significant financial troubles and survived its first months by selling the *Siddur Hashalom,* which was published in Moscow in 1956. Monthly operating expenses of the yeshiva came to 45,000–50,000 rubles: this included wages for the teaching and administrative staff, costs of the students' room and board, and monthly stipends for each student of 60–160 rubles, depending on the size of his family.[19]

Requests from Jewish groups abroad to donate significant sums to the yeshiva were turned down by the Soviet authorities; the issue of fundraising for the yeshiva from the registered congregations across the USSR was also left unclear. Whereas financing of training centers for religious service providers of other religions came from the nationwide institutions of each, the Jewish religion had no religious center; the yeshiva was, on one hand, a sort of national institute and, on the other, an entity associated with the congregation of Moscow's main synagogue. The yeshiva heads tried to involve rabbis from outside Moscow in the yeshiva's activities so as to strengthen its status as a national body, but the authorities seem to have frowned on this. Nevertheless, donations were organized for the yeshiva in many congregations, either through the coordination of various rabbis or the congregant's personal initiative; and in certain synagogues special collection boxes were set up bearing the words "Kol Yaakov Yeshiva."[20] But the SRA representatives were displeased with such boxes, and even forbade their use; in any case, the boxes did not raise nearly enough revenue to help sustain the yeshiva. Thus in the second half of its first year of existence, the yeshiva found itself in dire financial straits; yet in mid-1957, thanks largely to fundraising efforts by the Jews of Georgia, the situation improved somewhat. This republic had well-off Jews (especially those in commerce) who were willing to donate significant sums toward religious training. The yeshiva's second year of operation (1958), therefore, saw both an increase in the number of students and their funding, as well as a real improvement in the yeshiva's financial position.

Financing now came from three main sources: (1) Georgian Jews; (2) donations from tourists, who in part transferred funds raised by Jewish groups abroad; and (3) money collected by the Moscow congregation. In the subsequent couple of years, however, with the harsher Soviet stance on religion, the yeshiva again sank into difficulties. The number of students from Georgia dropped significantly, and correspondingly Georgian donations fell. The authorities also heightened their supervision of transfers of funds from abroad via tourists, and the fierce antireligion campaign of the late 1950s and early 1960s appears to have led to a drop in the donations from the Moscow congregation as well. Yet this crisis was manifested primarily in the reduced number of yeshiva students.

The candidates for study at the yeshiva rather disappointed Rabbi Levin because most came from the districts and only a few from Moscow itself. In 1957 the yeshiva had only ten students: their average age was thirty-eight and most had families with children. The following year the number of students doubled and their average age dropped, because more than a third were from Georgia. The Georgian yeshiva students had a different profile from that of their Ashkenazi mates: their average age was twenty-five, most had less than a high school education, and they had studied in the Georgian language. Prior to their arrival at the yeshiva, they had worked at simple jobs (e.g., as laborers in factories or warehouses or as shop clerks). Moreover, most had had some religious education, having learned to pray from their fathers or grandfathers.

Yet this uptick in yeshiva enrollment was brief, and by 1959 signs of deterioration were evident. The number of students decreased by 20 percent; by 1961, only ten students were studying at the yeshiva, nine of them from Georgia.[21]

Despite the obstacles in its path, the yeshiva continued to function as long as it had a quorum of students. But for reasons that are unclear, all the yeshiva students from Georgia returned home in early March 1962 and remained there for at least several months. The authorities exploited this situation to bring about the yeshiva's collapse without closing it officially. If in previous years the authorities in Georgia and Moscow had not insisted that all regulations be followed for obtaining a temporary residence permit in the capital, now the yeshiva students were required to provide all required permits from the Georgian and Muscovite governments—and the Georgian authorities maintained that the residence-permit applicants sought ends in Moscow other than study, using this claim to reject the applications. The Moscow police, who treated all comers from Georgia with special suspicion, also refused to grant residence permits in the capital to Georgian yeshiva students. When the US rabbi David Hollander visited Moscow in late 1962, only five students remained at the yeshiva,[22] among them two who had already finished their studies and were apparently serving as ritual slaughterers in Moscow.

In the five years of the yeshiva's existence only two of its students were ever ordained, and they did not serve as rabbis. In the mid-1960s the yeshiva shut its doors without the authorities having closed it officially.

The Kol Yaakov Yeshiva, which had opened in Moscow with a grand celebration and served as the focal point both within the USSR and mainly abroad of hopes for a renewed religious leadership in the Soviet Union, did not justify its existence. Unlike the seminaries for preparation of Christian religious functionaries, whose students were mainly young, most of the yeshiva students were adults caring for families, and only a few viewed themselves as being called to serve the religious public. After two generations of an antireligion climate that was often forbidding, it is unsurprising that only a tiny number of the USSR's Jews were interested in providing their children with any sort of religious instruction, particularly when such an education clashed entirely with the world around them—especially in the big cities—and would have produced a wide chasm in the children's souls.

CHAPTER THIRTEEN

Kosher Slaughter (*Shechita*) and Matzah Baking

Keeping kosher is an important commandment in the Jewish faith, and quite a few Jews who don't observe other commandments try in some fashion to keep kosher in their homes. Of course, adherence to this mitzvah is a private affair by its very nature, and in the USSR no special surveys were conducted on the matter, so assessing its scope is impossible. Yet even if keeping kosher is done primarily within the family, it has at least two public aspects: *shechita* (kosher slaughter) and the baking of matzah (unleavened bread) for Passover. Unsurprisingly, then, the congregations were usually involved directly or indirectly in both of these practices.

Shechita

In the USSR, the legal practice of religion was understood very narrowly as involving ceremonial rites, and the SRA chairman noted in his letter of April 1954 that "Kosher meat is not among the objects of ritual [*ne otnositsia k pred-metam kul'ta*] without which it is impossible to observe any religious obligation; it is rather a food [consumed by] a certain portion of the Jewish population."[1]

Since the SRA was of the opinion that *shechita* did not count as a "religious rite," it also did not consider itself as charged with overseeing this subject. The congregations, on the other hand, did feel that it was their duty to ensure the provision of kosher meat and would apply to the SRA representatives with requests on this issue.

With regard to kosher slaughtering, a distinction should be made between the slaughter of animals, large and small, and that of fowl. Slaughter of a cow or sheep usually required a slaughterhouse, as well as veterinary supervision to ensure that health standards were met. A single family generally did not consume all the meat from a large cow (especially given the lack of freezers and refrigerators in the USSR) and thus such slaughtering necessarily was associated with the sale of the meat. Since private commerce was forbidden in the USSR, the sale of kosher meat would take place in the government stores or cooperative chains, which were under the close supervision of the authorities. Thus in 1945 and 1946 the Gomel' congregation applied to the district SRA representative to allow the kosher slaughter of cattle, whose meat would be sold in the government butchery chain.[2] Such requests were almost certainly received from other congregations as well, so that the SRA chairman found it necessary to state as follows in an October 1945 circular:

> The SRA does not currently see a possibility of responding favorably to these requests, primarily because meat is a rationed product, so organizing the sale of kosher meat is a very complex affair. The soviet also takes into account that only a small circle of religious Jews consumes kosher meat.[3]

The authorities, then, seem to have had no objection in principle to kosher slaughter and meat sales, even as they acknowledged the practical difficulties it presented given that meat was sold in the government shops by coupon. But in late 1947 rationing officially ended in the USSR, providing the context for the April 1948 circular from the SRA chairman, in which he wrote:

> Commerce in kosher meat for religious Jews may be organized exclusively in the suitable consumer network of the consumer cooperative without any special designation for this purpose of shops or kiosks [kioski] and in agreement with the district consumer shop union [oblpotrebsoiuz]."

A similar response was given by the SRA representative to the Minsk congregation's request that it be allowed to supply kosher meat.[4] However, because the SRA did not, as stated, regard supplying kosher meat as a necessity of religious ritual, it warned its representatives not to get excessively involved in this subject. In this spirit, the Ukraine SRA representative instructed his subordinates that "this subject must be dealt with by the cooperatives and not the synagogues. If the heads of the district consumers' cooperatives apply seeking your opinion you may answer: 'We have no objection.' But kiosks or stands selling kosher meat are not to be allowed near the synagogue."

The authorities again stressed that the sale of kosher meat was not to be permitted in or near the synagogues,[5] but even so this practice didn't disappear completely. Thus, for example, in 1945 the authorities in Khar'kov allowed kosher slaughter to be carried out in the town slaughterhouse and the meat to be sold in a shed in the synagogue courtyard.[6] It may be presumed that Khar'kov wasn't the only city where this form of kosher meat sales took place, with the authorities turning a blind eye.

After rationing was officially canceled, the union of consumer cooperatives in the districts of Ukraine and certain cities of Russia were given explicit permission to sell kosher meat in the meat shops, and subsequently a congregation in the city of Chernovtsy came to an agreement with a cooperative to sell kosher meat in the latter's shops, with the sanction of the district authorities. Similar arrangements were made in Moscow, Kiev, Kherson, Romny,[7] and other areas. However, certain congregations were not satisfied with such agreements and sought greater involvement in the supply of kosher meat, whether from a desire to increase their kashrut supervision or to raise profits. Thus, for example, the Kremenchug congregation applied in July 1948 to the municipality with the following suggestion:

> Our slaughterer will kill the animal destined for slaughter on that day and if he arrives at the conclusion that the cattle is kosher, he will remove from it the amount of meat needed by the kosher meat consumers. This meat will be delivered to the slaughterer, who will pay your agent in accordance with the weight and price fixed by you. The slaughterer will take the meat and transport it to one of your shops, where he will sell it to all buyers without reference to their nationality.[8]

The proposed agreement would have involved the congregation, via the slaughterer, in the whole process of meat-supply, from slaughter to retail to the consumer. Though we don't have a record of the response to this proposal, the existing documentation does show that in quite a few towns in Russia and Ukraine, at least between 1944 and 1948, kosher slaughter of animals and sale of kosher meat took place through various complicated arrangements with the local authorities. Indeed, in 1948 the Moscow SRA representative reported that "currently in almost all cities, sales of kosher meat for religious Jews are taking place."[9] But with the rise of the campaign against religion, the number of cities where such sales took place decreased. Matters were slightly different in Central Asia and the Caucasus, where it was customary for large segments of the population to slaughter a goat or a sheep for themselves—a practice that made it easier for Jews to keep kosher if they chose to do so. A family or several families would buy a sheep, slaughter it using kosher methods, and divide the meat among the buyers or sell it to neighbors. The authorities ignored this all.

During the thaw, when the various cooperative bodies were given greater latitude to engage in local initiatives, the congregations renewed the various arrangements for sale of kosher meat as well. Thus, for example, in 1955 a Jew appeared in the Moscow SRA office complaining that, with Rabbi Shlifer's knowledge, kosher meat was being sold in the synagogue at exorbitant prices.[10] On the whole in Moscow, kosher slaughter expanded with the opening of a kosher restaurant, and some of the meat slaughtered supposedly for the restaurant was offered for sale to all comers. Moscow, the window through which the outside world viewed the Soviet Union, and Kiev, where many tourists visited, had *shechita* and kosher meat sales even during the final years of the Khrushchev regime, when a vigorous campaign against religion was under way. In 1960, two or three cows were being slaughtered a week in Moscow by kosher means,[11] a meager number for a Jewish population that, according to the 1959 census, numbered 240,000 souls.

The slaughter of fowl required no special permit: at the most the slaughterer had to pay taxes on his income. As a result, fowl slaughterhouses were set up in the yards of many synagogues, where the job was done for a fee. How the revenues were divided between the synagogue and the slaughterer is unclear, but the evidence suggests strongly that the slaughterer would give part of the profits to the congregation. Thus, the closure of some synagogues had implications, too, on the kosher slaughter of fowl. Though some slaughterers continued their work in the yards of their homes, this was a smaller-scale activity that, in any case, certain local authorities regarded as illegal. Thus, for example, the Bobruisk SRA representative reported that three Jews were engaging in the illegal slaughter of fowl, that they had been warned to desist, and that information had been passed to the "suitable agencies." Likewise, in Pinsk the SRA representative claimed that two butchers were not working efficiently and were spending "most of their time on affairs of kashrut [*zanimaiutsia prigotovleniem koshera*]."[12] The butchers therefore tried to find indirect ways to continue *shechita* on a wider scale, one integrated into the Soviet marketing system. Thus, for example, in the Vinnitsa district, some of the *shochtim* (slaughterers) were taken on at the "poultry industry factories" (*oblptitseprom*); they continued their kosher slaughter in the market stalls as workers of a Soviet enterprise. The district SRA representative considered such activity to contravene Soviet laws on religious affairs and demanded that the stalls be closed. Similar stalls were selling kosher meat in Minsk and Khar'kov: these were officially considered part of the subdistrict supply net (*raizag*) that provided feathers to the state. The slaughterers were thought by the authorities to be state institution workers, but they seem to have received no wages, earning a ruble or two from private customers for kosher slaughter of a bird. On the eves of Jewish holidays, they processed 450–500 birds a day, with their income reaching 500–600 rubles. The heads of the subdistrict supply network almost certainly received kickbacks from this arrangement, either through bonuses from the state for the extra supply of feathers or directly from the slaughterers. But in the early 1950s, when the SRA representative became involved, the Jewish slaughterer was removed from Minsk and replaced by a Russian woman. The dropoff in Jewish visits to the stalls resulted in a corresponding steep decline in feathers supplied to the state; non-Jews usually slaughtered their own fowl, so the feathers never reached the national authority. Nonetheless, the SRA representative in Minsk viewed the removal of the kosher slaughterers as an achievement. In Khar'kov, on the other hand, the Jewish poultry slaughterers maintained their role until the late 1950s, as they did in Mogilev-Podol'skii; the kosher slaughter of fowl was tolerated mainly on account of the feathers it supplied to the state.[13] Yet when the antireligion campaign intensified, the Khar'kov district SRA representative recommended ending this arrangement, claiming such a step "would halt the activity of another focus of encouragement for religious fanaticism and nationalism."[14] In other main cities like Moscow and Kiev, the kosher slaughter of fowl continued in structures built for the purpose in the synagogue yards. For the kosher slaughter of a fowl in Kiev, the customer paid fifty kopecks, 70 percent of which the slaughterer gave to the congregation.[15]

Throughout the 1941–1964 period, kosher slaughter of fowl occurred in most towns with a Jewish population. Yet the kosher slaughter of large animals and the sale of the meat through the public network depended largely on the regime's stance toward religion at a given time. In the years when the antireligion campaign was harsher, the kosher slaughter of cattle diminished significantly, although it never disappeared. The general impression is that fewer Jews demanded kosher meat from large animals as compared to chickens, especially as the holidays neared, Passover in particular.

Matzah

Like kosher meat, matzah was deemed to be apart from religious ritual by the Soviet authorities. In February 1954 the SRA chairman wrote:

[M]atzah is to be regarded as one of the bakery items [khlebo-bulochnye izdelia] consumed by religious Jews at specific times of the year instead of regular food. . . . It should not be counted as a necessity of religious rite without which it is impossible to observe certain religious ceremonies; but it is a necessary food item, the demand for which should be provided for.

The SRA chairman clearly knew that without matzah a Passover service, undoubtedly a religious ceremony, could not be conducted. The decision stemmed from a simplistic approach according to which only services conducted in the synagogue were "religious rites." This approach, of course, disregarded the possibility that in some religions certain rituals are conducted inside the home. Given this basic stance, the SRA didn't consider itself obligated to help supply matzah for Passover, and tried to hand the issue off to the local authorities.[16] However, the congregations did view matzah supply as one of their important activities, and they made appeals on this issue to the SRA, which couldn't completely evade it.

The congregations' involvement in matzah supply was especially tricky. On the one hand, in the 1930s and 1940s the practice was not banned by law, yet on the other, the Soviet economy was supposed to be planned and regulated, and it was not known for a surplus of flour and associated products, as demonstrated by the bread-rationing regime in effect from the late 1930s through 1947. During this period, flour could be obtained exclusively from the market (*kolkhoznyi rynok*), at high prices and in small quantities. The baking of matzah, therefore, likely did not occur in significant amounts outside the government framework.

After rationing ended, flour was supposedly sold on the free market, but the supply wasn't always regular and, especially in years of a poor wheat harvest, shortages occurred. With regard to the supply, a distinction was made between flour that came from the "state fund" (*gosudarstvennyi fond*) and flour that was sold freely: the "state fund" flour was supposed to ensure the supply of bread and other basic products to the populace, and its prices were considerably lower than that for flour on the open market.

Each public baking system was allocated a certain amount of "state fund" flour; the price of products made from that flour was fixed by the state according to general policy and usually did not reflect their actual cost. In line with the overall plan, which covered the smallest details, each bakery system had to use the "state fund" flour to bake goods of various types that were determined in advance. Matzah was included in the list of products that the public bakeries and cooperatives could produce,[17] so from the legal-official standpoint nothing prevented the baking of matzah. It is true that matzah baked from "state fund" flour came at the expense of other baked goods, the demand for which also exceeded supply, and no separate allocation of flour existed for matzah baking. Yet anyone or especially any institution needing baked goods for a specific event was allowed to bring the necessary amount of flour from the free market with which the public bakery could prepare the needed products. For such an arrangement, the phrase "given flour" (*daval'cheskaia muka*) took root. In principle this sort of flour was to be supplied personally by the individuals requiring the products, but in practice the supply of "given flour" for matzah was handled by the congregation or other entities working on behalf of the individuals and not by the individuals themselves. In many places where matzah was sold, a sign in Russian read, "given flour," a phrase that was meaningless for many matzah buyers.

Due to the conflict between the SRA policy holding that Passover matzah was not part of the religious ritual and the constant applications to produce matzah from the congregations, the Ukraine SRA representative sent a circular stating thus before Passover 1948:

> The believers of the Jewish faith are applying to us on the issue of matzah. . . .
> On this it should be made clear to them: matzah may be baked from "given flour." The state will not give any [flour from the state fund] toward the baking of matzah. . . . [I]f the national authority [for food] (*Pishchetorg*) turns to you for permission to bake matzah, you may reply in writing: "No objection."[18]

The SRA thus sought not to issue directives on matzah baking, stating that the matter should be arranged at the local level. But with the stringent anti-religion climate of the early 1950s, the SRA in the republics and districts alike sought explicit instructions from the central authority on matzah baking, showing a wariness to act alone in setting standards for the practice. Subsequently, the central SRA indeed held a meeting on the subject, and on February 17, 1950, rendered the following decision:

> 1. On the matter of baking matzah for the approaching Jewish religious holiday, Passover, it is to be suggested to the [SRA] representatives . . . that the problem be solved locally, in cooperation with the main Soviet institutions and in accordance with the local conditions.
>
> 2. The SRA for its part thinks as follows: (a) At times when the national institutions decline to bake and sell matzah for religious Jews, there should be no impediment to agreements reached between authorized religious congregations and the cooperatives over baking and selling matzah using the flour of the religious [people] or of the factories; nor should obstacles be raised in cases where groups of religious people bake matzah for their own needs in home conditions. (b) The baking of matzah within the synagogue perimeter, the commerce in [matzah], and the collection of funds for the purchase of matzah for free distribution to believers is not to be permitted. (c) The heads of the religious congregations and the factories baking matzah are to be warned that they are not to advertise the preparations for baking matzah and selling it; the manner of purchasing the matzah may be announced by the religious congregations only within the synagogue.[19]

The central authorities' ambiguous stance toward matzah baking, thus, seems not to have changed. The emphasis of the decision was on limiting information about matzah to Jews who needed it mainly for religious reasons and, at the same time, the broad Jewish public, who did not often come to the synagogues and bought matzah mainly as a symbol of national identification. The prohibition banning congregations from advertising where matzah could be purchased—while certain bakery window displays announced, "Buy *paskha* [traditional pyramid cookies for Easter] here"—roused the ire of quite a few Jews, who expressed this view in letters to the authorities; conversely non-Jews would express irritation whenever permission was given to bake matzah with "state fund" flour. Thus, for example, the Ukraine Communist Party secretary received an anonymous letter in 1957, stating:

> I write to you only because I hear on all sides the bitterness of the Russians and Ukrainians. . . . [T]he Jewish Passover is approaching and matzah is being baked specially for them. We think this is a waste of state [flour] funds. In many towns there isn't enough bread for our people and here in the capital [of Ukraine] they bake matzah for Jews. It would be better to give this harvest to the people who grew it.[20]

Such letters were corroborated by views expressed by Soviet bureaucrats in closed meetings. Thus, for example, at a 1958 council of propaganda departments of the Communist Party (Agitprop) in the Chernigov district, a question was raised: "Why do the cooperatives bake matzah?"[21] Unsurprisingly, when the central authorities began taking a harsher stand against religion, matzah baking became a prime target. The Vinnitsa district sra representative wrote as follows in 1960:

> Among Communists active in the subdistricts and districts . . . the justified question arises, why must the government institutions and cooperatives bake matzah and not the religious [people] themselves, as the Christians do? For the Orthodox, Catholics and others, no one bakes the *pascha* or the *kulich* [sweet items for the Easter holiday], so why do we give these privileges only to the religious Jews?[22]

Yet given the regime's lack of clarity and contradictions on baking matzah, on one hand, and the desire of the congregations to ensure a supply of this commodity, on the other, the issue depended largely on each town's authorities. Overall, the baking and supplying of matzah can be broken down into four components: (1) baking and selling by the state systems or the cooperatives (*arteli*); (2) baking and selling by a private organization connected to the congregation; (3) matzah baking in the family framework; and (4) receipt of matzah from abroad. Each of these four components can be elaborated as follows.

The Committee for Religious Affairs, which operated alongside the All-Russian Central Executive Committee (VtsIK), determined in February 1937 that the People's Commissariat for Food Industries (*Narkompisheprom*) could indeed bake and sell matzah through the general network.[23] However, supplying matzah this way caused two difficulties, one associated with Jewish law and the other with Soviet politics.

For the part of Jewish law, maintaining the kashrut of matzah baked in the national chain and sold unpackaged posed a great difficulty. It is therefore unsurprising that Jews of Leningrad complained to the authorities in 1937 that observant Jews were refusing to eat the matzah baked in the public bakeries. In quite a few cases, congregations sought to appoint supervisors to oversee the kashrut of matzah baked in national chains, with salaries to be paid by the factory. The Odessa congregation made such a request in February 1949, asking that the supervisors serve in the factory for a six-week period when the matzah was being baked for Passover.[24]

The Leningrad congregation made similar requests in 1955, stipulating as well that those occupied in matzah baking not work on the Sabbath. The Moscow SRA responded to the request with this ruling (among other thoughts): "No one has the right to demand a special day of rest from a public factory, beyond what is customary in the specific region. . . . Nor is it acceptable to demand the presence of an outside supervisor in food production departments."[25]

The response to this statement by many congregations was that a certain inadequacy in the kashrut of matzah must be accepted—it was better that Jews eat such matzah than no matzah at all. Yet it was not the halakhic aspect that was the main factor in preventing the baking of matzah in the public institutions.

At times of letup in the regime's campaign against religion, more factories were willing to produce matzah, yet during and after the war, the factories faced two separate and considerable difficulties: (1) the rationing of bread, with each person entitled to 400–800 grams a day, redeemed with a coupon; (2) the fact that the bread sold to the public was usually baked from rye and also often included oats, corn, potatoes, and the like. Matzah meanwhile had to be baked from pure wheat flour. Each bakery was given a certain amount of flour from the "state fund," and the bread produced was distributed to stores on the basis of the number of consumers it had listed. This raised two questions for matzah provision: (1) What should the relation be between the allotted daily ration of bread and the daily amount of matzah? (2) Is it legally permissible to sell enough matzah in advance to last several days? The authorities in the Kirovograd district answered these questions on August 5, 1946, as follows:

> [M]atzah is to be sold using coupons for white bread [*khlebnye talony na belyi khleb*] on the basis of the norm of fifty grams of matzah per one hundred grams of bread. The matzah may be sold fifteen days in advance . . . and as per the request of the buyers, when the matzah is sold it is permitted also to sell rye bread in advance for the same number of days.[26]

Until the late 1940s, then, the authorities appear to have allowed public institutions to bake matzah and to supply it in the baked-goods chains. The matzah supply was handled this way even during the famine year of 1942.

In December 1941, the USSR signed an agreement with the representative of the Polish government-in-exile to provide assistance to Polish citizens in the USSR, a deal that also involved the American Jewish Joint Distribution Committee. In this context the Joint sent about sixty tons of matzah from the United States to the USSR for Passover of 1942. This matzah was intended only for Polish refugees and did not actually reach the Jews native to the USSR.

Following this operation, the Lubavitcher Rebbe, who was based in New York, sent a letter to the Jewish organizations in many countries asking that at least 100,000 dollars be raised to aid the Jews of the USSR before Passover. But the Rebbe's appeal came too late to garner the amount requested, and as a result not enough matzah could be sent to the Soviet Jews. Nevertheless, some of the funds raised do seem to have reached the USSR, helping explain why the government food authority in Uzbekistan allocated a large amount of flour from the state fund for the baking of matzah before Passover 1942. In the city of Tashkent, four bakeries of the public food chain were made kosher and worked assiduously to supply matzah—not only to the Jews of Uzbekistan but also to Moscow and other cities.[27] For Passover of 1945, matzah was baked in the public institutions of Chernovtsy and sold at a price fixed by the congregation; some was also distributed to the poor. Likewise, for Passover of 1948 one of the city's cooperatives (*pishcheprodukt*) agreed to bake ten tons of matzah, but the authorities stressed that the flour for the matzah would be purchased by the cooperative and not by the congregation, so as to reduce the latter's involvement as much as possible. The trend toward reducing the congregation's involvement in matzah baking in the public or cooperative chain expanded with the increased persecution of religion in general and of the Jewish religion in particular toward the end of Stalin's regime. But during those years, the SRA also stressed that matzah was primarily an issue to be handled by the local institutions and not a matter of religion.[28]

During the late 1940s and early 1950s, the main effort was geared toward preventing the broader nonobservant public from demanding matzah for Passover. To this end the Ukraine SRA representative, in a special circular before Passover 1949, stated "that certain clerical elements of the Jewish religion are widely advertising the locations of matzah baking and are hanging notices of this in Russian and Yiddish. We must demand from the synagogue administrations to immediately take down such signs everywhere they are found."

Correspondingly, in 1949 the public institutions and cooperatives in Kiev, which had the largest Jewish population in Ukraine, did not agree to bake matzah.[29] In January 1951 the Minsk congregation applied to the SRA representative for permission to do so and received the usual reply: that it should reach agreements with the appropriate cooperatives. Two cooperatives indeed agreed to bake the matzah, but the Communist Party authority forbade them from honoring the agreement. In contrast with the failure experienced by the Minsk congregation, in 1952 the congregations of Vinnitsa, Chernigov, Zhitomir, and Rovno managed to reach matzah-baking agreements with the cooperatives, and we may assume that Jews in the neighboring districts bought their matzah from these sites. In the Kiev and Chernovtsy districts, by contrast, in 1952 no public bakery was found that was willing to bake matzah.[30]

In the late 1940s and early 1950s, therefore, no uniform policy appears to have governed the baking of matzah in public institutions or cooperatives. The public baking of matzah for Passover depended on the local conditions and the success of the Jews in persuading the local factories and local authorities to allow the baking to occur.

The level of interference in the baking of matzah did not change fundamentally during the years following Stalin's death. Thus, for example, the public bakeries in the city of Dnepropetrovsk refused to bake and sell matzah for Passover 1954 even though the chairman of the SRA had announced as follows in January 1954:

[B]ased on information received by the SRA from the management of the USSR Ministry of Commerce [*Upravlenie prodtovarami Ministerstva Torgovli SSSR*], there is no prohibition against selling matzah baked in the public bakeries and bread factories, if there is a demand for such.

Yet evidently this declaration was insufficient for the local food boards, which, while they agreed to sell matzah in their retail chain, maintained that they had no instructions from Moscow to bake them. And when instructions of this kind do seem to have been given, those same bodies maintained that they had no ovens free for such baking.[31]

For Jews, the main shift after Stalin's death was one of mood: many now dared to work more openly to win the needed permits for baking matzah. Whereas the Jews of Kiev had resigned themselves to the prohibition against baking matzah in 1952 and 1953, before Passover 1954, when the city authorities demonstrated the same inclination, the congregation sent emissaries to Moscow to demand that an immediate instruction be given to bake matzah from one hundred tons of state-fund flour. Ultimately an instruction was given to bake matzah from fifty tons of the state-fund flour and forty tons of given flour. Likewise, the Jews of Zhitomir complained loudly in response to the denial of their request to bake matzah, following which appropriate orders were given and matzah was baked for Passover of 1954.[32]

With the letup in the battle against religion, the central institutions tended increasingly to recommend or directly order that matzah be baked in the public chains or cooperatives; some of the latter, however, which probably didn't get the expected personal or factory kickbacks, resisted doing so. Thus, for example, when the rabbi of the Minsk congregation applied to have matzah baked for Passover of 1955, he was told that there would be no objection—but the bakery factories in the city did not want to comply.[33] The local bureaucracy, for its part, was reluctant to take responsibility and passed the subject from one official to the next, while never expressing a clear objection to the instructions from the central government. Such bureaucratic sidestepping is quite noticeable in the events in Kiev around Passover 1955. Early in that year congregation activists turned to the SRA representative to arrange for the supply of two hundred tons of matzah. The SRA representative passed the request to the secretary of the Ukrainian government, who responded that the local authorities must resolve the problem, all the while refusing to instruct them to do so. The SRA representative in Kiev then applied to the head of the propaganda department of the district Communist Party, who replied, "We don't oppose it; yet as this has to do with the city of Kiev, the decision must be made by the municipal party committee." Thus, the SRA representative turned to the city party's second secretary, who stressed that "there are big problems with matzah baking in Kiev, because the situation in the '[state] flour fund' is very bad." When presented, however, with the possibility of baking matzah from given flour, he replied that city hall must decide on such a proposition. The deputy mayor responded that "she had no objection to the baking of matzah in Kiev but would not give orders in this matter to the producing agencies as long as no order was received from above." The SRA representative then complained to the Ukraine party secretary on February 17, 1955, that the municipal and district agencies were avoiding taking responsibility and avoiding giving suitable instructions on matzah baking, although without objecting explicitly. Following this complaint, suitable instructions seem to have been given, and before Passover 1955, matzah was baked. That same year, the Zhmerinka congregation arranged with the bakery goods distribution network to bake matzah and sell it in the general chain, but toward Passover 1956 the authorities refused to allow the baking of matzah. The congregation complained to Moscow and on January 4, 1956, a directive was received from the SRA and from the USSR Ministry of Commerce that matzah baking should go forth. The cooperative's management, which naturally disagreed with the directive, did not dare refuse but instead sought to delay its implementation. Familiar with such a tactic, the congregation turned to Moscow on February 16 asking for an instruction to immediately commence the matzah baking; this request was passed to Ukraine, following which the matzah was baked.[34] In 1956 the Kiev authorities instructed the authorities of the town of Nikolaev to enable the public system to bake matzah, but this instruction was held up by the municipal agencies and issued only three days before Passover. In the same year, the Zhitomir congregation also came to an agreement with one of the cooperatives on matzah baking, with the congregation promising to pay to fix one of the factory's ovens for this purpose. But at the last moment the cooperative declared that the dough-rolling machine was broken. As a result, the Jews of Zhitomir and surrounding towns went without matzah that year.[35]

The Kiev congregation turned directly to the Ukrainian government, this time seeking an allocation of two hundred tons of flour from the state fund, or else the issuance of appropriate instructions to the city's seven bakeries to bake matzah from given flour. The request was granted, and the flour was provided from the state fund. Meanwhile the Zhitomir congregation, wiser for having experienced the previous year's avoidance tactic, was prepared for SRA foot-dragging in advance of Passover of 1957 and threatened to send a mission to Moscow. Eventually, a delegate from the congregation visited the Ukraine SRA representative, and the latter sent a letter to Zhitomir instructing that "possibilities be examined for baking matzah in the public factories in the cities [of] Zhitomir and Berdichev and for including this product in the March work plan." Still, the public bakeries refused to bake matzah, so the congregation bought flour, had it transported to towns where matzah baking was allowed, and brought the matzah back to Zhitomir and sold it to whoever wanted it. The complaint from the Nikolaev congregation as to its difficulties in getting matzah baked for Passover 1957 was answered by the SRA as follows: "We will pass the request from the religious association of the city of Nikolaev to our Ukraine representative whilst emphasizing that it would be best to answer the complaint positively if possible."[36] Returning to the scene in Kiev, the municipality instructed the baked-goods factories (*glavkhleb*) to bake two hundred tons of matzah. Over twenty-two days (March 5–27), some seventy-six tons were baked in Kiev, but on March 27 the Ukraine Ministry of Commerce ordered that matzah baking from state-fund flour cease immediately and be replaced by baking only from given flour. Considering the lack of access to given flour, matzah baking stopped; then, two weeks before Passover, the ministry delivered a new instruction reversing its previous order and allowing baking with state flour. Over those two weeks, some fifty tons of matzah were produced in the public bakeries. The resulting 125 tons of matzah were sold in eleven stores throughout Kiev.[37] In 1958, due to the generally positive attitude toward baking matzah in the public bakeries, matzah was produced in public factories in Kiev, L'vov, Dnepropetrovsk, Lugansk (Voroshilovgrad), Poltava, Odessa, Belgorod-Dnesterovskii, Balta, and Vinnitsa, as well as in other towns in Ukraine. In Moscow, too, several public bakeries made matzah (150 tons), but the supply apparently did not meet the demand. In Tbilisi, on the other hand, more matzah was baked than needed, and some of the surplus was sold in Moscow, available through the large chain of public stores.[38] Overall, it appears that 1957 saw no real shortage of matzah for Passover throughout the USSR.

In 1959 a negative shift appeared in the authorities' attitude toward matzah baking in public factories or cooperatives, stemming from both the antireligion campaign and the year's diminished grain yields.[39] The authorities thus tried to prohibit or greatly limit the amount of matzah baked in public factories and the supply of state-fund flour for this purpose. Yet precisely in this year, and through 1964, the USSR sought to consider more seriously the effects of Western public opinion. As a result, the authorities tried to allow the baking of matzah in cities more visible to the outside world. It is in this context that we can understand the positive response of the municipal trade director in Moscow to the request of the rabbi of the main synagogue for the allocation of 150 tons of state-fund flour for matzah baking. By contrast, the authorities in smaller towns that were less open to the outside world, such as Zhmerinka, Vinnitsa, and others, tried to prevent baking; it was only thanks to the vigorous efforts of the congregations that several such towns managed at the last minute to get permission for limited baking of matzah.[40]

So long as the battle against the Jewish faith intensified, the authorities sought to prevent the baking of matzah. Even as certain groups of Jews were able to arrange the baking of matzah in the framework of public cooperatives (e.g., in the town of Stalino), these cases were the exception.[41] A clear illustration of the situation was the refusal in 1963 of the Moscow bakeries to bake matzah for Passover "for technical reasons."[42]

Conflicts also arose at times between local authorities who took a more practical approach and party functionaries who considered it their duty to take a hard line on religion. Thus, for example, in Chernigov the congregation came to an agreement with the bakeries over the baking of matzah for Passover of 1959, and gained the support of the SRA representative and the district authorities, but the Communist Party district committee objected. The party committee even sent a complaint about the stance of the Chernigov district SRA representative to the Ukraine SRA representative in Kiev. One of the clearer illustrations of such a difference in attitude may be seen in the events leading to Passover 1959 in Kiev. The head of the congregation, S. I. Bardakh, made an official request to the city's vice mayor, who answered that "in Kiev all is ready for baking matzah, and matzah will be baked when the time comes." The vice mayor added in a discussion with the SRA representative that "the baked goods conglomerate . . . is prepared to bake matzah and [the vice mayor] herself is in favor of baking a limited quantity, but the city party committee . . . is opposed to matzah baking." The city party secretary declared outright that "matzah will not be baked in Kiev," and asked to have matzah removed from the list of products approved for production by the USSR Ministry of Food. He also demanded that packages of matzah received from the Israeli rabbinate be returned.[43] Part of the official apparatus in Kiev had difficulty accepting the relaxed Soviet antireligion policy as expressed through its permission to bake matzah in the public bakeries in 1955–1958; these agencies thus tended to take a stricter line whenever they felt a change in this policy was pending.

Baking matzah in the public bakeries had certain advantages over baking it in other ways. Much of this matzah was made from state-fund flour, which cost less than given flour. In addition, such matzah was sold in the general stores network, an advantage for Jews who for whatever reason preferred not to purchase it where matzah only was sold. But the congregations had a smaller involvement in the baking and selling of matzah under this arrangement, hence smaller profits; also there was less-strict oversight over the laws of kashrut.

PRIVATE ARRANGEMENTS CONNECTED TO THE CONGREGATION

In the 1930s, the religious associations were forbidden to engage in any economic activity; baking matzah for sale was considered economic activity even when the flour was provided by the customer. However, with the softening of antireligion policy, the local authorities tended to allow the formation of temporary bakeries for the production of matzah (*vremennye kustarnye pekarni*). Because the congregation was a main actor in the matzah supply, most initiators and organizers of such temporary groups or cooperatives came from among its ranks, and sometimes the baking and selling took place in the synagogue itself. As most matzah consumers were unaware of the legal distinction between the congregation and the temporary matzah bakery, they spoke of matzah baked by the congregation or even by the synagogue. Accordingly, we too shall use this phrase (but with quotation marks to distinguish the informal "congregation" from the official one). Because in the official sense the congregation was not considered the entity engaged in baking matzah, income from such baking was not listed in the congregation's account books. This made it possible for the authorities, when they so desired, to accuse the congregation of engaging in profiteering through the baking of matzah. Such an accusation was made often to extract concessions.

Unlike matzah made in the public factories, matzah baked by the "congregation" was subject to tax, which raised the price and gave the financial officials (*fininspektor*) considerable powers of extortion. This form of matzah baking became the most common following the cancellation of bread rationing, but it had also existed previously. In his response to the Khar'kov congregation's request, the SRA chairman wrote in March 1946: "So long as this regards the fulfillment of the religious needs of the Jews [with respect to] baking matzah this year we shall permit the religious congregations to bake matzah without interference using 'given flour' provided by the religious [people]."

And the chairman of the district commerce authority (*Oblotorgotdel*) of Kirovograd wrote on August 5, 1946, that "if the town bakeries do not have the facilities for baking matzah, the town authorities will issue a permit for temporary bakeries."[44]

Matzah baking by the "congregation" existed alongside production by public bakeries, whether because the latter did not meet the demand or because some Jews were willing to pay higher prices for matzah more rigorously supervised for kashrut. But when the government limited production in the public bakeries, the "congregations" turned into the main or the only supplier of matzah for Passover. Thus, for example, in Kiev in the years 1949–1951, the "congregation" paid an annual sum of 100,000–150,000 rubles in taxes for the matzah it baked.[45] Likewise, in Minsk in 1950 temporary baking cooperatives formed that sold matzah in private homes for twenty to twenty-five rubles a kilogram. After Passover the rabbi admitted that "there was enough matzah not only for the religious but also for the nonreligious." For Passover of 1951, the "congregation" of Dnepropetrovsk rented a house at the edge of town, built a special oven in it, and baked eighteen tons of matzah, which according to government estimates was meant to supply 2,200 families. For Passover of 1952, twenty-five tons of matzah were baked in the same way; and 3.25 rubles of tax were paid per kilogram—meaning that the "congregation" paid the state treasury more than 81,000 rubles that year for baking matzah.[46] The Priluki "congregation" was taxed 12,000 rubles in the same year for baking matzah, even though it claimed earnings of only 15,000 rubles. The Chernovtsy "congregation" baked (per its own account) only ten to twelve tons of matzah in 1952 but had to pay taxes of 200,000 rubles—that is, seventeen to twenty rubles for each kilo of matzah.[47] Before Passover of 1952 the Ukraine SRA representative announced that matzah baking would no longer be permitted in private temporary cooperatives (*chastnye arteli*), but rather only in the public network, while the Kiev municipality turned down the congregation's request to bake matzah, and in 1952 and 1953 matzah was not baked in an organized fashion in the city with the largest Jewish population in Ukraine.[48]

When the public bakeries in Dnepropetrovsk refused to bake matzah for Passover of 1954, the congregation appealed to Moscow and the verbal directive was issued "to allow [the 'congregation'] to bake matzah privately (*khozaist-vennym sposobom*) from 'given flour' and using equipment belonging to the congregation." A manager was appointed from the congregation—its deputy chairman—and twenty-five people worked for a week baking and selling the matzah. The revenue was supposed to be used, among other things, for re-furbishing the synagogue and "other goals." Though the baking was taxed by law, the city prosecutor decided to take the "congregation" to court for baking the matzah without a written permit, and the penalty was confiscation of the 60,536 rubles in the congregation's bank account, though legally the matzah had not been baked using these funds. The congregation appealed this sentence, and deliberations on the case continued at least until late 1957.[49]

Given the change in climate following Stalin's death, certain Jews in towns without an official congregation dared to bake matzah for sale in their homes, and the government, which knew about it, took no punitive measures at all.[50]

With the gradual relaxation of the antireligion struggle in the mid-1950s, signs emerged of a shift in the SRA's attitude toward baking matzah in "temporary cooperatives," known by most Soviet officials to be extensions of the congregations. This was the context for a letter by the Ukraine SRA representative in early 1954 to his superiors in Moscow:

> Since, according to laws of the ritual, the matzah must be baked in specially
> adapted bakeries, by special people and under supervision of a religious service
> provider, we do not think it would be expedient to burden the public factories

and cooperatives with such "production." . . . We, with the Kiev district sra representative . . . therefore suggest . . . that an agreement be granted the registered
association [i.e., the congregation] for a onetime baking of matzah from "given
flour" purchased by itself, while at the same time the sra representative will
transfer to the Finance Ministry a list of the persons engaged in baking matzah,
so as to levy income tax from them. . . . If a positive answer is received . . . the Kiev
religious association intends to bake matzah at four or five points in the city. . . .
We have informed the city and district [party] committee of Kiev of this. . . . We
request that [you] discuss this issue and give us appropriate instructions.[51]

This suggestion marks the first time, as far as the available documentation
indicates, that the congregation is mentioned as directly involved in baking
matzah, even if this arrangement is limited to one time. We may assume that
suggestions of this type were raised by other sra representatives and that they
led to a change in the predominant approach of the sra toward the role of the
congregation in baking matzah.

This new approach was apparent in the March 13, 1957, meeting between the
legal advisor of the sra in Moscow and the deputy director of the Tax Bureau
of the ussr Finance Ministry (*Zamestitel' nachal'nika Upravleniia nalogov Ministerstva sssr*). There, the sra representative asked that the Finance Ministry
issue instructions "not to impede the religious congregations from baking
matzah directly themselves, because it is about a ritual product for Passover."
In effect, the sra was declaring both that Passover matzah is part of religious
ritual and that the congregations could take charge of its baking. Minutes of
the meeting were forwarded to the Ukraine sra representative along with a
recommendation to discuss this subject with the Finance Ministry officials
in Ukraine.[52]

Having finally acknowledged that matzah is a part of Jewish religious ritual,
the sra needed to get involved in its supply. With the intercession of the sra
representative, the authorities allowed the Cherkassy congregation to bake
4,500 kilos of matzah in 1956. Furthermore, a letter from the sra in Moscow
to its Ukraine representative in 1957 noted:

In towns which do not allow this possibility of matzah baking [i.e., via the
"congregation"], the faithful travel to various cities in the neighboring districts,
turn to their relatives and receive by mail packets of matzah from hundreds of
kilometers away; they buy it, peddle in it, et cetera.[53]

Hence, allowing the "congregation" to bake matzah was viewed as better than its illicit transfer and sale. Thus in Minsk the "congregation" baked

24,000 kilos of matzah in 1958, and matzah was baked as well in Berdichev, Zhitomir, Nikolaev, and other Ukrainian cities.[54] That year the authorities allowed private associations for baking matzah to act in towns that didn't have registered congregations, such as Stalino, Khar'kov, Gomel', Mogilev, Borisov, Slutsk, and others.[55]

Baking matzah from given flour, after paying taxes, was not an illegal activity and was conducted rather openly and broadly until the late 1950s. However, at the end of the decade, two changes in Soviet policy impeded this means of matzah baking: (1) a vigorous regime-led campaign against the "black market" and (2) an intensified struggle against religion. Matzah baking was seen as a religious cover-up for commercial enterprise, and the people involved were referred to in SRA reports as "shady traders" (_temnye del'tsy_), "speculative elements" (_spekuliativnye elimenty_), and the like. This was the prevailing attitude when the Ukraine SRA representative wrote thus to the president of the republic before Passover of 1959:

> We view it as undesirable that the religious [people] be allowed to organize private bakeries and prepare matzah near the synagogues. . . . [N]ear these private bakeries Jewish clerics and speculator types gather to fan the flames of religious fanaticism and to profit personally at the expense of the religious portion of the population.

In this spirit the Ukraine SRA representative sent directions to the districts, demanding that they take appropriate steps to prevent organization for matzah baking.[56] This was the context in which many "congregations" were forbidden to bake matzah for Passover 1960–1961. Amid this climate, Western papers reported that eight Jews were arrested in Moscow in 1963 for baking matzah and accused of black-marketeering and illegal commerce in food.[57]

However, even during the antireligion campaign years, the baking of matzah at the initiative of the congregations, groups tied to them, and minyans did not cease. In Gomel', seven matzah-baking groups were active before Passover of 1959, some of which were recognized indirectly by the authorities once they paid their income tax. One of the heads of these groups, Rosa Rivina, was tried on marketeering charges and sentenced to two years in prison. In Rechitsa, matzah was baked that year in a similar fashion.[58] For Passover of 1961, a similar group formed in L'vov, but because the townspeople knew that the congregation was "in the spotlight," the congregation members didn't dare bake matzah without at least first making arrangements with the municipal financial officials. They therefore applied to the city's finance department, which replied that no permit was needed from the city department for short-term baking but rather one from the district authorities. In their application to the district authorities, the organizers expected to receive the reply typical of the time—that any Jew interested in having matzah was free to bake it at home—so their emphasis was as follows:

> A single individual, with the best of intentions, cannot bake matzah by himself: a group of no fewer than six persons and another four experts is required . . . for each baking station, because matzah baking necessitates special handling, that is, two kilos of dough must simultaneously be kneaded and passed from hand to hand . . . and within fifteen minutes the matzah comes out ready.

However, these arguments did not sway the district authorities, so the organizers appealed to the Ukrainian prime minister, who did not answer until the holiday had begun,[59] with the result that no organized baking of matzah seems to have happened in the city that year. In Chernovtsy, the authorities allowed the only remaining congregation in town to bake matzah for Passover 1961, but before the holiday in 1962 the heads of the congregation were summoned and warned not to do so again, and ordered also not to accept any matzah from Israel. In Moscow, matzah was baked for Passover 1962 by the "congregation" of the synagogue in Marina Roshcha, and for Passover 1963 two tons of matzah were baked by the "congregation" of the main synagogue.[60]

MATZAH BAKING IN THE HOME

The third form of matzah baking in the USSR occurred within the family framework. Certain families took this route either because the matzah from public sources did not satisfy them as being sufficiently kosher[61] or because of the growing official limitations on public matzah-baking. The authorities usually encouraged baking in private homes because such matzah was not destined to be consumed by a wider public. However, even in the years when the authorities did permit public matzah-baking, certain families baked it at home. In some locations (e.g., Chernovtsy and elsewhere), rabbis recommended home-baking[62] because they either believed this allowed for superior observance of kashrut or because they simply felt it was better to have matzah this way than not at all. Sometimes home-baked matzah was sold to neighbors and acquaintances, but home matzah-baking remained very limited in scope and had little significance for the wider Jewish public.

RECEIPT OF MATZAH FROM ABROAD

The fourth way of getting matzah to the Jews of the USSR was through importation in large quantities from abroad. Given that such an option required hundreds of tons of matzah to be shipped in an organized, planned fashion, the agreement of the government was clearly necessary. During Stalin's last years, with the Cold War at its peak, such an agreement would have been impossible, but the relaxation of interbloc tensions during Khrushchev's time perhaps may have allowed for such activity. Still, as far as we are aware, no such proposal was put forth by the large Jewish organizations; nor does evidence exist of pressure by the US authorities to link the matzah issue with that of produce sales to the USSR. Notably, in 1963, some fifty days before Passover, world Jewish leaders called upon their kinfolk to hold special prayers for the freedom of Soviet Jewry and twelve US Jewish organizations—religious and secular—appealed to the USSR via telegrams to Khrushchev and to the USSR ambassador to the United States, declaring their immediate willingness to fly large quantities of matzah at their own expense and to distribute it across the country. Their appeal met with no response, because the Soviet government viewed it, rightly, as mainly a propaganda ploy. On the other hand, for years the Israeli rabbinate and other Jewish bodies in various countries worked on sending small quantities of matzah, a gesture intended mostly to convey symbolism and not intended to meet even a fraction of the demand by the Jews of the Soviet Union. So we must look at this activity from the perspective of the developing connections between the Jews of the USSR and those of Israel and the world, which indeed is how Soviet Jewry and the Soviet authorities saw it.

Demand

The partial data available indicates that in 1958 the authorities tended to ease restrictions on the baking of matzah, with matzah baked in thirteen cities in Ukraine and at least four towns in Belorussia. In most locations, matzah was baked in the public bakeries. Isolated data on matzah-baking in the public network in four cities (Moscow, Kiev, Vinnitsa, and Zhmerinka) suggests that a total of 293,000 kilograms were baked in these cities during 1958.

Here the question arises: which part of the Jewish population was demanding matzah? The proportion of religiously observant Jews who did not eat bread during the Passover week was very small; nevertheless, a repeated shortage of matzah was evident because the demand came not only from the observant Jews. Quite a few Jews held a festive meal on the *Seder* night to commemorate the exodus from Egypt and the move from slavery to freedom; they strove to have matzah on their table at least for this one night. The Ukraine SRA representative described the situation in Kiev as follows:

Long queues snake wherever matzah is baked and sold. Profiteering sales of matzah at two to three times [the prices in the public shops] and the arrangement of private, illegal bakeries—all these show us that this religious custom is being maintained among the Jewish religious population, and that the demand for matzah remains high.[63]

Demand for matzah came also from Communist Party members, despite their supposedly strict ideological indoctrination. Thus, for example, the writer of the Ukrainian report mentions:

Most of the Jewish population consumes matzah, even the nonreligious and in some cases even Communists. In Kiev it was found that workers at the newspaper *Vechernyi Kiev* [Kiev Evening] the Communist Party members Alperin, Ozkar, Katzman, Rosen and Kaganovich—prepared some hundred kilos of matzah, exploiting their special status as newspaper workers. The matzah they purchased was kept in a storeroom of one of the furniture shops not far from the newspaper offices.[64]

Communists who bought matzah were dismissed from their posts; one of them (Alperin) was even removed from the party.[65] Along with showing the risks to party members, this case shows the extent to which matzah was in demand. As one journalist, a nonobservant Soviet Jew, put it to a Western correspondent: "I personally can manage without [matzah] but I'd like to have a few matzot to show my children and keep the tradition."[66] The demand extended to intermarried families, as was reported from Vinnitsa: "[N]ot only religious Jews bought matzah but also secular ones including Russians and Ukrainians from mixed families (with only the husband or the wife being Jewish)."[67]

In summary we may assert that the baking of matzah was never absolutely prohibited in the USSR, and that restrictions depended on a combination of four factors: (1) the Soviet attitude toward religion in general and toward the Jewish religion in particular at any given time; (2) the scarcity or abundance of flour and its products in particular years; (3) the attitude of the various local authorities directly or indirectly involved in matzah baking; and (4) the ability of the congregations in various locations to find appropriate channels for the supply of matzah, however partial, to the broader Jewish population.

CHAPTER FOURTEEN

Holiday Observance in the Private Sphere

The Jewish holidays were times when a special religious atmosphere was felt: the synagogue was painted and repaired, extra seats were added, and so on. Accordingly, in the 1920s and 1930s, the Soviet media tended to ramp up its antireligion propaganda during the holidays. Where for Christians the propaganda intensified on the eves of Christmas and Easter, for Jews this happened on the eves of the High Holidays and Sukkot (which officials called the "Jewish autumn festivals," *osennye prazdniki*) and on the eve of Passover. After the war, this intensification of antireligion activity was carried out less by the media and more by the SRA. Heightened attention was paid to religious activity and the behavior of the population in the SRA meetings around the holidays, and special reports were issued on the subject. The archival material thus affords us a peek at the behavior of part of the Jewish population and the attitude of the authorities in response to this behavior.

In any treatment of Jewish observance of the holidays, a distinction should be made, to the extent possible, between the public aspect and the private-family aspect. The public aspect found expression primarily in visits to synagogues and minyans and in the communal arrangements for Passover matzah baking. In this chapter we shall try to focus on the private-family aspect, which by its nature was kept hidden, especially from agencies that persecuted religion, and is thus reflected only in the most partial way in the internal Soviet documentation. Nevertheless, even this material suffices to broaden the characterization of religion in the communal experience of the Jews of the USSR in the period in question. We shall focus here on two components of the picture: (1) workplace behavior during the holidays and (2) different ways of celebration of the Jewish holidays within the family or other contexts.

Holidays, on the most basic level, are days of rest. Indeed, the official obligation to work on Shabbat and holidays troubled quite a few Jews in various countries, and a struggle for the right to choose a day of rest was waged in Russia and other countries over dozens of years. Freedom to choose one's day of rest was advocated by all the Jewish political parties throughout Eastern Europe, including nonreligious ones like the Bund. In the Soviet Union—from its outset an antireligious country that viewed rest on Shabbat as a manifestation of a Jewish-religious worldview—the issue took on special significance. Yet the problem was not so acute in the 1920s so long as there were still factories and private workplaces that could elect to close on Shabbat or holidays. This state of affairs changed in the 1930s, when nearly the entire Soviet economy became state-run; the various cooperatives (*arteli*) were no different in this respect from the state-run factories and institutions. Moreover, the obligation to go to work was imposed in effect on the entire working-age population: unemployment was considered parasitism and incurred a range of punishments. This helps explain why in the 1930s, and even more so after wwii, nearly all Jews worked on Shabbat, except for an isolated few who managed to evade doing so by various means. In Berdichev, for example, in the first postwar years, a certain cooperative was headed by a Communist Party member named Gikman. Most or all of this cooperative's workers were Jews, and by general agreement of labor and management the day of rest was transferred from Sunday to Saturday.[1] Yet this was an unusual case in the European ussr (although less uncommon in the Central Asia and Caucasus regions) and it lasted relatively briefly. Yet the Jewish holidays—when, like Shabbat, work was prohibited for observant Jews—took up only a few days a year, days often unknown to the local authorities, making it easier for Jews to evade work on them.

The simplest and most direct way of not working, at least on Rosh Hashana and Yom Kippur, was to ask permission to take unpaid leave or to use vacation days. Indeed in the Chernovtsy district, the rabbis' council applied to the sra representative on August 17, 1945, asking that factories and institutions announce that Jewish workers interested in taking leaves of absence be free to do so on both days of Rosh Hashana and on Yom Kippur. This request, reflecting ignorance of the realities in the Soviet Union, was of course rejected out of hand.[2] Yet we nevertheless find, in the first years following the war, quite a few cases in which Jews requested and were granted leave for at least one day of the Jewish holidays. A number of official institutions tended in those years to respond favorably to such requests, either because they did not identify an ethnic motivation or because they just chose to look the other way. Thus, for instance, in the town of Bershad' in 1952 the authorities ignored the warnings of agencies regarding Passover and granted leaves of absence for many of the Jews who sought them.[3] To minimize this phenomenon, sra representatives sent out circulars noting the dates of the Jewish holidays and asking that leave not be granted for those days.[4]

The more pressure grew to not grant Jews vacation time during the holidays, the more Jews made efforts to take sick leaves on those days. Quite a few Jews thus sought such authorizations from doctors, especially for Yom Kippur. So long as the battle against the Jewish faith remained relatively moderate, the authorities tended to ignore such requests in their internal correspondence, but once the battle intensified in the late 1940s and early 1950s, the authorities began to pay attention. Thus, for instance, the authorities in Zhmerinka, where the Jewish population numbered four or five thousand, discovered that on the last day of Passover 1952 (the day when a memorial service is held), 310 Jews "fell ill." These were not just workers in consumer cooperatives but also railroad workers, pharmaceutical workers, and so forth. Similar reports were made in Bershad'.[5] These examples indeed come from small communities, and it is unclear whether the phenomenon was typical in larger towns as well.

Jews were often employed in the various service-sector branches: shops, kiosks, stalls for clothing-repair, and so forth. These businesses had the right to choose a day or several days a year when they were permitted to be shut for a "cleaning day" (sanitarnyi den'). In businesses that had many Jewish employees, the workers, with the agreement of management, tended to choose Rosh Hashana and even more so Yom Kippur as a day on which the factory store would be closed; the authorities often looked the other way at such decisions. Yet with the intensification of the antireligion policy, an order was given to "representatives of the SRA in the districts . . . to examine whether there are cases of absenteeism on holidays."[6] Following this instruction, the SRA representative for Latvia reported that the director of a cooperative in the town of Krustpils, a Communist Party member named Lucats, had closed his establishment and sent workers home to celebrate the holiday, and that the directors of the workers' supplies unit (Otdel Rabochego Snabzheniia, or ORS) of the railroad and the consumer cooperative had done the same.[7]

An SRA representative reported that examination of three out of the six subdistricts (raiony) in the city of Odessa revealed that "thirty-five commercial stations were partially or completely inactive on Yom Kippur of 1949." The director of the commerce department in the city thus ordered that charges be brought against all those who failed to work on Yom Kippur, in accordance with USSR legislation of June 26, 1940, prohibiting unexplained work absences. A response to this order was signed by one of the heads of a furniture manufacture and sales cooperative (Prommebel'), Shekhter by name, retroactively declaring October 3 (that is, Yom Kippur) as sanitarnyi den—a day of rest.

Skipping work wasn't the only way in which people marked the holiday. Thus, for example, the SRA representative for Kiev noted that "when I went to political studies classes for Marxism-Leninism at the university on the eve of October 3 [Yom Kippur] I noticed that none of the Jewish students was present."[8] The people in question here were not religious and almost certainly not elderly; rather, they were Jewish youths seeking to express their identification with the memorialization of Babi Yar and with the protest against antisemitic policy. The SRA representative reported, with some exaggeration, that "on Yom Kippur, life in Zhitomir and other towns fell silent . . . the stalls, the shops, and the kiosks of various institutions in the market were closed."[9]

The SRA representative for the Bobruisk district observed that on Passover of 1951 in the district's capital city:

[M]any of the commercial stations [*torgovye tochki*] were closed, especially stalls and kiosks . . . whose managers were Jews. . . . All this was done with the pretext of a day of rest. . . . The managers of trade institutions were summoned by the district authorities [*oblispolkom*], and the schedule [*grafik*] of rest-days was examined for those commercial stations.[10]

In Kiev on Yom Kippur of 1951, "thirty-four commercial stations [were closed] because their workers were at synagogue that day." A committee studying the Yom Kippur problem in Chernovtsy found that "thirty-three workshops for the service of the public [*Masterskie bytovogo obsluzhivaniia*] were out of operation, and closed; fifty additional workshops had the partial presence of workers, the majority of whom came to work in holiday attire and moved about without doing a thing."

In addition, thirty-three commercial stations were closed that year in Belaia Tser'kov.[11] In Odessa, thirty-eight stores and shops (*larek*) were closed. In Chernigov, thirty-three workshops serving the public were closed and fifty others functioned only in part. A similar picture obtained in Zhitomir, where twenty-four commercial stalls and wine stores were shut on Yom Kippur. Even during Stalin's final years, then, Jews in large numbers appear to have found ways of skipping work on the Jewish holidays, especially Yom Kippur, or of working only partially or coming in festive attire to show identification with the holiday. Here we are not speaking of the elderly: retirement age was sixty for men and fifty-five for women. In turn, the SRA tried hard to influence local authorities and workplaces to prevent Jewish absenteeism on the holidays, which they defined as an infringement of "work discipline."[12]

This phenomenon of missing work on the holidays expanded after Stalin's death, especially after the formal announcement of the release of the doctors. In certain towns, Jews now even dared to keep their children home from school; thus, for example, a report from a school in Chernovtsy states that on Passover of 1954 several hundred Jewish children did not show up for school. Yet during this period, the SRA preferred to ignore the phenomenon and noted in its correspondence that "facts have not been discovered of violations of state work discipline by the religious."[13] Furthermore, even when presented with evidence of absenteeism from work on Jewish holidays, SRA officials treated the issue more leniently than they had in previous periods.[14] The reports during the thaw differed substantially from those of the previous period, as reflected by the following:

> During the holidays [of 1957] mass violations of work-discipline by the religious were not noted. Nevertheless in certain cities—Kiev, Vinnitsa, Zhitomir, Chernovtsy and others—there were such phenomena as officials of commercial networks and production cooperatives leaving their work on various pretexts and who were to be found at the synagogues and minyans.

The report author then relates that in Dubovoe (Zakarpat'e district), the bread supply was insufficient owing to the failure of Jews to come to work. In this district's settlements of Iasinia and Tiachevo, some of the cafeterias and workshops were closed on the High Holidays. The excuse was that repairs were being made to the establishments; as a result, food was not supplied to some of the transportation workers and those in the carpentry factory. In Malin (Zhitomir district), nearly all the stalls in the market were closed.[15]

As noted, Jews who for one reason or another did not wish to miss work on the Jewish holidays sometimes marked the dates by coming to work in festive clothing.[16]

When it came to children observing the holidays, even during this suppos- edly liberal period, the authorities took special notice. By the 1920s, a practice had taken root whereby the authorities would relay special instructions to the schools to take extra care to inform on Jewish children who did not come to school on the religious holidays. To that end it became customary to examine the attendance records from time to time; and when word spread, in the town of Ovruch (Zhitomir district), that many Jewish children were not attending the two respective schools on Yom Kippur (one serving ten grades, the other seven), the authorities asked to see the attendance sheets. This examination revealed that the teachers had "accidentally" missed taking attendance that day.[17] Here an understanding of sorts was reached between the Jewish teachers, who certainly were not religious in the typical sense of the word, and parents who did not send their children to school on Yom Kippur.

Failure to appear for work on the holiday or to send children to school, or even wearing the festive holiday attire, was not a clandestine behavior even if relatively few dared act in this way. Since such phenomena were more com- mon in the small towns, where every unusual behavior aroused notice, they were evidently known to the local authorities, who on the whole preferred to ignore them.[18] No less important, this behavior by a few granted many Jews an inner sense that these were holidays, even if they themselves did not give public expression to the fact.

With the increasingly strident antireligion policy of the late fifties and early sixties, the SRA officials, Communist Party apparatchiks, and various agencies again intensified their efforts to halt various practices associated with the holidays. Indeed, before the High Holidays of 1960 the SRA sent a special memorandum to party secretaries and mayors in Chernovtsy and Khotin ordering that they ensure no repetition occurred of such behavior as

> Jews coming to work in festive attire . . . and all day long [on Yom Kippur] not working and only pretending to do so by their presence. During work hours many of the Jews visit . . . the synagogue where they are to be found for an hour or two, after which they go back to work. They disguise their departure from the workplace and going to synagogue with claims that they went to the managers, the office and so forth.[19]

Such a passage shows that absenteeism, or other ways of marking the Jewish holidays in the work context, was a sufficiently widespread phenomenon and not one confined to the tiny groups of observant Jews who found sundry methods to avoid work on Saturdays as well. The motivations for such behavior doubtless varied from person to person but presumably included a mixture of memories from childhood, a desire to mark or identify with the tradition of a father or grandfather murdered in the Holocaust, and perhaps an intent to express ethnic identity by this means. Yet even Jews who for whatever reason were prevented from making such public identifications by taking a leave of absence made efforts to note the holidays within the family circle.

Many Jewish families celebrated the autumn holidays with a feast, which took place on the night of Rosh Hashana or one of the evenings near it. Thus, on the days before the holidays a special liveliness filled the shops. The Belorussia SRA representative, for instance, noted that on the eve of the holidays of 1949 and on the holidays themselves, the Jewish population of Gomel' purchased baked goods and delicacies and ordered special foods in the restaurants. An SRA official who conversed with the manager of the town market reported the manager's comment that the autumn holidays saw an increase in purchases by Jews of chickens, geese, fish, and calf meat. On these days, according to the manager, prices rose three- to fivefold for fowl, fish, and beef.[20]

The SRA representative for the Pinsk district found it worth mentioning that "[O]n September 17 and 18 [1953] a non-Jew could not buy fowl in the market since all the fowl had been bought by Jews and slaughtered by Fridman the slaughterer. A man who lives near the slaughterer attested that over a hundred birds were slaughtered." Another SRA representative noted in 1955 that in the markets of Minsk, Borisov and Slutsk, "prices doubled for fish, fowl and beef due to the great demand for them by local Jews."[21] Even if these reports seem to be blaming Jews for the rising prices and shortages of certain market products, they also indicate that many Jews were marking the holidays in some special way. The party secretary of Mozir attested that on the major holidays of 1949, "Jews of middle and advanced age wore their best clothes on the holiday." Meanwhile, the SRA representative in Belorussia noted in 1954 that "it's not just elderly Jews who celebrate religious holidays, as we tend to believe, but also Jews of other ages. This is manifest among other things in the fact that in many towns on the evening of the holiday a large number of people of the Jewish ethnicity walk about in the streets dressed in holiday attire." The SRA representative for the Mogilev district stressed in 1955 that during the holidays Jews were dressed in special finery; his colleague in the Vinnitsa district noted that during the holidays of 1958, people "strolled about the streets of town (the nonreligious too) in festive attire."[22] From Minsk came the report that "on the religious autumn holidays [of 1957] quite a few Jews turned out to stroll dressed in their fanciest holiday clothes." And the atmosphere in Gomel' on Simchat Torah of 1949 was described by the SRA representative thus:

> On the streets . . . one could see Jews strolling in a festive and happy mood, especially older people. . . . Jews walked about arm in arm, spoke and sang in Yiddish. On meeting them I asked why they were in such good spirits, and one answered me: "For us it is now a happy holiday [Simchat Torah]." Religious Jews are happy on this holiday and also drink.[23]

Lists of the food items purchased before the "autumn Jewish holidays," as well as accounts of the behavior of Jews during the holidays, make clear that not just observant Jews sought to mark the holidays but also broad swaths of the Jewish public, including many avowed atheists.

The holiday of Passover held a special place in Jewish family life, as was noted in a Soviet antireligious article of 1930: "Observance of the Pascal holiday is generally the final thread binding the freethinking Jew who is distancing himself from religion to the Jewish tradition." A Soviet newspaper described the atmosphere on Passover of 1939 in one of the Jewish kolkhozes of Belorussia as follows:

> The first day of Passover . . . falls on the first day of the planting season. . . . [A]ll members of the kolkhoz, the elderly included, left for work . . . yet in the kolkhoz

households Passover was celebrated. At the table sat . . . the extended family and the table was set with bread and matzah [a practice common in Israel and its kibbutzim as well].[24]

Indeed, the custom of family gatherings on the Seder night was retained after the Holocaust. In certain communities, mainly small ones, public Seders were even conducted in the synagogues. Yet with the intensification of the antireligion policy, the SRA chairman demanded, in March 1950, that congregation heads be summoned and warned "not to conduct the Passover Seder [*paschal'naia trapeza*] in the synagogue."[25] The public Seders seem to have stopped in the wake of such threats, but the practice of holding a festive meal in the family setting continued.

Many Jewish families considered it their duty to hold a festive meal to which relatives and acquaintances were invited, and took care to have matzah on the table. As a longstanding resident of the town of Ufa attested: "To this day I gather all my children and grandchildren to the Passover Seder and prohibit them at least for this evening from eating bread."[26] Even families that saved every penny at other times during the year adorned the holiday table with the finest foods, whatever the cost. On the Seder night, special baked goods would accompany matzah, as well as fish and foul. In the markets of towns with a large Jewish population, a special bustle was felt on the eve of Passover—and all the more so when the holiday fell close to Easter. As the Bobruisk district SRA reported in 1951: "Preparations for the religious holiday of Passover among the Jewish population of the town of Bobruisk began in the second half of the month of April . . . the Jewish population has begun to buy fowl, eggs, fish and so forth." The atmosphere in Minsk prior to Passover of 1955, where (according to the 1959 census) there were close to 40,000 Jews (8 percent of the total population), was described by the SRA representative as follows:

> The holiday atmosphere among the religious Jews [in town] can be confirmed also in that on the eve of Passover there was a clear rise in purchases by Jews in the market of wheat flour [apparently for baking matzah], oil, fresh fish, fowl, and other products called "kosher." . . . [I had] a conversation with the market manager of the town of Borisov . . . who told [me] that there is great demand in the market for fowl and fresh fish. . . . On the days of the Passover holiday one notices that many Jews have gone out to stroll, wearing festive attire.[27]

On the eve of Passover of 1958, Jews in the market of Gomel' purchased much fowl, noted the district SRA representative, and "on these days there was a line of fifteen to twenty women holding birds in their hands in the courtyard of

Sorkin [the slaughterer]. . . . The apartments in which religious Jews live have candles lit in them (on the Seder eve)." Similarly, the SRA representative's account of the days before Passover of 1959 tells that the courtyard "constantly had a line of twenty to thirty people." Yet unlike the previous year, the person took care to note, for slaughtering a bird the *shochet* demanded two rubles.[28] Likewise, the foreign reporters who visited on the eve of Passover of 1963 noted that, in the shops of Moscow in neighborhoods with many Jewish residents, one felt the particular bustle of holiday shoppers.[29] All the accounts thus indicate that celebration of this holiday was not confined to observant Jews, whose numbers were quite small, but rather encompassed broad circles of the Jewish public who held festive Seder meals in their homes.

In an autobiographical novel, the Russian-Jewish author Iurii Karabchevskii (b. 1938) describes a Seder held in his grandfather's home in Moscow: "They took out the furniture, arranged the chairs, assembled all the relatives; Grandfather was at the center of attention. It was time for the first Seder when the entire family would assemble. And indeed this was a great holiday, a holiday of general interest, a day of consolidation."[30]

From the material presented in this chapter, we can assert that quite substantial portions of the Jewish population in the Soviet Union tried, at least within the family realm, to preserve certain remnants of the Jewish tradition, at least during the holidays.

CHAPTER FIFTEEN

Charity and the Jewish Needy

The practice of giving aid to the poor, indigent, ill, and needy of various sorts is well rooted in Jewish tradition, and before the Revolution thousands of charitable organizations operated across Russia. Quite a few were connected with a synagogue, directly or indirectly. Yet after the Bolsheviks' seizure of power, the Commissary for Justice of Russia ruled as follows on August 24, 1918:

> All societies that limit membership to those of a single religion and that use the guise of charity will be closed. . . . Their aim is to extend direct aid and support to a particular religion. . . . And so will those that do not hide their religious purpose . . . and expend their monies on religious aims.[1]

This order was aimed at harming the religious institutions and limiting their influence on the population through the giving of charity; yet the ruling, like many others of those years, was mainly declarative in nature and had only a limited effect in practice. During the great famine of 1921, the All-Russian Central Executive Committee (VtsIK) announced in December that religious associations had the right to collect funds to aid the hungry. Jews too were permitted to establish charitable organizations in the 1920s, such as one named the Society for the Supervision and Care of the Jewish Elderly, Ill, and Street Children.[2] These and similar organizations were in effect the successors of the prerevolutionary charitable organizations, and the latter incarnations, too, were connected (if indirectly) with the synagogue.

The question of the involvement of religious entities in charitable acts came up explicitly in the mid-1920s, when the battle against religion had relaxed somewhat. During this time a religious association of the Greek Orthodox Church in Rostov-on-Don sought permission from the Executive Committee of the Russian Soviet Republic to engage in charitable activity. In May 1925, the Commissar of Justice responded that "since one of the commandments of the Christian religion is the performance of good deeds . . . especially the extension of material aid to their coreligionists, or charity," there is no reason why the religious associations should not engage in such. Moreover, charitable societies were cited as the preferred agents of such activity, as done among the Jews. Notwithstanding the twisted language of the response, the regime seems

to have acknowledged, during this period, the role of charity as a religious obligation and the role of religious associations to deliver it, even if through an
organ nominally separate from the religious entities.[3] Yet this approach—which
in effect allowed religious associations including congregations to engage in
charity work—underwent a fundamental change in the late 1920s.

As the decade turned, all formerly legal Jewish charitable societies were dissolved, and in the 1930s the authorities argued that no poor people required
assistance in the USSR, and that if they did, the state would provide for them.
Furthermore, acts of charity (*blagotvoritel'nost*) were deemed unnecessary—especially those of religious entities whose entire purpose was to increase their
influence on the public. Correspondingly, the 1929 laws on religious affairs did
not permit religious entities to engage in charity activity. These laws did not
mean that charitable acts ceased entirely in the 1930s—now, however, such
acts seem to have been done by individuals without the involvement, direct
or indirect, of congregations.

The picture changed once again during the Second World War, as a result
both of the shift in Soviet policy on religion and of the difficult economic
situation. After the war, vast numbers of Soviet subjects were in need, and
famine ravaged. In the liberated areas of Ukraine, famine, in some instances,
led to cannibalism. Because of the Holocaust, hundreds of thousands of Jewish
orphans, widows, people with handicaps, and the like had urgent needs. Given
the dire conditions throughout Eastern Europe, many Jewish organizations,
foremost of which was the American Jewish Joint Distribution Committee
(JDC, aka "the Joint"), launched widespread welfare projects in these countries.
The USSR did not permit such organizations to operate in its lands, but the
authorities also did not prevent various organizations from sending food to
private individuals and even to congregations. The JDC thus orchestrated a
broad system of food shipments from Tehran to the Soviet Union. In the United
States, the post-Holocaust years also saw a great revival of *landsmanschaftn*
who considered it their duty to send food packages to their communities of
origin. Quite a few private individuals[4] who turned to the congregation in the
USSR to locate relatives also themselves felt obligated to aid the congregation by
sending food packages. Certain congregations, mainly in territories annexed to
the USSR during WWII, and especially those of L'vov and Chernovtsy, received
thousands of packages in the first years after the liberation, some of which were
distributed to the needy. Others were sold, with the proceeds going to charity:
22 percent of the food packages that reached the L'vov congregation went to
the Jewish poor and needy, 18 percent went to those injured during the war
(including non-Jewish officers), 12 percent went to orphans and families who

lost their income-earner through service in the Red Army, 11 percent went to Jewish university students, 10 percent went to veterans of the Red Army and ex-partisans, 4 percent went to Jews who returned from Nazi concentration camps, and 2 percent went to the families of Jewish officers who were still serving in the Red Army.[5]

Charity work on a large scale was not limited to those congregations that received packages from abroad. Due to the growing feelings of fraternity among Jews following the Holocaust, Jews from many towns within the USSR contributed to the congregations in order to help their brothers. Some congregations even held public events (like cantorial evenings) to raise funds for the charities.[6] Donations were collected penny by penny from numerous Jews, alongside contributions of large sums. Thus, for example, on the eve of Passover 1946, Professor Zarakhovich of Khar'kov donated 10,000 rubles for charitable purposes to the congregation of Leningrad, which purchased a large quantity of potatoes and distributed it to Jews in need.[7] Likewise, Moscow's main synagogue was able to raise some 120,000 rubles for charity in 1946, which it distributed monthly to Jews in need. Such practices were likewise followed in those years by most other congregations that operated legally in the USSR. The authorities perceived charity as a legitimate function of the congregations, which listed related expenses openly in their account books.[8] As soon as 1946, however, a change began to be felt in Soviet policy toward this sort of activity.[9]

After the appointment of Shlomo Shlifer as rabbi of Moscow's main synagogue, the SRA representative told the rabbi that the congregation's charity box, put in place by his predecessor, Shmuel Chubrutskii, needed to be removed. If synagogue attendees wanted to contribute to charity, they could do so, but funds thus collected should be transferred to the state social welfare agency, which would distribute them to the needy without ethnic distinction. In response, the rabbi said that some people contribute specifically to the congregation out of a wish to aid their brethren; he sought a delay of a month for the elimination of the charity box. The ultimate removal of the charity box caused great resentment among the worshipers, who accused the rabbi of an inability to stand up to the authorities, unlike his predecessor. On December 26, 1946, the rabbi thus met with an SRA official and complained that the removal of the charity box was undermining his authority in the congregation. To this claim, the official replied:

> Since charity is one of the principles [*dogmat*] of the Jewish religion, the soviet does not object if funds collected by the synagogue as voluntary contributions of

the religious for this purpose . . . shall be transferred to a special organization for their distribution to the needy which by law is designated for doing so [i.e., the welfare ministry].[10]

The official was thus accepting the rabbi's argument that charity is a basic religious commandment but rejecting his specific request that aid be distributed to the needy through the congregation, since that would be a means for the congregation and religion to have an influence on the public. Accordingly, bowing to the pressure from the authorities, the Moscow congregation ended its formal use of a charity collection box.

In several provincial towns, by contrast, charity collection boxes of various sorts lasted a few years longer. In 1946, the Zhitomir congregation had a collection box that was used "systematically for the collection of means amongst wealthy and influential Jews: doctors, professors . . . as well as other responsible employees in the Soviet apparatus." The Mozir congregation distributed 200–250 rubles per month to needy Jewish families, aside from the 9,000 rubles it raised for the Red Cross to aid children orphaned during WWII. In Novograd-Volynskii, "between 1946 and 1948 the congregation arranged a systematic raising of funds for charitable purposes to ethnic standards. Until 1948, there was a charity box in the Vinnitsa congregation, labeled *bikur holim* (visitations to the sick), the funds from which went to aid the needy. In early 1948, however, the Vinnitsa district SRA representative ordered that "the gathering of funds to aid the poor, *tsedaka* [the Hebrew word was spelled in Cyrillic letters], be prohibited absolutely."[11] Even so, individual congregations did not hasten to give up this activity. Thus, for instance, before the High Holidays of 1950, the Nikolaev congregation sought donations from Jewish homes to aid the poor and the sick.[12] We may assume that other congregations did the same. The Berdichev congregation, for example, was accused of maintaining a collection box "for the aid to impoverished Jewish families"; this was one of the points supposedly used by the authorities to justify the congregation's dissolution. Likewise, until 1951 the Ashkenazi congregation of Tashkent distributed 13,000 rubles each month to needy Jews in and around town, despite an explicit prohibition on such a practice. And the charity and mutual support fund of the Kiev congregation, headed by Itsik Goichman, held 12,000 rubles in 1952.[13]

With *tsedaka* being explicitly forbidden, the language of the SRA on this subject grew increasingly harsh. Thus, in 1952 an SRA representative complained to his superior in Moscow that "on Yom Kippur [the Jews] grant donations to 'the poor' and contribute to *tsedaka*, and this is nothing more than an expression of Jewish nationalism and maybe even Zionism."[14]

In the years when the antireligion struggle eased, charitable activity almost certainly increased anew, supplemented by donations of tourists from abroad. Yet despite the change in climate, the SRA's position altered relatively little. For their part, congregations now also sought to assist those liberated from the gulag, among them religious Jews. Thus, for example, Rabbi Yaakov Yosef Berger of Minsk noted that during his absence from the synagogue, funds had been collected to assist "nationalists" arrested in 1950. Quite a few of those released were completely destitute and often had no families to assist them. In turn, some asked for the help of the congregations, many of which rose to the challenge. In these years, fundraising for charity also expanded. Thus it was reported that in 1957 activists of the Zhitomir congregation went house to house to collect funds for the aid of Jews in need.[15] Yet unlike in the 1940s, semiofficial charity boxes no longer dwelled in the synagogues; charity giving took place through private donations by rabbis and individuals.[16]

As part of the antireligion campaign of the late 1950s and early 1960s, the persecution of charities increased. Likewise, the Communist Party's antireligion resolutions of 1960 explicitly mentioned the giving of *tsedaka* as among the activities violating Soviet law.[17] In line with this ruling, one of the accusations against the directorship of the Korosten' congregation in 1962, and that led to its removal, was that it engaged in charity. The new management, too, was ultimately accused of the "sin" of running a sort of charitable organization called Bread for the Poor, which solicited donations from visitors to the cemetery.[18]

Collection of funds and distribution to needy families picked up during the periods before the autumn holidays and Passover. Aid even came in traditional forms, such as *maot hittim* ("wheat coins") or *kimcha depischa* (Passover flour). In the first postwar years, many congregations saw it as their duty to carry out the mitzvah of *kimcha depischa* by distributing matzah to the needy, despite the severe rationing of flour at the time. Thus, for example, when matzah was baked in the municipal facilities of Chernovtsy for Passover of 1945, the rabbis council issued special authorizations that matzah should be given without charge to Jews in need, and the official bakeries honored these authorizations. In this context, one can understand why the Khar'kov congregation sent a telegram to Stalin in advance of Passover of 1947, requesting that nine tons of flour from the "state fund" be allocated for matzah to be distributed to Jews in need. The SRA chairman responded to this request, stating that "the distribution of matzah to the Jewish poor by the congregation falls into the category of charity, which the congregation does not need to be engaging in. And consequently there is no room for allocating flour [for this purpose]."[19] The Berdichev congregation, like some others, distributed matzah to the needy without interference from the authorities. Yet on the eve of Passover 1948, the Ukraine SRA representative issued a directive that "the gathering of funds, *maot hittim* [the Hebrew words are spelled out in Cyrillic], for the sake of aid to the 'poor' is not to be permitted in any way." A memorandum to the same effect was sent by the SRA chairman to all his district subordinates before Passover 1950.[20] In the early 1950s, accordingly, the majority of congregations refrained from openly continuing the practice of *kimcha depischa*. Toward the end of the decade, though, with the easing of the antireligion strictures, the practice resurfaced. Thus, for example, before Passover of 1957 the Zhitomir congregation distributed two or three kilograms of matzah to every Jewish family in need, even though that year the matzah was not baked in town but rather imported from other cities.[21] In other towns, too, *kimcha depischa* was almost certainly distributed by congregations to needy families. These acts were disguised in various ways, although the authorities could identify them when needed as violations of Soviet regulations on religious affairs.

The small space into which permissible religious activity in the USSR was confined kept the congregation from fulfilling one of Judaism's important commandments—charity. All charity had to be arranged clandestinely, and the authorities could at any time accuse those involved with running "black market operations," which were against the law and could be used to dissolve the congregation and close the synagogue. All those involved, even the donors, thus risked incurring punishment. Even so, quite a few Jews saw it as their duty to aid their brethren in need. The funding of charitable activity, whether by continuous monthly support or only before the holidays, had the participation of many Jews. It was in this way, in the difficult years following the Holocaust, that thousands of Jewish families were saved.

CHAPTER SIXTEEN

Ritual Baths and Circumcision

Ritual Baths (Mikvas)

Until the Revolution, almost every town with a Jewish population had at least one ritual purification bath. But during the religious persecutions of the 1920s and 1930s, most of the *mikvas* were shut down on various pretexts, the most common of which was the claim, not entirely untrue, that they did not meet sanitation standards. Yet even in cases in which congregations were ready to remodel the baths so as to meet sanitary requirements, the authorities, on the whole, did not permit this. The few *mikvas* that still existed in the Soviet Union during the interwar period, as well as the much larger number in the annexed areas, were destroyed almost to the last; some of the remainder were converted to municipal bathhouses. To skirt the prohibitions, some Jews built *mikvas* in private courtyards, which would serve not only family members but also the few others who sought *mikva* purification.[1]

Shortly after the liberation of Soviet territories from Nazi occupation and the return of Jews to their former communities, certain congregations made efforts to install *mikvas*. The installation of new *mikvas* that could meet sanitary requirements was especially difficult at least for the first decade following the war, when the sewage and water supply systems in the big cities, and even more so in the midsize towns, were in ruins. The authorities generally took care to provide a flow of water to the public bathhouses, which most of the population used, and to remove the sewage water that resulted. And so in certain towns, the congregations reached agreements with the local authorities and bathhouse administrators to designate a special room in the bathhouse for a *mikva*. *Mikvas* of this kind existed in the municipal bathhouses of L'vov and Chernovtsy. In 1946 the Khar'kov congregation signed an agreement with the bathhouse trust (*Banno-prachechnyi trest*) to build two *mikvas* inside the municipal bathhouse.[2] These *mikvas* operated without impediment for about five years, but with the intensification of the anti-Jewish policy, and because Jews visiting the *mikvas* shared a common entrance with ordinary bathers, the Ukraine SRA representative sought authorization from his superior in Moscow to close the *mikvas* down. He received the following reply:

The soviet does not see a basis for closing the rooms with pools within the general bathhouses only because they can be utilized also in accordance with the laws of *mikva*-use. . . . Bathhouses usually contain facilities for various kinds of bathing: general, baths, showers and the like, and the soviet does not find reasons for objecting to bathhouses also containing rooms with special pools so that the religious from among the Jewish faith will be able to wash in them according to the laws of *mikva*. . . . It is right to arrange for such rooms in the public bathhouses so as to prevent the Jewish congregations from demanding that a *mikva* be built next to the synagogue, which would afford them also a commercial [opportunity]. . . . This ensures that in those rooms the general sanitary standards are maintained. . . . Accordingly, the soviet holds that elimination of the *mikva*s should not be sought in the places that the latter exists.

A similar response was given by the SRA representative to the Chernovtsy municipality. Yet he stressed that payment for using the *mikva* had to reach the baths office and that this must absolutely not turn into an additional source of income for the congregation.[3] Yet despite the reasoned arguments of the SRA chairman, the SRA representative in Ukraine held that "it is better that the *mikva* . . . be beside the synagogue and the *mikva*s in the bathhouses be closed."[4] The existence of *mikva*s within bathhouses, though not without certain flaws from a *halakhic* standpoint, permitted many more Jews to avail themselves of them.

Until the late 1940s, functioning *mikva*s existed in quite a few cities of the Soviet Union, such as Moscow, Mukachevo, Chernovtsy, Kiev, and others.[5] Yet with the intensification of antireligion policy, many of these *mikva*s were closed. The events in Kiev illustrate some of the steps the authorities took to shut down *mikva*s. In early 1953, to begin the process of closing the *mikva*, a three-person commission that included a Jewish doctor was sent to examine the situation. The commission found that the *mikva* was at a lower elevation than the municipal sewage system and, consequently, that its water was stagnant and not being cleansed. The commission also found that the boiler heating the water was of insufficient size, and that the room containing the *mikva* was dilapidated and being heated with an iron stove, presenting a fire hazard.[6] Evidence suggests that this description of the *mikva* was close to reality, yet it was not the sanitary conditions that bothered the critics and their superiors but rather the use of a *mikva* at all. However, just as the report was being written, some two weeks after Stalin's death, new winds began to blow in the Soviet Union.

With the new climate in 1954, the head of the L'vov congregation formally sought permission from the authorities to approve construction of a *mikva* in the synagogue, at the congregation's expense. The request was approved, and a *mikva* was built that met all sanitary standards.[7] Now smaller congregations, too, dared turn to the authorities to approve the construction of *mikva*s. Thus, for example, the Bershad' congregation noted in its application in 1954:

> When it was hot the Jewish population took advantage of the Latoritsa River, flowing through the center of town. Yet now that it's cold it's no longer possible to bathe and wash in the river. . . . Knowing that our request is legal we are seeking your permission to build a *mikva*.[8]

That year a group of Jews from Mukachevo (which did not have a registered congregation) also applied for permission to build a *mikva*. The district SRA representative, who in those transition years did not know what decision to make, argued that building a *mikva* did not require his permission and that the whole matter was in the jurisdiction of the local authorities. In those years, then, increasing applications may well have been made to the local authorities seeking permission to build *mikva*s. In the face of these requests, the SRA representative in Ukraine wrote to the Chernovtsy municipality in 1955 that objections are not to be raised against a congregation that seeks to build a *mikva*, provided technical and health standards are met.[9] Despite this tolerant attitude toward *mikva*-building in 1955–1958, when the antireligion struggle was relaxed, evidence exists only of permission granted to certain communities to build *mikva*s, rather than a widespread phenomenon.[10]

Construction of a *mikva* that could meet sanitary standards required that numerous bureaucratic hurdles be overcome and significant financial outlays made, even if relatively few people used the *mikva*. As a result, *mikva*-building did not hold a high priority amongst the congregations. Religiously observant women as well as men thus had *mikva*s built clandestinely in private houses, and those who visited them did so in secret.[11]

Circumcision

Unlike *mikva*s, which served only the most strictly observant Jews, circumcision was considered a definitive mark of belonging to the Jewish people. Until the Revolution, circumcision was practiced even by Jews who did not keep any other commandment or who had distanced themselves from religion. This tradition continued at least through the 1920s despite the vigorous campaign of propaganda against religion. In the twenties, it seems, most Jewish parents circumcised their children, including those who were unquestioned

Communists. Yet during the thirties, the fissures widened even in this realm, as a result of four main factors: (1) the widespread emigration of Jews from the "Pale of Settlement" regions to areas lacking any Jewish tradition; (2) the increase in mixed marriages among the young generation; (3) the desire to forestall unpleasant reactions to children from the surrounding society (in kindergartens, primary and secondary schools, the army, and so forth); and (4) a strict antireligion policy that viewed circumcision as a backward custom. The percentage of Jews in the European parts of the Soviet Union (matters were different in Asia and the Caucasus) who circumcised their sons in this decade thus fell; at the same time, a significant drop was noticeable in the number of *mohalim* (qualified circumcisors). Some of the *mohalim* abandoned the field, whether due to persecution by the authorities or to pressure by their children over the damage to their social or career prospects or to assorted personal reasons. The number of *mohalim* also diminished because many were murdered in the Holocaust or grew old or died by other means. Parents who wished to have their sons circumcised and did not belong to the very small circle of the religiously observant in the USSR thus had to invest resources and expenses to locate a *mohel.*

Yet in the context of the national reawakening following the Holocaust, more parents sought to circumcise their sons in order to add them to the leger of the Jewish people, who had suffered such heavy losses. For the same reason, some sought to escape identification as Jews and did so by avoiding circumcision for their children.[12]

Most circumcisions were done in secret or in private, and so by their nature are reflected only incidentally in the Soviet documentation. Nevertheless, as implied earlier, an SRA representative noted in 1947 that the number of circumcisions rose after the war. The *mohalim* are described by the representative as "dark characters," many of whom live in Gomel' and travel to other towns to conduct the ceremonies there.[13] Yet circumcisions were performed not only in the peripheral areas but also in the main cities of Russia. Thus, for example, in the first quarter of 1948, 150 circumcisions reportedly were performed in Leningrad. These cases were known by the authorities and arranged by nonreligious as well as religious parents.[14] In other cases, *mohalim* reached agreements to carry out the procedure in hospitals. Such arrangements prevented, at least in part, accusations that the procedures were done by unauthorized individuals and reassured parents that they occurred in suitable medical conditions. Thus, Rabbi Avraham Ben Shmuel Gorobanskii agreed with the hospital in Berdichev to perform circumcisions in the natal-care department. This arrangement evidently had the support of Jewish doctors, with the authorities looking the other way. Until the late 1940s, such circumcisions were being conducted in many Soviet towns; the authorities largely ignored them, and even nonobservant Jews including Communists circumcised their children. In 1949 the SRA chairman averred:

> Of late this ritual is being performed by nearly all the religious Jews. In all cities and towns in which even a small number of Jews reside, there is a special surgeon—the *mohel*—who performs this operation in the homes of the religious. This ritual is especially widespread among the clerics and elements having nationalist tendencies.... [T]hey seek to grant this ritual nationalist character, while trying to persuade people that a Jew who is uncircumcised cannot be considered Jewish. It should be noted that the practice of this ritual has increased significantly in the last years. Oftentimes it is performed also by nonreligious Jews and even by members of the party and the Komsomol [the Communist Youth movement].[15]

Persecution regarding circumcision intensified in the late 1940s, as it did in other areas. The documentation describes a case involving a journalist of the *Komsomol'skaia Pravda,* who until May 1947 lived in L'vov. Born in 1921, he had been a member of the Communist Party since 1944 and also belonged to the Writers' Union. In February 1947 he had a son, whom he had circumcised. Another writer, who apparently was present at the celebration, informed party authorities of the "contemptible" act of his colleague. In late 1948, the report was sent to Moscow, where the accused then resided and worked as a journalist for the *Literaturnaia gazeta.* Officials from the party and the Writers' Union, after discussing the issue in October 1948 and April 1949, booted the man from both entities, rejecting his pleas that the circumcision had been performed in response to pressure from his father.[16] In those years, detective activity targeting circumcisions also increased. Nurseries (*detskie konsultatsii*) were required to report babies who had been circumcised, along with their parents, especially if they were members of the Communist Party or the Komsomol. Often the accused were summoned for clarifications and sometimes they were punished. Thus, for example, the party committee in the town of Olevsk removed from its ranks two Jews who had circumcised their sons: one who served as party secretary in a factory, and another, a woman who worked as a teacher. In Korosten', too, several high-ranking Jews were kicked out of the party over the same "sin."[17] Dismissal from the party was a serious punishment, not only because it was a personal stain but also because it limited opportunities for career and social advancement. Faced with such prospects, fewer parents in the

European parts of the Soviet Union seem to have dared hold a circumcision ritual for their sons. Some now did this completely in secret.

In these years, another option, common previously in the 1920s, was for parents to leave the newborn with the grandparents, who would arrange the circumcision, allowing all the "blame" to be shifted to the elderly, who had not yet undergone Soviet education.[18]

In this period, too, matters were otherwise in Central Asia and the Caucasus. Thus, for instance, in the Georgian and European synagogues of Baku in 1951, thirty-one circumcisions were carried out openly; and in the synagogue of the mountain Jews in that town, another forty-three circumcisions took place.[19]

The persecution of the *mohalim* also increased in this period. In mid-April 1949 the SRA representative for Ukraine sent a letter to his district representative in Chernovtsy, where a good number of *mohalim* worked. He asked that the congregation rabbis identify those who were carrying out circumcisions "so as to be able to prosecute them in the event of complications following surgery." He also recommended approaching finance departments in order to impose suitable taxes on the *mohalim*. Indeed, the criminal law of the USSR stated:

> The engagement in the medical profession by a person without suitable medical training is punishable by incarceration for up to a year or a fine of one hundred rubles. If those activities lead to damage to health or death, the punishment is incarceration for up to five years.[20]

Every *mohel* was thus subject to punishment, which would be especially harsh if the baby required hospitalization. No wonder that only a very few dared take the personal risk of performing circumcisions; sometimes these were itinerant *mohalim* who would come from another town to carry out the rite and then return to their place of residence. Often the *mohalim* were the same people who handled *shechita*, as was the case in many towns of Eastern Europe before the Revolution as well. And sometimes the *mohel* was the rabbi.

The number of parents—especially members of the Communist Party and persons of stature in the Soviet apparatus—who agreed to have their sons circumcised dropped steadily, as was noted by Rabbi Avraham Gorobanskii in 1950: "This year I am performing no more than three to five circumcisions a month. In some cases Jews who work in the Soviet and party [apparatus] prefer to bring a surgeon for the job instead of me so as to avoid unpleasantness."[21]

With the thaw, increasing numbers of Jews seem to have circumcised their sons, though the Soviet sources do not mention this explicitly and the bureaucracy largely ignored the information that reached it on this subject. Yet during the antireligion campaign of the late 1950s and early 1960s, the Soviet media condemned the "barbaric rite of circumcision" and stressed that *mohalim* were raking in piles of cash. Many articles noted the inappropriate medical conditions that often jeopardized the health of the newborn, transmitted diseases, and so forth.[22] Again parents who agreed to circumcise their sons were condemned, especially members of the Communist Party and persons of status in the Soviet apparatus. Nevertheless, even during this period some high-ranking Jews continued the practice.

Not just "nationalist reactionaries," as the Soviet officials labeled them, but also broader classes of Jews believed that "circumcision is not only a religious ritual but a fundamentally nationalist one, and by means of circumcision a Jew can be distinguished from a non-Jew."[23] While the scope of the practice cannot be quantified in the USSR in 1941–1964, we can assert with reasonable confidence that circumcision was not confined to the tiny minority of observant Jews but rather extended to relatively broad sectors of the Jewish population.

CHAPTER SEVENTEEN

Cemeteries, Holocaust Memorials, & Burial Societies

Graveyards

In the Soviet Union, as elsewhere, graveyards were an important part of the life of a congregation, and upon forming, every Jewish community allocated space for one. For the authorities' part, they allocated parcels of land for graveyards to Jews, and the community usually covered the cost; sometimes the Jewish graveyards were adjacent to the Christian ones, but the two were always kept separate. The Jewish cemetery was usually fenced off and contained a structure called a "chamber" or "purification house," where the corpse would be washed and dressed in shrouds. In prerevolutionary Russia, burial and cemeteries were under the purview of the congregation, within which the burial society (*hevra kadisha*) served as the responsible agency.

Burial was considered among the most important mitzvot, one that the family of the deceased was obligated to perform rigorously. A person without relatives was considered a *met mitzvah*—that is, someone whose burial became the duty of the community. Most congregations made great efforts to bring each deceased Jew to a Jewish grave. The burial society, which supervised graveyard maintenance as well as burials, turned into the most important and influential charitable organization. Through this status, over time it acquired tasks not directly associated with burial. With the transformation of Russian Jewish society in the second half of the nineteenth century, the institution of the burial society drew increasing criticism, and its public and economic power waned. In particular, the *maskilim* (figures in the Jewish enlightenment movement) leveled harsh critiques against these societies, some of them justified. Still, under the tsarist empire, burial and cemeteries remained affairs of the Jewish public and the regime did not really intercede.[1] This situation changed once the Bolsheviks seized power.

Under Bolshevik rule, all cemeteries were nationalized and the religious associations were completely separated from the functions of burial and graveyard maintenance, the latter being assigned to departments of the local authorities. Even so, in practice the burial societies continued to function through the 1920s, and were regarded as private enterprises providing services. New regulations were issued in the 1930s that outlawed the continued existence of the burial societies. Officially, this status did not change during the war or after it, either.[2] But with the outbreak of the Soviet-German war, the municipal authorities found themselves increasingly stretched and preferred that the religious associations resume the task of operating the cemeteries. Yet in December 1946, when Rabbi Shlomo Shlifer sought permission from the SRA to have interment issues transferred to the congregation, the vice chairman replied that all burial affairs were the responsibility of the local authorities and the congregation should not play a part. Transport of the deceased, assignment of grave sites, and the like were the responsibility of the trust for the provision of burial services (*Trest pokhoronnogo obsluzhivaniia*), which operated at the behest of the local authorities.[3]

After the war the soviet for the Russian Orthodox Church and the SRA could not ignore the sorry state of the cemeteries, which elicited complaints and requests alike by the religious associations regarding burial and graveyard maintenance. Accordingly, on May 21, 1947, a discussion was held by representatives of the soviet of the Russian Orthodox Church and the SRA about the situation of cemeteries. In effect, this discussion was an indirect acknowledgment that the subjects of burial and cemeteries could not be completely divorced from their religious aspects. The legal entanglements and the many entities involved in burial and graveyard maintenance thus created facts that were rather different from those set forth in the Soviet laws and the regulations.

In the 1920s, most Jewish cemeteries continued to be cared for by the burial societies and almost all Jewish deceased were buried in them. In the 1930s, however, land for new cemeteries ceased to be allotted based on religion but rather became "internationalized." Many such graveyards had plots designated for the various religions, and family or friends who wanted their loved ones to be buried in a Jewish cemetery had them buried in these plots.[4] Villages and midsize towns, meanwhile, continued to have cemeteries distinguished by religion, and almost all the Jewish dead were buried in Jewish ones, the funeral rites being either Jewish or Soviet, with Soviet burials including music and speeches containing Communist slogans. Thus, despite the absence of official burial societies, until the Holocaust most locations with a significant Jewish population, especially in the former Pale of Settlement, had organizations that took care of burials with Jewish rites and saw to the maintenance of Jewish cemeteries. This situation changed radically once Germany invaded the USSR and captured many areas with a large Jewish population, causing hundreds of thousands of Jews to flee or evacuate to interior areas of the USSR.

Condition of the Cemeteries

With regard to the condition of the Jewish cemeteries, a distinction must be made between the areas under Nazi occupation and those not occupied. In the unoccupied areas, great differences also existed between settlements consisting mainly of Jewish refugees and those with a large prewar Jewish population and preexisting congregations. In many towns that in the 1930s had had a Jewish community with cemeteries of its own, the burial societies, which were directly connected with a congregation and whose workers were part of it, continued to operate during the war almost openly. Yet some towns that may not have had Jewish cemeteries at the war's outset established them during the war.[5]

In towns with a relatively large population of Bukharan Jews, an organized burial and graveyard maintenance system existed, a case that also applied for the mountain and Georgian Jews (living in Tashkent, Samarkand, Dushanbe, Baku, Makhachkala, Derbent, and elsewhere). All such sites had Jewish cemeteries and functioning burial societies, and usually also handled the burial of Jews who had arrived more recently. In places where differences of opinion separated the burial society of the Bukharan Jews and the Chabadniks, as in Bukhara and Samarkand,[6] the two burial societies worked in tandem.

Concentrations of refugees also existed in towns that had lacked Jewish cemeteries before the war, and where the Jewish population, under stress from immediate exigencies, had not ensured itself an allocation of a special area. Yet even in such towns, the deceased were brought to burial with Jewish rites. Thus, for example, interments in the remote town of Chaili in the Kazakh Republic were handled by Rabbi Levi Yitzhak Shneorson and in the town of Alpaevsk, in the Ural region, by Emmanuel Michlin.[7] However, as those towns lacked Jewish cemeteries, the deceased were buried in the general cemeteries or in the Christian or Muslim ones. The buriers in such cases tried to leave at least a symbolic spatial division between the Jewish graves and the others, but after a short time any markers meant to distinguish the Jewish plots disappeared. One of the unoccupied areas with a special history is the city of Leningrad, which, though never conquered, was besieged for many months. This city, which at the war's outset had more than 200,000 Jews, lost over a half million of its overall population to hunger during the siege, among them thousands of Jews. The congregation assumed responsibility for these Jews' burial in common graves in the Jewish cemetery. On January 15, 1942, the congregation signed an agreement with a cooperative that would bury the dead and manage lists of bodies brought to the synagogue and then taken for burial in common graves. The contractors' cooperative also committed to laying out the common graves and putting a metal plaque on each with the names of those buried. The synagogue thus turned into a sort of purification house, and a few Jews, during this time of duress, made sure that at least some of the dead Jews were buried in the Jewish cemetery.[8]

In Moscow, there were twenty-two cemeteries, of which only three met religious standards (Muslim, Armenian, and Jewish—the last in Vostrikovo). These were not separate cemeteries but plots within the general cemetery. Jews who did not bury their dead in Vostrikovo could bury them in one of four Jewish cemeteries in towns near Moscow: Saltykovka, Pushkino, Perlovka, and Malakhovka. Burials in the cemetery in Malakhovka involved the family paying for transport of the body and for the purification, shroud, and burial rites, as well as making a donation.[9] Unsurprisingly, then, only a few of Moscow's Jews chose to bury family members in those cemeteries.

All Moscow's cemeteries were, at least officially, under the management of the trust for the provision of burial services. In the Vostrikovo cemetery, there was no purification house; accordingly, in December 1945, Rabbi Shlifer sought permission from the SRA to erect a special structure for this purpose, at the congregation's expense. The reply to this application raised two issues: (1) cemeteries are under the jurisdiction of the municipality and the congregation shouldn't be involved; and (2) the new structure would be a branch of the synagogue or even an additional synagogue, and hence could not be allowed.[10]

Even towns not occupied by the Nazis sometimes had Jewish graveyards, which suffered from extreme neglect. Rabbi Shlifer described the condition of Moscow's Vostrikovo cemetery in 1945: "[T]he fence is destroyed, and animals are grazing on the graves." A 1947 report from the Ul'ianovsk district states that in both Jewish cemeteries the fences had been removed and the area had become a grazing field for cattle. Cemeteries, not only the Jewish ones, were also destroyed by the local inhabitants, as described in one of the SRA reports:

> Exploiting the lack of oversight over cemeteries, the population is looting every-thing which can bring any sort of income or use: wooden crosses and fences serve for firewood; stone fences and gravestones for construction and rehabbing; plots in the graveyards are plowed as vegetable gardens or turned into garbage dumps.[11]

The municipal departments officially responsible for graveyard mainte-
nance shirked their duty, and the other Soviet authorities likewise showed
little sensitivity toward cemeteries in general and Jewish ones in particular.
In the town of Saratov, for example, the Jewish population at the outset of
WWII was about seven thousand and roughly doubled by the census of 1959.
The town had a cemetery. In 1945 a preeminent actor in the local theater,
Ivan Slonov, died, and the authorities decided to erect a fancy tombstone to
mark his grave. As no suitable stone was available nearby, they took one from
the Jewish cemetery, where those murdered in the town's pogrom of 1905
were interred. The stone was returned only after a bitter protest by the city's
Jews.[12] On the whole, the authorities showed little respect not only for grave
markers of historic import but also for the resting places of the dead from the
previous war. Thus, for example, in efforts to level the ground near the Jewish
cemetery Preobrazhenskoe in Leningrad, mass graves of Jews from the war
were severely damaged; the work continued despite the appeals and protests
of the congregation. Ultimately, the area atop the mass graves was turned into
paths and roads.[13]

Whereas generally the condition of the Jewish and non-Jewish cemeteries
in the unoccupied areas were not significantly different from one another, the
towns liberated from Nazi occupation held an entirely different picture. In
those towns the fences surrounding nearly all the Jewish cemeteries had been
taken down, the purification houses dismantled, and most of the gravestones
smashed or stolen. Only a relatively small part of the destruction, as far as we
can ascertain, was done by the Nazi administration; most of it was done by the
local population, which stole whatever it could. What, after all, could be easier
than to seize fences and purification houses for firewood or headstones for
construction, when the very lives of any and all Jews were free for the taking?
While those interred in the Christian cemeteries had family and churches to
safeguard them, the entire Jewish population had been murdered or had fled.

During the German Fascist occupation all the Jewish graveyards in the
Zhitomir district were completely destroyed: the fences dismantled and the
stones knocked over, sometimes broken—or smashed to bits (in the cities of
Berdichev and Zhitomir). The Jewish cemeteries of Krivoi-Rog, Dnepropetrovsk, Shepetovka, Proskurov, and other towns were in a similar state.[14] Three
years after the end of the war, the Jewish cemetery in Pinsk was described as
"strewn with skulls and human bones, full of garbage, the gravestones smashed,
with gaping holes in the graveyard where clay was being mined." Worse still
was the situation in Kirovograd, where there are "no signs left of the former
Jewish cemetery—neither fences nor headstones."[15]

Along with theft and looting, the main causes of which were economic, the destruction of a Jewish cemetery was sometimes an expression of debasement. In quite a few towns, headstones were taken from Jewish cemeteries and used to pave sidewalks and roads. To punctuate the insult, the stones were placed with the engraving facing up, so that pedestrians would trample them and vehicles would drive over them. Thus, for example, the sidewalks of Shevchenko Street, a main street in Kamenets-Podol'skii, were paved with Jewish gravestones. In L'vov the Nazis paved the courtyard of a garage in Lenin Street with stones taken from the Jewish cemetery, as was described in early 1953: "Engraved on the tombstones are inscriptions with religious content, dedications to relatives who have passed away. Some of the inscriptions are in embossed metal. All this is on the surface—they are being walked and driven over."[16]

In many of the towns under Nazi occupation the Jewish cemeteries were destroyed, some permanently. But the destruction did not end with the occupation: hooligans of all sorts found refuge in the graveyards, the local population continued with the destruction, and even official Soviet entities used the Jewish cemeteries for their own purposes.

At the end of the war and in the years that followed, crime and hooliganism grew throughout the country. Purification houses and even open graves served as sleeping quarters for thugs. Furthermore, graves were sometimes dug up in the hunt for valuables, as a January 1947 report on the condition of cemeteries in Ukraine attests: "In the caves of graves [in Kiev] criminals and thieves arranged sleeping sites for themselves and they use some of the graves as toilets. . . . [I]n the absence of guards, criminal elements are busy digging and searching for valuables [in Babi Yar]."[17]

Looting and theft from the Jewish cemeteries took many forms. According to one source, "The stone fence around [the Jewish cemetery in Kiev] was dismantled by the local population as construction material." In addition: "The guard at the Jewish cemetery in Lubny plowed over part of the cemetery for a private vegetable garden."[18] And in the towns of Kremenchug, Poltava, Nezhin, Priluki, Chernigov, Belaia Tser'kov, and Chernobyl, the Jewish cemeteries were turned into public or private grazing lands.[19] The cemetery guard in Uman' converted the purification house into a chicken coop, and eventually took over the cemetery and sold gravestones. A report from early 1947 mentions that "in the closed Jewish cemetery in the city of Khar'kov the destruction of tombstones continues . . . tombstones taken from the Jewish cemetery in the city of Uman' were used to make a storehouse. . . . [T]he majority of towns have no fencing in the cemeteries and [where there is] the theft of fences continues."[20] In Rovno, "the fence is completely destroyed, animals wander around freely and the destruction of tombstones continues." Said one source, "In certain towns the guard houses [*storozhki*] of the cemeteries are taken over by people who have nothing to do with guarding the cemetery."[21] The state of the Ianovskii cemetery in L'vov, where many Jews murdered in a camp of the same name were interred during the Holocaust, was described by a Soviet clerk in 1953 in dry, factual language:

> Garbage is strewn on the old graves of the cemetery. Cars and carts ride over one part of the cemetery. Goats and cows graze there. One side of the cemetery isn't fenced and hence there is free passage for vehicles and cattle. The guard hut and the purification house are broken down, not refurbished, filthy, there's no electricity, no table, no chairs. There is no cemetery guard and the fence near the guard hut is used to hitch horses brought to the nearby veterinary clinic.[22]

The authorities not only failed to prevent the theft and looting, certain Soviet agencies participated in it:

> The old Jewish cemetery in Kiev is used as the practice field for army units . . . a road has been paved through it for vehicles. In 1945–1946 the burial administration of the municipality used a part of the cemetery, parceling it into vegetable gardens for its employees. To that end, all the headstones were removed.

Two cemeteries in Odessa offered a prospect no brighter: their fences were dismantled by the local residents, and Red Army units had removed gravestones for use in construction.[23] The head of the Kiliia congregation (Izmail district) complained in a letter to *Pravda* in 1951, which of course was not published, testifying that he himself saw "the representatives of city institutions taking headstones [from the cemetery] for their own use." In Nikolaev a "car park [was built] in the Jewish cemetery . . . and the access to it was blocked by equipment." At the Jewish cemetery in the hamlet of Sirotino in Belorussia, after the war, the Soviet authorities built a pigsty.[24]

The places where thousands of Jews were murdered during the Holocaust fared no better:

> Babi Yar, which entered history [as a symbol] of Fascist crimes in Ukraine [as the SRA representative wrote in early 1947], is not preserved at all and parts of it are exploited as a sand quarry. In some places the slopes are eroded by autumn rains and the bodies of the murdered [roll] in the area. . . . The common graves in the Grodzenskii Forest [Grodzenskii les] near Uman', where three thousand Soviet children under the age of ten were murdered, gets no attention at all from the municipality.[25]

The attitude of the local authorities, who by law were supposed to care for the cemeteries in their jurisdiction, was usually disparaging, but in certain cases their disdain escalated to pointed discrimination against the Jewish cemeteries. Thus, for example, in 1946 the Grodno district had 126 cemeteries, of which only the thirty-six Jewish ones were "in a neglected state . . . completely disregarded by the municipality," wrote the SRA representative.[26]

Based on an SRA report from 1947, the hostile, politically unbalanced standpoint of the municipal departments toward the cemeteries of the different religions also warrants mention. Thus, for example, the Priluki municipality devoted much attention to the maintenance of the Russian cemetery, but ignored the questions raised by the Jewish population on this issue.[27]

The discriminatory stance held by quite a few municipalities did not change for many years after the war, as reflected in a statement by the Jews of Vitebsk:

> We, citizens of Vitebsk of Jewish nationality, are angered by the attitude of the
> local authorities . . . toward the cemetery. The town of Vitebsk has [in 1961] one
> Jewish cemetery, which has existed for decades. After the Great Patriotic War,
> an area was allocated near the Jewish cemetery for burial of citizens of Russian
> ethnicity. The city fenced off this cemetery, and two guards are there to oversee it.
> But despite the fact that the Jewish cemetery has already been there for decades,
> it hasn't been fenced to this day, there is no regular guard, and gravestones are
> continually stolen. . . . Each year [the authorities] promise to fence the cemetery
> and place a guard there, but for some reason never fulfill the promise.[28]

The attitude of the authorities toward maintenance of the cemeteries was so disgraceful that during the thaw even some in the Soviet media condemned this "nihilistic" approach.[29] Yet unsurprisingly, even during the thaw many Jewish cemeteries remained neglected, as the Jewish population lacked the ability to rehabilitate them. Thus, for example, in 1955 the Jewish cemetery of Kherson was left "without a fence [and] the headstones [are] unprotected [and] ruined." The ensuing proposal to convene "all the town's Jews" to raise funds to fence the cemetery was forbidden by the authorities on the grounds that such an event would "raise the authority [of the congregation] in the opinion of the Jews."[30] One of the cemeteries in Chernovtsy wasn't "fenced, nor guarded by anyone and as a result, animals graze there, headstones disappear . . . [and in 1955] a group of people was found to be in the business of stealing, processing [and selling] the gravestones." The city did not deny these facts but claimed that the stones that had fallen over had been set up again and appointed a new manager to restore order.[31]

Apart from the neglect and destruction, "reassignment" also posed a problem after the war: by Soviet law cemeteries in which burials had not occurred for twenty years or whose land was required for public needs could be used for other purposes.

One instance of a reassignment that received special attention involved the burial site of the Gaon of Vilna. When news of the reassignment of the cemetery where the Gaon was buried reached Jews in other countries, the World Jewish Congress sent a telegram dated November 5, 1947, to the Jewish Anti-Fascist Committee in Moscow requesting that the Gaon's headstone be preserved, given its importance to world Jewry. The committee, in turn, passed the telegram to the Lithuanian Communist Party secretary, asking that he examine the matter. The Vilna municipality set up a special committee to look into the subject, comprising architects, experts in historical building preservation, as well as a researcher from the Jewish museum and the head of the congregation. The committee, which submitted its report in December 1947, concluded that the cemetery had been destroyed and that recently erected headstones of Jewish sages (the Gaon died in 1797) lacked historical value. It added that only the inscriptions incorporated in the *ohel* (tent) built over the grave sites had any such value. The committee thus recommended that the stones with inscriptions be concentrated in a small area of the cemetery and be integrated into the park planned to replace it. In line with these recommendations, the municipality decided in October 1948 to reassign the cemetery where the Vilna Gaon had been buried as well as to cease future burials in the Jewish cemetery of Rovnoe Pole Street. Later in the same month, on October 27, the city decided to reassign the Antakalnis Jewish cemetery as well. The Gaon's grave was moved to a new cemetery, and a "tent" was erected over his grave by the local Jews.[32] In justifying this latter reassignment, the authorities estimated that some 80 percent of the headstones in the Antakalnis cemetery, located in the city center, had been destroyed during the war, and their restoration would be a huge expense that the city was not willing to fund.

During the two years needed to dismantle the Antakalnis cemetery, the appropriate agencies were charged with drawing up a list of the grave sites of famous figures or those with historical value, which were then to be transferred to the new cemetery. The municipality was then to assist families seeking to move graves of their relatives to the new cemetery, while unrelocated headstones would be used for other purposes—buildings and so forth.[33]

In those same years, many Jewish cemeteries were dismantled in other places as well, but these cases did not attract interest either because they contained no famous grave sites or because news of their dismantling never reached the West. One such instance involved the Dorgomilskii Jewish cemetery in

Moscow. After plans for the dismantling were announced, Rabbi Shlifer sought permission from the SRA representative to relocate the grave of Grigorii Iollos (1858–1906), a Jewish member of the first national Duma, to the new cemetery. When asked by the SRA official if the interred man had been religious, the rabbi replied: "If he was a Jew and murdered by the 'Black Hundreds,' the synagogue should take part.... [I]ndeed all the Jews who fell in the war or were murdered by the nation's enemies are holy in the eyes of the synagogue, regardless of their religious convictions."[34]

With the thaw, reassignment of cemeteries spread. As part of a certain decentralization policy, the republics were allowed to pass their own legislation, which did not always conform with the central regime's 1929 regulations on religion. In July 1958, the National Planning Committee (*Gosplan*), in conjunction with the Ministry of the Interior of the Republic of Ukraine, issued instructions regarding the "system of burial and cemetery maintenance," according to which reassignment of a cemetery no longer required the passage of twenty years after the cessation of burials. This ruling was designed to give legal cover for the urban planning of many towns. In 1956, Khar'kov floated plans to reassign the Jewish cemetery. Upon learning of the proposal, the city's Jews sent a delegation to Moscow to protest. The delegation emphasized that burial in this cemetery had ceased only in 1950 and, as a result, its reassignment contravened Soviet regulations.[35] Yet after the new regulations were issued, this argument lost its basis and the cemetery was reassigned.

In the late 1950s and early 1960s, therefore, quite a few cemeteries were reassigned in Ukraine and in other republics too, where similar instructions seem to have been issued.[36] For its part, world public opinion paid special attention to the dismantling of the old Jewish cemetery of Kiev (Lukianovskoe Kladbishche), where famous rabbinical and political figures were interred.[37] The municipality had decided to reassign the cemetery in 1962, and passed a special resolution allowing family members to move graves to other cemeteries. Knowledge of the reassignment spread widely in the West because of the famous people buried there and because of media emphasis on its proximity to Babi Yar, which in those days had become well known due to Yevgeny Yevtushenko's poem "Babi Yar." With all the exposure, the subject acquired international significance and members of parliament, celebrities, and institutions appealed to their respective USSR-based embassies to voice concern. Accordingly, the head of the Ukrainian security services suggested to the Central Committee of the Communist Party that a special committee be formed to deal with relocating the graves of famous people from this cemetery to the new one; indeed following this flurry of activity, the remains of

Rabbi Shlomo Ben-Zion Twersky were relocated to a different cemetery and those of Rabbi Yosef Yozel Horowitz and Ber Borochov, one of the founders of Socialist Zionism, were brought to Israel. The lobbying efforts of the Israeli embassy in Moscow to have the remains of Zionist activist Max Mandelstam (1839–1912) brought from Kiev to Israel, however, were to no avail. Attempts to transport the grave of the founder of Chassidism, Israel Baal Shem Tov, from Medzhibozh to Israel likewise failed.[38] For less famous figures, the relocation of earthly remains depended mostly on finding family members who would assume the costs. Thus, in the course of a few years some 1,500–2,000 graves were relocated from the old Kiev Jewish cemetery to others. The cemetery was finally closed in 1964, and thousands of unclaimed gravestones or parts thereof were broken and ground up.[39]

Given the widespread tendency to decommission Jewish cemeteries in many USSR cities, three US-based associations were organized: Hesed shel Emet (True Kindness), Geder Avot (Wall of the Ancients), and Maalin Bakodesh (Uplifting of the Sacred). They dealt with erecting tombstones for famous rabbinical figures on their new grave sites as well as transporting certain graves to Israel. As part of this endeavor, a tombstone was erected in Kiev on the grave of Rabbi Sidarsky, son-in-law of Rabbi Israel Salanter.[40] Yet the activities of this coalition were limited to safeguarding graves of famous Jews, whereas the thousands of graves of simple Jews, who either had lost all their relatives in the Holocaust or whose relatives lived in different towns, disappeared entirely. In areas that once had Jewish cemeteries, buildings were erected, parks were built, and all traces of Jewish history were eradicated irretrievably.[41]

Jewish Activity for Rehabilitation and Maintenance of Cemeteries

Given the extreme neglect of and the discrimination against maintaining and rehabilitating Jewish cemeteries, the various municipalities' disinclination to involve themselves, and the preference of the local authorities "to get rid of cemetery maintenance . . . and hand it over to the religious associations,"[42] the degree of Jewish initiative in each given community held great importance.

Following the Holocaust, Jews worldwide felt increased sensitivity toward preservation and rehabilitation of cemeteries. This sensitivity stemmed from a shift in attitude toward previous generations and also from a sense of personal obligation to honor one's ancestors' graves. During the German occupation, the cemeteries in quite a few towns were used as sites to execute Jews.[43] Jewish efforts in this area took place on two related fronts: demanding from the authorities greater care for the cemeteries and, more crucially, rehabilitating and guarding cemeteries through the resources provided by the Jews themselves.

Especially vigorous activity to rehabilitate cemeteries was taken in the areas annexed by the USSR during the Second World War. Thus, for example, one of the first activities of Rabbi Aharon Shvartsman, on returning in 1945 to his hometown of Orgeev in Moldavia, was to solicit contributions for the rehabilitation of the destroyed cemetery. In L'vov, too, the graveyard was effectively in the care of the congregation, until this stewardship was forbidden by the authorities.[44] In addition, broad efforts to guard and rehabilitate cemeteries were made by congregations in Kiev, Zhitomir, Odessa, Vinnitsa, Nikolaev, Lubny, Khar'kov, Berdichev, Orel, Chernigov, Shepetovka, Proskurov, Kamenets-Podol'skii, Mozir,[45] and many other towns. In certain congregations the Jews were not satisfied with simply raising funds and did the rehabilitation work themselves. For instance, in the town of Smela (Kiev district) a workday (*voskrestnik*) was arranged and the town's Jews went out with tools to fix up the cemetery.[46] In Kiliia, a Jew named Bershadskii took upon himself the job of repairing and guarding the graveyard. He went from one Jewish apartment to the next to raise funds for a guard to prevent further looting and destruction. But with the intensification of the antireligion campaign, he was summoned to the authorities "and it was explained to him in great detail that the job of guarding the cemetery is one of the tasks of the municipality and that fundraising by visiting homes was strictly forbidden."[47]

In most towns—even the small ones—that had a Jewish population after the war, the local Jews took care of repairing (fencing and guarding) the cemetery, but in quite a few towns liberated from the Nazi conquest the resident Jewish population had completely vanished, or else the remaining Jews were unwilling to expend the necessary resources to cover guarding and rehabilitation, so the work fell mainly to the local authorities. In such towns the remnants of the Jewish cemeteries slowly disappeared.

Alongside the independent Jewish efforts, Jews also frequently petitioned the authorities about repairs and supervision of the cemeteries as well as allotment of grave sites for Jews. For example, in Vinnitsa the congregation made continuous, strenuous efforts to prevent the further destruction of the cemetery, and, in a complaint to the chairman of the SRA in June 1946, stated:

> Isn't it enough that the Jewish cemetery was destroyed by the Fascists during the German occupation—and now it's being dug up, vegetables are grown, while the tombs where our parents, relatives and dear ones [rest] are being smashed and desecrated. There has even been an attempt to allocate plots there [in the

cemetery] for private construction. . . . Rumors have spread that they want to take our cemetery from us. . . . The Jewish community is willing to assume the costs for [preserving and maintaining our cemetery—if the rumors are true]. Already last year we erected a fence which is now again destroyed.

In response to this complaint, the executive committee of one of the municipal regions (*Kirovskii raisovet*) resolved in April 1946 "to allocate a plot of land adjacent to the Jewish cemetery and to obligate the head of the municipality division . . . to not build houses in the Jewish cemetery, [and] to allow the Jewish religious congregation to build a structure" for purification. Accordingly, the congregation built a house of purification at the cost of 35,000 rubles and even reached an agreement with the city hospital to arrange for a Jewish burial following the death of a community member. The congregation also hired, at its own expense, two guards for the cemetery. Such details affirm that in Vinnitsa, for some years, all issues relating to burial were being handled by the congregation. But with the intensification of the antireligion policy, the district authority chairman wrote in 1949 that the purification structure must immediately be nationalized and that the guards' salary must be paid by the municipal authority and not by the congregation.[48]

Kiev's Jews sent many complaints about the continuing neglect of and thefts in the Lokianovka cemetery, and as a result a guard was posted there. The city of Odessa also agreed in 1946 that the congregation could fence the two Jewish cemeteries at its own expense, and even promised to supply building materials for this purpose.[49]

But such measures did not stop the destruction of the cemeteries, and in 1954, Odessa congregation head Y. Grintser complained about severe damage to the Jewish cemetery to the SRA chairman, who immediately passed the complaint to his representative in the district, demanding that the subject be discussed by the district executive committee and a report be issued on the steps taken. The discussion, it seems, had no concrete results and the assault on the cemetery continued. Hence, in July 1956 the congregation's rabbi submitted a complaint listing "irregularities" in the cemetery, which apparently did not disappear in years to come. In Kiev, meanwhile, in the first half of October 1958, forty-seven graves in the Jewish section of the cemetery were desecrated. Faced with the considerable bitterness of the city's Jews, and possibly fearing an international outcry, the city immediately undertook to rebuild the stones, at its own expense.[50] In Sirotino, only vigorous complaints by the Jews led to the removal of a pigsty from the cemetery area.[51] Five years of complaints and protests by the Jews of Kamenets-Podol'skii were needed before the authorities repaved Shevchenko Street (discussed earlier) and removed the tombstones from the surface. In L'vov, by contrast, even though "this situation generates [as witnessed by the SRA representative] harsh reactions, especially from the ... Jewish population, and many complaints,"[52] Jewish tombstones continued to serve as pavement at least until 1953.

In some towns, thanks to energetic activity by Jews, zones for Jewish burial were allocated; and when in 1954 the Voronezh congregation complained to the SRA about the local authorities' refusal to allocate a special parcel for Jewish graves, Moscow sent a directive stating that a parcel should be given for this purpose and no obstacles raised.[53] The Kiev congregation likewise demanded space for a Jewish cemetery, and the local authorities, to comply minimally, allocated a parcel of land that was far from the city and lacked access roads. The congregation refused to accept this parcel and continued to bury its dead between the rows of the old cemetery. Only in 1957 was a general cemetery built in the city near the Gostomel Road (Gostomel'skoe shosse) with a section granted to Jews that ultimately was augmented by a purification house.[54]

Despite the many difficulties and the different conditions in each town, until 1949 the authorities in general showed relative tolerance toward the congregations with regard to rehabilitation and guarding of cemeteries. But this attitude changed with the growth of the anti-Jewish policy. As the scene changed, the SRA worked to reduce the involvement of the congregations in management of cemeteries and was reluctant to allocate special plots for burial of Jews. Meanwhile certain local authorities, pursuing their self-interest (i.e., saving money) preferred to pass responsibility to the care of the congregations. These contradictions are clearly reflected in the events surrounding the land allocation to the Jewish cemetery in Voroshilovgrad. In 1951 a group of the city's Jews sought an allotment of land for the cemetery. After the SRA rejected the request, the municipality decided anyway on June 11, 1951, to respond in the affirmative. Thus emerged a conflict butting general Soviet policy, which did not view favorably the establishment of Jewish cemeteries or Jewish care of them, against the municipality, which wanted to be freed of this responsibility. Pressure was applied from above and the municipality revoked its previous decision, but by then the cemetery had already been established.[55] In this case the Jewish population had succeeded in exploiting the contradictions between the central government policy and the interests of the local authorities.

With the resolutions of November 10, 1954, stressing the need to respect religious sensitivities, Jewish complaints increased regarding damage and discrimination in the cemeteries. Thus, for example, the Jews of Nikolaev sought assistance in fencing the cemetery, the neglect of which "disrespected their sensibilities." The authorities budgeted 50,000 rubles for this purpose, although they took no action until 1957.[56]

Holocaust Memorials

Many Jews who had the means to restore, at least partially, the head-stones of their family members would sometimes also carve the names of relatives who perished in the Holocaust.[57] Such a practice was followed as well for those who passed away in the first years after the liberation. This all was usually done privately and did not attract any particular attention. But quite a few people were not content with these gestures and felt that memorialization of the Holocaust victims should have a public dimension. A public memorial would, they felt, give voice not only to their personal pain but also to their sorrow over the destruction of European Jewry in general and of Soviet Jews in particular. A common goal thus emerged, including personal and public elements, simple people and those of high status, religious and antireligious Jews, and Communists. The initiatives to memorialize the Holocaust were local and came from the grass roots.

By 1944 the Jews in the town of Bershad' had gathered the remains of those murdered by the Germans and buried them in the Jewish cemetery. In the town of Shchors, the remains were buried in a common grave, on which "was set a large stone of granite, etched on which was an inscription in Russian, 'Eternal remembrance of the victims of the German Nazi conquerors' . . . and [in Hebrew], 'Their blood shall I avenge.'"[58] Memorial stones for Holocaust victims were set up in the village of Nagartav (Bereznegovatoe subdistrict of the Nikolaev district), Tomashpol', Shargorod, Iampol', Iaruga, Ladyzhin, and Berdichev, where every year from 1944 to 1947 a memorial service was held—as was also done in Tarnopol' and Sorotino, and even in the town of Rechitsa, where a prewar Jewish population of more than seven thousand had dwindled to several dozen families after the liberation. Even in Lenin-grad, which had not been occupied, congregation activists Belous and Gedalia Pecherskii erected a monument to those who had perished during the siege.[59] So long as the memorial-related activities were done without ostentation, the authorities gave them no special attention, but when congregations sought to give the memorials a broad public significance the authorities vigorously opposed such a step.

One of the first attempts at wide-scale public Holocaust memorialization, to the best of our knowledge, was made in Odessa, where a congregation head asked to perform a symbolic burial of Holocaust victims. The authorities forbade this ceremony and even declared that the initiative was being nourished by a nationalist tendency, which the security services needed to address.[60] Yet such assemblies actually took place, and one of the first seems to have occurred in Khar'kov in January 1945. Similar assemblies, however, planned by the congregations of Riga, Novograd-Volynskii, and Kamenets-Podol'skii, were forbidden by the authorities.[61] The authorities viewed such Holocaust assemblies, which were difficult to supervise, as events that brought unity to the Jewish people, and so sought to prevent them.

With the thaw, hopes grew that the regime had changed somewhat, and these hopes intensified following the Twentieth Communist Party Congress in 1956. Certain congregations, thus, resumed their efforts to memorialize the victims of the Holocaust. For example, in 1958 the heads of the Zhitomir congregation asked to have the remains of Holocaust victims from the prisoner camp in the Bogonia region brought for a Jewish burial. The authorities, for their part, opposed the proposal on the grounds that "this would lead to activization of the Jewish public sphere."[62] This example suggests that, even during the thaw, the authorities did not appreciably change their negative posture toward granting public significance to burials of the remains of Holocaust victims.

Because in the USSR, unlike in other areas of Eastern Europe, Jews were not usually transported to extermination in special camps, but were rather murdered primarily near their places of residence, most of the scenes of murder remained neglected after the war. It was therefore only natural that the congregation would take upon itself the task of putting up monuments in those places.

In the first postwar years, the various regions held no unified policy toward initiatives of this sort. In the Baltic states the authorities tended to allow the monuments to be erected more than in other areas. In Lithuania, in 1946 the authorities agreed to the construction of a monument to the Jews murdered in Ponary (Ponar), near Vilna. Likewise in towns such as Dobele in Latvia, markers were placed on the sites where Jews were murdered.[63] In neighboring Belorussia, several attempts were made to remember the Holocaust with a monument. In Minsk, a monument was erected on the site of the murders with inscriptions in Russian and Yiddish—and despite the authorities' interdiction, a public gathering was held there. Influenced by the events in Minsk, in late 1945 the people of the minyan in Cherven', in the same district, initiated similar activities and raised funds to build their own monument from town natives now living in other cities. The few Jews who returned to the town of Glubokoe were able to erect a Holocaust memorial with Yiddish inscriptions, and near the town of Sirotino (Vitebsk district), a monument with inscriptions in Russian and Yiddish was erected at the site of the murders of most of the town's Jewish residents.[64]

Efforts were made to memorialize the victims of the Holocaust in at least sixteen cities and towns across Ukraine, including three cities in areas annexed to the USSR during WWII (L'vov, Tarnopol', and Chernovtsy). While in L'vov the efforts were not successful, in Tarnopol' a monument was erected over the grave of the victims, and in 1946 official representatives of the government even participated in its unveiling. In Chernovtsy, by contrast, the authorities forbade fundraising for this purpose, arguing that the subject was under the jurisdiction of the municipality since those murdered were not only Jews. Similar responses were given by the authorities in other towns.[65]

Despite the opposition of the authorities, this activity did not stop even in the late 1940s. The small Jewish population in the town of Pervomaisk worked through the unregistered congregation to erect a monument for those murdered in the Holocaust, as did the congregation in Poltava, which raised funds for the same purpose. The Kremenchug congregation stressed in its application to the authorities that "each Jew has the obligation to share in the erection of this type of historic monument." The tiny congregation of the town of Shepetovka arranged the communal graves of the Holocaust victims by itself. In Lubny, the little congregation made the modest request that the neglected place where the Holocaust victims were buried be handed over to its care. As a result, Leib Grinberg, who served as rabbi and congregation head, turned to the municipality for permission to have the congregation care for the burial site of the approximately three thousand murdered Jews of the community. This request elicited favorable answers from the local authorities, until it was overruled by the district SRA representative. Nevertheless, the rabbi was able to get a trench dug around the parcel, which let it serve as a sort of monument to the murdered; the area was marked off and the congregation cared for it for years. Likewise, in Uman' the congregation took it upon itself to rehabilitate the site in the north of the town where more than ten thousand Jews were murdered. In the main city of the Dnepropetrovsk district, the deputy head of the congregation (Shulman) tried to have a monument erected for the victims of the Holocaust, and recruited Jewish artists for the purpose, seeking also to exploit the difference of opinion between the Soviet authorities. These activities ultimately prompted him to leave town, fearing arrest.[66] Here, we get a picture of the broad and persistent efforts by Jews to erect monuments for victims of the Holocaust, exploiting to the maximum the lack of clear instructions forbidding it.

In the Zhitomir district, efforts were made to memorialize Holocaust victims in at least two cities: through a modest memorial in the town of Novograd-Volynskii, where the congregation arranged "four common graves . . . fenced them and erected gravestones with Yiddish and Russian inscriptions";[67] and a more substantial one in the city of Berdichev, where the congregation worked for years to put up a monument on the burial site of victims of the Holocaust.

Among the Jews in Berdichev and certain surrounding areas, most were murdered about four kilometers from the city on the road leading to the village of Romanovka, near a military airfield. A short while after the liberation of the city, the congregation began to work toward erecting a monument on the site of the mass murder. The municipality and the army opposed this plan, and in 1946 the head of the congregation, Metler, was summoned and ordered to cease such activity. In response, he declared proudly, "I acted for the religious and for Jews in general . . . in any case we shall build . . . monuments to the victims of Fascism." Denied the ability to set a monument on the site of the murder, the Jews of Berdichev placed symbolic gravestones for the Holocaust victims in the Jewish cemetery. But they did not give up on the monument at the murder site, and efforts to this end continued into the late 1940s and early 1950s. After much struggle, the congregation succeeded in early 1953 in having a monument erected on the site where the victims were buried, but this soon was removed. After Stalin's death the congregation renewed its efforts with respect to the murder site and in the mid-1950s resumed fundraising for it. Donors included Jews living in Moscow, Leningrad, Kiev, and other cities, and a monument was prepared with an inscription in Yiddish or Hebrew, with the Russian text below. The Russian inscription read, "Here rest the bodies of local residents and prisoners of war who were bestially shot by the Hitlerite Fascists in 1941–1942." The inscription, at least the Russian one, did not explicitly mention that most of those murdered were Jewish, though that fact was hinted at strongly by the presence of the Hebrew characters.

Having learned from the experience of the early 1950s, the congregation expended much effort to get explicit permission to erect the monument next to the airfield, exploiting family and personal connections with the airfield's commander. Eventually permission was obtained, and the public unveiling was set for June 2, 1958. Persons from the congregation were in touch with the municipal transportation authorities and arranged to have many buses available for transport to the opening ceremony; and according to the program several members of the congregation and some prominent local officials were to give speeches. But at the last minute the plan was scrapped, either on local orders or orders from Kiev. Erection of the monument was deemed illegal, and some of the people involved were harshly chastened in the town's Communist Party committee. Thereafter, the monument was moved to the Jewish cemetery, with the murder site left neglected until at least the early 1990s.[68] Thus, the Jews of Berdichev fought for twelve years to erect a monument on the common grave of their loved ones who were annihilated in the Holocaust, a struggle that involved many Jews from different levels of society and doubtless left a deep scar on quite a few.

The congregation therefore marked, throughout the years considered in this work, the sole locus for memorializing the Holocaust—and a significant one, which drew cooperation from Jews from different levels of society and in various forms, including donations, use of personal connections, and suchlike. Efforts often extended beyond town limits and contributed to the formation of ties among Jews of different locales.

Burial Societies (Hevrot Kadisha)

By Soviet laws and regulations religious burial services were permissible, and accordingly the SRA representative on December 26, 1946, answered an inquiry from Rabbi Shlifer as follows:

> No one is prohibiting performance of burial services in the cemeteries in accordance with religion, that is to say "purification" rites, wrapping the deceased in "shrouds," placing the body in a grave ("funeral") and holding burial prayers at the cemetery ("Maleh") [a reference to the prayer "El Maleh Rahamim"]. But in all that regards transportation of the body . . . and assigning plots in the cemetery, such matters are entirely the domain of the burial corporation. [Words in quotation marks were Hebrew in Cyrillic characters.][69]

Based on this explicit authorization, certain congregations employed workers defined as caretakers for burials. In other towns people who were not officially among the congregation's employees nevertheless handled the burials and were associated with the congregation or with minyans informally.[70] In some places that had Jewish cemeteries or in Jewish plots within general cemeteries, the local authorities employed Jews, at least some of whom were capable of performing religious burial rites. Each of these orientations can be regarded as a kind of "quasi–burial society." (We shall abandon the "quasi" in what follows, but retain the scare quotes.)

The existence of "burial societies" in the cemetery was the frequent cause of rivalry and accusation, such as that seen in Moscow during the first postwar years. The city council employed fifteen individuals to handle burials in the

Jewish cemetery, some of whom were qualified to hold burial services according to Jewish religious law (or at least thought to be so). Aside from these individuals, the congregation of the main synagogue employed seven workers to deal with the deceased and had a special office for the purpose. Each "burial society" complained that the other's gravediggers were charging fifty to a hundred rubles per deceased and three to five hundred rubles to perform the religious rites; each also complained that flowers were disappearing from the graves, even the ribbons and paper in which the flowers were wrapped, and being sold to visitors to the cemetery.[71]

"Burial societies" such as these were indeed permitted to demand payment for religious burial rites, but disputes frequently broke out between the family of the deceased and the "societies" over specific amounts. The "burial society" would also hold prayers in the cemeteries on the *yohrzeit,* the anniversary of the individual's death. The existence of "burial societies," and sometimes also of private individuals working in the Jewish cemeteries, was a gray area usually ignored by the authorities, so long as the prevailing central policy viewed religion with relative tolerance.[72] But as the antireligion policy worsened, the very existence of such "societies" was called into question, as is evident from this 1951 letter from the Belorussia SRA representative to his superiors:

> While examining the work of the Jewish congregations and religious groups, we encountered two phenomena for which we aren't sure of the correct solution, as there are no regulations or instructions for this matter. The first phenomenon is that the congregation and religious groups [i.e., minyans] take upon themselves the function of the burial agency. In the registered Jewish congregation in Minsk these people are employed, and in other unregistered religious groups there are individuals near the cemeteries who, during interments, conduct certain Jewish religious rites. . . . On my assumption that "experts" such as these are not part of the activity of the religious congregation, I propose removing them from the roster of congregation employees. . . . I ask the soviet [for Religious Affairs of the USSR] to issue instructions regarding what degree of connection should exist between burial issues and the religious congregations, and whether it is justified for certain local authorities to require resources from the religious population so as to maintain the cemeteries, and sometimes to completely hand control of them to the religious associations and groups.[73]

Where the Belorussia SRA official took a hesitant stance toward the "burial societies," his counterpart in Ukraine viewed them as a significant income source for the congregation, and thus opined that activities in the cemeteries should be more harshly supervised.[74]

Yet given the more favorable climate of the mid-1950s, seventy-four-year-old Aharon Kruglik, the head of the "burial society" in Voroshilovgrad, dared to launch a complaint to the SRA representative about municipal authorities who refused to allow him to charge a family for religious burial services. To this the SRA representative replied that religious burials are permitted and nothing should interfere with them, but that the question of payment is a private matter between the deceased's family and the provider of the service. A Jewish memoirist from the USSR describes the burial of his mother in the town of Orsha:

> On Friday, the ninth of August 1963, my mother died. I approached the head of
> the burial society . . . and he sent two people to take my mother from the bed. . . .
> [O]n Shabbat in the evening a woman came from the "burial society" and sewed
> a shroud . . . on Sunday they washed my mother and dressed her in white . . . in
> a bus, traveling slowly, we brought the body to the Jewish cemetery on Engels
> Street. I recited kaddish in the cemetery and one Jew said the prayer "El Maleh
> Rahamim."[75]

Funerals were not always so tranquil, including in the same town of Orsha, where the desires of family members for a Jewish funeral often clashed with those of the deceased's colleagues for a more "respectable" service—especially if the former held a high position, such as doctor or factory manager. The family usually relented, leaving its members not only aggrieved at the death but also hurt by the manner of his interment.[76]

"Burial societies" were usually the active element in the maintenance of cemeteries, and their chief concern was the purification houses. Thus, the "societies" were behind the initiative of the congregation of Kiev, which in 1957 sought permission to build a house of purification in the Jewish cemetery. According to "the instructions" from the SRA, a religious association was allowed to build a ritual structure (kul'tovoe zdanie) at its own expense, so long as the SRA approved it and the local authorities did not object. Accordingly the SRA chairman recommended that the Kiev congregation raise funds for this purpose (tselevoi sbor) in the synagogue, but ensure that only religious people donate. The building had to be built in accordance with specifications of the city engineer and other local authorities, and after construction would be listed as owned by the local authority.[77]

In Chernovtsy, "burial societies" encouraged one of the city's congregations to apply to the city authorities for the repair of the purification house, promising that the city would be paid fifty rubles by each family of the deceased washed in the structure. This arrangement lasted several years, but with the thaw, the congregation sought to change the terms and only pay rent on the building, a much smaller amount. In response, the authorities agreed to give up the structure to the congregation without any payment whatsoever. When the antireligion campaign of the late 1950s intensified, however, the subject of the purification house was again brought up in the Chernovtsy municipality, which demanded a rent payment.[78]

In Leningrad it was the deputy chairman of the congregation and one of the "burial society" activists who made sure that a special plot would be dedicated to Jewish burial in the new, soon-to-open general cemetery. The former even tried to get a house of purification included in the plans, the construction costs of which would be covered by the congregation. Though this plan didn't materialize, it does suggest that "burial societies" during this period were operating in ways beyond what was legally sanctioned.[79]

The "burial societies" did not distinguish clearly between payments to individuals for memorial services in the cemeteries and payments for Jewish last rites, the latter of which actually provided revenue meant for congregational goals. "Burial society" revenues, whether from funeral services or collection boxes in the cemeteries, were not always listed fully in the congregation's account books. This tactic enabled the congregation, on the one hand, to fund activities such as supporting the poor and sick—areas considered by the authorities to be outside the congregation's domain—and, on the other, laid the grounds for financial irregularities and assorted suspicious behaviors. In the late 1950s and early 1960s, then, when the Soviet authorities stiffened their antireligion campaign, they were able to exploit internal disagreements and mutual accusations having to do with the financial irregularities of the "burial societies." Thus, for example, the authorities accused the congregation in Nezhin (Chernigov district) of having "organized a burial society" and "taken money" from the families of the deceased—something forbidden by Soviet rules and regulations.[80]

The Soviet authorities also made sure to publicize broadly most reports, whether true or fictitious, of the activities of the "burial societies," whose participants purportedly lined their pockets with the cash contributed for funeral services and cemetery maintenance.[81] The authorities thus strove to disgrace the religion and cut into an important economic resource for religious activity. The more the "burial societies" lost prestige, the less they could work to obtain distinct burial sites for Jews. In Belorussia, accordingly, the Minsk municipality in 1962 issued the instruction that all the Jewish deceased be buried in the general cemetery. This decision was completely illegal, even by

Soviet rules and regulations on religious affairs, and the community leaders opposed it fiercely. In response to their protests:

> [W]e were summoned to the municipality [wrote congregation heads Gorelik and Shor] and they began lecturing us that separate burials of religious Jews are unethical and would have a negative effect on the Communist education of children who come to visit the graves of their relatives.

The extreme and unusual step taken in Minsk may have resulted from the unusually harsh line this republic took against Judaism as compared with others, and may have owed in part to animosity toward the town's Jewish deputy mayor, Y. B. Kazhdan. Yet such behavior was not a vast departure from the overall antireligion policy practiced in those years.[82]

After WWII the ancient graveyards gradually filled up and new ones were built. Allocations for new graveyards were not made based on religion, and in quite a few regions the number of Jewish cemeteries as well as Jewish parcels within general cemeteries declined. Yet in many communities the Jewish population, like the members of other religions, still succeeded in securing separate land allotments. Often these parcels are described as "Jewish cemeteries," but they were actually Jewish parcels in general cemeteries. And obtaining such parcels cost the Jews considerable effort (as in Minsk). Even in Moscow, a showcase for tourists visiting the USSR, the lobbying efforts of Rabbi Levin met with ill will. Nevertheless, the authorities told him that new parcels would soon be added to the existing cemetery and the problem would resolve itself. Indeed a new parcel was added, but from the first day it included bodies from various groups among the Jewish dead and in time the area became a general cemetery.[83]

The number of active Jewish cemeteries, or Jewish parcels in general cemeteries, thus steadily diminished. Yet they continued to exist in a series of towns, as was attested by a religious Jew who immigrated to Israel from Mogilev-Podol'skii in the late 1950s:

> In most of the towns of Ukraine there exist . . . separate cemeteries for Christians and for Jews. In places where the cemetery is in one area, the Jewish and Christian parts are divided by a stone wall or a fence. . . . The burials of the Jewish deceased are handled by a sort of "burial society" which is not described as such for fear of the evil eye.[84]

At the time, some were willing to expend large sums to have their relatives buried in Jewish cemeteries, and the formation of Jewish burial plots thus became an important income source for the congregation.

Most of the towns that had congregations, both official and sometimes unofficial, had some sort of "burial society" functioning in 1941–1964. The existence of these "societies" was possible both because of the authorities' lack of interest in handling burials and cemetery maintenance and because certain Jewish entities had the desire and will to support burial of Jews with Jewish last rites. These societies took care not only of ritual burials but also of the maintenance and guarding of the graveyards. Such "burial societies," though officially they did not exist, served as an important income source for the congregation and indirectly supported its charitable activity and other needs. In this respect this activity extended the historical function of the "burial societies." Yet the income steadily declined with the decrease in Jewish cemeteries in the USSR and the diminished call for their services from Soviet Jews. Furthermore, the complicated and restrictive Soviet rules encouraged irregular financial practices by the "societies," which the regime could exploit in its attacks on religious activity.

The Jewish cemeteries suffered from neglect and destruction, which intensified during the Holocaust and after, a result of both the plundering by the surrounding population and the policies of the local authorities. Where the Jewish population did not take action, the Jewish cemeteries essentially disappeared—and a corresponding decline occurred in the overall number of Jewish cemeteries or zones within general cemeteries. In the new cemeteries the authorities were disinclined to allocate special areas for Jews, and thus a symbol of Jewish community life in the Soviet Union gradually disappeared. Even Jewish efforts to memorialize victims of the Holocaust, for the most part, left few long-term traces owing to the opposition of the authorities.

In the first decade following the liberation of the Nazi-occupied territories of the USSR, many congregations engaged in broad efforts to memorialize the victims of the Holocaust. This activity, which was chiefly local in initiative, took various forms: from caring for and arranging the areas where Jews had been killed to erecting monuments and holding public funeral ceremonies for Holocaust victims. Such activities had the participation of Jews who filled important roles in the Soviet government and scientific apparatus, and whose joint work with the congregations in these campaigns was perhaps the sole expression of their Jewish identity.

CHAPTER EIGHTEEN

The Attitude of World Jewry and Israel to Judaism in the USSR

The attitudes held by world Jewry and the Jewish community in the Land of Israel (and later the state of Israel) toward Jewish religious life in the Soviet Union can be thought of as deriving from an overall interest in Soviet Jewry but also as having special characteristics. The congregations (synagogues), unlike other Soviet Jewish institutions (such as the Jewish Anti-Fascist Committee), were not formed by the authorities, and given their historical-ethnic authenticity they might have been expected to be the focus of world Jewish interest. Yet because these entities were both permitted and tolerated in a country that opposed religion, the congregations' activists had to cooperate to some extent with the authorities, earning them an ambivalent and suspicious response abroad. Unsurprisingly, then, until the late 1950s the congregations were not given their due in both the Jewish and general media in the West and in Israel.

World Jewry

The changing ties between religious institutions in the Soviet Union and world Jewry correspond to the various changes in the attitude of the Soviet authorities toward religion in general and the Jewish religion in particular.

The focus of world Jewry was first on the Holocaust and its implications, and later on the establishment of the state of Israel. The Jewish press focused on the murder of the Jews in the Nazi-occupied territories and on the lives of the hundreds of thousands who were expelled or managed to flee, somehow escaping destruction. Meanwhile, many worldwide Jews held a considerably positive attitude toward the USSR at the time, even those who were ideologically and politically remote from Socialist ideas. Thus, the calls of prominent Jewish figures inside the Soviet Union to "the Jewish brethren of the whole world," on Radio Moscow in August 1941, fell on ready ears. Correspondingly, the delegation of the Jewish Anti-Fascist Committee was given an enthusiastic reception in the United States, Mexico, Canada, and England in June–December 1943, with nearly all the Jewish organizations unified in their perception of a new page in relations between world Jewry and the Jews of the USSR. In the talks between the Jewish Anti-Fascist Committee delegation and representatives of various institutions of US Jewry, the latter expressed interest in broadening the direct contacts with the religious community in Moscow.[1] Presumably the delegation responded with the standard formula in those days: "There is nothing stopping us from doing so." But to the best of our knowledge, relations after the meeting did not differ at all from the situation beforehand. From the autumn of 1942 on, the Union of Russian Jews in New York remained in continuous contact with the head of the Moscow congregation, Shmuel Chubrutskii, and weekly telegrams were exchanged regarding the search for lost relatives, which helped reestablish ties between relatives on both sides of the Atlantic.[2]

In discussions in the United States with the delegation of the Jewish Anti-Fascist Committee, the Jewish organizations expressed a readiness to give material aid to the Jewish population of the USSR, yet the Soviet authorities consented only on condition that this be done through the Soviet Red Cross and with the aid distributed not only to Jews. The authorities promised that such aid would be directed to regions with especially large Jewish populations.[3] In assenting to this plan, the Joint Distribution Committee (JDC) in effect returned to its arrangement for humanitarian assistance with the Soviet regime that pertained in the first years following the Russian Civil War. Yet whereas in the early 1920s the JDC had representatives in the Soviet Union that also oversaw Jewish religious entities, during the Soviet-German war and the first years afterward, aid from the JDC flowed to Soviet agencies that did not allocate any assistance, direct or indirect, to the religious communities.

The later years of the war saw an increased interest in Soviet Jewry. Thus, in September 1944 the rabbinate of Great Britain sent a telegram (signed by Rabbi Solomon Shonfield) to the head of the Moscow congregation and to the Jewish Anti-Fascist Committee proposing to send a delegation to Moscow to discuss assistance and cooperation with Soviet Jewry. The telegram was passed on to the SRA, which replied, "[G]iven the absence of a single center for the Jewish religion . . . a visit by this sort of delegation is premature."[4] In November 1944 the World Jewish Congress (WJC) was set to convene in Atlanta, and a delegation of Soviet Jews was to be invited as well. Dr. Nahum Goldman (1895–1985), in a discussion with the Soviet ambassador to Mexico, Konstantin Umanskii, noted "that it is desirable that the delegation include not only representatives of the [Jewish] Anti-Fascist Committee, but also representatives of the Orthodox group, whose arrival will make a great impression on public opinion. [The ambassador] agreed that uniting [the actor Solomon] Mikhoels with a bearded Orthodox Jew was a great idea."[5] Yet in the end no delegation was allowed to leave the Soviet Union.

Toward the end of the war, Jewish organizations in the United States increased their efforts to provide material assistance to war survivors. This activity focused on those Eastern European countries that had active representation from organizations, mainly the Joint, that also supported the religious congregations. Activity of this kind was not permitted within the USSR. Still, given the interest of US Jews—especially immigrants from Eastern Europe and their descendants—in their countries of origin and their desire to learn which of their relatives had survived,[6] the activity of the landsmanschaftn also increased. These groups' members were mainly immigrants from the cities annexed to the Soviet Union during the war; there was almost no representation from emigres from communities cut off from the Jewish world after the Bolshevik seizure of power. The activists in the landsmanshaftn shared the traditional belief that the Jewish needy should be assisted by the congregation, and thus they, as well as private individuals, devoted themselves to sending food and clothing packages addressed to the congregations in eastern Galicia (mainly L'vov), northern Bukovina (mainly Chernovtsy), as well as various towns in Moldavia and the Baltic countries. The Joint, too, participated in these activities, sending food packages from Tehran not just to congregations in the annexed territories but also to several cities in the older parts of the USSR.[7] The Soviet authorities imposed high customs charges on the packages; these were paid in foreign currency, providing an income source for the state.[8] As part of the assistance effort, some landsmanshaftn also sent religious books and sacramental objects. A package of this kind was received in 1948 via the Pan-Soviet Society for Foreign Cultural Ties (VOKS—Vsesoiuznoe Obshchestvo Kul'turnoi Sviazi s Zagranitsei) and addressed to the registered congregation in Priluki. The Moscow customs officials sought advice from the SRA, which counseled that the package not be forwarded to its destination.[9]

The congregations, both registered and unregistered, that received food packages thus turned into centers for material assistance to the Jewish population in their towns. The central authorities looked unfavorably on the receipt of such packages, viewing them justifiably as a means for increasing the influence of the congregation on the Jewish population. Yet given the distress in the state and the desire to retain the sympathies of Western public opinion, the regime reconciled itself to the phenomenon. The local authorities, which profited both directly and indirectly from the aid sent from abroad, encouraged the practice. In quite a few towns at the time, there were no recognized congregations, yet permanent minyans operated almost openly and were popularly called the *kehilla,* or congregation (*obshchina*). When food packages reached such towns addressed to the Jewish congregation, the post officer normally would pass them to a Jew known locally as the head of such a "congregation."[10]

Toward Passover of 1946, the Union of Orthodox Congregations in the United States and Canada launched a campaign to send a million food packages to the Jews of Europe. In this context, some 15,000 packages were intended to be sent to the USSR, 15 percent of which were to be distributed by the congregations as they saw fit. Yet the government of the Soviet Union objected to the orderly transfer of aid to the Jews of its state. Nevertheless, the thousands of packages, or perhaps tens of thousands—we are not able to estimate the number precisely—that did arrive in these years from Jewish organizations and private individuals abroad did much to assist large numbers of Jews.[11]

During this time, ties of sorts were formed between certain congregations in the USSR and private individuals and Jewish organizations abroad, especially in the United States. Yet any relations with foreigners by the Jews of the Soviet Union were supposed to be formally handled by the Jewish Anti-Fascist Committee; indeed this was one of the main reasons for its formation. The Jewish organizations thus sought primarily to build relations with the committee, hoping it would invite and host Jewish personages from abroad. In this context, in 1946, Ben-Zion Goldberg (1895–1972), a journalist for the Yiddish New York newspaper *Der Tog,* visited the USSR. Goldberg was not especially interested in the synagogues and neither were his hosts; yet when he visited Kiev during Passover the poet David Hofshtein took him to the synagogue, where some 2,500 people were gathered. Goldberg was allowed to speak from the podium "and after the speech a question-and-answer discussion ensued." Yet the chairman of the congregation understood that the discussion would go in unwanted directions and therefore had collected and screened the questions in advance.[12] The presentation of questions, a common way of voicing opinions in the Soviet Union, was thus filtered by the head of the congregation, who knew the Soviet reality well and the limits of what the congregation would be allowed. This dynamic almost certainly characterized the few other encounters between foreigners and the heads of Soviet congregations and their rabbis. Yet even those feeble contacts ended in 1949.

With the steady closure of the Soviet Union to the outside world and the worsening of interbloc relations, in 1949 explicit guidelines were given to the SRA regarding ties between the religious associations and their coreligionists abroad. These guidelines affirmed that the Armenian-Georgian Church and the institutions of the Muslim faith would have no obstacles raised to their foreign ties, and that the situation for the other religions should be determined "according to concrete objectives and conditions; and vigorous action must be taken against attempts of religious organizations from abroad to influence the behavior of their coreligionists in the Soviet Union."[13]

The Jewish religion was not one of those groups for which the "concrete objectives"—that is, Soviet interests—justified allowing contacts with foreign elements. Hence the congregations were forbidden to continue the random contacts with world Jewry that some of them had formed in the first postwar years. Likewise the climate in the United States during the anti-Communist "witch hunts" led by Senator Joseph McCarthy (1908–1957) prevented American Jewish groups and individuals from maintaining any sort of ties with the Jews of the Soviet Union.

Yet even during these dark years, the Soviet authorities did not refrain from taking advantage of the Jewish religion for their propaganda purposes abroad. When, for example, a Communist delegation from Canada visited the USSR in 1951, its members were brought to the synagogue in Kiev, and the congregants presented a letter to the Jews of Canada in which they praised Stalin and freedom of religion in the Soviet Union.[14]

After Stalin's death and the improvement of interbloc relations, Jews from the free world displayed a certain widening of interest in their relatives in the USSR. Increasingly Jews were referred to the congregation of the main synagogue of Moscow in the search for relatives. Rabbi Shlifer thus sought permission to hang lists of people for whom international relatives were searching in synagogues across the country, yet permission was not granted for this, even as the rabbi was allowed to forward the letters he was receiving to his colleagues in other towns.[15]

In that same period, various initiatives were put forward to form ties between the congregations of the USSR and world Jewry; these had the participation of certain religious leaders of Eastern Europe. Thus, for example, the chief rabbi of Romania, Moshe Rosen (1912–1994), proposed to Rabbi Shlifer that a world congress of rabbis be convened in Warsaw in support of international peace. The Soviet authorities had issues with the proposal, and it was taken off the agenda.[16]

In 1955 Nahum Goldman proposed to the head of the congregation of Moscow's main synagogue that an official visit be made by a delegation of the World Jewish Congress. His suggestion was rejected.[17] In August of that year, Rabbi David Hollander, head of the Rabbinical Council of America, sought permission from the Soviet embassy in Washington for a delegation to visit the USSR, and in December a similar request was made by the New York Board of Rabbis. In 1956 permission was granted for a visit by a delegation of Orthodox rabbis from the United States, and over twenty-five days (June 21–July 16) the delegation visited ten congregations, four of them in Georgia. The delegation from the New York Board of Rabbis had to settle for visits to only four congregations.[18]

In advance of the visit by the delegations, the authorities gave instructions to the local rabbis on how they were to present themselves. They "advised" Rabbi Shlifer not to invite the delegation to his summer home (_dacha_), and suggested that whenever the visitors took an interest in the number of synagogues in the Soviet Union "these need not be divided into registered and unregistered ones."[19] In other words they hinted clearly enough that the rabbi was to augment the number of synagogues functioning legally. On June 25, 1956, Rabbi Shlifer presented a four-page report on the visit of the delegation to Moscow in which he noted, among other things, that "some people in the synagogues addressed the rabbis [from the United States] and told them that all they see is not reality, but only a window display [_pokazukha_]." In the same report the rabbi maintained that those people were provocateurs—Shmuel Chubrutskii's men.[20]

The two delegations returned home from the USSR with different impressions of their visits. The Orthodox delegation described religious life in the Soviet Union in sufficiently positive terms whereas the New York rabbis conveyed considerable criticism. The visits of the delegations of rabbis from the United States aroused certain hopes for the expansion of religious activity in the USSR. But, for their part, the Soviet authorities evidently did not reap the propaganda "benefits" they had hoped for and discontinued any future visits.

After these visits the Soviet authorities demonstrated less willingness to allow direct contact between the congregation heads in the USSR and their colleagues beyond its borders. In late 1957 a conference of European rabbis was about to convene in Amsterdam, and Rabbi Leib Levin was invited to attend. With the consent of certain Soviet authorities, he accepted the invitation and even requested a visa, but with the intervention, almost certainly, of the security services, the rabbi withdrew his offer of participation on the pretext of an illness and sent only his blessings.[21] That same year the World Jewish Congress, led by Nahum Goldman, sought to develop closer ties with congregations in the USSR. Goldman, who believed world Jewry had a duty to secure a religious and cultural life for Soviet Jews in their native land, repeated his effort from the previous year and invited representatives of the large congregations in the

Soviet Union to take part as observers in a meeting of the wjc.[22] The replies echoed that of the Minsk congregation, which said that "since our congregation is an explicitly religious one and does not involve itself in political matters, we decline absolutely to participate in the congress as observers. Dr. Goldman, we ask of you not to complicate our community with political affairs."[23]

The efforts of the head of the wjc to form ties between the Jewish congregations of the ussr and world Jewry ran counter to the concept of the state of Israel, and this led to friction between Goldman and the nascent state.

During the mid-to-late 1950s, international tourists to the ussr increased steadily, including many Jews.[24] The Jewish tourists included those who intended to visit relatives, as well as tourists sent at the recommendation of Nativ (an Israeli liaison organization that maintained contacts with Jews living in the Eastern bloc), with the explicit goal of meeting and forming ties with Soviet Jews,[25] a fact that did not go unnoticed by the security services.[26]

For example, the sra representative described a visit of American Jewish tourists to a synagogue on *Hol hamoed* of Passover 1959:

On the day of the holiday, April 25, the synagogue in Kiev was visited by *five American tourists* [emphasis in original], who during their visit announced to the head of the congregation . . . that they would not be praying as they had not enough time and wanted only to know about the conditions of the lives of the Jews in the ussr—is there no persecution of Jews, why are there no Jewish schools, how many Jews live in Kiev and whether religion here is not being suppressed.[27]

The reports by the congregation heads about every foreign visit to the synagogue were so detailed as to border on the ridiculous. Thus, for example, the rabbi and congregation head in Minsk, Yaakov Yosef Berger, wrote about the visit to the synagogue of two us tourists on September 10, 1954. The tourists were accompanied by two people, one of whom was the translator. One of the tourists turned to the rabbi and peppered him, in Yiddish, with a series of questions relating to religious life, the lack of Jewish culture, the miserable structure that served as the synagogue, and suchlike. To all the questions, the rabbi responded by toeing the Soviet propaganda line. At the end of the visit, the tourists asked permission to photograph the rabbi next to the forlorn synagogue building. This request worried the rabbi, who pretended not to understand and asked the translator for help as he tried to gain time. At that moment the tourists noticed that the fancy building next door had previously been a synagogue and they began to photograph it. The reality of this structure completely contradicted something the rabbi had told them earlier—that all the synagogues in Minsk had been destroyed during the war. To extricate himself from the embarrassing situation, the rabbi

approached them and stressed that this structure too had been destroyed and its skeleton had been offered to the Jewish congregation so as to make it suitable for a synagogue, yet the congregation declined since technically there was a risk of collapse, so that it was forbidden to hold gatherings for prayer there.

It is not hard to imagine the rabbi's feelings about the web of lies he was forced to weave and that he transmitted to the SRA representative a week after the visit. The SRA representative added for his part that "it is unknown whether all this happened or not, since the interpreter did not understand Yiddish.... Yet with my familiarity with Rabbi Berger and his very loyal attitude, it can be believed that he is telling the truth."[28] The rabbi was thus perceived as possibly suspicious both in the eyes of the tourists and the Soviet authorities. He and others in his position may therefore be regarded as tragic figures, whose lives grew more difficult as more foreigners came to the synagogues.

Because of the embarrassing situations caused by foreigners' visits to the synagogues, the Belorussia SRA representative sought to prevent future visits of this kind. Yet such a stance ran counter to Soviet policy during the thaw, when the regime sought to demonstrate that a significant change had taken place after Stalin's death, as exemplified by the opening of the state to tourism and Western media. Accordingly, a reply was received from Moscow that "artificial obstacles are not to be placed before tourists from abroad who visit the synagogue in Minsk." Yet the writer advised his subordinate in Belorussia to instruct the rabbi that he must report to the SRA prior to any visit of foreigners to the synagogue, and to ensure "that Rabbi Berger not receive foreigners privately but in the presence of one or two members of the board of the congregation" to be selected by the SRA representative.[29]

Many of the Jewish tourists visiting the synagogues tended to leave behind books and ceremonial objects. Yet world Jewry, led by Nativ, did not rest content with transmission of books and ceremonial objects via tourists, but developed a broad network for mailing materials of this kind directly to congregations and private individuals. Over the years Nativ had gathered numerous such addresses and used them without the Soviet authorities raising significant obstacles. However, this policy changed in 1959, and the mailing of prayer books, phylacteries, and prayer shawls—as attempted by Canadian Jews[30]—was disallowed; pressures were brought to bear on congregations and individuals to return these gifts to their senders.[31] The new measures taken by the Soviet authorities were harshly condemned by the Western media, and to counteract the criticism the Soviet authorities announced in mid-1962 that a workshop to manufacture prayer shawls had opened in Moscow and that congregations were requested to direct their orders there.[32] No such workshop seems to have ever opened, at least according to my searches.

Faced with pressure from the authorities, many congregations handed over the gifts left by tourists, out of fear the congregations would otherwise be dissolved. On October 7, 1959, the board of the Minsk congregation passed a resolution "to prevent the Jewish worshipers in the synagogue from receiving gifts from any one of the tourists or other visitors." In Ukraine the SRA representative instructed that all gifts brought by tourists be collected by the congregation management and transferred to the authorities.[33] The synagogues thus had become places that tourists, such as those from Nativ, tried to infiltrate with "undesirable literature," an endeavor that the Soviet authorities unsurprisingly sought to prevent.

Israel Before and After Statehood

In the years before Israeli statehood, the organized Jewish community in the Land of Israel (the Yishuv) and the Zionist movement made contact with Soviet officials in London, Ankara, Egypt, and the United States, mainly with the goal of explaining the importance of the Zionist project and reversing the negative Soviet attitude on the matter. Tied to this effort was the sense that the Soviets' postwar treaty with the democratic nations could lead to permission for Zionist activity within the USSR itself.[34]

Yet when the representatives of the Yishuv and the Zionist movement discussed with the Soviet representatives matters relating to Jews then living in the Soviet Union, the discussions were mainly limited to the Jews of Poland. The Zionist side sought to release thousands of Jews from the former Poland to immigrate to the Land of Israel. The focus was on Zionist activists and pioneers stuck in the annexed areas of the Soviet Union who had a stake in the Yishuv.[35] For Jews in the Soviet Union but *not* in these annexed territories, the Yishuv representatives sought to enable the exit only of several dozen elderly people who had relatives in the Land of Israel. They also sought freedom for the prisoners sentenced for Zionist activity in the 1920s or 1930s or those who were imprisoned trying to leave the country illegally during or after the Second World War. Whenever the Zionist representatives mentioned the immigration of Jews to the Land of Israel, they made no mention of the Jews of the Soviet Union, or else they noted explicitly that they were not speaking of Soviet citizens.[36] This approach stemmed, almost certainly, both from the representatives' desire not to antagonize the Soviets and from the fact that several shared the stance expressed by Zionist leader Chaim Weizmann, in a meeting with Ivan Maiskii (1884–1975), USSR ambassador to Britain:

[I]f in [the USSR] the present regime lasts, then in twenty or thirty years [the Jews] will assimilate. . . . The Soviet Jews will gradually integrate and be an inseparable part of the horizon of Russian life. . . . I may not like it, but I am ready to resign myself to it.[37]

In attempting to influence Soviet officials, the Yishuv and the Zionists sought mainly to secure Soviet support for the proposed UN partition plan to create a Jewish and an Arab state. Yet a November 1946 proposal by Yaakov Robinson (1889–1977) to the Council of American Zionists to launch a public battle in the United States was very quickly tabled.[38]

Indeed, on May 14, 1947, during the UN special session on Palestine, the USSR representative spoke of the enormous suffering of the Jewish people and its right to a state in the Land of Israel. Then, on September 30, 1947, a telegram was sent from the Soviet foreign minister supporting the establishment of the Jewish state (made public in a November 26 speech by Andrei Gromyko). Both gestures strengthened the Yishuv's positive attitude toward the Soviet Union. Also in this context may we view the letter of blessing for Hanukkah (sent December 22) by Israel's chief rabbi, Yitzhak Halevi Herzog, to the congregation of Moscow's main synagogue. Given the public change in the Soviet Union's stance toward the Yishuv, the letter was read from the podium of the synagogue.[39] The change in the Soviet posture toward the Jewish community in the Land of Israel was regarded by certain religious leaders in the USSR as the hand of God. And Rabbi Mendel, of the Chernovtsy synagogue, said as follows, according to an SRA report: "[T]he day will come when by the will of God a Jewish state shall arise and then the leaders of the world will not be able to vanquish us." The head of the Beregovo congregation expressed himself similarly in affirming that "the state of Israel arose thanks to our prayers and it has been granted to us by the Almighty."[40]

In spring 1948 the declaration of Israeli statehood roused great passions throughout the Jewish world, including in the USSR, where prayers of thanks were incanted in the synagogues. For instance, a week after statehood was declared flyers were posted in the streets of L'vov announcing that on May 23 a thanksgiving prayer would be held in the synagogue; a large crowd indeed participated. Encouraged by this example, on May 29 the Chernovtsy congregation sought permission from the authorities to conduct a special prayer for the peace of the state of Israel. Since the Soviet media was then stressing the

USSR's support for Israel, the local authorities saw no problem with holding such prayers. The chairman of the district authorities (*oblispolkom*), Markin, gave his prompt authorization, and on June 1 a thousand people attended the service, which ended with the prayer "El Maleh Rachamim" (O Lord Full of Mercy), in memory of those who fell defending the state.

The Jews' response to the declaration of statehood seems to have surprised Soviet authorities, and the security services were held responsible for not properly assessing the mood of the Jewish public. Later the security services were the first to seek prevention of public gatherings held in such a spirit, and as early as June 9, 1948, the Ukraine security services took the position, apparently on orders from Moscow, that "Zionists and clerical elements, without revealing their anti-Soviet perspectives and with a pretext of loyalty to the Soviet regime, are struggling to take advantage of the legal opportunities [i.e., the synagogue] to realize their hostile nationalist activity."

In this context it is not hard to understand the guidelines of the SRA representative for Ukraine "that prayers of [thanksgiving for the establishment of the state] are undesirable . . . since they are in essence mass assemblies, organized by nationalist elements, who seek to turn the synagogue into a sociopolitical organization."

On the basis of this instruction, the authorities rejected the requests of the congregations of Odessa and Kiev to hold thanksgiving prayers in their synagogues.[41] Yet since in those days there was a lack of clarity and perhaps even opposition of views among the different Soviet agencies regarding prayers for Israel, the authorities in Moscow tried to delay them on the pretext of the rabbis being ill, and the service was held only on June 26, 1948, by which time the security services had arranged for surveillance of all those who came.

In and around the Moscow main synagogue, masses gathered, with the tally estimated by authorities at 10,000. From the wall of the synagogue, two banners hung: one read, "May 14, 1948—Declaration of the State of Israel"; the second, "Am Yisrael Chai" (the Nation of Israel Lives). The hall was festooned with stars of David. After the prayers, telegrams sent to Stalin by Chaim Weizmann and Rabbi Yitzhak Halevi Herzog were read aloud from the podium.[42]

The synagogues thus became a focal point for Jews' expression of their identification with the state of Israel, in prayer or by other means. Thus, for instance, the secretary of the congregation in Uzhgorod suggested that religious Jews ask the authorities "to allow them to organize military units" to aid Israel. People from numerous congregations in Uzbekistan, according to a report from the republic's SRA representative, expressed an interest in the possibility of immigrating to Israel.

The head of the Leningrad congregation came to the SRA representative in his district accompanied by a famous doctor from the city, Filistovich, and the two proposed "to organize aid for the Jewish fighters in Palestine from the Jews of the Soviet Union and also to establish a Jewish Anti-Fascist Committee by the synagogue."[43] The proposers thus viewed the war in the Land of Israel as part of the anti-Fascist struggle that was then so much discussed. Other members of the congregations were not content to appeal to the authorities and commenced practical activities at their own initiative: for instance, the rabbi of the Chernigov congregation began raising funds for Israel.[44]

In late August 1948, the head of the Israeli diplomatic delegation, Golda Meyerson (later Meir), arrived in Moscow; and on September 10 she presented her credentials. The ambassador's advisor, Mordechai Namir, met with Rabbi Shlifer in the presence of the congregation secretary, Eliahu Davidov, and board member Krupitsky. In this meeting arrangements were made to prepare for the arrival of the entire embassy staff at the synagogue on Shabbat, September 11, 1948. Word of the pending arrival spread quickly in town, and on Shabbat more visitors came than usual. As outlined in the arrangements the embassy members were given *aliyot* to the Torah, and after the prayers had concluded the ambassador came down from the women's section and said her blessings to the rabbi. The congregation welcomed the embassy members with great excitement and applause.

Yet even as the Soviet newspapers were full of reports on the arrival of the Israeli ambassador and the delivery of her credentials, Stalin felt the time was right to stress to the Israeli leadership, and even more emphatically to the Jews in the USSR, that a complete separation must exist between the issues faced by Soviet Jews and Soviet policy toward Israel. In early September 1948, Stalin personally ordered that the author Ilya Ehrenburg compose an article clearly stating that there is no connection between Soviet support of Israel and any identification by the Jews of the USSR with the new state. This article was meant to be signed by several important Jews from the Soviet Union. As it happened, implementation of the order was delayed because Ehrenburg was out of town; only between September 15 and 17, 1948, did Lazar Kaganovitch, Piotr Pospelov, Leonid Il'ichev, and Georgii Malenkov meet and ask Ehrenburg to write the article. Ehrenburg presented the piece on September 18, and it was published on September 21 in *Pravda,* after Stalin's explicit authorization. The article, as Golda Meir characterized it, was "essentially pro-Israel and anti-Zionist."[45]

Such an account helps frame the Soviet policy designed to limit contacts between the Israeli embassy and the Jews of the Soviet Union, which primarily took place in the synagogues. The policy was implemented because the contacts, as the SRA chairman said, were meant to "heat up undesirable tendencies among a certain portion of the Jewish citizens of the USSR who visit the synagogue."[46] Accordingly, the authorities refused to permit the festive transfer of a Torah scroll sent from a synagogue in Tel Aviv to the Moscow synagogue, demanding that this be done only in the narrow circle of congregation activists. They also instructed Rabbi Shlifer not to respond to embassy requests for frequent meetings with him and to limit the contact to religious matters such as participation in synagogue prayers and assisting the embassy in keeping kosher.[47]

The Israeli embassy in Moscow was thus forced to deal with the tension and conflicts created by its dual role. Its primary purpose was to attend to the essential interests of the state of Israel, such as Soviet support in international forums to counter anti-Israel efforts (e.g., the Bernadotte Plan), acquisition of weapons essential for the Israel Defense Forces, increasing the Jewish community in Israel via immigration permits for hundreds of thousands of Jews from Romania and Hungary—states that fell within the USSR's sphere of influence—and broadening bilateral trade. To achieve these aims, the Israeli embassy had to demonstrate loyalty to the Soviet Union. The second purpose of the embassy was to link the state of Israel and world Jewry to the Jews in the USSR, an objective viewed by the Soviets as undesirable. Since the Israeli leadership, primarily David Ben-Gurion, considered the state's establishment as the most important historical event of recent generations, any activity considered likely to harm state needs had lower priority. For its part, the stance of the Israeli leadership ran against the deepest sensibilities of thousands of Jews in the USSR, despite their identification as citizens of the Soviet Union, as expressed in Ehrenburg's article.

Still, excitement among Jews over the state of Israel ran deep. When, for example, the Israeli embassy staff came to Moscow's main synagogue on the first day of Rosh Hashana (October 4) of 1948, some ten thousand people, according to the SRA estimate, gathered to greet them. Afterward, some accompanied Ambassador Meyerson in a procession to her hotel, and when the authorities sought to interrupt this spontaneous happening, the participants said: "We have been waiting for this event for two thousand years, how can you forbid us from expressing our feelings?"[48]

Warm relations between the USSR and Israel did not last long. In late 1948 the first signs of deterioration appeared, and the situation grew bleaker in 1949. In the Soviet press increasing numbers of articles attacked the state of Israel and its policies. In February 1949 the Soviet Foreign Ministry lodged an official protest to the Israeli delegation in Moscow for its "illegal activity" as manifest in its having sent its bulletin "to public Soviet organizations, Jewish congregations and Jewish kolkhozes."[49]

As Israel's leadership grew less convinced of any chance of a positive response to its overtures to the USSR, the decision evolved to raise with the Soviets the subject of immigration by the USSR's Jews to Israel. Yet even hinting at the issue in diplomatic meetings sharpened the sensitivities of the Soviet security services, which intensified their surveillance of the embassy staff to prevent any contact between Soviet Jews and Israel's representatives. This change was felt particularly during the visit of the Israeli embassy staff to the Moscow synagogue during the High Holidays of 1949. While this year, too, the staff members were given aliyot to the Torah and a memorial service was conducted for those who had fallen in the Israeli War of Independence, the audience kept a certain distance from the embassy staff, fearing whatever consequences awaited. In early 1951, unsurprisingly, the Israeli envoy to Moscow reported "that the irregular and the formal contacts that we'd had with the rabbi [Shlifer] have in effect completely ceased . . . and people in the congregation are treating us as outcasts."[50]

Even despite such reports, on August 18, 1951, Minister for Internal Security Semion Ignat'ev sought permission from the secretary of the Central Committee of the Communist Party, Georgii Malenkov, to arrest Rabbi Shlifer for having been in contact with the Israeli embassy and with the Jewish Anti-Fascist Committee.[51]

Against such challenges, the congregations understandably strove to institute a complete and utter separation between the worshipers and the foreigners. In 1952 the Israeli soccer team came to pray at the synagogue in Moscow and was seated in the section meant for visitors from abroad. When, due to lack of space, some regular congregation members tried to sit among them, they were asked by another member to find other seats.

Given the chilly state of USSR-Israel relations, some individuals among Israel's leadership grew ready to listen to suggestions about going beyond purely diplomatic activity. In particular, certain Israelis were trained in the methods of the so-called Illegal Aliyah and Brikha (Escape), an underground effort that in 1944–1948 worked to achieve the illegal repatriation of Jews from the Eastern bloc to the Land of Israel. Heading this organization was Shaul Avigur, who along with others was prepared to contribute his experience for operations among the Jews of Eastern Europe. Thus, in spring 1952 a special agency was created, which eventually was given the code name "Nativ." In its first years Nativ functioned as part of the Mossad for Intelligence and Special Operations; later it became an independent agency reporting directly to the prime minister.

For its first two or three years, Nativ continued in the tradition of the Brikha, handling the immigration of Jews from the USSR and Eastern Europe through smugglers, forged documents, and suchlike. The results of this effort were miniscule, though, and the agency drew harsh criticism. Although Avigur defended the agency he headed, he evidently understood that the methods used during the Brikha and the Illegal Aliyah could not simply be copied, and that Nativ must tap the potential offered by the formal representation of the sovereign state of Israel. He also saw clearly that, with regard to the Jews of the USSR, rapid results—that is, immigration to Israel—could not be counted on. Rather, a long-term strategy of strengthening Jewish identity had to be pursued, which eventually would lead to the desired outcome.

On February 11, 1953, while Nativ was still being organized and Nehemia Levanon and his associates were en route to Moscow posing as diplomats, the USSR cut its ties with Israel. In effect, then, Nativ's activities in the USSR began in December 1953, once diplomatic relations resumed. The Nativ members who at the time were sent to Moscow were not personally religious, yet:

> From the first it was clear to us [writes Levanon] that the synagogue was the sole place where Jews gather and that only there can local Jews have discussions with the members of the Israeli embassy. We hoped . . . that we would be able to build the significant contacts there.[52]

An inevitable tension thus developed between the Nativ figures and the heads of the synagogues. While the primary aim of Nativ in its synagogue visits was to form "significant contacts" with local Jews, the heads of the congregations saw it as their duty to safeguard the continued existence of the sole permitted Jewish institution in the USSR, through cooperation with the Soviet authorities.

To approach the congregations, Israel also tried the interfaith path. In 1954 the Ministry of Religion proposed to a delegation of the Russian Orthodox Church in Jerusalem that a delegation of rabbis be sent to the Soviet Union; the request went unanswered. During the thaw, too, Israel's chief rabbi turned to Rabbi Levin in Moscow to arrange for a group of Bratslav Chassidim to visit R. Nahman's grave in Uman'. The SRA, to whom the letter was referred, instructed that no response be given at all.[53] With all the rejections, the Israeli embassy in Moscow was left as a principal channel for contact with Jews in the Soviet Union.

During the interbloc thaw, the freedom of movement of members of the diplomatic corps widened beyond Moscow. The broadened mobility enabled Nativ to visit farther-flung towns, where the synagogues likewise served as one of the few locations enabling direct contact with Soviet Jews. In these meetings and through the contacts that developed from them, the Nativ members tried to disseminate information in various forms on the state of Israel and Jewish culture, as well as religious literature—prayer books, Haggadot, calendars, and so on.[54] Some of the local Jews who received these items redisseminated them, either for religious reasons or for profit.

After Nehemia Levanon was caught red-handed meeting with Soviet Jews in a private apartment, several Jews were arrested and, in 1955, Levanon and two other Nativ members (Moshe Mark and Moshe Kehat) were quietly expelled from the USSR. Their replacements likewise viewed the synagogues as central locations for forming contacts with Soviet Jews and distributing literature and religious objects. Even embassy staff who were not members of Nativ increasingly participated in this type of activity once it received the embrace of the ambassador himself (Yosef Avidar), who unlike his predecessor encouraged his staff to reach out to synagogues across the country.[55] Thus, for instance, in May 1956 the Odessa synagogue received a visit from the deputy secretary to the ambassador, Avraham Agmon—a Nativ member—and his wife. Agmon distributed manuscripts, postcards from Israel, and prayer books to synagogue attendees. When the rabbi and congregation head failed to report this activity, he was summoned to the SRA representative, who hinted that he would, as a result, have to relinquish one of his two roles. Diment argued in his own defense that he had seated Agmon near himself and Agmon's spouse near his own wife, so as to keep them away from the worshipers. The rabbi also stressed that the guests "handed out the gifts not in the synagogue but in the street, for which I can't be held responsible."[56]

Each visit of this kind thus caused a headache for the congregation activists, who were obliged to form a barrier between the guests and the public and to report exactly to the SRA on the contacts between the guests and public, as well as any other happenings. At the same time, every such visit drew a greater crowd to the synagogue, something the congregation activists welcomed. Thus, the congregation administrations' respective attitudes toward visits by embassy staffers were ambivalent and depended considerably on personalities, the local approach of the authorities, and the general policy toward religion in a given period. Rabbi Levin, for example, in September 1958 went at his own initiative to the SRA to complain that the Israeli embassy staff was traveling by car to the synagogue on Shabbat and that this was generating much resentment among the worshipers. He likewise related that when he spoke of the matter to Ambassador Avidar, the latter referred to it as a "provocation."[57]

The deterioration in relations between the USSR and Israel that followed the Sinai campaign in fall 1956 obliged the heads of the congregations and their rabbis to act more carefully. On November 6, 1956, correspondingly, Rabbi Shlifer went to the SRA and proposed, at his own initiative or perhaps after hints from certain officials, to publish a protest letter in the press against "Israeli aggression." The proposal was welcomed and the rabbi was asked to bring the draft, which he did on November 14; on December 6 the rabbi presented the SRA officials with a similar letter from the Georgian congregations.[58]

As the antireligion policy intensified, the authorities in various regions sought to reduce to the extent possible the visits of the Israel embassy staff to synagogues. On the eve of the holidays of 1962, an order was issued to the heads of the few remaining congregations in Ukraine "not to offer any honors to their coreligionists from abroad and to decline any gifts offered them." This order put the heads of the Kiev congregation in an awkward position when on the eve of Yom Kippur four members of the Israeli embassy came to town, led by Ambassador Yosef Tekoa. That evening Zvi Ofer, formally a trade attaché and actually a Nativ member, asked that Tekoa be given honors appropriate to a representative of the state of Israel. The congregation head, keeping to the instructions he was given, declined. Ofer then addressed the worshipers directly with the same request, but with no success. The next day all four guests came to the synagogue, and the official report indicates that "they conversed with the worshipers, handed out illustrated magazines, prayer books, symbols, and invited the Jews to immigrate to Israel." A demonstration of sorts coalesced around the synagogue, which the SRA representative, not without exaggeration, described as follows:

> Among the crowd that gathered in the street cries were heard, as if the Soviet regime "does not give freedom to Jews," limits the "rights of Jews" in employment and education. . . . Those shouting demanded that Israel's diplomatic representative "defend the rights of Jews. . . ." An even uglier scene showed itself when the Israelis went out to the street. The shouters, mainly the handicapped and old ladies, blocked the path of a vehicle [that chanced by] and demanded of its driver to "run them over," since "in the name of Jewish unity they are prepared to sacrifice their lives."[59]

Faced with scenes such as this during visits by Israel's representatives to the synagogues, SRA officials demanded that the Soviet Foreign Ministry halt or at least reduce such visits throughout Ukraine. Yet the Soviet Foreign Ministry refrained at that time from openly discriminating against the Israeli diplomats, as compared with their colleagues from other Western countries, and the visits to synagogues throughout the USSR and especially Ukraine continued.[60]

However, the authorities did tend at that time to take harsher actions against congregation heads for contacts with foreigners. This situation is reflected in the events at the Minsk synagogue on the eve of Tisha be Av (July 29, 1963), during which the ambassador and his family, on a visit to the synagogue of the Belorussian capital, left a prayer shawl and a book of lamentations. The SRA representative immediately reported as follows to his superiors:

> Members of the [synagogue] administration are receiving with great pleasure all sorts of "gifts" in the form of prayer shawls and prayer books, although we warned them not to receive any contributions [*podachki*], but these rag purveyors [*triapochiniki*] don't respect anything and thus debase the honor of Soviet citizenship.

The ambassador didn't limit himself to visiting the synagogue and the next day also visited the graveyard, where Jews often came to pay respects to their deceased relatives; there he could meet Jews free from the watchful eyes of the synagogue leaders.[61]

On special occasions, Israel embassy staff visited communities not usually reached by tourists at all. For example, the SRA representative received information from the "neighbors" (i.e., security services) that Korosten', Zhitomir, and Berdichev were about to be visited by staff members from the Israeli embassy. The congregation heads were immediately summoned and guided on how to behave when the guests arrived. Once the embassy staff booked hotel rooms, the date of their planned arrival spread quickly, and on Friday night, some two hours after Arieh (Liova) Eliav and Gorev (first name unknown) reached town, twice as many people as usual attended the synagogue. The two left on a table several books of psalms, Bibles, and calendars. The response of the worshipers was described in the report as follows: "For a while all this was left without anybody touching it and later a Jew [here his name appears] approached and took one prayer book[;] after that all the rest fell on it and grabbed the gifts that were on the table."

On February 1, the two emissaries reached Zhitomir, where a day later they were visited in the hotel by the congregation head and one of its activists. During the actual visit to the synagogue, about a hundred people gathered. The report delivered to the authorities by two congregation activists was presumably accurate, listing in great detail the gifts that the embassy representatives left behind, along with the names of the people who took them (including exact addresses) and the fact that the guests contributed to the synagogue charity box, which when opened was found to contain four hundred rubles.[62]

This account, cited in detail in the Soviet documentation, reflects accurately the sense of remoteness and fear felt by congregation activists in dozens of midsize towns, which were effectively cut off from the outside world. These activists were investing all their efforts to preserve the minimum amount of Jewish life they were allowed.

In towns lacking a synagogue the Nativ people tried to establish contact with the regular minyans, which had resumed almost-open operation during the thaw. Thus, for example, in December 1958 a Nativ member visited a minyan held in the home of Yisrael Mirkin in Vitebsk, where the former left religious books and material for learning Hebrew. Mirkin was summoned to the SRA, to which he handed over all the gifts.[63] When the antireligion campaign intensified and many minyans went underground, this sort of meeting with embassy officials seems to have ceased.

Whereas prayer shawls, phylacteries, and prayer books are used year-round, the Arbaa Minim (Four Varieties: *etrog, lulav, hadas, arava*) are used just once a year, during Sukkot. Thus, when the antireligion battle weakened in the mid-fifties, numerous congregations sought assistance from the Soviet authorities in obtaining *lulav*s and *etrog*s for the Sukkot holiday. Pursuant to these requests, and with the authorities seeking to demonstrate their liberal attitude toward religion, in 1956 the USSR embassy to Israel asked Israel's Foreign Ministry the cost to import a thousand *lulav*s and *etrog*s. Whether due to the quoted price (one thousand pounds sterling) or for other reasons, the USSR did not pursue this idea, and the SRA notified Rabbi Shlifer that owing to the shortage in foreign currency, supplying the congregations with *etrog*s would be difficult.[64] Yet while Israel's Foreign Ministry evidently viewed the supply of *etrog*s and *lulav*s as an ordinary commercial deal, the Nativ people felt that provision of these ceremonial items marking the fall harvest from Israel's chief rabbinate would strengthen ties with the Jews of the USSR, and that tiny as well as large congregations should be included in the effort. Provision of *lulav*s and *etrog*s to the Soviet congregations thus became a function of Nativ and its branches inside and outside the USSR, a function that steadily expanded.[65] A report of the SRA on the "autumn Jewish holidays" for 1956 notes that "unlike previous years, this year there was growth in the number of congregations . . . to which the Israeli rabbinate has sent packages including . . . *etrog*s." And in 1957 the SRA representative in Ukraine stressed:

> Each year Israel's rabbinate is increasing the number of packages which contain *etrog*s and *lulav*s . . . along with letters of blessings, which are sent to the congregation's address, and in this way in effect ties are formed with the religious service

providers and the religious activists, and this arouses fanaticism among the religious and promotes nationalist manifestations.[66]

Especially worrisome to the Soviet authorities was the fact that the *etrogs* and *lulavs* were sent not just to the legal congregations but also to the minyans, which the regime had less supervision over and knowledge about. Moreover, the congregations that were unable to get *etrogs* from Israel often were given them by other congregations, thus resulting in ties between congregations[67]—something various branches of the regime viewed as undesirable.

Given the excitement aroused by the *etrogs* arriving from Israel, the authorities did their best to reduce the number that reached their destination, especially in towns where contact with Jews of the outside world was particularly feeble.[68] Thus, for instance, when two packages from Israel's rabbinate reached Zhitomir before the holidays of 1957, the congregation head, Shulman, sought advice from the district SRA representative as to how to handle them. The congregation head was given a lecture on Israel's aggressive policies and the need for Soviet patriotism. The head of the congregation took the hint, and a few days later returned to the same official and informed him that the board had decided not to accept the packages from Israel.[69]

As the antireligion policy intensified, restrictions on receipt of *etrogs* also grew, and in 1959, 185 packages containing *etrogs* and religious books sent by Israel's chief rabbinate were returned. Yet the *etrogs* that did make it through the curtain were received with great excitement by quite a few Jews, as the Western press reported. Also, the more the authorities restricted the delivery of *etrogs*, the higher their prices rose on the black market, reaching 800 to 1,000 rubles apiece. Receipt of *etrogs* and *lulavs* thus turned into another point of contention between the Soviet authorities and the Western organizations that dealt with the Jews of the Soviet Union, mainly Nativ. The congregation activists, meanwhile, who hoped to let those visiting the synagogue fulfill the mitzvah, were caught between the two forces.[70]

Like the *etrogs,* the matzah packages sent to congregations and private individuals in the USSR were meant mainly to strengthen ties between their receivers and Israel or world Jewry—not to meet the practical demand for matzah. Those who received the matzah felt something like this: "[M]atzah [from Israel] was perceived as 'holy' and distributed in small pieces [to attendees at the synagogue] who waited in line."[71] This symbolism did not escape the notice of the authorities, and as early as 1957 the SRA representative in Ukraine proposed that receipt matzah be restricted:

From observation of the special attitude to matzah received from Israel, we have come to the conclusion that in sending matzah packages to the USSR Israel is attempting to arouse nationalist feelings among certain groups of religious Jews. . . . It is thus desirable to ensure that the congregation administrations refuse to accept the matzah packages.[72]

Yet the "matzah campaign" expanded anyway, and similar packages were received not only from Israel but also from the United States, England, and Sweden. In 1958 the Ukraine SRA representative reported:

[T]his year matzah packages from Israel's rabbinate were received by all the congregations . . . and many of the unregistered religious groups [minyans]. [The senders] know the addresses not just of the religious congregations and unregistered groups but also of rabbis and religious activists, congregation leaders and minyans.[73]

This state of affairs infuriated the SRA, yet out of consideration for world opinion it avoided formally restricting delivery of matzah, preferring to apply pressure to the congregations themselves to decline the packages. In 1959 the Ukraine SRA representative reported:

[T]his year, too, as in previous years, packages of "kosher" matzah from the rabbinate of the state of Israel reached the addresses of congregations and also those of unregistered groups of religious [minyans]. . . . Certain congregations . . . refused to accept the packages from abroad and they were returned. The congregations of Chernovtsy and Odessa received from Israel two packages of matzah and arranged their distribution to the religious.[74]

The congregation heads who were obligated to decline the gifts of matzah were greatly conflicted. On the one hand they fiercely desired to taste of the matzah *shmure* (guarded) from the Holy Land while on the other they feared being accused of maintaining ties with Israel, which might lead to closure of the synagogue. An embodiment of this conflict can be seen in the account of the behavior of Shulman, the head of the congregation in Zhitomir. On April 8, 1957, a week before Passover, he appeared in the office of the SRA representative and revealed that the congregation had received a notice from the post office about an unsolicited package from Israel. The official, after consultation with the security services, advised the congregation head to accept the package. And indeed, two days later the congregation head again appeared in the official's office, the unopened package in hand. The SRA official described the tragicomic scene as follows: "They laugh at us and send a kilogram of matzah as if to the poor [said Shulman]." After opening the package, he blurted out emotionally: "It's a special matzah for religious people and it should be delivered to the rabbi." Suddenly as if remembering [that he had said something he shouldn't have], Shulman remarked that "actually the best thing would be to send the package back." The package of matzah from the Holy Land was placed in the synagogue, and the attendees tasted small amounts. Having observed this attitude toward the matzah, the official stressed that it would have been better for the package not to have been accepted, and once received it would have been best if its contents were distributed to the congregation administration, as the Kiev congregation did, rather than include all the worshipers in the experience, since the latter just "excites Judaism and the revival of nationalistic feelings," serving Israel's aims.

Following the stance articulated by the SRA official in Zhitomir, most congregations in the district declined to accept the matzah sent to them for the Passover of 1958, and only the rabbi of the Novograd-Volynskii congregation dared to receive a package "and distributed matzah in the synagogue on the first day of Passover."[75] The matzah packages sent from Israel, or from other countries as arranged by Nativ, mainly were meant to give synagogue attendees, and through them other Jews, a sense of connection with the Jews of Israel and the world.

The feeble contacts between the staff of the Israeli embassy in Moscow and the congregation activists took place in an atmosphere of considerable tension and mutual reservation, stemming both from the different positions in which each found itself and from their different perspectives on the aims of their activity. While the staff of the embassy, including the Nativ members, had diplomatic immunity and could at worst be banished from the Soviet Union for their activities, the congregation activists, who remembered the terror campaigns of the late 1930s and early 1950s, had learned from experience that any contact with foreign entities stood to harm them and their families.

The congregation activists believed it was their responsibility to keep the final embers of Judaism in the USSR alive, so they worked to prevent anything that could harm the synagogue or lead to its closure. They understood that the existence of the synagogue as an authorized institution depended on the authorities and hence were ready to collaborate with them whenever necessary. Guaranteeing the continued existence of the synagogue was their entire aim. The Nativ people, on the other hand, viewed the synagogue as a framework that permitted contact with Soviet Jews as a means of strengthening their Jewish affiliation and their bonds to Israel, the ultimate purpose being immigration.

Although both sides were interested in deepening the Jewish sensibilities of Soviet Jews, often the Nativ workers viewed congregation activists as mere agents of the regime. Meanwhile, some congregation activists felt that the involvement of the embassy was threatening the very existence of the synagogue.

Relations between the synagogue activists and Israel and world Jewry were thus complex. Often one side or the other lacked sufficient consideration of the objectives and methods of operation of its counterpart, even though both were interested in the survival of Judaism, either as a continuation of Jewish history in Russia or as a long-term investment in the objective of immigration to Israel. The synagogues were often a focal point for the contest between the Western activists working on behalf of Soviet Jews, as led by Nativ, and the branches of the Soviet regime, with the congregation heads and the rabbis caught in between and earning the trust and appreciation of neither side.

|||| Conclusion

From its inception, the Soviet Union was run by an explicitly antire-ligious regime, which considered religion in all its forms as a harmful relic of the past that needed to disappear. The regime had established a sort of new religion of Communism, whose proponents viewed traditional religion as an undesirable and rival element; the new human being to be fashioned by Communism was to be a sworn atheist who fights off every manifestation of religion or any connection with it. Thus, for its entire duration the Soviet regime was engaged in a constant battle against religion. Yet the scope and intensity of this battle were determined to a great extent by the social and political context in which the country found itself at any given period, and to varying degrees the regime took into consideration the effect that religious persecution would have on the USSR's international standing. It is thus unsurprising that following the Nazi invasion of the Soviet Union, at a time when the regime sought, by any means, to recruit large masses of people into the war effort, a certain reprieve occurred in the battle against religion. This shift was also meant to serve Soviet foreign policy and to raise the standing of the Soviet Union in the public opinion of the Allied countries. Confronted with this new reality, the regime learned that despite its brutal persecution and suppression for some two decades, religion was still a significant social force that needed to be taken into account and preferably harnessed to achieve national objectives. Accordingly, in 1943 the government reached a sort of "concordat" with the Russian Orthodox Church, with permission to engage in religious activities extending to other religions as well. The agreement made necessary the 1944 establishment of a Soviet for Religious Affairs (SRA) to oversee these activities.

Even during the periods of supposed tolerance toward religion, the Soviet regime confined the permitted activity to the realm of sacred ritual, while many other issues essential to the commandments of the Jewish faith, such as charity, kosher food, matzah for Passover, and so forth, were deemed to be not part of such ritual. Moreover, the approach of the Soviet authorities toward religion was patterned on the model of the universalist faiths and did not at all correspond to Judaism, in which national-ethnic and religious aspects are so closely intertwined as to be inseparable. It follows that any change in the attitude of the authorities toward one of the realms—ethnic or religious—had implications for the other. This state of affairs set the stage for a conception by the authorities of Judaism-oriented activities as expressions of ethnic identity or even of ethnic nationalism. Hence, as the policy of suppressing the Jewish ethnic minority intensified and relations with the state of Israel worsened, the legal institutions of the Jewish faith also came under increasing pressure. The bond between Jewish religion and ethnicity gave the authorities cover when accusing Jews who performed certain rituals of doing so out of ethnic-national motives. Indeed, accusations of this kind were used to remove Communist Jews from the ranks of the party and harshly chastise other Jews who had attained status in Soviet society. Judaism, like the other religions, existed in the Soviet Union under the constant supervision of an antireligious regime that for reasons of necessity permitted the legal existence of religious institutions. It is no surprise, then, that most scholarly publications on the Jews in the Soviet Union have focused on the persecutions and close supervision of the Jewish faith. In this study, by contrast, an attempt has been made for the first time, on the basis of new archival documentation, to examine and assess, systematically and fairly, the persistence of some Jewish religious activity in spite of the vise of Soviet antireligious policy—and how this contributed to sustaining the identity of the broad Jewish public, nearly all of which was not religious.

Over the nearly twenty-five years dealt with in this work, congregations and synagogues were the sole Jewish institutions permitted to operate legally and with some independence at the local level. Such congregations spanned the length and breadth of the Soviet Union, and their number in certain years reached several hundred. Unlike the other Jewish organizations established by the Soviet regime, such as theaters, publishing houses, the Yiddish authors' sections, and the Jewish Anti-Fascist Committee, the congregations were continuations of sorts of the institutions of Jewish religion that predated the Bolsheviks' seizure of power. They were the sole legitimate Jewish institutions not ideologically identified with the Soviet regime, and they were perceived by the latter as tolerable at best. Maintaining these Jewish frameworks thus depended, at least to some extent, on the direct and indirect support of broad sectors of Jewish society. It also depended on the existence of groups of religious people willing to accept the challenges that legal existence posed as well as to press against the limits set by the regime for what counted as permitted rituals.

The wide public support enjoyed by the legitimate religious institutions in the first postwar years, as well as the existence of hundreds of permanent minyans that gathered almost openly, expressed the clear conceptual shift in mind-set that many Jews had undergone as a result of the Holocaust. The shift was driven by three factors: (1) The tragic fate met by most Jews of the towns—where at least some of the Jewish traditions had been preserved, mainly by the older generation—led to a reestimation, in thought and sentiment, of relations toward this tradition by the intermediate generation and even by some of the younger generation. The contempt of and ridicule toward religion that many Jews had expressed prior to the war now disappeared. (2) The brutal murder of such great masses of Jews, carried out in plain sight of the surrounding population in each town and hamlet, eroded the faith of Jews in the brotherhood of man and increased the alienation they felt toward the surrounding society. This alienation intensified as the Jews encountered antisemitism when they returned to areas liberated from Nazi occupation. (3) The sense of alienation and orphanhood experienced by so many Jews brought them together, despite differences in social status, education, and even worldview.

As a result of this national awakening, many nonreligious Jews, some of them directly and others behind the scenes, participated in efforts to form congregations and obtain structures for synagogues. These efforts, made in hundreds of towns across the Soviet Union and sometimes lasting for years, focused the energies of an extremely broad Jewish public, most of which had never visited a synagogue, yet that rose in reaction to the discrimination and oppression of the Jewish religion. To overcome obstacles and permit the opening of synagogues, some members of this public exploited their connections with the local Soviet establishment, whose interests did not always correspond to those of the central administration. This public was also the primary source of funds for the great expenditures needed to rehabilitate and restore synagogue structures. By this means many Jews expressed their ethnic identity.

Not surprisingly, with the establishment of the state of Israel the synagogues became a magnet for thousands of nonreligious Jews, who visited to express their identification with the nascent state. Some even sought to turn the congregations into centers for contributions and assistance for embattled Israel.

The response of the administration to this national awakening was not long in coming. The authorities worked to keep nonreligious people away from the synagogues, as part of the anti-Jewish policy embraced by the regime in the late 1940s and early 1950s. This policy was manifested in a complete cessation of Soviet Jewish cultural activity, the arrest of most Jewish-Yiddish cultural activists, and a broad campaign of removal of Jews from positions in administration, culture, and technology. Indeed, the fears that then prevailed in the state led many nonreligious Jews to dissociate themselves from the congregation framework. Yet when Jews sought to express their identity or to protest antisemitic policies, there was no place to do so except at the synagogue. And thus, on Yom Kippur and Rosh Hashana, large masses of Jews would gather around the synagogues, among them sworn Communists and high-ranking figures in Soviet society. These demonstrations were not at all to the liking of the regime, and, as a result, in early 1953, in connection with the Doctors' Plot, all synagogues in the Soviet Union were on the verge of complete closure. Only Stalin's death and the thaw that followed averted this fate.

With the thaw and the greater openness of the USSR to the world, synagogues became one of the few places in which nonreligious Soviet Jews could meet tourists or members of the Israeli embassy. This again made the synagogue attractive to secular Jews. The regime, for its part, strove to limit such contact by intensifying direct supervision of the synagogues as well as insisting that congregational leaders prevent foreign contacts or report them exactly. The congregations' compliance with such demands, in turn, seems to have led the nationalist and nonreligious Jewish public to view the congregational establishment as collaborators with the regime. Even so: in those years, too, the synagogues and their environs were the gathering place for vast numbers of Jews during the High Holidays. Likewise, the new generation of Jewish youths, who sought to give voice to their national sentiments in ways similar to their non-Jewish contemporaries, chose the festival of Simchat Torah and the synagogue grounds as the most appropriate site for conducting a Jewish "happening." Some of those youths who gathered around the synagogue on Simchat Torah and kept apart from the formal religious establishment of the congregations, in time, became the spokesmen of the Jewish national movement. In that role they helped validate the underappreciated work of the legal religious establishment and its contribution to the survival of Judaism in the Soviet Union.

The official institutions of the congregations consisted mainly of elderly Orthodox Jews, and usually included a rabbi, a *gabbai,* the congregation administration, and several other individuals. Many such leaders had clear memories of the attacks on the Jewish religion in the late twenties and early thirties, and now they were ready to dedicate themselves to preserving legalized religious activity permitted thanks to a softening in the regime's antireligion campaign. These individuals viewed the synagogue as the final brake that could slow assimilation, the last breeze that could restore some faint life to the latent embers of Judaism. Unlike the groups of Chassidim, which were tiny, mostly insular, and had little influence with the broad Jewish public, the congregational activists reasoned that only the legally existing synagogues could let even Jews distant from religion gain any taste of their heritage. Such legal existence meant keeping in continuous contact with the authorities and responding to their demands, while at the same time constantly trying to widen the scope of Jewish activity. To that end, the congregation activists used the traditional methods of personal connections with members of the local Soviet establishment, exploitation of conflicting interests among the various official branches, applications to the various authorities in person and in writing, and even bribery when needed.

Because the Jewish religion, unlike the other faiths, does not have a central establishment, each and every congregation in the USSR could use only its own resources to address requirements and opportunities alike that varied from place to place and at times did not accord with central USSR policy. By various tactics the congregation activists were able, during one of the most difficult periods in Soviet Jewish history and in complete isolation from the rest of the Jewish world, to keep hundreds of synagogues running across the state. For this purpose, they drew on some of the energies of the reawakened nationalism unleashed among broad swaths of the nonreligious public by the Holocaust. Some members of that public involved themselves with the congregations, both directly and indirectly. Some did so only through financial contributions that permitted restoration of synagogue structures. Yet thanks to this activity, centers were created in hundreds of towns of the USSR that not only let Jews make contact with one another but also let them protest the discrimination against them by engaging in mass demonstrations.

Although prohibited throughout almost the entire period covered by this book, congregation activists placed charity boxes in the synagogues to which nonreligious Jews could also contribute. These collection boxes were not only a means for synagogue workers to uphold a key commandment of Judaism—but, in particular, they let congregations assist the elderly and needy and Jews who returned broken in body and spirit from their hiding places in the Nazi-occupied USSR or from the Nazi concentration camps themselves. Certain congregations also tried to assist those few Jews who were released in the mid-1950s from the Soviet gulag, where they had been interned for their religious activism.

Congregation heads were also central actors in the efforts to memorialize victims of the Holocaust and to maintain the Jewish cemeteries—activities that drew the participation and support of an extremely broad Jewish public, given the great sensitivity that the entire Jewish population felt toward such issues in the context of the Holocaust. These and similar activities created a broad infrastructure for cooperation—sometimes explicit but usually informal—between synagogue activists and Jews from social classes remote from religious observance. The synagogues thus deviated from pure ritual as defined by the Soviet authorities, and in effect became frameworks for building Jewish national identity and an underground infrastructure for Jewish communal life.

It was also thanks to the activity of the congregations that kosher slaughter of fowl, at least, continued for all those who kept kosher or who simply sought by this means to mark the festivals of Judaism. Likewise, the congregation administrations did their best to exploit the various opportunities to supply Passover matzah, both to Jews who did not eat *hametz* and to those who wanted at least some matzah on their Seder tables for symbolic purposes.

All these efforts were made on the fine line between legal and illegal, as determined by the often-changing whims of the regime. An activity perceived to be at least tolerated in one period became a serious infraction in another. The legal status also depended quite a bit on the interpretation given by the local bureaucracy to the shifts in the regime's attitude toward religion. Most of the time, then, a sword of Damocles hung over the heads of community activists; violations of the Soviet laws on religious affairs could easily lead to their personal banishment or even to closure of the synagogues.

Naturally, activism under these circumstances gave rise to tensions and mutual suspicion. To these we may add the personal factors of competition for influence and prestige, disputes over how best to guarantee the continued existence of the synagogue, and quarrels over the activities on which the congregation should focus. Some of these disputes were not unique to congregations in the Soviet Union, but others derived from the special conditions under which the Soviet congregations functioned. Nearly every dispute of this sort was brought to the authorities, who became the arbiters of the internal affairs of the congregations. This permitted those authorities to exploit the divisions for their own purposes, to put their preferred people into the congregation administration, and to form a comprehensive network of informers.

The activists of the congregations and the synagogues have hitherto not earned the appreciation due them. They were neither heroes nor even Zionists, and their necessary cooperation with the authorities prevented them from winning an excess of enthusiasm and support from Jewish entities abroad. Furthermore, these activists' modes of operation involved continual compromise with the demands of the authorities, so their behavior was closer in kind to traditional Jewish intercessionary behavior than to modern Jewish communal politics.

Lack of appreciation for these activists has been sustained for decades in Western historiography. At least until the appearance of the Jewish national movement, Soviet Jews were described invariably as "the Jews of silence." Yet, as this text has shown, Jewish activity, while not always overtly public, was widespread throughout the country, at least since the start of the Soviet-German war. What's more, much of Western historiography has failed to recognize the changes wrought by the experience of the Holocaust on the identity and sensibilities of many Soviet Jews in the immediate postwar period that prompted many to identify—and act—as Jews. Thus, the Jewish national movement was portrayed as creation ex nihilo rather than being rooted in the congregations and synagogues that preceded it.

Indeed, the leaders and activists of the congregations and synagogues kept alive the faint embers of Judaism under the extremely difficult conditions of a regime committed to opposing religion. In turn, they permitted broad sectors of the Jewish public in the Soviet Union, each in its own way and with its own understanding, to give an expression, small or large, to their Judaism, and thereby to contribute to the survival of Jewish identity in the Soviet Union.

Notes

References to material in archives of the former Soviet Union are identified by collection (coll.), inventory (inv.), file, and page.

Introduction

1. For the approaches to periodization see Shkarovskii, 1999, pp. 7–10.

2. Illustrations of this are given by the indictment and verdict of Rabbi Shalom Twersky, TsGOOU, coll. 623, inv. 1, file 5883, pp. 24–25, 35.

3. This was the context in which the antireligion propaganda developed in earnest, and the director of the Cultural Department of the Central Committee of the Communist Party rightly complained that "antireligion propaganda has nearly ceased in recent years." Of thirteen antireligion publications, ten had ceased. Russkaia, 1996, pp. 316, 319.

4. Congress, 1939, p. 135.

5. Odintsov, 1995, p. 38.

6. Ibid., p. 39.

7. In this context the Jewish scholar in Soviet Belorussia, Leon Dushman, completed a manuscript in Yiddish, meant mainly for the Jews in the annexed areas, titled *Jewish Anti-Religious Folklore.* This book was not published because of the war. See MA thesis of Daniel Romanovskii at the Hebrew University of Jerusalem; see also Kak, 1940, p. 31; Kischkowski, 1960, pp. 69–75.

8. Smilovitskii, 1999, p. 92.

9. Rumors spread abroad of a "seminary for red rabbis" in Kamenets-Podol'skii (*Hatzofeh,* February 19, 1941), but we have found no confirmation of this.

10. Pechenik, 1943, p. 36.

11. Ibid., pp. 37–38.

12. Rozenblat, 1997, p. 32; Levin, 2001, p. 79.

13. Levin, 1989, pp. 177–190; *Hatzofeh,* January 15, 1941.

14. Gershuni, 1981, p. 116. On the questions asked at the time of the Gaon of Tishebin residing in L'vov, see Landoi, 1967, pp. 97–98.

15. Mikhailov, 1941, p. 17.

16. It is estimated that at the time only 350–400 Russian Orthodox churches were functioning within the USSR's old borders. Shkarovskii, *Jewish Chronicle,* August 29, 1941; Tratsiak, 2000, p. 173.

CHAPTER ONE. Soviet Religious Policy in the Wake of the Nazi Invasion, 1941–1948

1. The first such call was made by the highest levels of the Russian Orthodox Church in the Soviet Union on June 22, 1941: Kashevarov, 1995, p. 119. For documentation see Odintsov, 1995a, pp. 55–59.

2. Odintsov, 1995a, pp. 61–63.

3. For documentation see ibid., pp. 49–50, 64; cf. Kuroedov, 1984, pp. 81–93; Kuroedov, 1973, pp. 28–31; Odintsov, 1999, pp. 279–297.

4. On the call made by the leaders of the Islamic faith on May 15, 1942, and by the leaders of the Old Believers (Staroobriadtsy) Church in December 1942, see Odintsov 1995a, pp. 52–54, 60–61.

5. *Jewish Chronicle*, January 2, 1942, p. 2.

6. Ibid., February 5, 1943, p. 8. On the telegram to Stalin (January 6, 1943) from the Kuibyshev community, see GARF, coll. 8114, inv. 1, file 910, p. 41.

7. Ehrenburg, 1998, p. 61.

8. Gosudarstvo, 1995, pp. 120–121; cf. a May 28, 1948, report of the SRA Ukraine representative for January to March 1948, TsGAOOU, coll. 1, inv. 23, file 5069, p. 153; and cf. GARF, coll. 6991, inv. 3s, file 47, p. 206.

9. On the establishment of a synagogue in the town of Stalinsk-Novokuznetskii, in Western Siberia, see Kaganov, 1994, p. 49.

10. *Jewish Chronicle,* September 11, 1942, p. 7. On Passover services in areas with refugee concentrations in the Central Asian republic of Uzbekistan see ibid., April 17, 1942.

11. Ibid., October 10, 1941, September 25, 1942.

12. Ibid., December 11, 1942.

13. The league was formally disbanded only in 1947, but had been inactive since mid-1941.

14. *Davar,* August 8, 1941.

15. *Hamashkif,* August 22, 1941.

16. Fireside, 1971, pp. 131–165; Shkarovskii, 1999, pp. 119–183. On churches in Ukraine where the situation was especially complicated, see Lisenko, 1996.

17. Odintsov, 1995a, pp. 51–52, 56.

18. Roï, 2000, p. 184.

19. Karpov (1898–1967) was employed for many years by the security services (NKVD) and during the thaw was accused of having used illegal methods against detainees in 1937–1938 in Leningrad and Pskov, for which a severe reprimand was written into his party file. During the war he was active in Ukraine, and in the rank of colonel (*polkovnik*) he was brought to Moscow a short while before the meeting. While working in the security services, Karpov was involved in supervision of the religious associations.

20. Odintsov, 1995a, pp. 41–47; see also Corley, 1996a, pp. 138–147.

21. Karpov served as chairman of the soviet for the affairs of the Russian Orthodox

Church from 1943 to 1960. See Karpov, 1994; Zubkova, 2000, pp. 102–110; Shkarovskii, 1999, p. 205.

22. This is indicated by the questions Stalin posed to Karpov during the night meeting, such as the following: What would be the nature of the foreign relations allowed to the Russian Church in the Soviet Union? What is known about the patriarch of Jerusalem, and the condition of the Orthodox Church in Bulgaria, Yugoslavia, and Romania? Many details may be found in Curtiss, 1953, pp. 304–325.

23. See Karpov, 1994, and Kischkowski, 1960, pp. 75–112. For a thorough summary on the regime and the Russian Orthodox Church that is based on substantial archival material, see Chumachenko, 1999.

24. GARF coll. 6991, inv. 3s, file 61, pp. 166–167; Kuroedov, 1973. Letter of the Chairman of the SRA to his subordinates of March 1945, NARB, coll. 952, inv. 2, file 1, p. 24. This instruction received much attention in the foreign press, and certain newspapers wrote that an order had come from Stalin to appoint military rabbis and supply the religious needs of Jewish soldiers. *Hatzofeh,* March 15, 1944.

25. Cahana, 1986, pp. 31, 33.

26. GARF, coll. 6991, inv. 3s, file 47, p. 204.

27. Luchterhandt, 1993.

28. GARF, coll. 6991, inv. 4, file 1, pp. 1, 3–5. See also the top-secret report from Polianskii to Kaptanov, Alexandrov, and Abakumov, July 1, 1947, ibid., inv. 3s, file 47, p. 206.

29. On this issue see Ro'i, 2000, pp. 171–175.

30. Report of the SRA representative in Uzbekistan for the first nine months of 1947. GARF, coll. 6991, inv. 3s, file 35, p. 194.

31. Instructions of the SRA of 1945, ch. 7, paragraph 3. NARB, coll. 952, inv. 2, file 1, p. 2.

32. GARF, coll. 6991, inv. 3s, file 47, p. 206.

33. Polianskii's letter, dated 1947, ibid.

34. GARF, coll. 6991, inv. 3s, file 47, p. 208; report by Polianskii for 1947 and the first quarter of 1948, file 53, pp. 38–39; SRA report for August–October 1946, TsGAOOU, coll. 1, inv. 23, file 4555, p. 391. Serova, 1999, p. 189.

35. GARF, coll. 6991, inv. 3s, file 47, p. 208.

36. Piotr Vil'khovyi completed a teachers' seminar in 1920. From 1926 on, he was a reporter for the newspaper *Kolgozpne selo* and in 1935–1940 he served as chief editor of literary publications in Kiev—that is, as a sort of censor. During the war he was sent to Uzbekistan, where he served as secretary of the Communist Party unit of the Writers' Union. In July 1944 he returned to Ukraine and became chairman of the Kiev broadcasting service. In February 1945 he was appointed SRA representative for Ukraine, in which role he served until 1959. See Mitsel', 1998, p. 11.

37. Private and secret letter by the Belorussia SRA representative, NARB, coll. 952, inv. 2, file 2, p. 28.

38. NARB, coll. 952, inv. 1, file 1, p. 57. For example, the SRA representative for the Pinsk

district was appointed in early 1948, but before he managed to begin his post he was sent several times to "ready the forest" (*lesozagotovki*). On the SRA visit to the Pinsk district from early 1948, see ibid., file 11, p. 56.

39. In a letter accompanying instructions to the SRA representative for the republic of Belorussia, in April 1945, Polianskii noted that "it is absolutely forbidden to rely in any way on the instructions in discussions with religious citizens or providers of ritual services . . . the instructions are kept in a special vault of the SRA representative." Ibid., inv. 2, file 1, p. 11.

40. Memorandum to the government of the Soviet Union, 1947. GARF, coll. 6991, inv. 3s, file 47, p. 208.

41. General assembly meeting of the SRA, July 9, 1948, authorizing the report of this institution's activities from 1947 and the first quarter of 1948. Ibid., inv. 3s, file 53, p. 12.

42. Ibid., file 47, p. 208; file 53, p. 14.

43. Ibid., file 47, p. 207.

44. Ibid., p. 209.

45. Mikhlin, 1986, p. 85; Chazan, 1990, p. 140.

46. The signatories were the following rabbis, some of whom were from towns under Nazi occupation at the time: Mordechai Nurok, Avraham Twersky, M. P. Grande, Beniamin Kalker, Yosef Shtitsberg, Meir Fridman, Faivel Gorodetski, Eliahu Sandler, Yosef Reikhvarg, Moshe Roginskii, Moshe Bernshtein, Kapotkin, and Uziel Twersky. See RGASPl, coll. 17, inv. 125, file 188, pp. 45–46.

47. Greenbaum, 1994, p. 57; Greenbaum 1999; Mikhlin 1986, pp. 78–103; Redlich 1995, pp. 28, 34.

48. Report of the SRA chairman to Soviet prime minister Molotov, GARF 6991, inv. 3, file 10, p. 141. Gosudarstvo 1995, p. 134.

49. *Hatzofeh,* July 17, 1945.

50. Mikhlin, 1986, pp. 103–104.

51. Report of the SRA representative in the republic of Uzbekistan for quarters one through three of 1946. GARF, coll. 6991, inv. 3s, file 35, p. 194.

52. Report of the Ukraine SRA representative for January–March 1946. TsGAOOU, coll. 1, inv. 23, file 2846, p. 21.

53. One supporter of this idea was the Yiddish poet David Hofshtein. Ibid., p. 22.

54. GARF, coll. 6991, inv. 3s, file 47, p. 218.

55. Instructions to the SRA for 1948–1949. Ibid., file 52, p. 45.

56. Kostyrchenko, 1992.

57. *Hatzofeh,* March 15, 1944.

58. GARF, coll. 6991, inv. 4, file 58, p. 139. Rabbi Shlifer's hopes that the Soviet regime would endorse a center for the Jewish faith were also reported to the delegation of US rabbis in July 1956. Ibid., file 70, pp. 142–143.

59. Protocol of the meeting of Rabbi Levin with SRA representatives on November 11, 1957. GARF, coll. 6991, inv. 4, file 75, p. 172; file 88, p. 123.

CHAPTER TWO. The Legalization of Congregations and Synagogues

1. See Orleanskii, 1930, pp. 7, 26–43.

2. Ibid., p. 27.

3. Ibid., pp. 10–11, 36.

4. Thus, for example, in 1947 the Dnepropetrovsk district SRA representative maintained that the leaders of the town's congregation had been improperly chosen and suggested that new elections be held, apparently so that persons more amenable to the authorities would be elected. TsGAVOU, coll. 4648, inv. 2, file 33, p. 33.

5. SRA directive of 1945. The requirement to obtain a permit from the SRA representative as well, included in the directive, became law in December 1962, once the Supreme Soviet Presidency of the RSFSR decided to alter the decisions from 1929 on this subject. GARF, coll. 6991, inv. 4, file 119, p. 3.

6. "On the Manner of Opening a Religion's House of Prayer." See GARF, coll. 6991, inv. 3s, file 1, pp. 29–32. The application for a structure for prayer had to be signed by twenty men and women living in town, and was presented to the district authority. The decision of the local institutions was then sent to the SRA representative.

7. Persons applying to register as a religious association (congregation) had to present four main documents: (1) a list of the people seeking to form the association; (2) the names of the chosen leaders; (3) signatures of at least twenty persons seeking to register the congregation, as long as these individuals had never been prosecuted in a Soviet court; (4) exact details of the "religious service provider [*sluzhitel' kul'ta*]" who would conduct the religious rituals.

8. Report on the Jewish religion in 1948. GARF, coll. 6991, inv. 4, file 23, p. 19.

9. On the formal process for opening a prayer house for a religion, as authorized by the USSR government on November 19, 1944, see NARB, coll. 952, inv. 2, file 1, pp. 54–55. See also Smilovitskii, 1995, p. 44. SRA lists for June 1, 1947, show 6,873 religious associations throughout the USSR (for all religions except the Orthodox Church); of these only 320, or 4.7 percent, were considered new associations. From the launching of the SRA until June 1, 1947, 1,963 requests for recognition of new religious associations were filed and only 16.3 percent were permitted. GARF, coll. 6991, inv. 3s, file 47, p. 207.

10. Letter from the Belorussia SRA representative to city hall of Orsha, September 23, 1947, citing directives from Moscow. NARB, coll. 952, inv. 2, file 11, p. 259, file 12, pp. 174–176; also see a letter from the SRA to the Belorussia representative, August 1947, ibid., inv. 1, file 7, p. 223.

11. Thus, for example, the SRA determined that the town of Romny (Sumy district) had 132 religious Jews in 1946–1947 and only 54 in 1948; in Konotop (Sumy district) the figures were 70 and 300, respectively. GARF, coll. 6991, inv. 4, file 23, p. 25.

12. GAVO, coll. 2700, inv. 19, file 33, p. 23.

13. The Poles'e district SRA representative stated clearly in his report about the activity

from April 15 until December 15, 1945: "Religious Jewish congregations did not exist in the areas temporarily captured by the Germans, but associations of Christians and Baptists did." NARB, coll. 952, inv. 2, file 2, p. 263.

14. Ibid., file 12, p. 162. The circular was approved by the SRA board on April 23, 1948. GARF, coll. 6991, inv. 3s, file 53, p. 2.

15. Report by the Belorussia SRA representative on the final quarter of 1946. NARB, coll. 952, inv. 2, file 10, p. 92. Reports of the Poles'e district SRA representative for 1946, file 5, p. 55; file 10, pp. 91–92.

16. Correspondence on this topic between the Chernovtsy district SRA representative and his superior in Kiev, 1947. TsGAVOU, coll. 4648, inv. 2, file 28, pp. 37, 124; file 31, pp. 121–122; file 33, pp. 101, 196, 198, 206, 211, 245, 252; file 37, p. 7. Letter from the chairman of the SRA to the Vinnitsa district representative, August 26, 1947. GAVO, coll. 2700, inv. 19, file 33, p. 48.

17. This calculation is based on a report on the Jewish religion in 1948. GARF, coll. 6991, inv. 4, file 23, p. 20.

18. NARB, coll. 952, inv. 2, file 9, p. 275.

19. GARF, coll. 6991, inv. 3s, file 8, p. 143.

20. Report by the Georgia SRA representative. Ibid., file 83, pp. 17–18.

21. Ibid., file 55, p. 47.

22. In 1947 there were 10,425 active religious associations (excluding those of the Russian Orthodox and Armenian churches), 1,536 of which (about 15 percent) were unregistered. Ibid., file 47, p. 208.

23. Letter from the Vinnitsa district SRA representative to the head of the district Department of Agitation and Propaganda of the Communist Party (Agitprop). GAVO, coll. 2700, inv. 19, file 35, p. 25. Letter from the chairman of the Vinnitsa district authority (*oblispolkom*) to the subdistricts, March 11. Ibid., file 38, pp. 4–5.

24. Report by the Vinnitsa district SRA representative of November 29, 1945. Ibid., file 33, p. 31. The report of this district's SRA representative of July 26, 1946, states as follows: "[T]he total counted [*vziato na uchet*] was seventeen congregations, only two of which were registered. . . ." Ibid., p. 74. Report by the Zaporozh'e district SRA representative from late 1947. TsGAVOU, coll. 4648, inv. 2, file 20, p. 24. On the Jews of the Zakarpat'e (Karpatorus') district, see Freilich 1959.

25. Correspondence regarding the congregations of Borisov and Polotsk. NARB, coll. 952, inv. 1, file 7, pp. 263, 382; inv. 2, file 12, p. 162; file 14, p. 14.

26. Thus, for example, the Belorussia SRA representative said of his representatives in the districts in 1947 that "[members of the unregistered congregations] bring [the SRA representatives] butter and eggs . . . and say, 'Take! These aren't bribes, just presents.'" Ibid., inv. 1, file 7, p. 303.

27. GARF, coll. 6991, inv. 3s, file 47, p. 208. NARB, coll. 952, inv. 2, file 27, pp. 120–121.

28. GAVO, coll. 2700, inv. 19, file 33, p. 75.

29. Report by the Belorussia SRA representative for the last quarter of 1947. NARB, coll. 952, inv. 2, file 19, p. 49.

30. SRA directives of 1945. Ibid., file 1, p. 11.

31. Orleanskii, 1930, pp. 8, 13, 21, 28.

32. The Belorussia SRA representative wrote to the Gomel' district authorities (July 26, 1947) that no special decision was needed regarding ownership of the building purchased by the congregation, since by law the local authority was automatically the building's owner. NARB, coll. 952, inv. 1, file 7, p. 90.

33. GARF, coll. 6991, inv. 3s, file 61, p. 58; inv. 4, file 23, p. 24. TsGAVOU, coll. 4648, inv. 2, file 48, p. 31.

34. Ibid., file 17, p. 137; file 44, p. 2.

35. NARB, coll. 952, inv. 1, file 17, pp. 202, 215.

36. Signatories to the agreement to receive a building for religious needs had to insure it against fire hazards. Orleanskii 1930, p. 15. Directives of 1945. NARB, coll. 952, inv. 2, file 1, p. 15. A religious association was required to pay local taxes on the use of a prayer house that was not its property. Orleanskii 1930, pp. 69–71; see also the October 31, 1968, addendum to the agreement for use of a building for religious purposes. Zakonodatel'stvo 1971, p. 74.

37. Thus, for example, the town of Krichev in Belorussia's Gomel' district, had five synagogue buildings remodeled for use as various Soviet institutions. NARB, coll. 952, inv. 1, file 11, p. 262. In Vetka, in the same district, five synagogues were expropriated: two became cultural clubs, one a workers' restaurant, one a sewing workshop, and one was demolished. Ibid., p. 261. Prewar Braslav had four synagogue structures: two of them were destroyed by fire and the remaining two were converted into warehouses after the war. Ibid., file 29, p. 157.

38. In Nadvornaia (Stanislav district) the Nazis deliberately damaged three synagogue buildings beyond repair; the Soviet authorities demolished them in 1947. TsGAVOU, coll. 4648, inv. 2, file 25, pp. 43, 126–127, 129, 146. In Ovruch (Zhitomir district) the Germans burned six wooden structures that once had served as synagogues. Ibid., file 52, p. 151.

39. Report by the Ukraine SRA representative for January–March 1948. TsGAOOU, coll. 1, inv. 23, file 5069, pp. 184–185.

40. Shkarovskii, 1999, pp. 170–172.

41. TsGAOOU, coll. 1, inv. 23, file 5069, pp. 184–185.

42. Letter from the Jews of Gomel', with thirteen signatories, September 1947. NARB, coll. 952, inv. 1, file 9, pp. 160–161.

43. Letters from the Moscow SRA, March 3 and 31, 1947. TsGAVOU, coll. 4648, inv. 2, file 28, pp. 27, 44.

44. Directives of 1945. NARB, coll. 952, inv. 2, file 1, p. 2.

45. The Belorussia SRA representative states in his reports for 1946 and 1947 that "the Jewish population's activity [aktivizatsiia] in forming synagogues . . . is growing daily and this fire has now spread to the Western districts of [the republic of Belorussia]." He stressed that the "Jewish religious associations have become more active of late and have cropped up in every city and town, even those where few Jews live." Ibid., file 2, p. 295; file 10, pp. 92, 236; file 11, p. 173.

46. Report by the Belorussia SRA representative for the final quarter of 1947. Ibid., inv. 2, file 13, p. 68. Similar statements are made in ibid., inv. 1, file 2, p. 9.

47. GARF, coll. 6991, inv. 3s, file 13, p. 9.

48. Letter from the SRA chairman, December 1947. TsGAVOU, coll. 4648, inv. 2, file 43, p. 13.

49. Correspondence on the synagogue in Odessa. Ibid., file 28, p. 107; file 37, p. 54; file 43, p. 86; file 44, p. 67. TsGAOOU, coll. 1, inv. 23, file 5069, p. 202.

50. Correspondence regarding the opening of a second synagogue in Vinnitsa. TsGAVOU, coll. 4648, inv. 2, file 33, pp. 11, 14, 16; file 37, pp. 20–23, 27,

51. GARF, coll. 6991, inv. 3s, file 13, p. 8; TsGAVOU, coll. 4648, inv. 2, file 28, p. 78; file 43, p. 96; TsGAOOU, coll. 1, inv. 23, file 5069, p. 170.

52. Reply of the mayor of Voroshilovgrad to the district SRA's demand to give the Jews a structure for a synagogue, March 26, 1946. TsGAVOU, coll. 4648, inv. 2, file 12, p. 16.

53. For correspondence on this subject, see GAVO, coll. 2700, inv. 19, file 31, pp. 18, 20, 23–24, 43, 89; file 33, pp. 50–51.

54. NARB, coll. 952, inv. 2, file 2, p. 54; file 12, p. 8. TsGAVOU, coll. 4648, inv. 2, file 28, p. 107; file 37, p. 54; file 43, pp. 13, 86; file 50, p. 41.

55. Letter from the SRA deputy chairman to his representative in Bobruisk, February 20, 1946. NARB, coll. 952, inv. 1, file 4, p. 44; file 8, p. 33. The synagogue building was confiscated and in the early 1950s served as the archive of Bobruisk. Ibid., inv. 2, file 48, p. 218; inv. 4, file 10, pp. 234–235.

56. GARF, coll. 6991, inv. 3s, file 10, p. 106.

57. Report by the Belorussia SRA representative for the third quarter of 1946. NARB, coll. 952, inv. 2, file 6, p. 73. Report for the fourth quarter of 1946. Ibid., file 10, p. 92.

58. Reports by the Belorussia SRA supervisor on his 1947 visit to Bobruisk and Gomel'. Ibid., inv. 1, file 7, p. 67; file 8, p. 58. Letter from the Belorussia SRA representative to the SRA chairman, July 25, 1947. Ibid., file 7, pp. 70–71. Letter from the executive committee of the Gomel' district, July 26, 1947, requesting agreement to remodel the synagogue building as a residence. Ibid., p. 89.

59. Report by the Belorussia SRA supervisor on his visit to the Vitebsk district from November 25 to December 9, 1947. Ibid., file 7, p. 352. Report by the Belorussia SRA representative to the prime minister of the republic. Ibid., file 12, pp. 2.

60. Reports by Belorussia SRA representatives of various districts, 1946. Ibid., inv. 1, file 8, p. 57; inv. 2, file 6, p. 73.

61. Report by the Mogilev district SRA representative, second quarter of 1947. Ibid., file 11, p. 7.

62. Report about Jewish religious activity in 1948. GARF, coll. 6991, inv. 4, file 23, pp. 23–24. Short survey on the Jewish religion, 1949. Ibid., inv. 3s, file 61, pp. 58, 159.

63. Report by the Belorussia SRA supervisor on his visit to the Vitebsk district from November 25 to December 9, 1947. NARB, coll. 952, inv. 1, file 7, pp. 351–352; file 12, pp. 48–53; file 18, pp. 171–173.

64. Reports by the SRA representative of the Polotsk district. Ibid., inv. 2, file 9, p. 71; file 10, p. 126. Letter from the same of December 22, 1947, to his superior in Minsk. Ibid., inv. 1, file 7, p. 369.

65. This decision was also approved by the SRA chairman, who claimed that not only was the building unsuitable for such a purpose but also that two of the signatories had rescinded their signatures. Letters from the Ukraine SRA representative and the central SRA of January and May 1947. TsGAVOU, coll. 4648, inv. 2, file 28, pp. 7, 74; file 70, p. 20.

66. Summary by the SRA representative on this subject and the *oblispolkom* of Dnepropetrovsk of December 1947. Ibid., file 31, pp. 22–23.

67. Ibid., file 52, pp. 70–71.

68. Ibid., file 31, p. 23; file 40, p. 3.

69. Kaganov, 1994. pp. 47–48.

70. NARB, coll. 952, inv. 2, file 10, pp. 37–38.

71. TsGAVOU, coll. 4648, inv. 2, file 12, p. 2; file 25, p. 7; file 31, pp. 11–12.

72. Letter from Jews of Orsha to prime minister of Belorussia, November 19, 1947, signed by 360 men and women. NARB, coll. 952, inv. 1, file 7, pp. 187, 250; file 11, pp. 38, 259; inv. 2, file 12, pp. 174–175.

73. Ibid., inv. 2, file 9, p. 275. An SRA member from Moscow made an almost identical statement in an August 1947 letter to the Ukraine representative. TsGAVOU, coll. 4648, inv. 2, file 28, p. 156.

74. Ibid., file 25, p. 6; file 33, p. 44; file 40, p. 17. GAOO, coll. 2700, inv. 19, file 35, p. 19.

75. TsGAVOU, coll. 4648, inv. 2, file 25, pp. 4–5; file 31, pp. 9, 132–135; file 37, p. 37.

76. Ibid., file 28, p. 46; file 31, p. 52.

77. Report by Polotsk district SRA representative, fourth quarter of 1948. NARB, coll. 952, inv. 2, file 16, p. 125.

78. GARF, coll. 6991, inv. 4, file 23, pp. 29–30.

79. Thus, for example, the Chernovtsy district SRA representative was fired in 1947 because he "often enough would visit the Jewish congregation's rabbi at his home . . . and the guest was given 'gifts' of packages sent from abroad by Jewish Zionist organizations. . . . [The man] helped Glozman [possibly a congregation member] obtain an apartment in a house belonging to the Evangelist Union . . . for which he received five thousand rubles." TsGAOOU, coll. 1, inv. 23, file 4137, pp. 2–4. Description of a failed attempt to bribe the Zhitomir SRA representative. TsGAVOU, coll. 4648, inv. 2, file 301, p. 73.

CHAPTER THREE. **The Formation of Prayer Groups (Minyanim)**

1. Rothenberg, 1971, p. 45.

2. Report of the Mogilev district SRA representative for the second half of 1957. NARB, coll. 952, inv. 4, file 10, p. 232.

3. Review on the Jewish religion for 1948. GARF, col. 6991, inv. 4, p. 21. Short review on the Jewish religion for 1949. Ibid., inv. 3s, file 61, p. 154.

4. Letter of the SRA chairman to his representative in Dnepropetrovsk. May 1955,

TsGAOOU, coll. 1, inv. 23, file 194, p. 74. See also TsGAVOU, coll. 4648, inv. 2, file 198, p. 57.

5. Narullaev, 1989, p. 61.

6. GARF, coll. 6991, inv. 4, file 23, p. 21. See also ibid., inv. 3s, file 61, p. 57, as well as instructions for lectures on antireligious subjects from November 1947. NARB, coll. 952, inv. 2, file 12, pp. 200, 225–226.

7. Correspondence with regard to Torah scrolls in Ostrog between the Rovno SRA representative and the deputy SRA representative for Ukraine, March 1946. TsGAVOU, coll. 4648, inv. 2, file 17, p. 68; file 19, p. 6.

8. GAVO, coll. 2700, inv. 19, file 33, p. 35. See also the report of the Vinnitsa district SRA representative from November 29, 1945. Ibid., file 31, p. 43.

9. Report of the Belorussia SRA representative, third quarter of 1949. NARB coll. 952, inv. 2, file 20, p. 76; inv. 1, file 16, p. 132.

10. GARF, coll. 6991, inv. 3s, file 39, pp. 121–122. Report of SRA activities for 1947 and the first quarter of 1948, file 53, p. 30, inv. 4; file 23, p. 21; file 350, pp. 10–12.

11. NARB, coll. 952, inv. 1, file 7, pp. 345–346. TsGAVOU, coll. 4648, inv. 2, file 296, p. 87.

12. Zonenfeld, 1990, pp. 163–164.

13. Letters of the Vinnitsa district SRA representative from 1945 and March 1946. GAVO, coll. 2700, inv. 7, file 31, p. 61; file 70, p. 15.

14. Sergiichuk, 1998, p. 89.

15. Letters of the Vinnitsa district SRA representative, 1945–1946. GAVO, coll. 2700, inv. 7, file 70, p. 15; inv. 19, file 31, p. 61.

16. Report of the Belorussia SRA representative, second half of 1954. NARB, coll. 952, inv. 2, file 45, p. 244.

17. TsGAVOU, coll. 4648, inv. 2, file 14, p. 4.

18. Letter from 1948 of the Vinnitsa district SRA representative to the director of Agitprop. GAVO, coll. 2700, inv. 19, file 35, p. 26.

19. Letter of the Belorussia SRA representative of July 25, 1947, to his superior in Moscow. NARB, coll. 952, inv. 1, file 7, p. 70. Order of the Belorussia SRA representative to all his representatives in the republic, November 26, 1947. Ibid., inv. 2, file 12, p. 198. Between 1945 and 1947 regular minyans were held in the Minsk district even in settlements with relatively small Jewish populations. Ibid., file 5s, p. 12. GARF, coll. 6991, inv. 4, file 23, p. 21.

20. TsGAOOU, coll. 1, inv. 23, file 4556, p. 131.

21. NARB, coll. 952, inv. 2, file 2, p. 125; file 11, p. 262.

22. TsGAOOU, coll. 1, inv. 23, file 4556, p. 131. NARB, coll. 952, inv. 2, file 8, p. 58.

23. In all the SRA reports available to us, we have not found a single instance of criminal trials for organizing a minyan.

24. TsGAOOU, coll. 1, inv. 23, file 4556, p. 131.

25. Letter from the Kiev SRA representative to the town's treasury official. TsGAVOU, coll. 4648, inv. 1, file 33, p. 95. See also NARB, coll. 952, inv. 1, file 7, pp. 371–372; inv. 2, file 11, p. 260; file 12, p. 191; file 13, p. 153.

26. GARF, coll. 6991, inv. 4, file 23, pp. 22–23. TsGAOOU, coll. 1, inv. 23, file 5667, pp. 59, 61, 94.

27. Report on the condition of the Jewish religion in Ukraine from July 1947. TsGAOOU, coll. 1, inv. 23, file 4556, p. 131. Report on the condition of the Jewish religion in the Soviet Union in 1948. GARF, coll. 6991, inv. 4, file 23, p. 22.

28. Report of the Belorussia SRA representative for the third quarter of 1949. NARB, coll. 952, inv. 2, file 20, p. 66.

29. Report of the SRA supervisor for Belorussia on his visit to the districts of Vitebsk and Polotsk from February 2–12, 1948. Ibid., inv. 1, file 11, p. 42.

30. Report of the Ukraine SRA representative, April–June 1947. TsGAOOU, coll. 1, inv. 23, file 49555, p. 330.

31. TsGAVOU, coll. 4648, inv. 2, file 19, p. 21; file 37, pp. 39–41.

32. TsGAOOU, coll. 1, inv. 23, file 5667, pp. 95–96.

33. GAChO, coll. 623, inv. 2, file 28, p. 10.

34. NARB, coll. 952, inv. 1, file 7, pp. 345–346; file 8, p. 244; file 11, pp. 3, 38, 60, 64; file 16, pp. 4–6, 128, 132; inv. 2, file 16, pp. 5–9; file 20, pp. 119, 126; file 23, p. 250; file 33, pp. 79, 83; inv. 4, file 68, pp. 62–64. GARF, coll. 6991, inv. 4, file 23, p. 21.

35. TsGAVOU, coll. 4648, inv. 2, file 49, p. 97; file 52, p. 108.

36. Ibid., file 3, p. 20; file 114, pp. 49–50. GARF, coll. 6991, inv. 3s, file 61, p. 57; inv. 4, file 23, p. 22. GAVO, coll. 2700, inv. 19, file 38, pp. 1,7; Ro'i, 1995, p. 268.

37. NARB, coll. 952, inv. 2, file 9, p. 74; file 12, p. 171; file 17, p. 191.

38. Ibid., file 19, p. 26.

39. Ibid., file 11, p. 227; file 14, pp. 45, 72. TsGAVOU, coll. 4648, inv. 2, file 49, p. 172; file 52, p. 137.

40. NARB, coll. 952, inv. 3, file 11, p. 174; file 12, p. 171.

41. TsGAVOU, coll. 4648, inv. 2, file 52, p. 151. TsGAOOU, coll. 1., inv. 23, file 5667, pp. 94–95. Ro'i, 1995, p. 268.

42. TsGAOOU, col. 1, inv. 23, file 5667, p. 94.

CHAPTER FOUR. Jewish Spiritual Needs in the Aftermath of the Holocaust

1. On the committee and its activities, see recent research that is based on broad archival material. Redlich, 1995, pp. 186–202, 413–464.

2. The poet David Hofshtein gave voice to this sentiment in his letters to his family in the United States in 1946. See Altshuler, 1979, pp. 154–155. Y. Kipnis, "On Hochmes, On Heshboines," *Dos naiye lebn,* May 19, 1947.

3. The literary-political almanac *Birobidzhan* had four issues published in 1946–1948 in runs of 3,000–5,000 copies. The almanac *Der shtern* had seven volumes published in Kiev in 1947–1948 in runs of 4,000–5,000 copies; seven similar compilations under the name *Heimland* appeared in Moscow in the same years in runs of 5,000 copies.

4. Letter in Hebrew by Malka Shekhtman; manuscript department of the Jewish National Library, Jerusalem, Kresl collection.

5. Altshuler, 1995.

6. Sergiichuk 1998, p. 89.

7. Svirsky attests that the book was written in the USSR and that the original version, in Russian, was published in Paris in 1974, after his immigration to Israel in 1972. Svirsky 1976, pp. 3–32.

8. See Altshuler, 1993.

9. GARF, coll. 6991, inv. 3, file 10, p. 140.

10. Lecture on the functions of SRA representatives. Ibid., inv. 3s, file 39, p. 76.

11. Ibid., file 47, p. 63.

12. Ibid., p. 217.

13. Report by the Ukraine SRA representative on the situation of the Jewish religion, July 25, 1947. TsGAOOU, coll. 1, inv. 23, file 4556, p. 130. This opinion was repeated by the SRA representative in another report. Ibid., file 455, p. 56.

14. Report by the Moldavia SRA representative at a meeting of the SRA in Moscow, January 23, 1948. GARF, coll. 6991, inv. 4, file 22, pp. 18–19.

15. Minutes of the assembly of the L'vov congregation, January 5, 1947. TsGAVOU, coll. 4648, inv. 2, file 33, p. 152.

16. GARF, coll. 6991, inv. 3s, file 39, p. 125.

17. Ibid., file 53, p. 30.

18. NARB, coll. 952, inv. 2, file 11, p. 174. See also ibid., file 13, p. 67.

19. Letter from the SRA chief to his representatives in the Belorussian republic, August 4, 1947. Ibid., file 12, p. 162. This stance was reiterated by the SRA chief in his letter to the Belorussian representatives, September 6, 1947. Ibid., file 9, p. 275.

20. Minutes of the SRA meeting in Moscow, November 1947. Ibid., inv. 1, file 7, p. 299.

21. Report by the Belorussia SRA supervisor on his visit to Mogilev, February 20 to March 13, 1948. Ibid., file 11, p. 64.

22. Report by the Ukraine SRA representative for October–December 1948. TsGAOOU, coll. 1, inv. 23, file 5667, p. 59.

23. Ibid.

24. Report of July 5, 1947. Ibid., file 4556, p. 130.

25. Report by SRA chairman to USSR prime minister Molotov, December 7, 1945. GARF, coll. 6991, inv. 3, file 10, p. 141.

CHAPTER FIVE. Stalin's Final Years, 1949–1953

1. Certain scholars give the earlier date of 1947 for the shift in the authorities' stance toward religion (see Ro'i, 2000, pp. 34–36). This perspective is based mainly on a memorandum on an antireligion campaign and the formation of an organization, "Znanie," to disseminate information. Two general comments are in order on this point: (1) Although in mid-1947 Dmitri Shepilov, a leader of the young party activists who had qualms about the government's policy toward religion, indeed proposed a resolution to launch an antireligion campaign, no decision was reached and the proposal, apparently on Stalin's orders, was not discussed at all and was sent to the archives. (2) In 1947 the Union of

Militant Atheists was formally disbanded; it had in fact ceased to function by the start of the Soviet-German war and was replaced by Znanie, which naturally included an antireligion plan as part of its program. Yet, in practice, Znanie did not initiate publication of antireligious literature at least until Stalin's death. At any rate, the documentation available to us does not show any difference in the behavior of the authorities in 1948 as compared to the previous year.

2. Altshuler, 1998b, p. 27.

3. See Bociurkiw, 1996.

4. Religiia, 1965, p. 56. Alekseev, 1992, pp. 195–208.

5. See Zubkova, 1998, p. 35. In this period very few articles were published that dealt with the Jewish religion. Pinkus, 1973, pp. 1–31, 48–51, 76; see also Haustein, 1989, p. 252.

6. Zubkova, 1998, p. 36. Report of the Ukraine SRA representative for January–March 1949. TsGAOOU, coll. 1, inv. 23, file 5607, pp. 149–150. An identical formulation was used by the SRA chairman in his report on activities in 1948 and the first quarter of 1949. GARF, coll. 6991, inv. 3s, file 61, p. 53.

7. *Isvestiia,* May 13, 1952; and see *Zhurnal Moskovskoi Patriiarkhii,* 1952, nos. 6–8.

8. The draft of the speech by Rabbi Shekhtman was approved by the SRA chairman. TsGAVOU, coll. 4648, inv. 2, p. 5; file 131, pp. 5, 48–50.

9. GAVO, coll. 2700, inv. 19, file 36, p. 61. Report of the SRA on the autumn Jewish holidays, 1949. GARF, coll. 6991, inv. 3s, file 61, pp. 185–186.

10. Circular of the SRA chairman before the 1950 Passover holiday. GAVO, coll. 2700, inv. 19, file 39, p. 12.

11. Report on religious activity in Ukraine in 1949. TsGAOOU, coll. 1, inv. 23, file 5667, p. 92.

12. Report of the Zhitomir district SRA representative on his 1949 visit to Berdichev. TsGAVOU, coll. 4648, inv. 2, file 65, p. 24.

13. For a report of this kind by a Jew who reached Kiev, see Zonenfeld, 1990, p. 100, as well as the Kiev district SRA representative's report on the issue of lodging people in synagogues and times when synagogues could remain open. TsGAVOU, coll. 4648, inv. 2, file 71, p. 86.

14. Letter of the SRA chairman to the Ukraine representative, April 4, 1951. Ibid., file 110, p. 63.

15. Before the war Rabbi Isaac Ozband was the head of the Telz yeshiva in Lithuania. In 1940 he fled after the Nazi invasion and spent the war in Uzbekistan. In 1950 he reached the United States, where he served as one of the heads of the Telz yeshiva in Cleveland and continued to maintain ties with Jews in the Soviet Union.

16. The response (in Hebrew, undated) was to a question posed by a member of the Chernovtsy congregation; see Bick, 1973, p. 54.

17. Letter of July 2, 1951. GAVO, coll. 2700, inv.19, file 40, p. 23.

18. TsGAVOU, coll. 4648, inv. 2, file 328, p. 110. Pinkus, 1993, p. 184.

19. Report of the Ukraine SRA representative for the third quarter of 1950. TsGAOOU, coll. 1, inv. 24, file 783, p. 2.

20. Report of the Ukraine SRA representative for the fourth quarter of 1952. Ibid., inv. 23, file 2741, p. 64.

21. Ibid., inv. 23, file 2471, p. 65.

22. Ibid., inv. 24, file 783, p. 370.

23. Reports of the Ukraine SRA representative for the third quarter of 1950 and on the 1952 High Holidays. Ibid., p. 20, file 1572, p. 312.

24. Memorandum on the Jewish faith from July 2, 1951. GAVO, coll. 2700, inv. 19, file 40, pp. 24–25. Report from Ukraine on the Jewish holidays from November 6, 1952. TsGAVOU, coll. 4648, inv. 2, file 62, p. 85.

25. GAVO, coll. 2700, inv. 19, file 44, p. 23. TsGAVOU, coll. 4648, inv. 2, file 179, pp. 131–139.

26. GARF, coll. 6991, inv. 3s, file 73, p. 6; file 100, pp. 48–49; file 475, p. 362. TsGAOOU, coll. 1, inv. 24, file 2741, pp. 73–74; file 3531, p. 33. Kostyrchenko, 1994, pp. 160–161; Kostyrchenko, 2001, p. 496. Ro'i, 1995, p. 269. Zonenfeld, 1990, pp. 191–202. Gottlieb, 1985, pp. 65–95.

27. NARB, coll. 952, inv. 2, file 68, pp. 221–232.

28. Report of the Latvia SRA representative on the Passover holiday of 1950. GARF, coll. 6991, inv. 3s, file 475, p. 27.

29. In late 1949 the SRA chairman detailed to his officers three methods for wiping out the minyans: (1) summonses and warnings to the organizers and apartment owners; (2) stiff tax penalties against those who continue with this practice; (3) activation of the police against those continuing to engage in the activity, and to that end utilizing neighbors' complaints about noise and so forth. NARB, coll. 952, inv. 2, file 21, p. 258.

30. Ibid., file 17, p. 34; file 21, p. 121. GAVO, coll. 2700, inv. 19, file 38, pp. 4–5.

31. Letter of the Vinnitsa district SRA representative to the *raispolkom* of Nemirov, March 12, 1949. GAVO, coll. 2700, inv. 19, file 36, p. 13.

32. NARB coll. 952, inv. 1, file 22, pp. 131–132; file 25, p. 33; inv. 2, file 24, p. 166. GARF, coll. 6991, inv. 3s, file 258, pp. 129–130. TsGAOOU, coll. 1, inv. 24, file 1572, p. 154.

33. GAVO, coll. 2700, inv. 19, file 26, p. 26; file 38, p. 40. NARB, coll. 952, inv. 2, file 39, pp. 64–70. Vasil'ev, 2005, pp. 255–284.

34. Applications of this kind were made in the towns of Rogachev, Slutsk, Voroshilovgrad, Kadeevka, and others. NARB, coll. 952, inv. 1, file 18, pp. 191, 199–200. TsGAVOU, coll. 4648, inv. 2, file 70, p. 19. TsGAOOU, coll. 1, inv. 24, file 783, p. 371.

35. TsGAVOU, coll. 4648, inv. 2, file 70, p. 19; file 76, p. 73. GAChO, coll. 623, inv. 2, file 29, pp. 48–49. NARB, coll. 952, inv. 2, file 23, p. 84.

36. One of the SRA representatives noted in 1953 that "the Jews have descended to a deeper underground . . . and there are rumors they are gathering somewhere for prayers." NARB, coll. 952, inv. 2, file 37, p. 147.

37. Ibid., file 23, pp. 128–129; file 24, pp. 166–168.

38. Report of the Baranovichi district SRA representative for 1950. Ibid., file 23, pp. 177–178.

39. Report of the Belorussia SRA representative, first quarter of 1950. GARF, coll. 6991, inv. 3s, file 258, pp. 130–131.

40. NARB, coll. 952, inv. 2, file 20, p. 122. TsGAOOU, coll. 1, inv. 24, file 783, pp. 371, 375–376. TsGAVOU, coll. 4648, inv. 2, file 88, p. 43. GARF, coll. 6991, inv. 3s, file 61, p. 154.

41. TsGAOOU, coll. 1, inv. 24, file 783, p. 386.

42. Ibid., file 1572, p. 154. NARB, coll. 952, inv. 2, file 39, p. 15.

43. TsGAVOU, coll. 4648, inv. 2, file 150, pp. 31–33. TsGAOOU, coll. 1, inv. 24, file 2741, p. 66.

44. Memorandum of the Belorussia SRA representative on the religions, December 10, 1950. NARB, coll. 952, inv. 2, file 23, p. 251. See also GARF, coll. 6991, inv. 4, file 23, p. 21.

45. Report of the Ukraine SRA representative for January–March 1950. TsGAOOU, coll. 1, inv. 24, file 12, p. 204.

46. GAChO, coll. 623, inv. 2, file 28, p. 10. TsGAVOU, coll. 4648, inv. 2, file 62, pp. 81, 89; file 63, p. 111. GARF, coll. 6991, inv. 4, file 24, pp. 39–40.

47. Report of the Vinnitsa district SRA representative of April 9, 1953. GAVO, coll. 2700, inv. 19, file 42, pp. 29–30. See also TsGAVOU, coll. 4648, inv. 2, file 62, p. 174.

48. Report of the Ukraine SRA representative for July–September 1949. TsGAOOU, coll. 1, inv. 23, file 2667, pp. 367–368.

49. TsGAVOU, coll. 4648, inv. 2, file 112, p. 64. See also ibid., inv. 1, file 194, pp. 135–136.

50. Opinion of the district SRA representative, September 16, 1951. TsGAVOU, coll. 4648, inv. 2, file 113, pp. 90–91.

51. TsGAOOU, coll. 1, inv. 23, file 5607, p. 153; inv. 24, file 783, p. 382.

52. TsGAVOU, coll. 4648, inv. 2, file 62, p. 158; file 63, p. 169; file 71, pp. 29, 31; file 76, pp. 45–47; file 83, p. 15; file 110, p. 61; file 114, pp. 90, 101; file 215, p. 169.

53. Letter of the Nikolaev district SRA representative to the chairman of the municipal soviet, August 1, 1949. TsGAVOU, coll. 4648, inv. 2, file 72, p. 27.

54. GAVO, coll. 2700, inv. 19, file 36, pp. 39–40.

55. TsGAVOU, coll. 4648, inv. 2, file 62, pp. 9–10.

56. Ro'i, 1995, p. 265.

57. GARF, coll. 6991, inv. 3s, file 53, p. 40.

58. TsGAOOU, coll. 1, inv. 24, file 783, p. 90; file 1572, pp. 313–314.

59. GAVO, coll. 2700, inv. 19, file 42, pp. 15, 45. TsGAOOU, coll. 1, inv. 2, file 2741, pp. 326–327.

60. Between January 1949 and January 1953, the number of houses of prayer in the Soviet Union decreased by 1,183, of which 820 were Orthodox churches, 69 were mosques, and 294 were those of other religions. GARF, coll. 6991, inv. 3s, file 73, p. 30.

61. Report of the Georgia SRA representative for 1951 and the first quarter of 1952. GARF, coll. 6991, inv. 9, file 83, p. 18.

62. Altshuler and Chentsova, 1993, pp. 59–63; Mitsel', 1998, p. 59. TsGAOOU, coll. 1, inv. 24, file 2773, p. 60.

63. Altshuler, 2001, pp. 64, 74.

64. TsGAVOU, coll. 4648, inv. 2, file 144, p. 14; file 151, pp. 24–26.

65. GARF, coll. 6991, inv. 3s, file 35, p. 190; file 92, p. 20.

66. Mitsel', 1998, pp. 77–78.

67. Mironenko, 1999, pp. 113, 171.

68. Report of the SRA chairman on the Passover holiday, April 22, 1953. GARF, coll. 6991, inv. 3, file 93, p. 2.

69. Cahana, 1986, pp. 157–158.

70. For a wider discussion of this topic, see Altshuler, 2001. GARF, coll. 6991, inv. 3, file 93, pp. 1–2.

71. NARB, coll. 952, inv. 4, file 158, pp. 182–185.

CHAPTER SIX. **Public Displays of Jewish Identity**

1. GARF, coll. 6991, inv. 3s, file 61, p. 186.

2. Between 8,000 and 10,000 people gathered in and around the Riga synagogue on the High Holidays of 1947—according to the authorities' appraisal, "mainly out of [ethnic-] national sentiments." Ibid., inv. 3, file 472, p. 284.

3. As an example, the informant lists five names and places of employment of Communists ages forty-two to forty-five who attended the synagogue in Berdichev, and two members of the Komsomol. Ibid., inv. 3s, file 61, pp. 186–189.

4. TsGAOOU, coll. 1, inv. 24, file 12, p. 84.

5. Ibid., pp. 85–86.

6. Report by the Belorussia SRA representative for the third quarter of 1949. NARB, coll. 952, inv. 2, file 20, p. 123.

7. Report by the Belorussia SRA representative for the second half of 1952. Ibid., file 33, p. 78. "During the 'autumn holidays' the heads of the synagogue in the town of Nikolaev, despite warnings from the SRA representative, "organized tours in the apartments of Jewish families so as to convince them that they should come to the synagogue irrespective of their religiosity so as to collect a donation toward helping poor Jews." GARF, coll. 6991, inv. 3s, file 73, p. 35.

8. By the authorities' estimate, 4,000–4,500 people gathered within and outside the two Riga synagogues that year. Ibid., file 475, p. 96.

9. A survey of the Jewish religion in 1950. Ibid., file 73, pp. 30–31.

10. Reports of the "autumn holidays" by SRA representatives. TsGAOOU, coll. 1, inv. 24, file 782, p. 373; file 783, pp. 374–375.

11. Report by SRA representative about religious activity in 1951. GARF, coll. 6991, inv. 3s, file 85, p. 177.

12. It is reasonable to assume that steps were taken against these people or that they were at least summoned to certain offices and warned not to repeat these doings. Report

by the Ukraine SRA representative for the last quarter of 1949. TsGAOOU, coll. 1, inv. 24, file 12, p. 88.

13. Report by the Ukraine SRA representative for the third quarter of 1951. Ibid., file 783, p. 386.

14. Memorandum from the Ukraine SRA representative on the "Autumn Holidays of the Jews," November 30, 1951. Ibid., file 2741, p. 372.

15. Report by the SRA representative for the second quarter of 1952. NARB, coll. 952, inv. 2, file 33, p. 80.

16. Letter from the Chernigov district SRA representative from early September 1951. TsGAVOU, coll. 4648, inv. 2, file 116, p. 96.

17. Letter of the SRA representative to the vice premier of the republic, November 28, 1951. TsGAVOU, coll. 4648, inv. 2, file 116, p. 97. Memo from the Ukraine SRA representative on the autumn Jewish holidays. TsGAOOU, coll. 1, inv. 24, file 2741, pp. 370–371.

18. Survey of the Jewish religion in 1950. GARF, coll. 6991, inv. 3s, file 73, p. 35.

19. Ibid., p. 31. Utershtein, 1999, p. 37.

20. Report by the Ukraine SRA representative about the autumn holidays of 1952. TsGAOOU, coll. 1, inv. 24, file 1572, pp. 317–318.

21. TsGAVOU, coll. 4648, inv. 2, file 150, pp. 101–102.

22. TsGAOOU, coll. 1, inv. 23, file 5607, pp. 326, 329; file 5667, pp. 345–346. TsGAVOU, coll. 4648, inv. 2, file 72, p. 14. Makhnovetskii was head of the L'vov congregation from April 1947 to October 1960, at least.

23. Letter from the head of the MVD personnel department. TsGAOOU, coll. 1, inv. 23, file 5607, pp. 345–346. Memo from the Ukraine SRA representative to the secretary of the Communist Party and the vice premier of the republic. Ibid., p. 326.

24. For more on this subject see Altshuler, 2001.

25. Mitsel', 1998, pp. 197–198.

CHAPTER SEVEN. Khrushchev's "Thaw," 1954–1959

1. TsGAOOU, coll. 1, inv. 24, file 2741, pp. 27, 360.

2. Religiia, 1965, pp. 71–77.

3. Some claim that none other than Nikita Khrushchev was behind this decision. Alekseev, 1992, pp. 212–214.

4. Report of the Belorussia SRA deputy representative on his visit to the Gomel' district, September 27 to October 2, 1954. NARB, coll. 952, inv. 2, file 48, p. 171.

5. Religiia, 1965, pp. 77–82.

6. GARF, coll. 6991, inv. 4, file 37, p. 14.

7. Anderson, 1994, p. 9.

8. In this context a delegation of Baptists visited the Soviet Union in July 1955 and met with religious leaders. *London Times,* December 21, 1955, p. 9.

9. One of the examples is the construction of the Catholic church in Klaipeda, some of the funds for which were transferred by various means from abroad.

10. GAVO, coll. 2700, inv. 7, file 404, p. 10. For a photo of the handwritten Hebrew calendar for the year 1960, which also contained the kaddish written in Cyrillic, see Shmeruk, 1961, pp. 20–21.

11. GARF, coll. 9661, inv. 3, file 262, p. 227.

12. TsGAOOU, coll. 1, inv. 24, file 4038, pp. 258–259. GARF, coll. 6991, inv. 4, file 71, p. 108. This was a synagogue building in the city center, known as the "Brodsky synagogue," which resumed functioning as a synagogue only in the late 1990s.

13. Report of the SRA representative of Ukraine for 1957. TsGAOOU, coll. 1, inv. 24, file 4704, p. 81.

14. TsGAVOU, coll. 4648, inv. 2, file 216, pp. 57–69, 88. During Passover prayers in Odessa in 1958, a stone was thrown at the synagogue window and youths who passed on bicycles shouted "beat the Jews." TsGAOOU, coll. 1, inv. 24, file 4704, p. 103.

15. Joseph Bernshtein (b. 1876) completed his studies at the Berdichev yeshiva at age twenty and worked for most of his life as an accountant; after his retirement he became active in the Kiev congregation. On Bernshtein's applications to open a second synagogue in Kiev, see TsGAVOU, coll. 4648, inv. 1, file 194, pp. 17–22, 76–79.

16. Ibid., inv. 2, file 171, pp. 14, 40, 45–46, 119–121; file 172, pp. 15–19, 34–38; file 173, pp. 81–85, 106; file 215, p. 197; file 320, pp. 49–53.

17. Ibid., file 173, p. 106; file 198, pp. 81–82; file 199, p. 108; file 216, pp. 29–31, 107.

18. October 1957 letter of the Kherson district SRA representative to the Ukraine SRA representative. TsGAVOU, coll. 4648, inv. 2, file 234, p. 56.

19. GAVO, coll. 2700, inv. 7, file 460, pp. 63–64. TsGAVOU, coll. 4648, inv. 2, file 250, p. 68.

20. This aspect was also stressed by the congregations of Zaporozh'e and Mozir. Ibid., file 171, p. 126; file 179, pp. 30, 32, 40; file 212, p. 89; file 235, pp. 86–87, 89, 93, 277, 284; file 277, pp. 6–9. GARF, coll. 6991, inv. 4, file 58, p. 110.

21. *Jerusalem Post,* August 30 and October 12, 1956; *Lamerhav,* October 31, 1956.

22. TsGAVOU, coll. 4648, inv. 2, file 215, pp. 3–4.

23. Ibid., file 171, pp. 52, 55–56, 115–118; file 172, pp. 86–88, 96–103, 109; file 180, pp. 145–146, 148–153; file 182, pp. 15–17; file 194, p. 116; file 202, p. 2; file 213, pp. 120, 123; file 216, pp. 154, 157–159, 162–165.

24. TsGAOOU, coll. 1, inv. 24, file 4038, pp. 130–131.

25. TsGAVOU, coll. 4648, inv. 2, file 236, p. 150.

26. GARF, coll. 6991, inv. 4, file 38, pp. 171–172; file 56, pp. 126–127, 152–153, 162–163.

27. Ibid., file 37, p. 71.

28. TsGAVOU, coll. 4648, inv. 2, file 211, p. 4. At issue was a structure purchased under the name of private individuals that had functioned as a synagogue up until 1949. After the formal registration of the Vinnitsa congregation, the congregation filed a complaint against the security services (MGB) demanding that the holy books confiscated during the closure of the synagogue be returned. This request was denied on the grounds that too much time had passed. Ibid., file 269, p. 16.

29. Ibid., file 245, p. 7; file 249, pp. 16–18; file 252, pp. 64–66, 74–75.

30. TsGAVOU, coll. 4648, inv. 2, file 212, pp. 244–245; file 213, pp. 154–155; file 217, pp. 12, 49–50; file 221, p. 242; file 236, p. 184.

31. Ibid., file 215, pp. 169–170.

32. Report of the SRA representative of Ukraine for the second half of 1954. TsGAOOU, coll. 1, inv. 24, file 4038, p. 243.

33. On the autumn Jewish holidays of 1956 in the Soviet Union, see GARF, coll. 6991, inv. 4, file 71, pp. 105–106.

34. *Al Hamishmar,* September 30, 1956. GARF, coll. 6991, inv. 4, file 71, p. 104.

35. *Unzer vort,* September 26, 1958; *Maariv,* September 12, 21, and 25, 1958; *Jewish Chronicle,* September 12, 1958. NARB, coll. 952, inv. 4, file 18, pp. 168–171; GAZhO coll. 4994, inv. 4s, file 1, p. 175. GARF, coll. 6991, inv. 4, file 73, p. 92.

36. TsGAVOU, coll. 4648, inv. 2, file 216, p. 56. GARF, coll. 6991, inv. 4, file 71, pp. 103–104. TsGAOOU, coll. 1, inv. 24, file 4494, p. 327. *Unzer vort,* September 26, 1958; *Maariv,* September 21 and 25, 1958; *Jewish Chronicle,* September 12, 1958.

37. NARB, coll. 952, inv. 2, file 45, p. 5. In Bobruisk more than ten minyans were active, and in Gomel' the number was similar. Ibid., file 48, pp. 217, 221. By the authorities' estimate Belorussia had some forty-five permanent minyans in 1957. Ibid., inv. 3, file 7, p. 33; inv. 4, file 1, pp. 107–108.

38. During the High Holidays of 1956, Moscow had thirty-four minyans known to the authorities; the city of Gorkii had fifteen; the Vinnitsa district had eighty-five; and Simferopol' had eleven. GARF, coll. 6991, inv. 4, file 71, p. 107.

39. TsGAVOU, coll. 4648, inv. 2, file 233, p. 40; file 249, p. 5. GAZhO, coll. 4994, inv. 4s, file 1; pp. 66, 195–196.

40. TsGAVOU, coll. 4648, inv. 2, file 249, p. 5.

CHAPTER EIGHT. The Public Campaign against Religion

1. NARB, coll. 952, inv. 4, file 19, p. 203.

2. Ibid., file 24, p. 24.

3. GARF, coll. 6991, inv. 4, file 123, pp. 5–14. TsGAOOU, coll. 1, inv. 24, file 5116, p. 303. TsGAVOU coll. 4648, inv. 2, file 339, p. 6. Religiia, 1965, pp. 82–83. Anderson, 1994, pp. 33.

4. GARF, coll. 6991, inv. 4, file 1, p. 45.

5. Statement by Leonid Ilitchev, secretary of the Central Committee of the Communist Party, *Pravda,* June 19, 1963.

6. Filatov, 1964. Kozlov, 1999, pp. 217–227.

7. The number of antireligious articles in the main newspapers rose from fourteen in 1957 to some one hundred in 1959, and leveled out at sixty-five per year in the early 1960s. The number of lectures on antireligious subjects rose about eightfold between 1956 and 1963. Powell, 1975, pp. 88, 105. In 1963 a special institute for scientific atheism was formed in the Academy for Social Sciences. Anderson, 1994, p. 38; Thrower, 1983, pp. 143–147.

8. *Radianska Ukraina,* January 19, 1962; *Partiinaia zhizn',* 1962, no. 10, p. 24. Anderson, 1994, p. 42. TsGAOOU, coll. 1, inv. 24, file 5116, p. 303.

9. *Ukrains'ky istorychny zhurnal,* 1964, no. 6, p. 87. Anderson, 1994, p. 46.

10. On seminars of this sort in Ukraine and Kyrgyzstan in 1964, see *Sovetskaia Kirgiziia,* November 29, 1964; *Znamia kommunizma,* October 27, 1964; *Voiovnychyi ateist,* 1964, no. 12, p. 27. A. Berman, a member of the editorial board of the main newspaper in Lithuania, complained that insufficient attention was being devoted to anti-Jewish propaganda. *Sovetskaia Litva,* February 26, 1964; *Kommunist Moldavii,* 1964, no. 12, pp. 68–69.

11. *Volzhskaia kommuna,* September 30, 1961.

12. GAVO, coll. 2700, inv. 7, file 494, p. 19.

13. *Agitator,* 1960, no. 18, p. 63. *Voiovnychyi ateist,* 1964, no. 3, p. 39. *Birobidzshaner shtern,* January 26, 1964.

14. Shakhnovitch, 1960, p. 25.

15. *Nauka i religiia,* 1960, no. 9, pp. 26–31; *Radians'ka Bukovina,* July 7, 1961, and August 31, 1962; *Desnians'ka pravda,* August 5, 1960; *Naddniprians'ka pravda,* January 11, 1961; Belenkii, 1963, pp. 140–141.

16. Kichko, 1963, p. 2.

17. The data are based on issue 29 of the bibliographic publication *Knizhnaia letopis',* which was devoted to books and pamphlets on religion and antireligious publications. See also Altshuler, 1970, pp. 46–50.

18. Prichiny, 1965, pp. 40–41, 118, 123.

19. NARB, coll. 952, inv. 4, file 20, pp. 48, 54. TsGAVOU, coll. 4648, inv. 2, file 265, p. 58; file 402, pp. 6–10. Mr. Kozlov's visit to the United States is covered in *Jews in Eastern Europe* (London), 1959, no. 1, pp. 7–10.

20. Congregation heads were instructed to report on any visits to a synagogue by tourists from abroad as well as to warn the worshipers not to accept gifts from the tourists, including religious artifacts. Any gift received by a worshiper had to be handed over to the congregation head for transfer to an SRA representative. TsGAOOU, coll.1, inv. 24, file 5205, pp. 89–90.

21. Ibid., file 5488, pp. 231–232.

22. Center for Research and Documentation of Eastern European Jewry at The Hebrew University, Pecherski collection.

23. TsGAOOU, coll. 1, inv. 24, file 5205, p. 371.

24. TsGAVOU, coll. 4648, inv. 2, file 40, p. 63; file 299, p. 157.

25. Report of the Ukraine SRA representative on the autumn Jewish holidays of 1960. TsGAOOU, coll. 1, inv. 24, file 5205, p. 331.

26. Calculation based on a topic search for "religion" in the publication *Evrei i evreiskii narod: Materialy iz sovetskoi pechati* (London), vols. 1–18.

27. *Ukrains'kyi istorychnyi zhurnal,* 1963, no. 6, p. 31; *Nauka i religiia,* 1960, no. 4, p. 37; *Kommunist Moldavii,* 1960, no. 7, pp. 73, 75; *Zaporizhska pravda,* February 19, 1960; *Radians'ka Bukovina,* June 7, 1961, and August 31, 1962; *Radians'ka Zhytomyrshchyna,* September 7, 1960.

28. *Sovetskaia Moldavia,* April 8 and August 6, 1960; *Voiovnychyi ateist,* 1960, no. 1, p. 29;

Kommunist Moldavii, 1960, no. 7, pp. 73–75; *Radians'ka Bukovina,* September 9, 1960, and May 30, 1961; *Naddniprians'ka pravda,* January 11, 1961; *Jews in Eastern Europe* (London), 1960, no. 6, pp. 6–12; GAZhO, coll. 623, inv. 2, file 258, pp. 83–85. TsGAVOU coll. 4648, inv. 2, file 299, pp. 167–168. GAZhO, coll. 4994, inv. 4s, file 6, p. 55.

29. For more on the blood libel in Buinaksk (Dagestan), see Altshuler, 1990, pp. 145–146, 550–553; on the case in Georgia see Neishtat, 1970, p. 96; and on that in Chernovtsy (Ukraine), see TsGAVOU coll. 4648, inv. 2, file 299, p. 163. On similar phenomena in Uzbekistan and Lithuania, see *Jews in Eastern Europe* (London), 1963, no. 2, pp. 34–39; no. 3, pp. 37–38.

30. On the throwing of stones at the Moscow synagogue and the arson attack on the guardhouse in Malakhovka as well as at the synagogue in Tskhakaia in Georgia, see *Forverts,* October 22, 1962; Neishtat, 1970, p. 90; GARF, coll. 6991, inv. 4, file 71, p. 109; *Jews in Eastern Europe* (London), 1959, no. 2, pp. 9–13; *Canadian Jewish News,* October 26, 1962; and *Herald Tribune,* October 21 and November 4, 1962.

31. *Minskaia pravda,* March 4, 1961; *Leninskii put',* May 27, 1961; *Golos Rigi,* August 13, 1960.

32. TsGAVOU coll. 4648, inv. 2, file 370, p. 39; file 376, p. 79; file 382, pp. 39, 79, 81, 86, 90–96.

33. *National Jewish Monthly,* October 19, 1962.

34. TsGAVOU coll. 4648, inv. 2, file 297, p. 94. GARF, coll. 6991, inv. 4, file 130, pp. 22–23.

35. For example, five Jews wrote to the Khotin municipality as follows: "We have not forgotten the brutality against the Jews of the German Fascists who murdered hundreds of thousands of innocents[.] [W]here was God then?" On these grounds, supposedly, the authorities demanded the closure of the town's synagogue. Similar letters with similar formulations were signed by an additional 170 of the town's Jews. TsGAVOU coll. 4648, inv. 2, file 327, pp. 129–140.

36. These included synagogues in the following towns: Rovno, Piriatin, and on Barbius Street in Chernovtsy. Ibid., file 274, pp. 103–104; file 275, pp. 159, 207; file 291, p. 2; file 293, p. 69; file 296, pp. 22–24; file 300, p. 79. See *Jews in Eastern Europe* (London), 1959, no. 1, pp. 4–5.

37. Including the following towns: Nezhin, Korostishev, Kremenchug, Kirovograd, Shepetovka, Lubny, and Drogobych. TsGAVOU coll. 4648, inv. 2, file 291, pp. 23, 42, 58–59, 98; file 293, pp. 15, 46; file 296, pp. 92–93; file 297, pp. 29, 93–99; file 299, pp. 46, 58, 68–74, 102–104; file 301, pp. 85–87; file 302, pp. 84, 99, 101; file 303, pp. 113, 119, 121; file 307, pp. 84, 97; file 325, pp. 43 82–83. TsGAOOU, coll. 1, inv. 24, file 5116, p. 303.

38. GAChO, coll. 623, inv. 2, file 169, pp. 60, 62, 65, 69–70, 74, 110, 112–114, 118, 120–123. TsGAVOU coll. 4648, inv. 2, file 27, p. 106; file 319, pp. 13, 74; file 321, pp. 84–86; file 324, p. 105; file 325, pp. 43, 82–83; file 327, pp. 18–24, 106–107; file 329, pp. 95–97; file 333, pp. 21–22; file 334, pp. 4, 6–9, 16, 115, 116; file 370, p. 87; file 371, pp. 55, 81–82; file 379, pp. 82–86.

39. Ibid., file 325, p. 83. GAChO, coll. 623, inv. 2, file 169, pp. 113–114.

40. Ibid., file 311, p. 30. TsGAVOU coll. 4648, file 319, p. 31; file 325, pp. 22–23; file 330, pp. 93, 96.

41. In 1960 two services were held in the synagogue every morning. For Sabbath prayers about a hundred people came. Ibid., file 319, pp. 7–8; file 324, pp. 11–19; file 328, pp. 24, 29, 86–88, 91–118.

42. GAOO, coll. 2700, inv. 7, file 514, p. 4. TsGAVOU, coll. 4648, inv. 2, file 296, pp. 1–2; file 300, pp. 7, 23; file 377, pp. 28–31, 44, 46, 53–56; file 401, p. 43; file 408, pp. 53–58. TsGAOOU, coll. 1, inv. 32, file 2846, pp. 42–44.

43. Thus, for instance, in justifying the closure of the synagogue in the town of Khotin, in 1961, the authorities stressed that in 1958 the congregation had purchased a matzah-baking machine and had been operating it ever since. TsGAVOU, coll. 4648, inv. 2, file 327, p. 127; file 65, p. 25.

44. Ibid.

45. NARB, coll. 952, inv. 3, file 36, p. 265.

46. Ibid., file 29, pp. 14–19; file 32, pp. 2, 258–259, 268, 273–274; file 36, pp. 23–25, 279.

47. TsGAVOU, coll. 4648, inv. 2, file 245, p. 1; file 249, p. 12; file 252, pp. 68–69; file 272, p. 35.

48. Ibid., file 291, p. 101; file 299, pp. 83–85; file 306, pp. 151–152; file 319, p. 18; file 324, pp. 92, 105–107; file 329, pp. 118–119.

49. TsGAVOU, coll. 4648, inv. 2, file 407, pp. 28–31, 46–48, 63–65. *Herald Tribune,* November 27, 1961.

50. GARF, coll. 6991, inv. 4, file 108, pp. 3–7, 39–44. Rabbi Levin hinted at the disputes and the use of informers in one of his sermons in the synagogue. Bick, 1973, p. 60. *Tog morgn zhurnal,* October 17, 1962. See also *Haboker, Lamerhav, Herut, Davar,* and *Hatzofeh,* October 18, 1962.

51. TsGAVOU coll. 4648, inv. 2, file 291, p. 115; file 299, pp. 113–116; file 307, pp. 95–96.

52. Ibid., file 274, p. 82; file 370, p. 20; file 376, pp. 1–3; file 406, pp. 143–150. *Jews in Eastern Europe* (London), 1959, no. 1, p. 5.

53. A USSR report to the UN in mid-1956 tells of 450 synagogues in the Soviet Union. In mid-1959 Soviet sources in the West reported the existence of 400 to 451 synagogues. Meanwhile, in 1960 a radio broadcast in the United States told of 150 active synagogues, whereas the rabbi of Moscow's main synagogue spoke of only 96. *Jews in Eastern Europe* (London), 1963, no. 2, p. 10; no. 3, p. 33.

54. TsGAVOU, coll. 4648, inv. 2, file 273, pp. 85–86; file 302, p. 16.

55. A report on minyans held in Zhitomir was handed in by the "support groups," an event that led to the minyans' closure. GAZhO, coll. 4994, inv. 4s, file 8, p. 2. TsGAOOU, coll. 1, inv. 24, file 6007, pp. 72, 109.

56. NARB, coll. 952, inv. 3, file 19, pp. 100–103; file 28, pp. 110–111, 195–196; inv. 4, file 21, p. 72.

57. Complaint by the Jews of Vitebsk to the prime minister of Belorussia, September 1959, and the answer of the *oblispolkom* (district authority). Ibid., inv. 3, file 28, pp. 77–78.

58. Letter by the *oblispolkom* of Vitebsk of November 13, 1959. Ibid., p. 104.

59. On November 14, 1946, a representative of the Soviet government issued an order to the censors to examine the libraries in the prayer houses of all religions and to confiscate books, pamphlets, and pictures having anti-Soviet content. GARF, coll. 9425, inv. 1s, file 403, pp. 116–117. This instruction seems mostly to have related to churches that had functioned during the Nazi occupation and not to synagogues, and this most likely explains why we have not found references to this subject in the available documentation. TsGAVOU, coll. 4648, inv. 2, file 228, p. 39; file 234, pp. 91–101; file 272, p. 93; file 278, pp. 49–51, 53. *Tog morgn zhurnal,* March 5, 1963. See also *Potul'nitskaia,* 2001, p. 120. *Jews in Eastern Europe* (London), 1959, no. 1, pp. 4–5.

60. Report of the Zakarpat'e SRA representative on the closure of houses of prayer, April 9, 1959. TsGAVOU, coll. 4648, inv. 2, file 272, p. 35.

61. Application of the Khar'kov Jews to the SRA chairman in Moscow, April 1959, with thirty-eight signatures. Ibid., file 277, pp. 7–9, 11; file 265, pp. 53–55.

62. Ibid., file 305, p. 21.

63. *Jewish Chronicle,* May 6, 1960.

64. Report of the SRA representative in Ukraine for 1964. TsGAOOU, coll. 1, inv. 24, file 5607, pp. 109–110.

65. Eliav, 1965, p. 68.

66. *Di yidishe tsaitung,* November 19, 1959; *Maariv,* October 18, 1960; *Yediot Aharonot,* October 18, 1960; *Forverts,* October 22, 1962.

67. See the December 7, 1962, editions of *Haboker, Lamerhav, Tog morgn zhurnal,* and *Di letste nayes.* See also *American Examiner,* December 13, 1962; *Jewish News,* December 14, 1962.

68. For an account of the atmosphere near the synagogue in Moscow on the Simchat Torah holiday, see Wiesel, 1967, pp. 48–71.

CHAPTER NINE. Rabbis and the Congregational Establishment

1. For a general survey on the rabbis in the USSR, see Yodfat, 1972.

2. On the "official rabbis" in tsarist Russia, see Shochat, 1976.

3. GARF, coll. 6991, inv. 3s, file 23, p. 72.

4. Ibid., file 24, p. 4.

5. Ibid., file 23, p. 74.

6. NARB, coll. 952, inv. 2, file 1, p. 28.

7. TsGAVOU, coll. 4648, inv. 2, file 72, p. 31.

8. Letter of Piotr Vil'khovy to his representative in the Poltova district, January 28, 1946. TsGAVOU, coll. 4648, inv. 2, file 17, p. 60.

9. Report of the SRA representative in Uzbekistan for quarters one through three of 1946. GARF, coll. 6991, inv. 3s, file 35, p. 194.

10. GAChO, coll. 623, inv. 2, file 3, pp. 34, 82; file 6, pp. 36–37. TsGAVOU, coll. 4648, inv. 2, file 299, p. 159. GARF, coll. 6991, file 1036, p. 165.

11. TsGAOOU coll. 1, inv. 32, file 4555, p. 60.

12. GARF, coll. 6991, inv. 4, file 1036, p. 165.

13. Ibid., inv.3s, file 13, p. 8; file 95, p. 3. TsGAVOU, coll. 4648, inv. 2, file 215, p. 203; file 233, p. 40; file 248, p. 22; file 253, pp. 14, 19, 28.

14. TsGAVOU, coll. 4648, inv. 2, file 72, p. 38. GAOO, coll. 2600, inv. 5, file 330, p. 174. GARF, coll. 6991, inv. 3s, file 95, pp. 3, 56. Osipova, 2002, p. 230. Mironenko, 1999, p. 116. *Hatzofeh,* August 20 and October 2, 1962; *Tog morgn zhurnal,* August 8, 1962; *Herut,* August 9, 1962; *Davar,* August 20, 1962.

15. Levin, 1989, pp. 165, 277. Hacohen, 1983, p. 206. Mitsel', 1998, p. 241. *Hatzofeh,* January 25, 1963.

16. GARF, coll. 6991, inv. 4, file 75, pp. 9–10. Bystriakov, 2002, pp. 71–72.

17. GARF, coll. 6991, inv. 3s, file 95, p. 49; inv. 4, file 74, pp. 160–161. Greenbaum, 1994, p. 8. Koten, 1964, p. 9.

18. Bick, 1973, p. 59.

19. GARF, coll. 6991, inv. 3s, file 95, pp. 50–54. According to one testimony the rabbi served as a conduit for funds arriving from the United States to aid Jews in need and those seeking to immigrate to Israel. YVA, file 03/5630. Greenbaum, 1994, p. 32. Osipova, 2002, p. 248. Beizer, 1989, pp. 252–253. *Hatzofeh,* October 2, 1962. *Kol Torah,* 1959, nos. 9, 11.

20. GARF, coll. 6991, inv. 3s, file 39, p. 165.

21. NARB, coll. 952, inv. 2, file 7, p. 61; file 49, pp. 60–61. GARF, coll. 6991, inv. 3s, file 95, pp. 2, 50. Davidson, 1985, p. 407.

22. NARB, coll. 952, inv. 4, file 17, pp. 32–33.

23. GARF, coll. 6991, inv. 3, file 83, p. 17.

24. Ibid., inv. 3s, file 95, p. 59. Greenbaum, 1994, p. 19.

25. Baazova, 1992, p. 181.

26. GARF, coll. 6991, inv. s3, file 95, pp. 50, 61. Interview conducted by Professor Dov Levin, January 6, 1964. Oral History Division, Institute of Contemporary Jewry, Hebrew University of Jerusalem.

27. GARF, coll. 6991, inv. 4, file 22, pp. 20–21. REE, 1994–2000, vol. 3, p. 462–463. Cohen, 1971, pp. 925, 943. Slipoi, 1971, p. 878. *Kommunist Moldavii,* 1960, no. 7, pp. 73–75.

28. On December 3, 1946, the Soviet government passed a resolution "on taxation arrangements for religious service providers." This resolution did not specify unequivocally which section of the tax laws applied to these providers. Only on March 13, 1963, was it established that those employed by religious associations who were *also* members of labor professional unions would be assessed taxes according to Section 5. Such individuals did not include rabbis, cantors, and the like. GARF, coll. 6991, inv. 4, file 119, p. 11. NARB, coll. 952, inv. 2, file 14, p. 142.

29. GARF, coll. 6991, inv. 4, file 99, p. 20.

30. Ibid., pp. 2, 21–22.

31. Biographical details on all these rabbis may be found in the Hebrew version of this book.

32. Eight rabbis in the USSR issued calls against US policy on atomic weapons; rabbis and congregation heads also condemned Israel's Sinai campaign. *Izvestiia,* November 11, 1956.

33. NARB, coll. 952, inv. 4, file 10, p. 234; file 19, p. 240.

34. Ibid., inv. 2, file 50, p. 18; file 52, pp. 207–209. *Gomel'skaia pravda,* July 24, 1960.

35. Lukin, 2000, p. 363. REE, 1994–2000, vol. 3, p. 455.

36. NARB, coll. 952, inv. 1, file 8, p. 57; inv. 2, file 12, p. 78.

37. Ibid., file 27, p. 193; file 38, p. 219; file 40, p. 223; file 52, p. 292. Levin, 1989, pp. 214, 233, 315.

38. NARB, coll. 952, inv. 4, file 21, p. 53.

CHAPTER TEN. **Cantors for Hire**

1. In early 1953 Moscow's synagogues had three permanent cantors. Other towns with permanent cantors were Irkutsk, Baku, Briansk, Kuibishev, Rostov-on-Don, Stalinabad, Leninabad, Tallinn, and the villages of Vani and Bandza. GARF, coll. 6991, inv. 3s, file 95, pp. 53–54, 58, 60–62. See also TsGAOOU, coll. 1, inv. 42, file 4704, p. 375; TsGAVOU, coll. 4648, inv. 2, file 251, p. 45; file 253, p. 1.

2. GAVO, coll. 2700, inv. 7, file 460, p. 67; inv. 19, file 42, p. 28.

3. GAChO, coll. 623, inv. 2, file 29, pp. 33, 36; file 135, p. 56. GAVO, coll. 2700, inv. 5, file 330, pp. 48, 151, 175. TsGAOOU, coll. 1, inv. 42, file 4704, p. 375. TsGAVOU, coll. 4648, inv. 2, file 173, p. 3.

4. Report by the Ukraine SRA representative on the autumn Jewish holidays in 1957. TsGAOOU, coll. 1, inv. 42, file 4494, p. 330.

5. TsGAVOU, coll. 4648, inv. 2, file 380, p. 103; file 407, pp. 41–45.

6. Consultations of this sort were usually held orally, and only occasionally do the SRA representatives mention having discussed matters with the "neighbors" and having authorized the out-of-town cantor only after meeting no objections from such informants. GAZhO, coll. 4994, inv. 4s, file 1, p. 174.

7. In 1945 several congregations in Chernovtsy held cantorial concerts. On August 4–7, 1949, the cantor S. I. Keizerman performed in Berdichev, and, in the authorities' characterization, gave "religious concerts" in the synagogue. In May 1949 an actor from Latvia by the name of Khaiat Utkas performed in a synagogue in Berdichev. TsGAVOU, coll. 4648, inv. 2, file 16, p. 56; file 65, p. 25; file 247, p. 9; file 299, p. 159. TsGAOOU, coll. 1, inv. 32, file 4555, pp. 328–329. GARF, coll. 6991, inv. 3s, file 8, p. 92.

8. TsGAVOU, coll. 4648, inv. 2, file 88, p. 43. TsGAOOU, coll. 1, inv. 24, file 1572, pp. 153, 316. GARF, coll. 6991, inv. 3s, file 73, pp. 32–33.

9. GAZhO, coll. 4994, inv. 4s, file 1, pp. 173–174; file 2, p. 178. GARF, coll. 6991, inv. 4, file 71, p. 104. TsGAVOU, coll. 4648, inv. 2, file 270, p. 79. TsGAOOU, coll. 1, inv. 42, file 4038, p. 258; file 4704, pp. 373–375.

10. For the holidays of 1957, the Irkutsk congregation invited a cantor and paid him five thousand rubles; the Kalarash congregation paid eight thousand that year for its cantor, and a cantor from L'vov was paid ten thousand rubles. GARF, coll. 6991, inv. 4, file 73,

p. 89. TsGAOOU, coll. 1, inv. 42, file 4038, pp. 166, 258; file 4494, pp. 230, 330. GAVO, coll. 2700, inv. 19, file 46, p. 12.

11. GAVO, coll. 2700, inv. 7, file 494, pp. 60–61; file 514, p. 50. GAZhO, coll. 4994, inv. 4s, file 6, pp. 29, 57; file 7, pp. 11–12.

12. GAChO, coll. 623, inv. 2, file 59, pp. 97, 103. GAVO, coll. 2700, inv. 19, file 35, p. 27. TsGAVOU, coll. 4648, inv. 2, file 50, p. 200; file 70, p. 39.

13. TsGAOOU, coll. 1, inv. 23, file 5607, pp. 171–174. GAVO, coll. 2700, inv. 19, file 36, p. 64; file 38, pp. 18, 23.

14. Letter by the SRA to the tax department of the district and city of Chernovtsy, January 22, 1959. GAChO, coll. 623, inv. 2, file 135, p. 3.

CHAPTER ELEVEN. Financing Religious Activities

1. A report by the chairman of the SRA of the USSR on its activities in 1946 noted that "the soviet does not deal especially with the issue of [financial] accounts." GARF, coll. 6991, inv. 3 s, file 47, p. 47. An SRA representative in the Zhitomir district noted that "it is not to be ruled out that the management of the Jewish congregation of Berdichev is concealing its revenues." GAZhO, coll. 4994, inv. 4s, file 8, p. 14. See also Orleanskii, 1930, pp. 22, 28.

2. TsGAOOU, coll. 1, inv. 24, file 5205, pp. 90–91.

3. Orleanskii, 1930, pp. 21, 28.

4. TsGAVOU, coll. 4648, inv. 2, file 49, p. 77.

5. Orleanskii, 1930, p. 28. Report from 1951 by the SRA supervisor for the Poles'e district. NARB, coll. 952, inv. 2, file 30, p. 2.

6. GAVO, coll. 2700, inv. 5, file 330, p. 50. Making donations in this form when receiving the honor of *aliya* to the Torah was an innovation of sorts in the traditions of most Eastern European synagogues.

7. TsGAVOU, coll. 4648, inv. 2, file 198, pp. 112–113.

8. During the High Holidays in the congregations of Kiev, Zhmerinka, Cherkassy, Bershad', Chernovtsy, and Iampol', a total of 73,100 and 87,100 rubles were collected in 1951 and 1953, respectively.

9. GARF, coll. 6991, inv. 3s, file 47, p. 218; inv. 4, file 23, p. 35.

10. Orleanskii, 1930, p. 28. GAVO, coll. 2700, inv. 19, file 36, pp. 2, 4, 64. TsGAVOU, coll. 4648, inv. 2, file 69, pp. 18–19; file 72, p. 51.

11. TsGAOOU, coll. 1, inv. 24, file 2741, p. 102.

12. GARF, coll. 6991, inv. 4, file 25, p. 18.

13. GAChO, coll. 623, inv. 2, file 15, pp. 30–32, 39–40. NARB, coll. 952, inv. 2, file 10, p. 237; file 14, p. 141; file 68, pp. 22–23.

14. TsGAVOU, coll. 4648, inv. 2; file 62, pp. 18–19. GAVO, coll. 2700, inv. 19, file 36, pp. 4, 7.

15. The commonly accepted meaning of the term *vocher* is a loan with very steep interest rates. However, the term less commonly implies a fixed weekly payment to Torah students. Information on this sense of the term, articulated by a very few Yiddish writers, was con-

veyed to me by Dr. Yossef Guri, an editor of the unpublished *Academic Yiddish Dictionary.* I am grateful for his insight.

16. Report by the Belorussia SRA deputy representative on an audit for the Minsk congregation, September 1949. NARB, coll. 952, inv. 1, file 16, pp. 103–110.

17. In October 1949 the SRA issued an order to end the practice of selling Hanukkah candles in Jewish homes. GAVO, coll. 2700, inv. 19, file 36, p. 77. TsGAOOU, coll. 1, inv. 42, file 2741, p. 65.

18. TsGAVOU, coll. 4648, inv. 2, file 65, p. 22; file 233, pp. 37–39.

19. GAVO, coll. 2700, inv. 19, file 36, pp. 2, 4. TsGAVOU, coll. 4648, inv. 2, file 62, pp. 18–19.

20. TsGAOOU, coll. 1, inv. 42, file 1572, p. 313.

21. Thus, for instance, the congregation of the main synagogue in Chernovtsy and the choir that led services during the High Holidays and Sukkot of 1946 were paid some 31,000 rubles. GAChO, coll. 623, inv. 2, file 15, pp. 30–32, 39–40.

22. TsGAVOU, coll. 4648, inv. 2, file 72, p. 38.

23. GAChO, coll. 623, inv. 2, file 15, pp. 30–32, 39–40. TsGAVOU, coll. 4648, inv. 2, file 303, p. 110.

24. TsGAVOU, coll. 4648, inv. 2, file 303, p. 101.

25. TsGAOOU, coll. 1, inv. 24, file 2741, p. 102.

CHAPTER TWELVE. Religious Studies and the Moscow Yeshiva, 1957

1. Orleanskii, 1930, p. 11. See also Odintsov, 1997, pp. 72–79. Mendl, 1997, p. 15. Levin, 1989, p. 442. Osipova, 2002, pp. 243–244, REE, 1994–2000, vol. 3, p. 265.

2. Landoi, 1967, pp. 102–104.

3. *Davar,* March 22, 1945.

4. Menahem-Mendel Puterfas was born in Belorussia and from 1925 to 1929 studied at the Chabad yeshivas in Khar'kov, Nevel', and Vitebsk. Early in the Soviet-German war he fled the Moscow area, eventually settling in Samarkand. In 1946 he moved to L'vov and from there attempted to cross into Poland; in 1947 he was sentenced to ten years in prison. After the liberation he lived in Chernovtsy until immigrating to Britain in 1964 and then Israel in 1972. He passed away in London in 1995. On the man and the teachers at the yeshivas, see Levin, 1989, pp. 337, 442; Osipova, 2002, pp. 225, 243–244, 252–253, 268–269; REE, 1994–2000, vol. 3, p. 265.

5. Levin, 1989, pp. 331–338.

6. *Hatzofeh,* March 15, 1944; Cahana, 1986, p. 31; GAChO, coll. 623, inv. 2, file 5, p. 1; file 6, pp. 15, 19. GARF, coll. 6991, inv. 3s, file 61, p. 160.

7. Ibid., file 29, p. 61.

8. GARF, coll. 6991, inv. 4, file 22, p. 27.

9. TsGAVOU, coll. 4648, inv. 2, file 20, pp. 21–22; file 272, pp. 36–37; file 296, p. 87. TsGAOOU, coll. 1, inv. 23, file 5069, p. 329. GARF, coll. 6991, inv. 3s, file 53, p. 37; file 61, p. 161. Criminal codex, 1952, section 122. Ro'i, 1995, p. 270.

10. Report by the Ukraine SRA representative for the first half of 1956. TsGAOOU, coll. 1, inv. 42, file 4038, p. 278.

11. Ibid., inv. 32, file 5667, p. 61. TsGAVOU, coll. 4648, inv. 2, file 72, p. 78. GARF, coll. 6991, inv. 3s, file 61, p. 161.

12. TsGAVOU, coll. 4648, inv. 2, file 72, p. 2. TsGAOOU, coll. 1, inv. 32, file 5667, p. 61. GAVO, coll. 2700, inv. 19, file 36, p. 1.

13. Letter of the Odessa district SRA representative from 1949. TsGAVOU, coll. 4648, inv. 2, file 72, p. 75.

14. GARF, coll. 6991, inv. 4, file 37, pp. 6, 68. For a wider treatment of the history of the yeshiva, see Altshuler, 2003.

15. TsGAVOU, coll. 4648, inv. 2, file 213, pp. 214–215. GARF, coll. 6991, inv. 4, file 71, pp. 33–35, 84; file 88, pp. 89–90. The first list of eleven candidates for study at the yeshiva included only one eighteen-year-old; the rest were adults. All the candidates were married and nearly all had children. Of the eleven, eight were natives of the areas annexed by the Soviet Union during WWII.

16. GARF, coll. 6991, inv. 4, file 58, pp. 138–139; file 71, p. 30; file 74, p. 26. *Hatzofeh,* March 29, June 12, and August 20, 1957; *Al Hamishmar,* February 9; 1957; *Davar,* January 25 and February 18, 1957; *Lamerhav,* March 3, 1957; JTA, February 18 and June 12, 1957; *Jewish Chronicle,* June 7, 1957. Michlin, 1986, p. 177.

17. *Al Hamishmar,* June 17, 1957; *Hatzofeh,* June 18 and September 10, 1957, and February 4 and 25, 1958; *Unzer wort,* February 8, 1958. The weekly *Davar Hashavua* published an article with photographs on the Moscow yeshiva in its May 7, 1958, issue. *Jewish Chronicle,* June 14, 1957, and January 16, 1959. *Jewish Life* (New York), August 1957, pp. 9–12.

18. GARF, coll. 6991, inv. 4, file 74, pp. 160–161; file 98, p. 38. *Yediot Aharonot,* August 22, 1957.

19. GARF, coll. 6991, inv. 4, file 84, p. 187.

20. TsGAVOU, coll. 4648, inv. 2, file 299, p. 163.

21. *Forwerts,* November 14, 1961; *Unzer wort,* November 18, 1961; Jerusalem Post, February 3, 1961.

22. *Tog morgn zhurnal,* April 9, August 7, and October 5, 1962. *Di letste nayes,* August 7 and 28, 1962. *Kanader odler,* August 9, 1962. *Der tog,* September 2, 1962. *Forwerts,* June 30, 1962. *Unzer vort,* July 9, 1962. *Yediot Aharonot,* April 9, August 7, and August 31, 1962. *Haboker,* April 9, 1962; *Al Hamishmar, Haaretz,* and *Herut,* August 7, 1962; *Davar,* July 6, 1962; *New York Post,* June 29, 1962; *Daily Herald,* August 7, 1962; *Jerusalem Post,* August 7, 1962; *Jewish Times,* August 9, 1962; *Jewish Exponent* (Philadelphia), August 17, 1962; *Jewish Chronicle,* July 6, August 3, and September 31, 1962; *Canadian Jewish News,* July 13, 1962; *Diario Israelita,* July 13, 1962; *Chicago News,* July 6 and August 9, 1962; *Bulletin* (Philadelphia), August 7, 1962; *News Post* (Baltimore), August 6, 1962; and *Herald Tribune,* August 6, 1962.

CHAPTER THIRTEEN. Kosher Slaughter (*Shechita*) and Matzah Baking

1. TsGAVOU, coll. 4648, inv. 2, file 179, p. 7.

2. NARB, coll. 952, inv. 1, file 5, pp. 315, 318.

3. GARF, coll. 6991, inv. 3s, file 23, p. 74.

4. NARB, coll. 952, inv. 1, file 14, pp. 171–173.

5. GARF, coll. 6991, inv. 3s, file 53, pp. 8–9; TsGAVOU, coll. 4648, inv. 2, file 50, p. 69.

6. Report by the SRA representative for Ukraine for the second quarter of 1946. GARF, coll. 6991, inv. 4, file 1036, p. 166.

7. GAChO, coll. 623, inv. 2, file 21, pp. 4, 15–16. GAVO, coll. 2700, inv. 19, file 35, p. 11. TsGAVOU, coll. 4648, inv. 2, file 52, p. 50.

8. Ibid.

9. GARF, coll. 6991, inv. 4, file 23, p. 33.

10. Ibid., file 98, p. 75.

11. *Al Hamishmar*, August 9, 1959. *Tog morgn zhurnal*, October 4, 1962. *Unzer veg*, October 21, 1960.

12. Report by the Bobruisk district SRA representative for the second quarter of 1951. NARB, coll. 952, inv. 2, file 27, p. 201; file 29, pp. 83, 193.

13. GAVO, coll. 2700, inv. 19, file 38, p. 48. NARB, coll. 952, inv. 2, file 27, pp. 123–125. *Lamerhav*, October 11, 1959.

14. TsGAVOU, coll. 4648, inv. 2, file 277, p. 12.

15. *Tog morgn zhurnal*, October 4, 1962. *Jewish Chronicle*, September 18, 1959.

16. TsGAVOU, coll. 4648, inv. 2, file 171, pp. 67, 106; file 180, p. 14; file 234, p. 71. GAVO, coll. 2700, inv. 7, file 404, p. 84.

17. The Zakarpat'e district SRA representative informed the congregation delegates that the Ministry of Trade had ordered that matzah be baked like every other baked product. However, the entities involved with sales of baked goods wrote that they feared there would not be sufficient buyers. TsGAVOU, coll. 4648, inv. 2, file 232, p. 85.

18. GAVO, coll. 2700, inv. 19, file 35, p. 11.

19. GARF, coll. 6991, inv. 4, file 25, p. 20.

20. TsGAOOU, coll. 1, inv. 24, file 12, p. 203; file 4494, p. 161.

21. TsGAVOU, coll. 4648, inv. 2, file 256, p. 75.

22. Ibid., file 300, p. 8.

23. In April 1935 the chairman of the Committee for Religious Affairs of the All-Russian Central Executive Committee (VtsIK) declared that baking of matzah should be permitted in Ukraine. GARF, coll. 5263, inv. 1, file 73, p. 238; file 47, p. 101.

24. Ibid., file 990, p. 127. TsGAVOU, coll. 4648, inv. 2, file 72, p. 39.

25. GARF, coll. 6991, inv. 4, file 37, p. 27.

26. TsGAVOU, coll. 4648, inv. 2, file 17, p. 12. Letters with a similar formulation were

sent by several institutions in the district, suggesting they were ordered by Moscow. GAVO, coll. 2700, inv. 19, file 31, pp. 12, 16, 66.

27. Litvak, 1988, pp. 215–225. Levin, 1989, pp. 225–226, *Jewish Chronicle,* 3, April 17, 1942.

28. GAChO, coll. 623, inv. 2, file 8, p. 8; file 21, pp. 1–2. GAVO, coll. 2700, inv. 19, file 35, p. 11. TsGAOOU, coll. 1, inv. 42, file 1572, p. 147.

29. TsGAVOU, coll. 4648, inv. 2, file 114, p. 99. Letter of Piotr Vil'khovy to SRA representatives of March 30, 1949. GAVO, coll. 2700, inv. 19, file 38, p. 7.

30. NARB, coll. 952, inv. 2, file 27, pp. 121–122. TsGAOOU, coll. 1, inv. 42, file 1572, pp. 146–147.

31. TsGAVOU, coll. 4648, inv. 2, file 171, pp. 34, 79.

32. Ibid., file 174, pp. 14–15; file 179, p. 8; file 182, pp. 12–13; file 196, p. 16.

33. NARB, coll. 952, inv. 2, file 50, pp. 29, 98, 105–106.

34. TsGAVOU, coll. 4648, inv. 2, file 196, p. 15; file 215, pp. 8–9. TsGAOOU, coll. 1, inv. 42, file 4038, pp. 183–187. GAVO, coll. 2700, inv. 7, file 404, p. 83.

35. TsGAVOU, coll. 4648, inv. 2, file 228, p. 13. GAZhO, coll. 4994, inv. 4s, file 1, pp. 56–57.

36. GAZhO, coll. 4994, inv. 4s, file 1, pp. 72, 149; file 218, pp. 57, 64, 126. TsGAVOU, coll. 4648, inv. 2, file 228, p. 13.

37. Ibid., file 233, p. 25; file 235, pp. 5–6.

38. *Hatzofeh,* April 10, 1958.

39. According to the seven-year plan, the grain harvests were meant to increase, from 1958 until 1965, by 6.33 percent (from 134.7 million to 180 million tons). As it turned out, the yields dropped by 10.1 percent, and although the USSR purchased grain from the West, certain areas still had bread shortages. Nove, 1992, pp. 264–362, 372–377.

40. GARF, coll. 6991, inv. 4, file 108, p. 8. Twenty-two hundred kilograms of matzah were baked in Zhmerinka, and thirteen tons were baked in Vinnitsa. GAVO, coll. 2700, inv. 7, file 478, pp. 48–49.

41. TsGAVOU, coll. 4648, inv. 2, file 180, pp. 58–59.

42. *Hatzofeh, Haboker, Herut,* and *Davar,* April 10, 1963.

43. TsGAVOU, coll. 4648, inv. 2, file 266, p. 8; file 273, pp. 11–13; file 277, pp. 101–102.

44. TsGAVOU, coll. 4648, inv. 2, file 17, p. 12; file 28, p. 43.

45. TsGAOOU, coll. 1, inv. 42, file 12, p. 202. TsGAVOU, coll. 4648, inv. 2, file 196, p. 15. GAVO, coll. 2700, inv. 19, file 38, p. 7.

46. GARF, coll. 6991, inv. 3s, file 258, p. 129. TsGAOOU, coll. 1, inv. 42, file 1572, p. 148; file 2741, p. 64.

47. TsGAVOU, coll. 4648, inv. 2, file 171, pp. 87–88. GAChO, coll. 623, inv. 2, file 52, p. 42.

48. TsGAOOU, coll. 1, inv. 42, file 1950, p. 1. TsGAVOU, coll. 4648, inv. 2, file 196, p. 15.

49. TsGAVOU, coll. 4648, inv. 2, file 173, pp. 59–60, 94; file 178, pp. 93, 95; file 215, pp. 5–6; file 228, pp. 53–56.

50. Initiatives of this kind were enacted in Borisov, Gomel', and elsewhere. NARB, coll. 952, inv. 2, file 48, pp. 37, 221.

51. TsGAVOU, coll. 4648, inv. 2, file 171, p. 17.

52. Ibid., file 228, pp. 15–18.

53. The authorizations for matzah baking were given by three agencies: the district Finance Department, the Department of Health, and the local fire department. TsGAVOU, coll. 4648, inv. 2, file 213, pp. 193–195; file 228, p. 29.

54. NARB, coll. 952, inv. 2, file 15, pp. 212–213; inv. 4, file 15, p. 171. GAZhO, coll. 4994, inv. 4s, file 1, p. 91.

55. TsGAOOU, coll. 1, inv. 42, file 4704, p. 96. TsGAVOU, coll. 4648, inv. 2, file 253, p. 131. NARB, coll. 952, inv. 2, file 51, pp. 134–135; inv. 4, file 15, p. 233.

56. TsGAVOU, coll. 4648, inv. 2, file 266, p. 9. In 1959 the Western media reported that matzah was baked in Moscow and Leningrad but that Kiev, Odessa, and Khar'kov had "severe shortages of matzah" (*Jewish Chronicle,* May 22, 1959).

57. TsGAVOU, coll. 4648, inv. 2, file 302, p. 18. NARB, coll. 952, inv. 3, file 28, pp. 4–6. GAVO, coll. 2700, inv. 7, file 514, p. 37. *Tog morgn zhurnal,* April 1963.

58. NARB, coll. 952, inv. 4, file 15, p. 151; file 21, pp. 71–72.

59. TsGAVOU, coll. 4648, inv. 2, file 331, pp. 51–53.

60. GAChO, coll. 623, inv. 2, file 172, pp. 48–49. *Hatzofeh, Haboker, Herut,* and *Davar,* April 10, 1963.

61. On home baking and sales of matzah in the postwar years in Kiev, see Zonenfeld, 1990, pp. 78–81.

62. TsGAOOU, coll. 1, inv. 24, file 1572, p. 148. GAVO, coll. 2700, inv. 7, file 404, pp. 83–84.

63. TsGAOOU, coll. 1, inv. 42, file 4704, p. 96.

64. Ibid., p. 27.

65. Ibid., p. 96. Mitsel', 1999, p. 183.

66. *Hatzofeh, Haboker, Herut,* and *Davar,* April 10, 1963.

67. GAVO, coll. 2700, inv. 7, file 478, p. 49.

CHAPTER FOURTEEN. **Holiday Observance in the Private Sphere**

1. TsGAVOU, coll. 4648, inv. 2, file 65, p. 27.

2. Letter by Rabbi Shiber to the Chernovtsy district SRA representative, August 17, 1945. GAChO, coll. 623, inv. 2, file 4, p. 13.

3. TsGAOOU, coll. 1, inv. 42, file 1572, p. 156.

4. TsGAVOU, coll. 4648, inv. 2, file 110, pp. 59–60; file 179, pp. 64–66; file 234, pp. 74–75. TsGAOOU, coll. 1, inv. 24, file 1572, p. 156.

5. Ibid., p. 153. GAVO, coll. 2700, inv. 19, file 46, pp. 79–83. GARF, coll. 6991, inv. 3s, file 1058, pp. 116–117.

6. The SRA chairman's instructions with regard to the autumn Jewish holidays. NARB, coll. 952, inv. 2, file 21, p. 231; file 40, p. 207. GAChO, coll. 623, inv. 2, file 28, p. 48.

7. GARF, coll. 6991, inv. 3, file 474, p. 220; inv. 3s, file 61, p. 164.

8. Ibid., inv. 3s, file 61, p. 164. TsGAOOU, coll. 1, inv. 23, file 5667, p. 369.

9. Ibid, inv. 24, file 12, p. 87.

10. NARB, coll. 952, inv. 2, file 27, pp. 201–202.

11. TsGAOOU, coll. 1, inv. 2, file 1950, p. 1; inv. 24, file 783, pp. 373, 376. GAChO, coll. 623, inv. 2, file 53, p. 3.

12. TsGAOOU, coll. 1, inv. 24, file 1572, pp. 98, 155.

13. One school in the Shevchenko region had 4,305 pupils: of these, 114 Jewish pupils failed to attend school on the eve of the first day of Passover (April 17), along with 117 on the first day and 272 on the last day of the holiday. Ibid., inv. 24, file 3531, p. 153, file 4038, p. 261.

14. GAVO, coll. 2700, inv. 5, file 330, p. 175; inv. 7, file 460, pp. 32, 69. GAZhO, coll. 4994, inv. 4s, file 1, pp. 175–176.

15. Report by the Ukraine SRA representative on the autumn Jewish holidays in 1957. TsGAOOU, coll. 1, inv. 24, file 4494, p. 334.

16. Report by the Zhitomir district SRA representative on the autumn Jewish holidays of 1958. GAZhO, coll. 4994, inv. 4s, file 2, p. 181.

17. TsGAOOU, coll. 1, inv. 24, file 4704, p. 379.

18. GARF, coll. 6991, inv. 4, file 71, p. 104.

19. GAChO, coll. 623, inv. 2, file 135, pp. 43, 46–47; file 158, pp. 52–53.

20. NARB, coll. 952, inv. 1, file 16, pp. 133–134.

21. Ibid., inv. 2, file 40, p. 223; file 51, p. 98.

22. Ibid., inv. 1, file 16, pp. 133–134; inv. 2, file 43, p. 72; file 51, pp. 275, 284. GAVO, coll. 2700, inv. 7, file 460, p. 69.

23. NARB, coll. 952, inv. 1, file 16, p. 134; inv. 4, file 10, p. 130.

24. Evreiskaia 1930. Ro'i, 1989. Mikhailov, 1941, p. 14.

25. Circular of the SRA chairman from March 1950. NARB, coll. 952, inv. 2, file 24, p. 49.

26. Shkurko, 1999, p. 215.

27. NARB, coll. 952, inv. 2, file 29, p. 83; file 51, pp. 98–99.

28. Ibid., inv. 4, file 15, p. 152; file 21, p. 72.

29. *Hatzofeh, Haboker, Herut,* and *Davar,* April 10, 1963.

30. Karabchevskii, 1991, p. 124.

CHAPTER FIFTEEN. **Charity and the Jewish Needy**

1. Gidulianov, 1926, pp. 622–623.

2. "Obshchestvo popecheniia i prizreniia prestarelykh, bol'nykh i besprizornykh evreev" (booklet), *Nizhnii Novgorod,* 1927.

3. Gidulianov, 1926, pp. 234–235.

4. Zonenfeld, 1990, p. 71.

5. TsGAVOU, coll. 4648, inv. 2, file 33, pp. 132, 136. TsGAOOU, coll. 1, inv. 23, file 4556, p. 133.

6. Similar activities took place in Leningrad, Chernovtsy, and other cities. GARF, coll. 6991, inv. 3s, file 47, pp. 229, 237. TsGAVOU, coll. 4648, inv. 2, file 16, p. 56; file 299, p. 159.

7. TsGAOOU, coll. 1, inv. 23, file 4555, p. 393. GARF, coll. 6991, inv. 3s, file 47, p. 229.

8. GARF, coll. 6991, inv. 3s, file 8, pp. 92–93. Thus, for instance, the account books of one of the synagogues of Chernovtsy show that, in late 1956, 10,820 rubles were spent on charity and 2,300 rubles were spent on other assistance. GAChO, coll. 623, inv. 2, file 15, pp. 30–32, 39–40.

9. In 1946 the Ukraine SRA representative sent a memorandum to his subordinates noting that he had received information indicating that the congregations in various towns were gathering funds for charitable needs and that this was a violation of Soviet laws on religious affairs that must be stopped. TsGAVOU, coll. 4648, inv. 2, file 17, pp. 48–49.

10. GARF, coll. 6991, inv. 3s, file 8, pp. 88–92.

11. TsGAOOU, coll. 1, inv. 23, file 4555, p. 329. TsGAVOU, coll. 4648, inv. 2, file 62, p. 174; file 296, p. 86; file 301, p. 77. GAVO, coll. 2700, inv. 19, file 35, p. 11. NARB, coll. 952, inv. 2, file 10, p. 94.

12. TsGAOOU, coll. 1, inv. 24, file 783, p. 92.

13. TsGAVOU, coll. 4648, inv. 2, file 65, p. 22. GARF, coll. 6991, inv. 3s, file 83, p. 135.

14. TsGAOOU, coll. 1, inv. 24, file 1572, pp. 313, 315; file 2741, p. 64.

15. NARB, coll. 952, inv. 2, file 45, pp. 203–204. GAZhO, coll. 4994, inv. 4s, file 1, p. 150.

16. Michlin, 1986, pp. 110–122.

17. Anderson, 1994, pp. 33.

18. GAChO, coll. 623, inv. 2, file 8, p. 8. TsGAVOU, coll. 4648, inv. 2, file 28, p. 43.

19. Ibid.

20. TsGAVOU, file 65, p. 22. GAVO, coll. 2700, inv. 19, file 35, p. 11; file 39, p. 47.

21. GAZhO, coll. 4994, inv. 4s, file 1, p. 88.

CHAPTER SIXTEEN. **Ritual Baths and Circumcision**

1. TsGAVOU, coll. 4648, inv. 2, file 406, pp. 143–145. Gershuni, 1970, pp. 105–106.

2. GAChO, coll. 623, inv. 2, file 29, p. 47. TsGAOOU, coll. 1, inv. 23, file 4555, p. 393.

3. TsGAVOU, coll. 4648, inv. 2, file 63, p. 93. GAChO, coll. 623, inv. 2, file 14, p. 71; file 29, p. 62.

4. GAChO, Coll. 623, inv. 2, file 29, p. 50.

5. TsGAVOU, coll. 4648, inv. 1, file 194, p. 110; file 201, p. 93; inv. 2, file 179, p. 141. GAChO, coll. 623, inv. 2, file 65, pp. 53–54.

6. TsGAVOU, coll. 4648, inv. 2, file 150, p. 69.

7. Ibid., file 179, pp. 129–130, 140; file 182, p. 39. Shoshkes, 1961, p. 151.

8. TsGAVOU, coll. 4648, inv. 2, file 173, p. 37.

9. Ibid., p. 36. TsGAOOU, coll. 1, inv. 24, file 4038, p. 102.

10. In those years a *mikva* was built in the town of Rostov-on-Don at a cost of 40,000 rubles. GARF, coll. 6991, inv. 4, file 130, pp. 22–23.

11. Zonenfeld, 1990, pp. 121–122.

12. Thus, for example, a Russian Orthodox priest in Minsk related that in 1946 several Jewish youths, male and female, came to him seeking to convert, and he indeed obliged them. NARB, coll. 952, inv. 2, file 10, p. 206.

13. Ibid., file 11, p. 174; file 13, p. 49. GARF, coll. 6991, inv. 3s, file 61, pp. 156–157.

14. GARF, coll. 6991, inv. 4, file 23, p. 33.

15. TsGAVOU, coll. 4648, inv. 2, file 65, p. 26. GARF, coll. 6991, inv. 3s, file 61, p. 156.

16. Leushin, 1995, pp. 93–94.

17. TsGAOOU, coll. 1, inv. 23, file 5667, p. 371. GARF, coll. 6991, inv. 3s, file 61, p. 157.

18. Zonenfeld, 1990, p. 171.

19. GARF, coll. 6991, inv. 3s, file 83, p. 14.

20. GAChO, coll. 623, inv. 2, file 28, p. 18. *Ugolovnoe zakonodatel'stvo,* 1963, vol. 1, p. 387.

21. TsGAVOU, coll. 4648, inv. 2, file 65, p. 26. Zonenfeld, 1990, pp. 102–103.

22. Gershovich, 1960, pp. 43–45; Altshuler, 1962, pp. 52–55. See also L. Katsman, "Pod svodami sinagogi," *Sovetskaia Belorussia,* February 4, 1960. E. Pavlenko, "Pod sen'iu sinagogi," *Sovetskaia Moldaviia,* April 28, 1960; N. Karmalinskii, A. Fel'dman, "Iakhve teriaet svoikh posledovatelei," *Nauka i religiia,* 1961, no. 3, pp. 85–86. N. Proskuriakova, "Marnovirstvo—vorog zdorov'ia," *Voiovnichyi ateist,* 1963, no. 8, p. 13.

23. GARF, coll. 6991, inv. 3s, file 73, p. 40.

CHAPTER SEVENTEEN. Cemeteries, Holocaust Memorials, and Burial Societies

1. Levitats, 1956; Levitats, 1981, pp. 58–60, 69–73, 170–173.

2. On the legal status of the graveyards and their condition between the World Wars, see Altshuler, 2002a.

3. GARF, coll. 6991, inv. 3s, file 8, pp. 89, 92.

4. Michlin, 1986 p. 149.

5. On the Jewish graveyard in Irkutsk in Eastern Siberia, see GARF, coll. 5263, inv. 1, file 9, p. 20; coll. 6991, inv. 4, file 19, p. 233. On the graveyard in Perm' (Molotov in the years 1940–1957), see ibid., p. 232.

6. On graveyards in Tashkent see Yehoshua, 1999; Taiar, 1987, pp. 22, 36, 49, 60, 68. On those in Bukhara see Terkel, 1963, pp. 249–253. On Samarkand see Sasonkin, 1988, pp. 243–244; Gottlieb, 1972; pp. 209–210; Gottlieb, 1985, pp. 157–163.

7. Gottlieb, 1976, pp. 207–208. Michlin, 1986, pp. 83.

8. Center for Research and Documentation of Eastern European Jewry at The Hebrew University, file 16. Lukin, 1993; Gessen, 2000, pp. 156–164.

9. GARF, coll. 6991, inv. 4, file 19, p. 219.

10. Ibid., inv. 3s, file 8, pp. 89, 92.

11. Ibid., p. 92; inv. 4, file 19, pp. 218, 221, 227.

12. TsGAOOU, coll. 1, inv. 23, file 4555, p. 63. GARF, coll. 6991, inv. 4, file 19, p. 224.

13. Center for Research and Documentation of Eastern European Jewry at The Hebrew University, file 16.

14. TsGAVOU, coll. 4648, inv. 2, file 14, pp. 19–20; file 16, pp. 64, 77.

15. NARB, coll. 952, inv. 1, file 11, p. 61. TsGAVOU, coll. 4648, inv. 2, file 17, pp. 26–27. Utershtein, 1999, pp. 18.

16. TsGAVOU, coll. 4648, inv. 2, file 37, p. 46; file 52, p. 92. GAVO, coll. 2700, inv. 19, file 47, p. 14. Mitsel', 1998, pp. 196.

17. TsGAVOU, coll. 4648, inv. 2, file 37, p. 46; file 52, p. 92. GAVO, coll. 2700, inv. 19, file 47, p. 14. Mitsel', 1998, p. 196. On conditions in Berdichev see *Jews in Eastern Europe,* September 1959 (London), no. 1, p. 4.

18. TsGAVOU, coll. 4648, inv. 2, file 14, p. 16. GARF, coll. 6991, inv. 4, file 19, p. 10.

19. GARF, coll. 6991, inv. 4, file 19, pp. 10, 16. TsGAVOU, coll. 4648, inv. 2, file 28, p. 101; file 199, p. 41. TsGAOOU, coll. 1, inv. 23, file 4555, p. 63.

20. TsGAVOU, coll. 4648, inv. 2, file 17, p. 71; file 45, pp. 12–13.

21. Ibid., p. 15.

22. Mitsel' 1998, p. 196.

23. TsGAVOU, coll. 4648, inv. 2, file 13, p. 7; file 28, p. 101; file 45, p. 4; file 174, p. 33. TsGAOOU, coll. 1, inv. 23, file 4555, p. 63. GARF, coll. 6991, inv. 4, file 19, p. 16.

24. TsGAVOU, coll. 4648, inv. 2, file 117, pp. 10, 43. Mindlina, 1997, p. 135.

25. TsGAVOU, coll. 4648, inv. 2, file 82, p. 101. In 1948 the minister for municipal affairs of Ukraine wrote to that republic's Communist Party secretary that "Babi Yar, the place where Soviet citizens were shot en masse[,] is in neglect." Ibid., file 45, pp. 12–13.

26. NARB, coll. 952, inv. 1, file 5, p. 319.

27. TsGAVOU, coll. 4648, inv. 2, file 38, p. 8. TsGAOOU, coll. 1, inv. 23, file 455, p. 63.

28. NARB, coll. 952, inv. 3, file 28, pp. 193, 196. Podlipskii, 1996, p. 195.

29. Gerodnik, 1964, no. 4, pp. 48–49.

30. TsGAOOU, coll. 1, inv. 24, file 4038, p. 97.

31. TsGAVOU, coll. 4648, inv. 2, file 201, pp. 89–90. GAChO, coll. 623, inv. 2, file 68, p. 2; file 111, pp. 12–13. GARF, coll. 6991, inv. 4, file 75, p. 20.

32. LVOA, coll. 1771, inv. 11, file 274, pp. 1–5, 9–15. *Tog morgn zhurnal,* September 1, 1961.

33. LVOA, coll. 1771, inv. 11, file 274, pp. 20–21.

34. At the same time Jewish cemeteries were dismantled in Zhitomir, Drogobych, and other towns. TsGAVOU, coll. 4648, inv. 2, file 33, p. 48; file 63, p. 174. GARF, coll. 6991, inv. 3s, file 61, p. 160.

35. GARF, coll. 6991, inv. 4, file 56, pp. 178–179.

36. Jewish cemeteries were dismantled in the following towns: Ostorog, Kirovogrod, Gaisin, Voronezh, Ufa, Rodin, Tbilisi, and others. TsGAVOU, coll. 4648, inv. 2, file 199, p. 59. NARB, coll. 952, inv. 3, file 11, pp. 116–118. Lukin, 2000, p. 206. Shpizel, 1999, p. 112. Shkurko, 1999, pp. 215–217. *New York Times*, June 19, 1959, p. 5; *Jews in Eastern Europe* (London), 1959, no. 1, p. 3.

37. Buried in this cemetery were many of the famous rabbis of Chernobyl (of the Twersky family), along with Yosef Yossele Horowitz, who was among the founders of the Mussar movement; the head of the yeshiva of Novo Grodek; and Zionist leaders such as Ber Borochov and Max Mandelstam.

38. TsGAVOU, coll. 4648, inv. 2, file 309, p. 50; file 402, pp. 2–3. Zonenfeld, 1990, pp. 236–245.

39. TsGAVOU, coll. 4648, inv. 2, file 372, pp. 17–18; file 402, pp. 4–5; file 407, p. 26.

40. *Tog morgn zhurnal,* November 30, 1961; January 27, 1963; March 13, 1963; March 28, 1963; November 12, 1965; and January 18, 1966. *Haaretz, Kol Haam,* January 29, 1963. *Forverts,* January 27, 1963.

41. *Jews in Eastern Europe* (London), September 1959, no. 1, p. 3.

42. TsGAVOU, coll. 4648, inv. 2, file 14, p. 16. GARF, coll. 6991, inv. 4, file 19, p. 19.

43. Rozenblat, 1997, pp. 72, 114, 141, 158.

44. TsGAVOU, coll. 4648, inv. 2, file 33, p. 109. *Sovetskaia Moldaviia,* June 8, 1960.

45. TsGAVOU, coll. 4648, inv. 2, file 14, p. 17; file 16, p. 77; file 17, p. 43; file 45, p. 16; file 46, p. 22; file 52, p. 93. TsGAOOU, coll. 1, inv. 23, file 455, pp. 61, 64; file 4555, p. 391. NARB, coll. 952, inv. 2, file 10, p. 94; file 11, p. 54. GARF, coll. 6991, inv. 3, file 798, p. 69; file 799, pp. 33–37, 53; file 800, p. 26; inv. 4, file 19, pp. 29, 233.

46. TsGAOOU, coll. 1, inv. 23, file 455, p. 64.

47. TsGAVOU, coll. 4648, inv. 2, file 88, pp. 45–46.

48. GAVO, coll. 2700, inv. 19, file 31, pp. 102, 109; file 35, p. 26; file 38, p. 22.

49. GARF, coll. 6991, inv. 3s, file 12, p. 40. TsGAVOU, coll. 4648, inv. 2, file 13, p. 7.

50. GARF, coll. 6991, inv. 3s, file 173, p. 75; file 213, p. 31; file 248, p. 16. *Jews in Eastern Europe* (London), 1959, no. 1, p. 3. *Jewish Observer Newsletter,* March 1959, p. 12.

51. Mindlina, 1997, p. 135.

52. TsGAVOU, coll. 4648, inv. 2, file 37, p. 46; file 52, p. 92. Mitsel', 1998, p. 196.

53. A parcel for the burial of Jews was allocated in Kirovogrod. TsGAVOU, coll. 4648, inv. 2, file 17, pp. 26–27. GARF, coll. 6991, inv. 3s, file 12, pp. 297–298.

54. TsGAVOU, coll. 4648, inv. 2, file 199, pp. 41–42; file 228, p. 25; file 253, pp. 47–48; file 273, pp. 5–6. TsGAOOU, coll. 1, inv. 24, file 4497, p. 327.

55. Ibid., file 783, pp. 371, 385.

56. TsGAVOU, coll. 4648, inv. 2, file 199, pp. 105–106; file 208, p. 14. GARF, coll. 6991, inv. 4, file 74, pp. 98–99.

57. On Jewish efforts to memorialize Holocaust victims during Stalin's rule, see Altshuler, 2002b.

58. Lukin, 2000, p. 140. Rybakov, 1997, pp. 233–235.

59. Ziabko, 1997, pp. 22–23. Lukin, 2000, pp. 259, 263, 371, 435, 450, 482–484, 498, 547. TsGAVOU, coll. 4648, inv. 2, file 65, pp. 21–22. TsGAOOU, coll. 1, inv. 23, file 4556, p. 131. Arad, 2004, pp. 348, 508, 513–514, 607. Mindlina, 1997, pp. 136–138. Center for Research and Documentation of Eastern European Jewry at The Hebrew University, Pecherski collection.

60. TsGAVOU, coll. 4648, inv. 2, file 17, pp. 57–58; file 19, p. 40. TsGAOOU, coll. 1, inv. 23, file 4556, p. 132.

61. GARF, coll. 6991, inv. 3, file 474, pp. 240–241. TsGAVOU, coll. 4648, inv. 2, file 37 p. 64; file 52, p. 92; file 301, p. 77. TsGAOOU, coll. 1, inv. 70, file 1172, p. 5. *Jews in Eastern Europe* (London), 1959, no. 1, p. 3.

62. GAZhO, coll. 4994, inv. 4s, file 3, p. 46. Grossman, 1980, p. 438. Grossman, 1991, pp. 502–503.

63. LVOA, coll. 181, inv. 1, file 26, p. 77. One testimonial indicates that a monument was erected in Ponar and taken down in 1952. Atamuk, "Ee nazivali Sara Krasnaia," *Evreiskii kamerton,* 29, June 2000. Gitelman, 1988, p. 185.

64. NARB, coll. 952, inv. 2, file 6, pp. 41, 73. Cholavski, 1988, p. 248. Smilovitskii, 1998, pp. 223-231. Central Archives of the Jewish People (Jerusalem), p. 199. Altshuler, 2002b, pp. 280-281. Gitelman, 1988, p. 189. Mindlina 1997, pp. 134-139.

65. Nearly identical replies were given to the Jews of Priluki and Kodyma. TsGAVOU, coll. 4648, inv. 2, file 33, p. 138; file 50, p. 199; file 116, pp. 93-94. TsGAOOU, coll. 1, inv. 23, file 455, pp. 61-62, 132. GARF, coll. 6991, inv. 3s, file 61, p. 160. Testimony of S. Kleiman, YVA, file 033/4394. Mitsel', 1998, p. 180.

66. TsGAVOU, coll. 4648, inv. 2, file 14, p. 20; file 50, pp. 45, 71, 73-74. TsGAOOU, coll. 1, inv. 23, file 4555, p. 391; file 5667, pp. 59-60, 92-93; inv. 24, file 3531, p. 33. GARF, coll. 6991, inv. 4, file 19, p. 229; file 23, pp. 31-32. YVA, file M-52/14.

67. TsGAVOU, coll. 4648, inv. 2, file 301, p. 74.

68. TsGAOOU, coll. 1, inv. 23, file 4555, p. 392. TsGAVOU, coll. 4648, inv. 2, file 65, pp. 21-22. GARF, coll. 6991, inv. 3, file 1103, p. 80. GAZhO, coll. 4994, inv. 4s, file 4, pp. 37-40. Gerrard, 1996, pp. 175-176, 247.

69. GARF, coll. 6991, inv. 3s, file 8, p. 89.

70. GAVO, coll. 2700, inv. 19, file 38, p. 23.

71. GARF, coll. 6991, inv. 4, file 19, p. 218.

72. Thus, for example, the burial society of the synagogue on Mitchkevitch Street in Chernovtsy demanded between five hundred and a thousand rubles for the burial of the former rabbi's wife; the family refused to pay and the body remained unburied for several days. TsGAVOU, coll. 4648, inv. 2, file 33, p. 248. TsGAOOU, coll. 1, inv. 23, file 4555, p. 392. GAChO, coll. 623, inv. 2, file 13, pp. 9-10; file 15, pp. 4, 33.

73. NARB, coll. 952, inv. 2, file 27, pp. 122-123.

74. GAVO, coll. 2700, inv. 19, file 36, p. 50.

75. TsGAVOU, coll. 4648, inv. 2, file 201, pp. 201, 203. Kreier, 1993, p. 45.

76. Lapidus, 1962.

77. TsGAVOU, coll. 4648, inv. 2, file 228, p. 25.

78. TsGAOOU, coll. 1, inv. 1, file 194, p. 88; inv. 24, file 4038, p. 102. TsGAVOU, coll. 4648, inv. 2, file 273, p. 2; file 278, pp. 47-48. GAChO, coll. 623, inv. 2, file 59; pp. 62-64, file 65, p. 68.

79. M. Beizer, "Stroitel'stvo iudeiskikh kul'tovykh sooruzhenii v Leningrad," *Ami,* April 14, 1999.

80. TsGAVOU, coll. 4648, inv. 2, file 273, pp. 68-69; file 299, pp. 103-104. Lukin, 2000, p. 201. Ia. Bukhbinder, "Dikii vid religii," *Radians'ke Podillia,* November 11, 1960.

81. M. Barykin, "Pod svodami sinagogi," *Volzhskaia kommuna,* September 30, 1961. E. Abramovich, M. Kriuger, "Bedlam v Sinagoge," *Sovetskaia Kirgiziia,* January 4, 1961. L. Irzhanskii, "Ne mozhu molchati," *Naddniprians'ka pravda,* January 11, 1961. M. Bilkun, Glazman, I. Kleiner, "Mulem," *Vechernii Kiiv,* September 21, 1963. Thus, for instance, one

witness in the April 1960 public trial held against the religious congregation in Faleshty, Moldavia, claimed that the local rabbi demanded a large sum for the burial of his wife. E. Pavlenko, "Pod sen'iu sinagogi," *Sovetskaia Moldaviia,* April 28, 1960. For a similar complaint from Chernigov, see A. Gurevich, "Molitva za 50 karbovantsiv," *Desnians'ka pravda,* September 8, 1961.

82. NARB, coll. 952, inv. 3, file 36, pp. 30–31.

83. TsGAOOU, coll. 1, inv. 25, file 186, p. 66. Gerodnik, 1964, p. 37. Michlin, 1986, p. 149.

84. *Lamerhav,* October 11, 1959.

CHAPTER EIGHTEEN. The Attitude of World Jewry and Israel to Judaism in the USSR

1. Kostyrchenko, 1994, p. 32.

2. Through both this organization and funding from the Joint, food packages were sent to 3,700 Jewish families in the USSR from May 1943 to June 1944. Brutskus, 1944, pp. 474–478.

3. Redlich, 1995, pp. 73–97.

4. GARF, coll. 6991, inv. 3s, file 1, p. 39; file 6, pp. 58–64.

5. Sovetsko-Izrael'skie, 2000, book 1, p. 99.

6. Thus, for example, the L'vov congregation alone received some 12,000 letters involving searches for relatives. TsGAOOU, coll. 1, inv. 23, file 455, p. 133.

7. The congregation of Staro-Konstantinov and other communities received packages from the Joint. TsGAOOU, coll. 1, inv. 23, file 4555, p. 392.

8. In 1947, 15,845 packages were sent from the Land of Israel to the USSR, and the customs charges levied reached 1,056,000 rubles; see Sovetsko-Izrael'skie, 2000, book 1, pp. 92, 328–329.

9. GARF, coll. 6991, inv. 3s, file 47, pp. 82–83.

10. GAVO, coll. 2700, inv. 19, file 38, p. 1.

11. Golod, 1996; Golod, 1998.

12. TsGAOOU, coll. 1, inv. 23, file 2846, p. 22.

13. GARF, coll. 6991, inv. 3s, file 53, p. 41.

14. TsGAVOU, coll. 4648, inv. 2, file 115, pp. 59, 61–62.

15. GARF, coll. 6991, inv. 4, file 58, pp. 13–15.

16. Ibid., file 37, pp. 90–92, 100–101.

17. Ibid., inv. 3, file 138, pp. 4, 6; inv. 4, file 38, pp. 197–198.

18. Charnyi, 2002, pp. 213–214. GAVO, coll. 2700, inv. 19, file 50, p. 17.

19. GARF, coll. 6991, inv. 4, file 57, p. 21. Given such "advice," it is unsurprising that, in response to a question about the number of active synagogues in the Soviet Union from a tourist visiting in 1956 from Indiana, USA, Rabbi Shlifer's reply was "about five hundred." Ibid., file 71, pp. 1–4.

20. Ibid., file 57, pp. 68–69.

21. GARF, coll. 6991, inv. 4, file 75, pp. 159, 163–164. *Hatzofeh,* November 15, 1957. *Al Hamishmar,* October 30, 1957. *Jewish Chronicle,* September 20, 1957, November 8, 1957.

22. JTA announcement, November 5, 1957.

23. NARB, coll. 952, inv. 4, file 22, p. 40; file 23, pp. 29-30. *Hatzofeh,* July 21, 1959.

24. By certain estimates, in 1953-1954 seven tourists visited the synagogues in the USSR annually, a number that rose to forty-three in 1955. Charnyi, 2002, p. 212.

25. On visits by tourists of this kind in the various cities of Ukraine, see TsGAOOU, coll. 1, inv. 24, file 4038, p. 261; file 4704, p. 377. GAOO, coll. 2000, inv. 5, file 330, pp. 114–115; inv. 19, file 50, p. 27.

26. TsGAVOU, coll. 4648, inv. 2, file 302, pp. 170–171. TsGAOOU, coll. 1, inv. 24, file 6007, p. 110.

27. Chernaia, 1998, p. 70.

28. NARB, coll. 952, inv. 2, file 43, pp. 61–64.

29. Ibid., p. 102.

30. GARF, coll. 6991, inv. 4, file 37, pp. 30, 68. *Maariv,* December 9, 1957. *Di letste nayes,* December 28, 1959; *Jewish Chronicle,* December 18, 1959.

31. On March 11, 1960, the JTA announced that for the first time the Soviet postal service had returned to the senders ritual objects sent by mail. *Maariv,* March 19, 1963. In early 1962 letters were received from Jews in the USSR asking their relatives not to send ceremonial objects, as the addresses were regarded with suspicion by the authorities. *American Examiner,* March 22, 1962.

32. *Hatzofeh,* July 24, 1962. JTA, July 23, 1962. *Tog morgn zhurnal,* July 24, 1962. *National Jewish Monthly* (Washington), October 1962.

33. NARB, coll. 952, inv. 3, file 19, p. 120. TsGAOOU, coll. 1, inv. 24, file 5297, pp. 43–45.

34. Sovetsko-Izrael'skie, 2000, book 1, p. 38.

35. In July 1941 the topic of material aid to the needy was also raised, yet it became irrelevant once the Polish government-in-exile signed its agreement with the USSR, through which aid was sent to Polish citizens including Jews. In the August 31, 1942 meeting between David Ben-Gurion and the first secretary of the Soviet embassy in Ankara, the latter asked whether the emigration of Soviet citizens was under discussion, to which Ben-Gurion replied: "At issue is solely refugees from Poland and the territories occupied by the Nazis." To enable this emigration, the Zionist spokesmen requested that a delegation from the Land of Israel be allowed to visit the USSR, a request that the Soviet authorities declined. Ibid., p. 18, 20, 24, 28, 51–52, 66, 72. Kles, 1989; Kles, 1994.

36. Sovetsko-Izrael'skie, 2000, book 1, pp. 16, 20, 25–26, 31, 37, 40, 51, 80–83.

37. Ibid., p. 16.

38. Ibid., pp. 165–167.

39. *Folks Shtime,* December 1, 1948.

40. TsGAOOU, coll. 1, inv. 23, file 4555, p. 327; file 5069, pp. 97–98. GARF, coll. 6991, inv. 3s, file 85, p. 177.

41. Sovetsko-Izrael'skie, 2000, book 1, pp. 306, 308–314. Ro'i, 1991, pp. 19–20, 26. Pinkus, 1993, pp. 182–185. TsGAOOU, coll. 1, inv. 23, file 5069, pp. 267–268; file 5667, pp. 61, 63, 365. VUChKA . . . NKVD, 1998, p. 39.

42. Michlin, 1986, pp. 229–230. Golda Meyerson estimated in her telegram that the

thanksgiving service in Moscow drew some 20,000 people. Sovetsko-Izrael'skie, 2000, book 1, p. 362. GARF, coll. 6991, inv. 4, file 23, p. 27. The SRA representative suggested removing the banner that read "Am Israel Chai," but the request was not honored and the banner stayed up. Ibid., inv. 3s, file 61, p. 155. Gershuni, 1970, p. 190.

43. GARF, coll. 6991, inv. 3s, file 61, pp. 28, 56, 155; inv. 4, file 23, pp. 28–29, 56. TsGAOOU, coll. 1, inv. 23, file 5667, p. 63. Ro'i, 2003.

44. TsGAOOU, coll. 1, inv. 23, file 5667, p. 64.

45. Sovetsko-Izrael'skie, 2000, book 1, pp. 375–383.

46. Ibid., p. 434.

47. GARF, coll. 6991, inv. 3s, file 56, p. 117.

48. Pinkus, 1993, pp. 495–498. Ro'i, 1991, pp. 13–38. Sovetsko-Izrael'skie, 2000, book 1, p. 400.

49. The bulletin was sent to thirty congregations and three kolkhozes; 140 copies were disseminated. Sovetsko-Izrael'skie, 2000, book 1, pp. 460–461, 468. GARF, coll. 6991, inv. 3s, file 1038, p. 32.

50. In a meeting on December 12, 1948, between Israel's foreign minister Moshe Sharett and USSR deputy foreign minister Andrei Vishinskii, the former devoted much time to the subject of immigration to Israel from the countries of Central Europe but did not mention the Jews of the USSR. Sovetsko-Izrael'skie, 2000, book 1, pp. 436–443. Yet during the meeting of Sharett in 1949 with the acting Soviet foreign minister, Iakob Malik, the former did raise the subject of the immigration of 30,000–50,000 Soviet Jews. Ibid., book 2, pp. 86, 119. When Ben-Gurion met with Soviet ambassador Pavel Ershov in late December 1948, the latter asked whether Israel intended to include Jews from the USSR, to which Ben-Gurion replied, "At this time we are referring primarily to the Jews of Romania and Hungary." Ibid., book 1, p. 447, book 2, pp. 84, 232.

51. Kostyrchenko, 1992, pp. 138–139.

52. Boaz, 2001, pp. 259–260. Levanon, 1995, pp. 53, 54.

53. GARF, coll. 6991, inv. 3, file 105, p. 165; inv. 4, file 88, pp. 180, 184–186.

54. Between 1953 and 1955 Nativ staff visited Odessa, Leningrad, Kiev, Yalta, Simferopol', Sochi, Sukhumi, Tashkent, Kokand, and Kuibishev. Levanon, 1995, pp. 66–73, 93–106, 125–130. In late 1955 Nativ had at least a dozen permanent addresses of Jews in Moscow, Odessa, Kiev, Leningrad, Kishinev, and Sizran to which propaganda was sent. Ibid., p. 106. See also Kamenetskii, 1998, pp. 22–25.

55. On visits of embassy staff to synagogues in various towns, see TsGAOOU, coll. 1, inv. 24, file 4038, pp. 134, 260. TsGAVOU, coll. 4648, inv. 2, file 299, pp. 165–166. NARB, coll. 952, inv. 3, file 12, p. 20; file 19, p. 121; inv. 4, file 20, pp. 66–67. Chernaia, 1998, p. 70.

56. GAOO, coll. 2000, inv. 5, file 330, p. 115.

57. GARF, coll. 6991, inv. 4, file 88, pp. 230–232; file 108, pp. 96–97, 99, 106–107.

58. Ibid., file 58, p. 138.

59. TsGAOOU, coll. 1, inv. 24, file 5205, p. 91; file 5488, p. 234.

60. Ibid., p. 91; file 5297, p. 85; file 5663, p. 107.

61. NARB, coll. 952, inv. 3, file 33, pp. 80–81.

62. Report on the visit of Israeli embassy staff to Korosten', Zhitomir, and Berdichev in early 1959. GAZhO, coll. 4994, inv. 4s, file 4, pp. 53–59.

63. NARB, coll. 952, inv. 4, file 16, pp. 170–171; file 18, p. 107.

64. GARF, coll. 6991, inv. 4, file 57, pp. 17, 108. *Maariv,* August 29, 1956. JTA, September 23, 1956.

65. TsGAOOU, coll. 1, inv. 24, file 4038, pp. 163–164, 259. GAOO, coll. 2000, inv. 5, file 330, p. 177. NARB, coll. 952, inv. 4, file 18, p. 225.

66. According to partial data, in 1956 sixteen packages were received containing 114 *etrog*s. GARF, coll. 6991, inv. 4, file 71, p. 104. See also: TsGAOOU, coll. 1, inv. 24, file 4494, p. 328; file 4704, pp. 81, 374–376. GAOO, coll. 2000, inv. 5, file 330, pp. 3, 175. GAVO, coll. 2700, inv. 7, file 460, p. 66. NARB, coll. 952, inv. 4, file 16, p. 85.

67. TsGAOOU, coll. 1, inv. 24, file 4494, pp. 328–329. TsGAVOU, coll. 4648, inv. 2, file 299, p. 161.

68. In December 1958 the Western press reported that Rabbi Levin had been investigated for several days with regard to the *etrogs* he received from the Israeli embassy in Moscow. *Der Moment,* May 12, 1958. These reports, however, are unconfirmed.

69. GAZhO, coll. 4994, inv. 4s, file 1, p. 180.

70. On March 10, 1960, the JTA announced that the "Arbaa Minim" packages sent by the Israeli rabbinate had been returned. *Yediot Aharonot,* December 25, 1959. *Maariv,* March 10, 1960. TsGAOOU, coll. 1, inv. 24, file 5663, p. 106.

71. Ibid., file 4038, p. 130; file 4494, p. 221; file 4704, p. 82. GAZhO, coll. 4994, inv. 4s, file 1, p. 88. See also chapter 13.

72. Report of the Ukraine SRA representative on Easter and Passover of 1957. TsGAOOU, coll. 1, inv. 24, file 4494, p. 221.

73. Ibid., file 4038, pp. 134–135; file 4704, p. 97. The list of addresses of Jews in the USSR increased considerably following the second repatriation to Poland in the 1950s, when many of the repatriated left for Israel and Nativ was able to obtain addresses from them.

74. NARB, coll. 952, inv. 4, file 2, p. 53; file 15, p. 213; file 18, p. 106. Chernaia, 1998, p. 69.

75. GAZhO, coll. 4994, inv. 4s, file 1, pp. 13–14, 74, 95–97; file 3, p. 80.

Bibliography

Archives

The names of archives cited in the notes are abbreviated as follows.

GAChO Gosudarstvennyi Arkhiv Chernovitskoi Oblasti (State Archive of Chernovtsy District)

GAOO Gosudarstvennyi Arkhiv Odesskoi Oblasti (State Archive of Odessa District)

GARF Gosudarstvennyi Arkhiv Rossiiskoi Federatsii (State Archive of the Russian Federation)

GAVO Gosudarstvennyi Arkhiv Vinitskoi Oblasti (State Archive of Vinnitsa District)

GAZhO Gosudarstvennyi Arkhiv Zhitomirskoi Oblasti (State Archive of Zhitomir District)

LVOA Lietuvas Visuomenis Orgonizaciju Archyvas (Lithuanian Archive of Public Associations)

NARB Natsional'nyi Arkhiv Respubliki Bialorus (National Archive of the Bialorus Republic)

RGASPI Rossiiskii Gosudarstvennyi Arkhiv Sotsial'no-Politicheskoi Istorii (Russian State Archive of Socio-Political History)

TsGAOOU Tsentral'nyi Gosudarstvennyi Arkhiv Obshchestvennykh Obedinenii Ukrainy (Central State Archive of Public Associations of Ukraine)

TsGAVOU Tsentral'nyi Gosudarstvennyi Arkhiv Vysshikh Organov Vlasti i Upravleniia Ukrainy (Central State Archive of the Highest Government Bodies and Directorates of Ukraine)

YVA Yad Vashem Archive

Books and Articles

The following sources are alphabetized by the abbreviated form of the citation given in the notes.

Akademiia (1996). Rossiiskaia Akademiia Gosudarstvennoi Sluzhby pri Prezidente. *Gosudarstvenno-tserkovnye otnosheniia v Rossii, Opyt proshlogo i sovremennoe sostoianie* (State-church relations in Russia: The experience of the past and the present situation), Moscow, 1996.

Alekseev, V. A. (1992). '*Shturm nebies: Otmeniaetsia? Kriticheskie ocherki po istorii bor'by s religiei v SSSR* (Is the storming of heaven being put off? Critical essays on the history of the fight against religion in the USSR), Moscow, 1992.

Altman, I., and I. Arad, eds. (1993). *Neizvestnaia chernaia kniga* (The unknown black book), Jerusalem-Moscow, 1993.

Altshuler, M. (1962). "Komu eto nuzhno" (Who needs this?), *Nauka i religiia*, 1962, no. 1.

Altshuler, M. (1968). *Chto est' iudaizm* (What is Judaism?), Moscow, 1968.

Altshuler, M., ed. (1970). *Pirsumim Rusiim Bibrit Hamoatzot al Yehudim Veyahadut, 1917–1967* (Russian publications on Jews and Judaism in the Soviet Union, 1917–1967), Jerusalem, 1970.

Altshuler, M., and Lifschits, eds. (1979). *Briv fun Yiddishe Sovetishe Shraybers* (Letters of Soviet Yiddish writers), Jerusalem, 1980.

Altshuler, M. (1990). *Yehudei Mizrach Kavkaz* (The Jews of the Eastern Caucasus), Jerusalem, 1990.

Altshuler, M. (1993). "Antisemitism in Ukraine toward the End of the Second World War," *Jews in Eastern Europe*, 1993, no. 3 (22).

Altshuler, M., and T. Chentsova (1993). "The Party and Popular Reaction to the 'Doctors' Plot,'" *Jews in Eastern Europe*, 1993, no. 2 (25).

Altshuler, M., l. Arad, and S. Krakovskii, eds. (1993). *Sovetskie evrei pishut Il'e Erenburgu* (Soviet Jews write to Ilya Ehrenburg), Jerusalem, 1993.

Altshuler, M. (1995). "The Unique Features of the Holocaust in the Soviet Union," (ed. Yaacov Ro'i), *Jews and Jewish Life in Russia and the Soviet Union,* Great Britain, 1995.

Altshuler, M. (1998a). "The Soviet 'Transfer' of Jews from Chernovtsy Province to Rumania, 1945–1946," *Jews in Eastern Europe*, 1998, no. 2 (36).

Altshuler, M. (1998b). *Soviet Jewry on the Eve of the Holocaust,* Jerusalem, 1998.

Altshuler, M. (2001). "The Synagogue in the Soviet Union on Passover 1953," *Jews in Eastern Europe,* 2001, no. 3 (46).

Altshuler, M. (2002a). "Jews' Burial Rites and Cemeteries in the USSR in the Interwar Period," *Jews in Eastern Europe,* 2002, nos. 1–2 (47–48).

Altshuler, M. (2002b). "Jewish Holocaust Commemoration in the USSR," *Yad Vashem Studies,* 2002, vol. 30.

Altshuler, M. (2003). "Ten Years of the Yeshiva in Soviet Moscow (1955–1965)," *Jews in Russia and Eastern Europe,* 2003, no. 1 (50).

Altshuler, M. (2004). "Itsik Kipnis—The 'White Crow' of Soviet Yiddish Literature," *Jews in Russia and Eastern Europe,* 2004, no. 2 (53).

Anderson, J. (1994). *Religion, State, and Politics in the Soviet Union and Successor States,* Cambridge, 1994.

Arad, Y. (2004). *Toldot Hashoah Bibrit Hamoatzot Ubashtachim Hamesupachim* (History of the Holocaust—Soviet Union and annexed territories), Jerusalem, 2004.

Baazova, L. (1992). "Yehudei Gruzia Betkufat Hashilton Hasoveti" (Georgian Jews in the Soviet period), in *Toldot Yehudei Gruzia Vetarbutam* (The history and culture of Georgian Jews) (ed. Rahel Arbel), Tel Aviv, 1992.

Baazova, L. (1995). "Synagogues and Synagogue Life in Georgia in the Postwar Era," *Jews and Jewish Life in Russia and The Soviet Union* (ed. Y. Ro'i), Great Britain, 1995.

Balevits, Z. V. (1967). *Pravoslavnaia tserkov' Latvii pod sen'iu svastiki (1941–1944)* (The Eastern Orthodox Church of Latvia under the sign of the swastika, 1941–1944), Riga, 1967.

Beizer, M. (1989). *Evrei v Peterburge* (Jews in Petersburg), Israel, 1989.

Beizer, M. (2002). *Sinagogy SNG v proshlom i nastoiashchem* (CIS synagogues: Past and present), Moscow, Jerusalem, 2002.

Belenkii, M. (1963). *Chto takoe talmud* (What is the Talmud), Moscow, 1963.

Bick, S. (1973). "Safrut Toranit Vehagut Datit Ivrit Bibrit Hamoatzot (Jewish religious literature in Hebrew in the Soviet Union), *Shvut*, 1973, no. 1.

Bilas, I. (1994). *Represivno-karatel'na sistema v Ukraine, 1917–1973* (The repressive-punitive system in Ukraine, 1917–1973), Kiev, 1994.

Boaz, A. (2001). *Alum Venochah Bakol, Sipur Hayav shel Shaul Avigur* (Unseen yet always present: The life story of Shaul Avigur), Tel Aviv, 2001.

Bociurkiw, B. R. (1986). "The Suppression of the Ukrainian Greek Catholic Church in Postwar Soviet Union and Poland," *Religion and Nationalism in Eastern Europe and the Soviet Union* (ed. Dennis J. Dumm), London, 1986.

Bociurkiw, B. R. (1996). *The Ukrainian Greek Catholic Church and the Soviet State (1939–1950)*, Edmonton, Toronto, 1996.

Bredli, D. (1994). "Dobrovol'nye obshchestva v sovetskoi Rossii, 1917–1932 gg." (Voluntary associations in Soviet Russia, 1917–1932), *Vestnik Moskovskogo Universiteta,* Seriia istoriia, 1994, no. 4.

Brutskus, I. (1944). "Deiatel'nost' Soiuza Russkikh Evreev v New Yorke" (The activity of the Union of Russian Jews in New York), *Evreiskii mir*, 1944 collection.

Bystriakov, A. (2002). *Evrei Ekaterinoslava-Dnepropetrovska (XX vek)* (The Jews of Ekaterinoslav-Dnepropetrovsk in the twentieth century), Dnepropetrovsk, 2002.

Cahana, C. M. (1986), *Pirkei Haim-Eidut Haia Ligzeirot Hanazim Beshnot Hashoah Vehasevel Tahat Shilton Hasovietim* (Life stories: Testimony on the Nazi edicts and the suffering under Soviet rule), Jerusalem, 1986.

Charnyi, S. (2002). "Vneshnie sviazi evreiskikh religioznykh obshchin v period ottepeli" (External ties of Jewish religious communities during the period of the "thaw"), *Judaica Rossica,* Moscow, 2002, no. 2.

Chazan, A. (1990). *Deep in the Russian Night,* New York, London, 1990.

Chernaia (1998). *Chernaia kniga Ukrainy: Zbirnik dokumentiv, arkhivnikh materialiv, listiv* (The black book of Ukraine: Collection of documents, archival materials, and letters), Kiev, 1998.

Cholavski, S. (1988). *Besufat Hakilayon—Yahadut Belorussia Hamizrahit Bimilhemet Haolam Hashniya* (In the eye of the hurricane—The Jews in Eastern Belorussia during World War II), Jerusalem, 1988.

Chumachenko, T. (1999). *Gosudarstvo, Pravoslavnaia Tserkov', veruiushchie, 1941–1961 gg.* (The state, the Russian Orthodox Church, and religious believers, 1941–1961), Moscow, 1999.

Cohen, Y. (1971). "Pirsumim Beivrit Ubeyiddish" (Publications in Hebrew and Yiddish), *Yahadut Bessarabia: Enciclopedia Shel Galuyot, Sifrei Zikaron Leartzot Hagolah Veedoteha* (Bessarabian Jewry: Encyclopaedia of Diasporas, Memorial Books of the Diaspora Lands and Communities), Jerusalem, Tel Aviv, 1971.

Conference (1952). *Conference in Defense of Peace of All Churches and Religious Associations in the USSR.* Held in Zagorsk on May 9–12, 1952.

Congress (1939). XVIII s"ezd VKP(b), Stenograficheskii otchet (Eighteenth Congress of the All-Union Communist Party [Bolsheviks], stenographer's report), Moscow, 1939.

Corley, F. (1996a). *Religion in the Soviet Union: An Archival Reader,* London, Macmillan Press, 1996.

Corley, F. (1996b). "The Armenian Church under the Soviet Regime," *Religion, State, and Society,* 1996, no. 4 (24).

Curtiss, J. Sh. (1953). *The Russian Church and the Soviet State, 1917–1950,* Boston, 1953.

Dagel' P. (1962). "Otvetsvennost' za posiagatel'stvo na lichnost' i prava grazhdan pod vidom ispolneniia religioznykh obriadov" (Responsibility for infringement [of the rights] of the individual and civil rights under the guise of fulfilling religious rites), *Sovetskaia iustitsiia,* 1962, no. 22.

Danilova, S. A., ed. (2000). *Iskhod gorskikh evreev: razrushenie garmonii mirov* (The exodus of the mountain Jews: Destruction of the harmony of worlds), Nal'chik, 2000.

Davidson, D. (1985). *Meaz Vead Hena: Minsk Ir Vaeym* (Minsk: Jewish mother-city) (ed. Even Shoshan), Jerusalem, 1985, vol. 2.

Dickinson, A. (2000). "A Marriage of Convenience? Domestic and Foreign Policy Reasons for the 1943 Soviet Church-State Concordat," *Religion, State, and Society,* 2000, no. 4.

Eliav, B. A. (1965). *Ben Hapatish Vehamagal, Nisayon Ishi Bekerev Yehudei Brit Hamoatzat* (Between the hammer and the sickle: Personal Experiences among Jews in the Soviet Union), Tel Aviv, 1965.

Ehrenburg, I. (1998). *Razluka* (The separation), Israel 1998.

Erusalimchik, G. (1999). *Raznye sud'by obshchaia sud'ba* (*Iz istorii evreev Cheliabinska*) (Different fates [but] a common fate [from the history of the Jews of Cheliabinsk]),1999.

Evreiskaia (1930). "Evreiskaia paskha, ee proiskhozhdenie i znachenie" (The Jewish Passover, its origin and meaning), *Antireligioznik,* 1930, no. 3.

Filatov, A. N. (1964). *Rol traditsii i privichek v sokhranenii religioznykh perezhitkov v SSSR: o nekotorykh osobennostiakh sovremennoi religioznoi ideologii* (The role of tradition and habit in the preservation of religious vestiges in the USSR: On some features of contemporary religious ideology) (ed. I. D. Pantskhava), Moscow, 1964.

Fireside, H. (1971). *Icon and Swastika: The Russian Orthodox Church under Nazi and Soviet Control,* Cambridge, 1971.

Fletcher, W. C. (1973). *Religion and Soviet Foreign Policy, 1945–1970,* London, 1973.

Garashchenko, A. N. (1992). "Kratkaia istoriia kamennogo zdaniia sinagogi v Irkutske" (Short history of the stone building of the synagogue in Irkutsk), *Sibirskii evreiskii sbornik,* Irkutsk, 1992.

Gelber, Ch. (1962). "Die Repatriierung der Bukowiner Juden in den Jahren 1944–1946," *Geschikhte der Juden in der Bukowina* (ed. H. Gold), Tel Aviv, 1962.

Gendel'man, Zh. (2000). "Religioznaia istoriia evreev Ukrainy XX stoletiia—(K voprosu k periodizatsii)" (The religious history of the Jews of Ukraine in the twentieth century—About the issue of periodization), *Etnosy Ukrainy Evreiskii svit*, Kiev, 2000.

Genina, E. S. (2000). "Kompaniia po bor'be s kosmopolitizmom v Kuzbase v kontse 40-kh-nachale 50-kh gg." (The campaign of the fight against cosmopolitanism in Kuzbas in the late 1940s and early 1950s), *Evreiskie obshchiny Sibiri i Dal'nego Vostoka*, Tomsk, 2000.

Gerodnik, G. (1964). "Razdumia o parkakh dobrykh vospominaii" (Reflections on parks of good memories), *Nauka i religiia*, 1964, nos. 4, 6.

Gerrard, J. (1996). *The Bones of Berdichev*, New York, 1996.

Gershovich, S. (1960). "Obrezanie" (Circumcision), *Nauka i religiia*, 1960, no. 2.

Gershuni, A. A. (1970). *Yehudim Veyahadut Bibrit Hamoatzot* (Jews and Judaism in the Soviet Union), Jerusalem, Feldheim Press, 1970.

Gershuni, A. A. (1981). *Kiddush Hashem: Parshiot Mesirut Nefesh Etzel Yehudim Bibrit Hamoatzot* (Jewish martyrdom: Real stories of self-sacrifice among Jews in the USSR), Jerusalem, 1981.

Gessen, V. I. (2000). *K istorii Sankt Peterburgskoi evreiskoi religioznoi obshchiny* (Toward a history of the St. Petersburg Jewish religious community), St. Petersburg, 2000.

Gidulianov, P. (1926). *Otdelenie tserkvi ot gosudarstva v SSSR: Polnyi sbornik dekretov, vedomstvennykh rasporazhenii . . .* (The separation of church and state in the USSR: Complete collection of decrees and authoritative orders . . .), Moscow, 1926.

Gitelman, Z. (1988). *The Jews of Russia and the Soviet Union, 1881 to the Present: A Century of Ambivalence*, New York, 1988.

Gladysh, K, and E. Tsirul'nik (1996). *Poltava—Pamiatniki Evreiskoi kul'tury* (Poltava—Monuments of Jewish culture), Poltava, 1996.

Gol'dshtein, R. I. (1992). *Materialy k istorii evreiskoi obshchiny Dnepropetrovshchiny* (Materials for the history of the Jewish community of the Dnepropetrovsk area), Dnepropetrovsk, 1992.

Golod (1996). *Golod v Ukraini, 1946–1947: Dokumenti i materiali* (Starvation in Ukraine, 1946–1947: Documents and materials), Kiev, 1996.

Golod (1998). *Golod 1946–1947 rokiv v Ukraini: prichini i nasledki* (Starvation in the years 1946–1947 in Ukraine: Causes and consequences), Kiev, 1998.

Gosudarstvo (1995). "Gosudarstvo i tserkov v gody voiny" (State and church during the war years), *Istoricheskii arkhiv*, 1995, no. 4.

Gottlieb, N. Z., ed. (1973). *Sefer Yahadut Hadmamah: Pirkei Gvura Muflaim, Parshiot Meratkot Vesipurim Madhimim* (The silent Jewry: Episodes of wondrous heroism, fascinating episodes, and amazing tales), Jerusalem, 1973.

Gottlieb, N. Z. (1976). *Sefer Toldot Levi Yizhak* (History of Levi Yizhak), Brooklyn, 1977.

Gottlieb, N. Z. (1985). *In the Shadow of the Kremlin*, New York, 1985.

Greenbaum, A. (1989). "The Moscow Yeshiva," *Jews and Jewish Topics in the Soviet Union and Eastern Europe*, 1989, no. 2 (9).

Greenbaum, A. (1990). "Harabanut Bebrit Hamoatzot Aharei Milhemet Haolam Hashniya" (The Soviet rabbinate after World War II), *Shvut*, 1990, no. 14.

Greenbaum, A. (1994). *Rabbanei Brit Hamoetzot Ben Milhamot Haolam* (Rabbis of the Soviet Union between the World Wars), Jerusalem, 1994.

Greenbaum, A. (1999). "Rabbi Shlomo (Solomon) Shlifer and Jewish Religious Life in the Soviet Union, 1943–1957," *Shvut,* 1999, no. 8 (24).

Greko (1996). "Greko-Katolits'ka tserkva v 1944–1991 rr" (The Greek Catholic Church from 1944 to 1991), *Ukrainskii istorichnyi zhurnal,* 1996, no. 4.

Grossman, V. (1980). *Chernaia kniga* (The black book), Jerusalem, 1980.

Grossman, V. (1991). *Chernaia kniga* (The black book), ed. V. Grossman and I. Ehrenburg, Kiev, 1991.

Gurevich, M. (1995). "Dom na Internatsional'noi" (The house on International Street), *Korni,* 1995, nos. 3–4.

Hacohen, R. N. (1983). *Sefer Lubavitch Vehayaleha* (Lubavitch and its soldiers), Kfar Chabad, 1983.

Harkavy, Z., and A. Shauli, eds. (1966). *Shomrei Hagahelet, Divrei Torah Merabanei Brit Hamoatzot Veartzot Hademocratia Haamamit* (Glowing embers, ritual responsa of rabbis in the Soviet Union), New York, Jerusalem, 1966.

Haustein, U. (1989). *Die Jedenheit auf dem Boden des Russischen Reiches: Religion in der USSR,* 1989.

Hoffman, C. E. (2002). *Red Shtetl: The Survival of a Jewish Town under Soviet Communism,* Jerusalem, 2002.

Kaganov, V. (1994). "Nelegal'nye evreiskie obshchiny Kuzbassa" (Illegal Jewish congregations of the Kuzbass), *Vestnik evreiskogo universiteta v Moskve,* 1994, no. 2 (6).

Kak (1940). "Kak stroit' lektsiiu na temu 'Iudaizm i ego reaktsonnaia rol' (Materialy k lektsii)'" (How to construct a lecture on the topic of "Judaism and its reactionary role [materials for a lecture]"), *Antireligioznik,* 1940, nos. 8–9.

Kamenetskii, Y. Y. (1998). *Harabi "Vehamossad": Prakim Alumim Behistoria shel Chabad* (The rabbi and the "Mossad": Unknown chapters in the history of the Chabad movement), Kfar Chabad, 1998.

Kamenetskii, Y. Y. (1998). *Arei Yaldut: Nikolayev, Yekaterinoslav-Dnepropetrovsk* (Towns of childhood: Yekaterinoslav-Dnepropetrovsk), Kfar Chabad, 1998.

Kanfesi (1998). *Kanfesi na Belarusi* (Religions in Belorussia), Minsk, 1998.

Karabchevskii, I. (1991). *Toska po domu* (Homesickness), Moscow, 1991.

Karpov, G. G. (1994). "Russkaia pravoslavnaia tserkov' stala na pravel'nyi put'—Dokladnye zapiski predsidatelia Soveta po delam Russkoi pravoslavnoi tserkvi pri SNK SSSR G. G. Karpova I. V. Stalinu, 1943–1946 gg." (The Russian Orthodox Church has set out on the right path—Reports from G. G. Karpov, the chairman of the Council of the Russian Orthodox Church, to J. V. Stalin, 1943–1946), *Istoricheskii arkhiv,* 1994, nos. 3, 4.

Kashevarov, A. N. (1995). *Gosudarstvo i tserkov': Iz istorii vzaimootnoshenii sovetskoi vlasti i Russkoi pravoslavnoi tserkvi, 1917–1945 gg.* (State and church: From the history of the relations between the regime and the Russian Orthodox Church, 1917–1945), St. Petersburg, 1995.

Khrushchev, N. (1961). *Otchet Ts.K. Kommunisticheskoi Partii Sovetskogo Soiuza XXII s"ezda partii* (Report of the Central Committee of the Communist Party of the Soviet Union on the Twenty-second Party Congress), Moscow, 1961.

Kichko, T. K. (1963). *Iudaizm bez prykras* (Judaism without embellishment), Kiev, 1963.

Kischkowski, A. (1960). *Die Sowjetische Religionspolitik und die Russische Orthodoxe Kirche,* Munich, 1960.

Kiselgof, Z. (1971). *Bemeitzar: Hadranim Udrashot* (Beseiged: Sermons and homilies), Mossad Harav Kook, 1971.

Kizhner, D. M. (2000a). "Istoriia vozniknoveniia sinagog v Tomske" (The history of the establishment of synagogues in Tomsk), *Evrei v Sibiri,* state collection, Tomsk, 2000.

Kizhner, D. M. (2000b). *Istoriia evreiskikh obshchin Sibiri i Dal'nego Vostoka: Materialy regional'noi nauchno-prakticheskoi konferentsii* (The history of Jewish [religious] communities of Siberia and the [Soviet] Far East: Materials of a regional scientific and practical conference), Tomsk, 2000.

Kles, S. (1989). *Gvulot, Mahteret Ubricha: Peilut Zionit-Halutzit Bibrit Hamoatzot Uksharim Im Hayishuv Baaretz, 1941–1945* (Borders, underground, and flight: Zionist pioneer activity in the USSR, 1941–1945), Tel Aviv, 1989.

Kles, S. (1994). *Bederech Lo Slula: Toldot Ha"Bricha," 1944–1948* (On an Unpaved Path: The History of the *Bricha* [1944-1948]), Jerusalem, 1994.

Kokurin, A. I. (1997). *Liubianka: VchKA, OGPU, NKVD, MGB, KGB, Spravochnik* (The Lyubianka: the Cheka, the NKVD, the MGB, and the KGB: A guide), Moscow, 1997.

Kostyrchenko, G. (1992). "From a Report Concerning the Jewish Religion in the USSR in 1946," *Jews and Jewish Topics in the Soviet Union and Eastern Europe,* 1992, no. 3 (19).

Kostyrchenko, G. (1994). *V plenu u krasnogo faraona* (Imprisoned by the red pharaoh), Moscow, 1994.

Kostyrchenko, G., ed. (1996). *Evreiskii Antifashistskii Komitet v SSSR, 1941–1948: Dokumentorovanaia istoriia* (The Jewish Anti-Fascist Committee in the USSR, 1941–1948: A documented history), Moscow, 1996.

Kostyrchenko, G. (2001). *Tainaia politika Stalina: Vlast' i antisemitizm* (Stalin's secret policy: The regime and antisemitism), Moscow, 2001.

Koten, B. (1964). "The Optimism of My Soviet Jewish Friends," *Jewish Currents,* May 1964.

Kotliar, E. (1997). "Kharkovskaia khoral'naia sinagoga" (Kharkov's choral synagogue), *Istoki,* 1997, no. I.

Kozlov, V. (1999). *Massovye besporiadki v SSSR pri Khrushcheve i Brezhneve* (Mass riots in the USSR under Khrushchev and Brezhnev), Novosibirsk, 1999.

Kreier (1993). *Pechal'naia rasposadnia* (A sorrow nursery), Minsk, 1993.

Kudritskii, A. V., ed. (1982). *Kiev: Entsiklopedicheskii spravochnik* (Kiev: Encyclopedic reference book), Kiev, 1982.

Kuroedov, V. A. (1973). "Iz istorii vzaimootnoshenii Sovetskogo gosudarstva i tserkvi" (From the history of the relations between the Soviet state and the church), *Voprosy istorii,* 1973, no. 9.

Kuroedov, V. A. (1984). *Religiia i tserkov' v Sovetskom obshchestve,* Izdanie vtoroe, dopolnen-
noe (Religion and the church in Soviet society), Moscow, 1984.

Landoi, B. (1967). *Hagaon Mitshabin—Rishumei Zikaron Lederech Hayav Vepoalo* (The Gaon
of Tshabin—Memoirs of his way of life and works), Jerusalem, 1967.

Lapidus, A. (1962). "Kak ia khoronil diadiu Natana" (How I buried Uncle Nathan), *Nauka i
religiia,* 1962, no. 12.

Leushin, M. (1995). "Zaiavlenie o ritual'nom obriade podtverdilos'" (The statement about
the ritual ceremony was confirmed), *Istochnik,* 1995, no. 5 (18).

Levanon, N. (1995). *Hakod—"Nativ* ("Nativ" was the code name), Tel Aviv, 1995.

Levavi, Y. (1965). *Hahityashvut Hayehudit Bebirobidzan* (Jewish colonization in Birobidzan),
Jerusalem, 1965.

Levin, S. D. (1989). *Toldot Chabad Berussia Hasovietit Bashanim 1917–1950* (History of
Chabad in the USSR, 1917–1950), Brooklyn, Otzar Hasidim, 1989.

Levin, D. (1989). *Tkufa Besograyim: 1939–1941, Tmurot Behayeii Hayehudim Baezorim
Shesufchu Librit Hamoatzot Bithilat Milhemet Haolam Hashniya* (The Jews in the Soviet-
annexed territories, 1939–1941), Jerusalem, Tel Aviv, 1989.

Levin, D. (2001). "A Report of the NKGB on Jewish Nationalist Activity in Lithuania,
1940–1941," *Jews in Eastern Europe,* 2001, no. 1 (44).

Levitats, I. (1956). "Hevra Hayehudit Berussia" (The Jewish community in Russia), *Heavar,*
1956, vol. 4.

Levitats, I. (1981). *The Jewish Community in Russia, 1844–1917,* Jerusalem, 1981.

Lisenko, O. E. (1996). "Khristianstvo v umovakh Drugoi Svitovoi Viini—Istoriosofs'ka
retrospektiva" (Christianity in the agreements of World War II: A historiographic ret-
rospective), *Druga Svitova Voina i Ukraina* (Materials of a scientific conference, June
27–28, 1995), Kiev, 1996.

Lisenko, O. E. (1998). *Tserkovne zhittia v Ukraini, 1943–1946* (Life of the church in Ukraine,
1943–1946), Kiev, 1998.

Litvak, Y. (1988). *Plitim Yehudim Mipolin Bibrit Hamoatzot, 1939–1946* (Polish-Jewish
Refugees in the USSR, 1939–1946), Jerusalem, 1988.

Liuteranskaia tserkov' (1997). *Liuteranskaia tserkov' v Sovetskoi Rossii: Dokumenty i mate-
riaky* (The Lutheran Church in Soviet Russia: Documents and materials), Moscow, 1997.

Luchterhandt, O. (1993). "The Council for Religious Affairs," *Religious Policy in the Soviet
Union* (ed. P. Ramet), Cambridge, 1993.

Lukin, V. (1993). "Evreiskie kladbishcha" (Jewish cemeteries), *Istoricheskie kladbishcha
Peterburga,* St. Petersburg, 1993.

Lukin, V., and B. Khaimovich, (1997). *100 evreiskikh mestechek Ukrainy* (100 Jewish shtetls
of Ukraine), vol.1, Jerusalem, St. Petersburg, 1997.

Lukin, V., A. Sokolova, and B. Khaimovich (2000). *100 evreiskikh mestechek Ukrainy* (100
Jewish shtetls of Ukraine), vol. 2, St. Petersburg, 2000.

Mendelevich, E. (1995). "Dva etiuda istorii evreiskoi obshchiny v Orle" (Two studies of the
history of the Jewish community in Orel), *Korni,* 1995, nos. 3–4.

Mikhailov, V. (1941). "Sovremennyi iudaizm" (Contemporary Judaism), *Antireligioznik*, 1941, no. 3.

Mikhailov, I. (1964). "Prestupleniia protiv lichnosti i prav grazhdan, sovershaemye v srede religioznykh grupp" (Crimes against the individual and against civil rights committed in the milieu of religious groups), *Sovetskaia iustitsiia*, 1964, no. 10.

Michlin (1986). *Hagahelet* (The ember), Jerusalem, 1986.

Mindlina, K. (1997). "K istorii odnogo pamiatnika" (Toward the history of one monument), *Evrei Belarusi, istoriia i kultura*, Minsk, 1997, collection 1.

Mironenko, S. V. (1999). *58-10—Nadzornye proizvodstva prokuratury SSSR po delam ob antisovetskoi agitatsii i propagande—Anotirovannyi katalog, mart 1953-1958* (58-10 of the criminal code—supervision of the operation of the public prosecutor of the USSR concerning cases of anti-Soviet agitation and propaganda—an annotated catalogue, March 1953-1958), Moscow, 1999.

Mitsel', M. (1998). *Obshchiniy Iudeiskogo verosipovedaniia v Ukraine: Kiiv, L'vov: 1945-1986* (Congregations of the Jewish religion in Ukraine: Kiev and L'vov: 1945-1986), Kiev, 1998.

Mitsel', M. (1999). "Shtetl-Kiev v 1958 godu" (The Shtetl-Kiev in 1958), *"Shtetl" kak fenomen evreiskoi istorii* (The "shtetl" as a phenomenon of Jewish history), Kiev, 1999.

Mitsel', M. (2004). *Evrei Ukrainy v 1943-1953 gg.—Ocherki dokumentirovannoi istorii* (The Jews of Ukraine in the years 1943-1953: Essays of documented history), Kiev, 2004.

Narullaev, A. A. (1989). "Leninskii printsip edinstva veruiushchikh i neveruiushchikh trudiashchikhsia v bor'be za sotsializm" (Lenin's principle of the unity of religious and non-religious workers in the fight for socialism), *Voprosy istorii KPSS*, 1989, no. 7.

Neiman, A. (1999). "Zhizn' i tragediia Romenskikh evreev" (The life and tragedy of the Jews of Romny), *"Shtetl" kak fenomen evreis 'koi istorii* (The "shtetl" as a phenomenon of Jewish history), Kiev, 1999.

Neishtat, M. (1970). *Yehudei Gruzia* (The Jews of Georgia), Tel Aviv, 1970.

Nidergofer, B. (2001). *Doroga smerti* (The road of death), Tel Aviv, 2001.

Nove, A. (1992). *An Economic History of the USSR*, England, 1992.

Odintsov, M. I. (1995a). "Religioznye organizatsii v SSSR: nakanune i v pervye gody Velikoi Otechestvennoi voiny, 1938-1943 gg.—Dokumenty" (Religious organizations in the USSR on the eve of and during the first years of the Great Patriotic War, 1938-1943—Documents), *Otechestvennye arkhivy*, 1995, no. 2.

Odintsov, M. I. (1995b). "Religioznye organizatsii v SSSR v gody Velikoi Otechestvennoi voiny, 1943-1945 gg.—Dokumenty" (Religious organizations in the USSR during the years of the Great Patriotic War, 1943-1945—Documents), *Otechestvennye arkhivy*, 1995, no. 3.

Odintsov, M. I. (1997). "Gosudarstvennaia politika'otdleniia shkoly ot tserkvi' v SSSR: Istoricheskii analiz i politiko-pravovoi aspekt" (The government policy on "the separation of school and church" in the USSR: Historical analysis and political and legal aspects), *Religiia, tserkov' v Rossiii i za rubezhom: Informatsionno-analiticheskii biulleten'*, 1997, nos. 9-10.

Odintsov, M. I. (1999). *Russkie Patriarkhy XX veka* (The Russian patriarchs of the twentieth century), Moscow, 1999.

Orleanskii, N. (1930). *Zakon o religioznykh obedineniakh RSFSR i deistvuiushchie zakony, instruktsii, tsirkuliary s otdel'nymi komentariami po voprosam, sviazannym s otdeleniem tserkvi ot gosudarstva i shkoly ot tserkvi v SSSR* (Law on religious associations of the RSFSR and operative laws, instructions, and circulars with separate commentaries on issues connected with the separation of church and state and school and church in the USSR), Moscow, 1930.

Osipova, I. I. (2002). *Khasidy: Istoriia khasidskogo podpol'ia v gody bol'shevitskogo terora* (Chassidim: The history of the Chassidic underground during the Bolshevik terror), Moscow, 2002.

Pechenik, A. (1943). *Tsionizm un yiddishkayt in sovetn rusland* (Zionism and Judaism in Soviet Russia), New York, 1943.

Peknyi, A. (1994). "Istoriia penzenskoi sinagogi" (History of the Penza synagogue), *Korni*, 1994, no. 1.

Peris, D. (1998). *Storming the Heavens: The Soviet League of the Militant Godless,* Ithaca (NY), 1998.

Pinkas Hakehilot (1980). *Encyclopedia of Jewish Communities—Polin* (Poland), vol. 2, Jerusalem, 1980.

Pinkas Hakehilot (1980). *Encyclopedia of Jewish Communities—Rumenia* (Romania), vol. 2, Jerusalem, 1980.

Pinkus, B., ed. (1973). *Evrei i evreiskii narod, 1948–1953, Sbornik materialov iz Sovetskoi pechati, kniga 1: Evreiskaia religiia i kul'tura* (Jews and the Jewish people, 1948–1953: Collection of materials from the Soviet press, Book 1: Jewish religion and culture), Jerusalem, 1973.

Pinkus, B. (1993). *Tehia Vetekuma Leumit: Hazionut Vehatnua Hazionit Bibrit Hamoatzot, 1947–1987* (National rebirth and reestablishment: Zionism and the Zionist movement in the USSR, 1947–1987), Sde Boker, 1993.

Podlipskii, M. Ryvkin (1996). "Evreiskie kladbishcha v Vitebske" (Jewish cemeteries in Vitebsk), *Vozrozhdenie*, 1996, nos. 2, 3.

Pospielovsky, D. V. (1988). *Soviet Antireligious Campaigns and Persecutions* (vol. 2 of *A History of Soviet Atheism in Theory and Practice and the Believer*), Macmillan Press, 1988.

Potul'nitskaia, T. (2001). *Iudaika iz fondov L'vovskogo muzeia istorii religii* (Judaica from the collections of the L'vov Museum of the History of Religion), L'vov, 2001.

Powell, D. E. (1975) *Antireligious Propaganda in the Soviet Union: A Study of Mass Persuasion,* Cambridge, 1975.

Prichiny (1965). *Prichiny sushchestvovaniia i puti preodoleniia religioznykh perezhitkov* (Reasons for the existence of and ways to overcome religious vestiges), Minsk, 1965.

Ramet, P. (1987). *Cross and Commissar: The Politics of Religion in Eastern Europe and the SSR,* Bloomington, 1987.

Reb Mendl (1997). *Reb Mendl—Sipuro Shel Hasid, Mashpia Umekushar* (Reb Mendl—The story of a Chassid, influential and connected), Kfar Chabad, 1997.

Redlich, S. (1995). *War, Holocaust, and Stalinism: A Documented History of the Jewish Anti-Fascist Committee in the USSR*, Boston, 1995.

REE (1994–2000). *Rossiiskaia Evreiskaia Entsiklopediia* (Russian Jewish encyclopedia), Moscow, 1994–2000.

Religiia (1965). *O religii i tserkvi: Sbornik dokumentov* (On religion and the church: Collection of documents), Moscow, 1965.

Ro'i, Y. (1989). "Hag Hapesach Mul Hamishtar Hasovieti" (The Passover holiday versus the Soviet regime), *Studies in the History and Culture of Eastern European Jewry*, annual publication of Bar-Ilan University, 1989.

Ro'i, Y. (1991). *The Struggle for Soviet Jewish Emigration, 1948–1967*, Cambridge, 1991.

Ro'i, Y. (1991). "The Role of the Synagogue and Religion in the Jewish National Awakening," *Jewish Culture and Identity in the Soviet Union* (ed. Ro'i and Beker), New York, 1991.

Ro'i, Y. (1995). "Jewish Religion after World War II," *Jews and Jewish Life in Russia and the Soviet Union* (ed. Y. Ro'i), England, 1995.

Ro'i, Y. (2000). *Islam in the Soviet Union from World War II to Perestroika*, London, 2000.

Ro'i, Y. (2003). "The Religious Life of the Bukharan Jewish Community in Central Asia after World War II," *Jews in Russia and Eastern Europe*, 2003, no. 2 (51).

Rothenberg, J. (1971). *The Jewish Religion in the Soviet Union*, New York, 1971.

Rozenblat, E., and I. Elenskaia (1997). *Pinskie evrei, 1939–1944 gg.* (The Jews of Pinsk, 1939–1944), Brest, 1997.

Russkaia (1996). *Russkaia Pravoslavnaia Tserkov' i kommunisticheskoe gosudarstvo, 1917–1941, Dokumenty i fotomaterialy* (The Russian Orthodox Church and the Communist state, 1917–1941: Documents and photographic materials), Moscow, 1996.

Rybakov, A. (1997). *Roman vospominanie* (Novel memoir), Moscow, 1997.

Sankt (1992). *Sankt Peterburg, Petrograd, Leningrad, Entsiklopedicheskii spravochnik* (St. Petersburg, Petrograd, Leningrad: Encyclopedic reference work), St. Peterburg, 1992.

Sasonkin, N. S. (1988). *Zichronotay* (My memoirs), Jerusalem, 1988.

Serhiichuk, V. (1998). *Desiat' buremnikh lit, Zakhidno Ukrains'ki zemli v 1944–1954 rr. Novi dokumenti i materali* (Ten stormy years: the western Ukrainian territories in 1944–1954: New documents and materials), Kiev, 1998.

Serova, I. (1999). "Sovet po delam religioznykh kul'tov pri Sovete Ministrov SSSR v 1953 g." (The Council for Religious Affairs by the Council of Ministers of the USSR in 1953), *Rossiiskoe gosudarstvo i obshchestvo, XX vek*, Moscow, 1999.

Shaevich, A. (1997). "Mibirobidzhan Likehunat Rav Rashi Berussia" (From Birobidzan to the role of chief rabbi of Russia), *Yehudei Brit Hamoatzot Bemaavar* (Soviet Jewry in transition), 1997, no. 3 (18).

Shakhnovich, M. (1960). *Reaktsionnaia sushchnost' iudaizma* (The reactionary essence of Judaism), Moscow, Leningrad, 1960.

Shakhnovich, M. (1965). *Zakat iudeiskoi religii* (The decline of the Jewish religion), Leningrad, 1965.

Shapiro, R. (1993). "Yizker-Bikher as Sources on Jewish Communities in Soviet Belorussia and Soviet Ukraine during the Holocaust," *The Holocaust in the Soviet Union,* (ed. L. Dobroszytski and J. S. Gurock), New York, 1993.

Shkarovskii, M. (1999). *Russkaia Pravoslavnaia Tserkov' pri Staline i Khrushcheve: Gosudarstvenno-tserkovnye otnosheniia v SSSR v 1939–1964 godakh* (The Russian Orthodox Church under Stalin and Khrushchev: State-church relations in the USSR between 1939 and 1964), Moscow, 1999.

Shkurko, E. (1999). *Ocherkii evreev Bashkirostana* (Essays on the Jews of Bashkirtostan), Ufa, 1999.

Shmeruk, H., ed. (1961). *Pirsumim Yehudim Bibrit Hamoatzot, 1917–1960* (Jewish publications in the Soviet Union, 1917–1960), Jerusalem, 1961.

Shochat, A. (1975). *Mossad "Harabanut Mitaam" Berussia* (The crown rabbinate of Russia), Haifa, 1975.

Shoshkes, H. (1961). *Fun Moskve Biz Ever Hayarden* (From Moscow to Transjordan), Jerusalem, 1961.

Shpizel, R. (1999). "Ostrozhskomu evreiskomu kladbishchu ispolnilos' 550 let" (The Jewish cemetery of Ostrog is 550 years old), *"Shtetl" kak fenomen evreiskoi istorii* (The "shtetl" as a phenomenon of Jewish history), Kiev, 1999.

Slipoi, M. (1971). "Agudat Yisrael Bebessarabia" (Agudat Israel in Bessarabia), *Yahadut Bessarabia: Enciclopedia Shel Galuyot, Sifrei Zikaron Leartzot Hagolah Veedoteha* (Bessarabian Jewry: Encyclopaedia of Diasporas, Memorial Books of the Diaspora Lands and Communities), Jerusalem, Tel Aviv, 1971.

Slutski, Y., ed. (1967). *Sefer Zikaron Lekehilat Bobruisk Ubnoteha* (Bobruisk memorial book), Tel Aviv, 1967.

Smilovitskii, L. (1995). "Jewish Religious Life in Bobruisk, 1944–1954," *Jews in Eastern Europe,* 1995, no. 2 (27).

Smilovitskii, L. (1998). "Eto bylo v Chervene" (It was in Cherven), *Evrei Belarusi—Istoria i kul'tura* (Jews in Belorussia—History and culture), Minsk, 1998, collection 3–4.

Smilovitskii, L. (1999). "Jewish Religious Leadership in Belorussia, 1939–1953," *Shvut,* 1999, no. 8 (24).

Smoliar, H. (1973). "'Kabalat Panim' Lepartizanim Yehudim": Zichronot mi-1944 Beminsk Hameshuchreret" (Unfriendly reception of the Jewish partisans: Memoirs on Minsk after the 1944 liberation), *Shvut,* 1973, no. 1.

Sovetsko-Izrael'skie (2000). *Sovetsko-Izrael'skie otnosheniia, Sbornik Dokumentov, tom 1, kn. 1: 1941–mai 1949, kn. 2: mai 1949–1953* (Soviet-Israeli relations: Collection of documents, vol. 1, book 1: 1941–May 1949; book 2: May 1949–1953), Moscow, 2000.

Stalin (1993). *Iosif Stalin v ob'iatiiakh sem'i, Iz lichnogo arkhiva: Sbornik dokumentov* (Joseph Stalin in the embraces of his family, from a personal archive: Collection of documents), Berlin, Moscow, 1993.

Starodinskii, D. (1991). *Odesskoe getto* (The Odessa ghetto), Odessa, 1991.

Svirsky, G. (1976). *Hostages: The Personal Testimony of a Soviet Jew,* Great Britain, 1976.

Taiar, I. (1987). (Shlomo Ianovskii) *Sinagoga razgromlennaia no nepokorennaia* (The synagogue [is] devastated but not subdued), Israel, 1987.

Terkel, B. (1963). *Di Zun Fargeyt baym Amu-Daria* (Sunset on the river Amurdaria), Buenos Aires, 1963.

Thrower, J. (1983). *Marxist-Leninist Scientific Atheism and the Study of Religion and Atheism in the USSR,* Berlin, 1983.

Tratsiak, I. (2000). "Religiinaia i natsyianal'naia polityka KP(b)B u Zakhodniai Belarusi v 1939–1941 gg." (Religious and ethnic policy of the Communist Party (Bolsheviks) in Western Belorussia between 1939 and 1941), *Bialoruskie Zeszyty Historychne,* Bialystok, 2000, no. 13.

Tzizuashvilli, G. (1979). "Yehudey Gruzia" (Georgian Jewry), *Haintelligentzia Hayehudit Bibrit Hamoatzot* (The Jewish intelligentsia in the Soviet Union), 1979, vol. 3.

Ugolovnoe zakonodatel'stvo (1963). *Ugolovnoe zakonodatel'stvo Soiuza SSR i soiuznykh respublik v dvukh tomakh* (Criminal legislation of the USSR and the Union republics, in two volumes), Moscow, 1963.

Ugolovnyi kodeks (1952). *Ugolovnyi kodeks RSFSR, Ofitsial'nyi tekst s izmeneniiami na 1 ianvaria 1952 goda* (Criminal code of the RSFSR: Official text with changes as of January 1, 1952), Moscow, 1952.

Utershtein, T. (1999). *Evrei Taganroga* (The Jews of Taganrog), Taganrog, 1999.

Vasil'ev, V. (2005). *Kommunisticheskaia vlast' protiv religii Moiseia* (The Communist regime against the religion of Moses), Vinnitsa, 2005.

Vekselman, M. (1999). "The Lubavich Hasidim in Uzbekistan, 1918–1995," *Shvut,* 1999, no. 8 (24).

Vol'f, E. (2001). *Vospominaniia byvshikh uznikov Zhmerinskogo getto* (Memoirs of former inmates of the Zhmerinka ghetto), Jerusalem, 2001.

VUChKA-GPU-NKVD, KGB-Iz Arkhiviv (The All-Union Cheka . . . NKVD, from the archives), 1998, nos. 3–4.

Waisman, B. (1973). *Yoman Mahteret Ivri Mibrit Hamoatzot* (A Hebrew diary from the Soviet Union), Ramat Gan, 1973.

Weinberg, R. (2002). "Birobidzhan After the Second World War," *Jews in Eastern Europe,* 2002, no. 3 (49).

Wiesel, A. (1967). *Yehudey Hadmama* (The Jews of silence), Tel Aviv, 1967.

Wilkowski, K. (1980). "Yom Kippur in Moskve" (Yom Kippur in Moscow), *Jerusholaimer Almanach,* 1980, no. 11.

Yehoshua, B. T. (1999). Bishlihut Hatzalah shel Sfarim Vekitvei Yad Beuzbekistan (On a mission to rescue books and manuscripts in Uzbekistan), *Hauma,* 1999, no. 135.

Yodfat, A. Y. (1972). "Rabbis and Jewish Clergy in the USSR, 1917–1970," *Judaism,* 1972, no. 82

Zakonodatel'stvo (1971). *Zakonodatel'stvo o religioznykh kul'takh, sbornik materialov i dokumentov* (Legislation on religious cults, collection of materials and documents), Moscow, 1971.

Ziabko, M. (1997). "Evrei Nagartava posle fashisstskoi okkupatsii" (The Jews of Nagartav after the Fascist occupation), *Evreiske naselennia Pivdennoi Ukraini: Istoriia ta suchastnist* (The Jewish population of southern Ukraine), Zaporizhiia, 1997.

Zonenfeld, S. Z. (1990). *Kol Badmama Nishma: Masechet Hayim Heroit Shel Mishpacha Shomeret Mitzvot Berussia Hacommunistit, Sipra Batya Barg* (A voice heard in the silence: A heroic episode of a religious family in Communist Russia, as told by Batya Barg), Jerusalem, 1990.

Zubkova, E. I. (1998). "Mir mnenii sovetskogo cheloveka, 1945–1948 gody, Po materialam TsK VKP(b)" (The world of opinions of the Soviet person, 1945–1948, according to materials of the Central Committee of the All-Union Communist Party), *Otechestvennaia istoriia,* 1998, no. 3.

Zubkova, E. I. (2000). *Poslevoennoe sovetskoe obshchestvo: Politika i povsednevnost' 1945–1953* (Postwar Soviet society: Politics and daily life, 1945–1953), Moscow, 2000.

Index